HOSPITALS
THE PLANNING AND DESIGN PROCESS

HOSPITALS

THE PLANNING AND DESIGN PROCESS

Second Edition

OWEN B. HARDY, FACHE, FAAHC
Ernst & Whinney
Chicago, Illinois

LAWRENCE P. LAMMERS, AIA, FAAHC
Lammers + Gershon Associates, Inc.
Reston, Virginia

AN ASPEN PUBLICATION®
Aspen Publishers, Inc.
Rockville, Maryland
Royal Tunbridge Wells
1986

Library of Congress Cataloging in Publication Data

Hardy, Owen B.
Hospitals, the planning and design process.

"Aspen publication."
Includes bibliographies and index.
1. Hospitals—Planning. 2. Hospitals—Design and construction. I. Lammers, Lawrence P.
II. Title. [DNLM: 1. Hospital Design and Construction. 2. Hospital Planning. WX
140 H271h] RA967.H25   1986   362.1′1′068   85-26756
ISBN: 0-87189-249-9

Editorial Services: Ruth Bloom

Library of Congress Catalog Card Number: 86-26756
ISBN: 0-87189-249-9

Printed in the United States of America

1 2 3 4 5

Dedication

To the advancement of functional planning and design of hospitals and related health care facilities and to the professional associates with whom we have worked over the past 15 years at Friesen International, Inc.; Medicus Planning, Inc.; Ernst & Whinney; and Lammers + Gershon Associates, Inc.

Table of contents

List of figures

. . .and exhibits

. . .and tables

Preface

Since publication in 1977 of the first edition of this book, many changes have occurred and are continuing to occur in the health care field in the United States. Each of these changes will affect, either directly or indirectly, hospital construction in terms of both type and scope, and each reflects concern—within the federal government and in the public and private sectors—over the rising costs of health care delivery.

Early governmental efforts to stabilize hospital costs included restricting the number of beds per 1000 population and placing controls over provisions of other hospital services. Restrictions on these aspects of hospital construction and function were greatly reduced concomitant with the withdrawal of federal funding for health planning under the National Health Planning and Resources Development Act of 1974 (Public Law 93-641). Nevertheless, governmental regulation remained the rule. In the early 1980s, however, the Reagan administration and a supporting Congress, after having seen little success under regulation, apparently decided that measures to spur competition among providers would be more effective in controlling costs than governmental restrictions. Subsequently, competition among hospitals has increased to a level never before experienced, which promises to continue into the foreseeable future.

Federal health care expenditures will probably be cut further by the Tax Equity and Fiscal Responsibility Act of 1982 (TEFRA) and by Title VI of the Social Security Amendment of 1983, better known as "Prospective Payment for Medicare Inpatient Hospital Services." These laws, which limit payment to hospitals for Medicare and Medicaid patients, will more than likely have a major impact upon hospital revenues. The cornerstone of the prospective payment system introduced by these laws is a fixed fee per diagnosis-related grouping (DRG) of illnesses. Prospective payment for care per DRG will force hospitals to shift from a management strategy of revenue maximization to one of cost and utilization management. At present, only hospital inpatient operating costs are covered by the Medicare prospective payment rate, but as more experience is gained under the system, other costs, such as capital, may be included.

Other changes in the health care field are a direct consequence of adverse public reaction to the high cost of hospital care. Many organizations have banded together in business coalitions to plan ways to reduce expenditures for health care. Hospitals are now responding by forming "preferred provider" groups, which discount, in one form or another, the charges to employees of a given organization in return for the business generated by employee health care utilization required by employees of that organization. The net effect will be to stimulate competition among providers and to cause them to be more efficient.

Health maintenance organizations (HMOs) continue to increase enrollments. Since HMOs are geared to providing necessary care but with avoidance of excessive utilization of expensive inpatient care, they tend to reduce overall utilization of in-hospital care per unit of population.

Furthermore, to help curtail utilization of hospital care, and expensive inpatient care in particular, many third-party payors (insurance companies) are including disincentives to utilization in their health care policies. These usually take the form of deductibles that the patient must pay directly to the hospital or other provider at the outset of an illness or over the course of a specific time period. There is evidence already recorded that such disincentives are effective to some extent.

Still other changes in the health care field stem from efforts by hospitals and similar facilities to assure internal cost effectiveness. Thus, owing to many factors, not the least of which are competition and the necessity to respond to public rebellion against the high cost of inpatient hospital care, the delivery of health care has assumed a growing ambulatory character. In addition, the vertical integration of modes of care delivery is now giving rise to related programs of pre-acute care, acute care, and post-acute care. Such programs have important implications for the character of hospital and other health care facility constructions in the future.

Hospital systems, both horizontally and vertically integrated, continue to expand and proliferate. The stand-alone hospital of the 1960s and 1970s is rapidly disappearing. Owing to the sharing of many centralized services and the vertical integration of others, responses must occur in the character of facilities, thus affecting the outcome of planning and design.

Like all constructions for human habitation, hospitals and related facilities for health care delivery continue to feel the impact of the energy crisis that was so dramatically called to the nation's attention in 1973–1974. Planning and design have been directly affected and must continue to reflect provisions for energy conservation.

Finally, technological sophistication has advanced rapidly, and new modalities of diagnosis and treatment continue to appear. Accommodations in terms of both facilities and equipment must be provided through the planning and design process.

All these changes will affect the output of strategic planning by hospitals and other health care providers for years to come, which, in turn, will affect the types of facilities provided to accommodate sponsored programs. How will facilities themselves change? Certainly, there will be a nearly universal attempt to increase the productivity levels of employees, and to become more operationally efficient in general. The physical efficiency of buildings themselves will receive greater emphasis. Optimum functionality and more intense building and equipment usage will have important implications for both planners and designers. At the same time, we do not expect to see any basic diminution in requirements for patient protection and comfort, or for the comfort and convenience of employees, physicians, and the visiting public.

Although hospital construction will continue to dominate, other related facilities will be provided to accommodate programs of pre- and post-acute care. Such constructions will probably be of a highly modular nature owing to the lack of established protocols to predict demand, as well as the necessity to make provision for change. Technological advancements will require the housing of sophisticated equipment in space properly and precisely allocated and designed. Thus, new challenges related to the complexity of such demands await tomorrow's planners and designers.

How will the planning and design process itself change? Does the process outlined in the 1977 edition of this book still possess sufficient validity for use in tomorrow's environment? We believe that it does. Although increased sophistication in planning algorithms will be necessitated to determine more accurately facility requirements of all types, the broad process will continue to achieve recognition for its appropriately sequenced steps and its complete rationality. Undoubtedly the *output* of the process will change rather dramatically owing to the unprecedented extent of change in the ways health care is delivered, but the process itself will not be radically altered.

In this edition we have revised to a considerable extent every chapter in the book; the chapters on strategic planning (role and program planning) and on space programming, in particular, have been dramatically improved. References have been diligently researched again to assure that every page reflects the most advanced planning methodologies in use today. In addition, insights gained in our experience with over 100 additional projects since publication of the first edition have been incorporated where appropriate.

Despite the possibility that close regulatory controls may be abandoned altogether by federal and state agencies, we have added a chapter on regulatory planning. All the major nations of the world are now regulating the delivery of health care and the constructions incidental thereto; conceivably a corresponding change in federal administration and congressional attitudes could bring about even closer controls than before.

Our primary objective, as in the original edition, is to bring logical order to the entire planning and design process for hospital constructions, based on state-of-the-art methodologies in an emerging environment. We sincerely hope that our work will provide a helpful resource for hospital executives, students in hospital administration and planning, architects, engineers, construction managers, investment bankers, financial feasibility consultants, functional planners, governing board members, and all others who may be connected with hospital constructions.

The original edition of *Hospitals: The Planning and Design Process* received the American Association of Healthcare Consultants' first annual Award of Merit. For this recognition by our peers we remain truly grateful, and in the preparation of this edition we have tried to hold to the high professional standards so clearly upheld by that prestigious organization.

Owen B. Hardy
Lawrence P. Lammers

Acknowledgments

Over the course of revising this text and the graphic illustrations, a number of people have helped us. For this we are truly grateful. We wish to thank especially our wives. Others who have given assistance are named below:

James Morell
John Abendshien
Kathy McInerney
David Shanahan
Linda Simon
James Lifton
Linda Barber

Howard Gershon
Joe Strauss
David Spahr
Jo Ellen Campbell
Dawn Hyland
Ellen Goldman
Guillermo Moreno

In addition to the active assistance we have received, there have been many friends who have extended us a great deal of moral support, which was equally necessary. Especially do we wish to name the following:

R. C. McWhorter
Paul Rutledge
Peter Rogan
John Fidler
Norman D. Burkett

Frederick H. Gibbs
Robert C. Harrison
Edward Romieniec, FAIA
George T. Mann, AIA
James Phalen

1

The Planning and Design Process

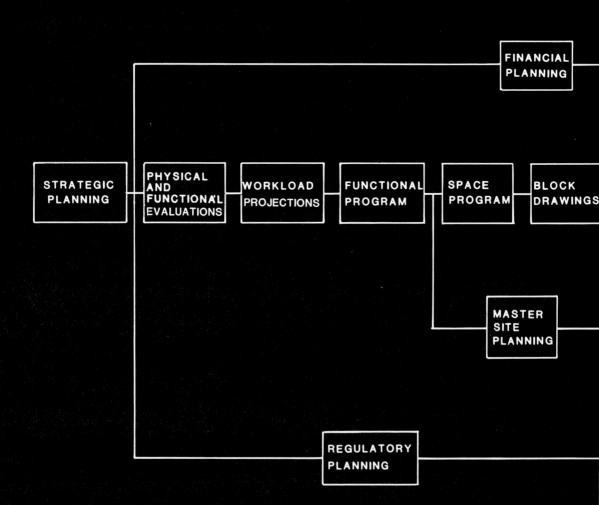

FINANCIAL
PLANNING

STRATEGIC
PLANNING

PHYSICAL
AND
FUNCTIONAL
EVALUATIONS

WORKLOAD
PROJECTIONS

FUNCTIONAL
PROGRAM

SPACE
PROGRAM

BLOCK
DRAWINGS

MASTER
SITE
PLANNING

REGULATORY
PLANNING

A perspective of planning and design

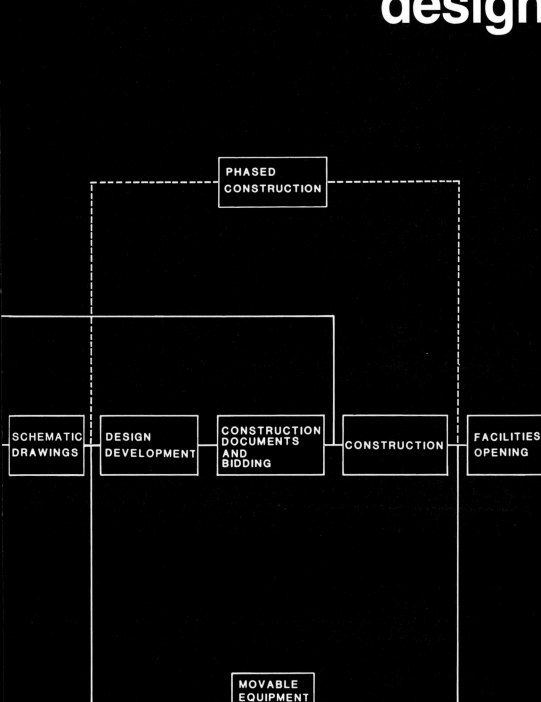

The future will see a continued strong demand for construction of health care facilities, including completely new or replacement facilities and projects involving major additions and modernization. Although the total annual value of health care construction projects may decline slightly in the immediate years ahead owing to deferments related to the reduced financial feasibility of some projects, demand for facilities will continue unabated. Therefore, planning and design will continue to merit prime emphasis among the several responsibilities of hospital officials.

As in the past, the expenditure of capital funds for planning, design, and construction will be largely by hospitals. The character of facilities required by hospital corporations is currently changing owing to the emphasis upon vertical integration and a trend toward the creation of health care delivery systems, but such corporations (and their medical staffs) will continue to dominate the delivery of health care in this nation. Because of the changing character of facilities and the continuing increase, on balance, in their complexity, planning and design will assume greater importance than ever before. Thus, planners, architects, builders, hospital executives and board members, medical staff representatives, and others who possess responsibility for undertaking hospital construction projects should have a basic understanding of planning processes and of appropriate concepts of hospital and related health care facility design objectives.

This chapter has two purposes: (1) to define and delineate the planning process from both academic and practical viewpoints and (2) to present a design philosophy for health care construction.

The planning process

Role of decision making

"Planning in its broadest sense has been accorded a variety of definitions, and there still exists considerable disagreement with regard to its scope within the overall management process. . . . Most authorities agree, however, that it invariably involves the future and that it is basically a process wherein decision making plays a vital role."[1]

Brown and Moberg, two noted authorities on "macro" approaches to management, have stated:[2]

> We shall define planning as the specification of the means necessary for the accomplishment of goals and objectives before action toward those goals has begun. . . . Planning involves a particular kind of decision making. As usual, it involves specifying alternatives and choosing among them. . . . The whole planning process is initiated by the establishment of goals. Once goals are set, alternative plans can be examined in the context of the opportunities and constraints facing the organization.

Another writer, John Argenti, has said:[3]

The two [planning and decision making] appear to be identical; indeed they *are* identical in logic. They are distinguished in practice only in one respect—the extent to which a manager takes deliberate and conscious care over a decision. When a manager makes a decision in an instant, we say he has taken a decision. When he makes a decision carefully, deliberately, systematically and formally, we say he has planned.

Robert M. Fuller, a Trinity University Professor of Business, confirmed agreement with many other planning authorities when he wrote, "Planning is, of course, decision making because it involves selecting from among established alternatives."[4] Fuller has also stated, "Since Henri Fayol's pioneering treatise on management in 1916, planning (or *prevoyance* as he called it) has involved two considerations: (1) assessing the future and (2) making provision for it. . . . Decisions about future activities can be no better than the assumption or premises upon which those decisions were made."[5]

Thus the opinions of most authorities, past and present, confirm the central role of decision making in planning. Certainly not all decision making can be called planning, since many decisions involve only simple choices, many of which are not oriented toward taking future actions. However, all planning *does* embrace the methodologies of decision making, and planning can be best accomplished through the proven techniques of decision making.

Decision-making approaches

Rational process

The *rational process* of decision making, described throughout classical management literature, follows a simple planning outline. Four steps or phases are usually cited as composing the process:[6]

1. diagnosing the problem and defining the mission, objective, or goals

2. determining and setting forth alternative courses of action

3. analyzing and testing the relative feasibility of each alternative solution or course of action

4. selecting the most feasible plan.

"Creative" decision making has sometimes been described as a process separate from the rational process, but thoughtful interpretation will reveal that creativity is a function of the individual mind, emerging as the steps of the rational process are pursued.

Reflective thought process

The *reflective thought process*, which philosophy John Dewey first outlined in 1910 and further elaborated in the early 1930s, also constitutes an outline for planning and in fact has been taught in a number of universities as such. The central idea in this process is the testing of alternative courses of action or decisions against facts, authoritative opinion, or the findings of research, in order to select the most feasible one.[7]

In his now-famous book *How We Think*, Dewey, after discussing a five-phase process of reflective thought, states:[8]

> . . . it has been suggested that reflective thought involves a look into the future, a forecast, an anticipation, or a prediction and this should be listed as sixth aspect or phase. As a matter of fact, every intellectual suggestion or idea is anticipatory of some possible future experience, while the final solution gives a definitive set toward the future.

Dewey repeatedly refers to "analysis and synthesis," "conception and definition," "control of data and evidence," "scientific thinking," and "systematic method," all of which are terms widely used and discussed in the jargon of today's planners. Although Dewey's approach to education processes, to which a major portion of his life's work was devoted, has been somewhat controversial, the reflective thought process that he outlined in great detail still stands preeminent, and its essence has been the subject of a number of recent lectures and articles on how to think (sadly, without due recognition of Dewey's work). Dewey's outline of reflective thought, as a process, can easily be adapted to group planning and frequently has been used for this purpose, whether consciously or unconsciously.

The systems approach

The *systems approach*, or modifications of it called by other names, has now been widely adapted to planning processes. Originally used for the development of new operational systems (e.g., space reentry) in the early 1960s, it now forms the basis for a variety of planning approaches, most notably strategic planning in the health care field.[9]

The systems approach is characterized by three basic concepts:

1. Problem solving and planning are tackled according to a deliberate methodology (the steps of the systems approach, as shown in Figure 1–1).

2. Planning problems are usually analyzed as a total process, rather than on a piecemeal basis, and conclusions drawn are utilized in the decision making inherent in planning.

3. An interdisciplinary team, rather than an individual, is employed in problem-solving tasks.

Figure 1–1 graphically outlines the process. As shown, the development of alternative approaches to attaining the objectives and the evaluation of these objectives form the basis of the systems approach.

Preparing to plan

In undertaking any complex activity, it is well to examine the experience of others in similar situations, if such information can easily be found and properly interpreted. Why respective successes or failures occurred is a worthwhile subject for examination. In dealing with approximately 300

Steps within systems approach to planning

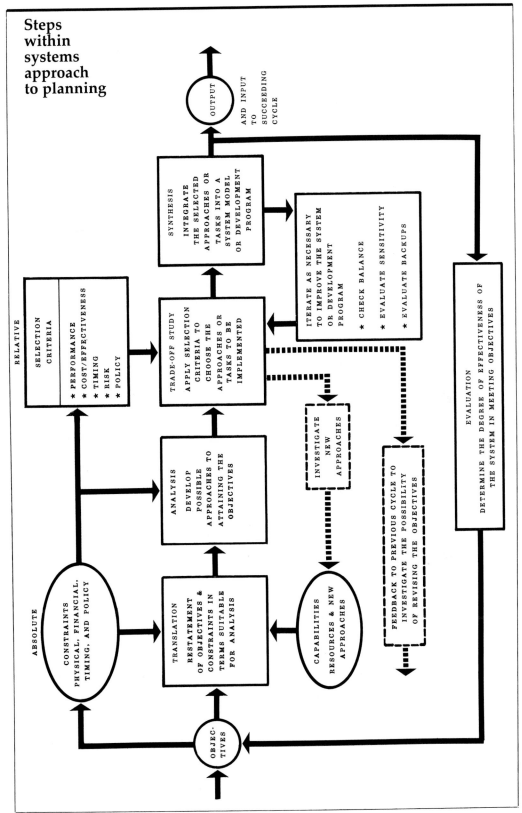

planning projects of one type or another over the two preceding decades, we have been able to summarize the major reasons for success or failure as the outcome. These reasons follow.

Successes

1. An appropriate planning methodology was adopted at the outset and followed throughout the planning program.

2. Hospital officials approached the planning activity with a high degree of objectivity.

3. Decisions were made on the basis of sufficient factual information relevant to the situation at hand.

4. Those involved with implementation of goals and objectives were also involved in their formulation.

5. Rather than with an academic orientation, the process was pursued with the anticipation of action results.

Failures

1. Key officials—usually, the chief executive officer, powerful board member(s), or certain medical staff members—subverted the process owing to a conflict of interest or subjectively held intuitions.

2. A formal process leading to sound decisions was not adopted, or the selected process was not followed.

3. Planning was given a low priority in the overall scheme of management.

4. Decisions were based on either insufficient, erroneous, or misapplied information.

5. Persons charged with the responsibility for the planning were not competent to perform the tasks inherent to the process or were unable to draw appropriate conclusions flowing from a complex data and information base.

As we have noted, one basis for success is the adoption of an appropriate planning process, and for failure, the absence of such a process. Certainly, the adoption of a systematic planning process is imperative in any hospital facility planning and design process, even in one of modest proportions. Team direction, timely action, error avoidance, objectivity, orderliness, control, and goal achievement all will be enhanced when the team is organized according to guidelines agreed upon by all members. Although there is no guaranteed prescription for molding the efforts of individuals into a single achievement, a definitive methodology for proceeding, plus expert direction, will afford vast improvement over disorganized planning characterized by instinctive reactions.

Every hospital should fix the responsibility for planning by title and position; authority to perform should be vested, whether or not a definitive facility planning program is imminent. Beginning with strategic planning, a planning format should be adopted, planning guidelines promulgated, and tasks fixed by individual or groups headed by an individual. When it becomes clear that a facility planning and design program will be considered, all facets of planning then in place should be reconsidered, owing to the fact that skills possessed by strategic planners may not include those needed for facility planning. Also, strategic planning is a far more simple and direct subprocess than is the more inclusive facility planning and design process.

The authors espouse no universal academic planning model inasmuch as needs vary from one building program to another, according to size, duration, and complexity. However, it is quite definite that in every instance, the methodology must be able to yield decisions of quality that are optimal in light of objectively identified considerations. Generally, derivations of either the rational decision-making process, the reflective thought process, or the systems approach, alone or in combination, can be adapted to individual situations so that an acceptable circumstantial "fit" will result.

With regard to practical aspects of accomplishing a building project of appreciable proportions, we believe that the process outlined in this text can be adjusted easily, with a high degree of success, to such a project.

Architectural design

Importance of design

The basic design of a hospital or related health care facility usually rests with only one or two individual architects, who reflect the labors of the entire planning team in a series of drawings. Thus the quality of the facility planning effort is ultimately dependent upon designers, who, it is to be hoped, are capable of interpreting complex relationships, internal traffic flows (personnel and supplies), technological requirements, and operational procedures to the extent that a product of beauty, reasonable cost, and optimal utility will result. No other activity in the planning continuum is more important than that occurring in the design phases.

Design represents the most definitive act of planning for construction with regard to a single building phase and has great impact on any succeeding phases; in it rests the final choice among alternatives, and consummated design represents decisions made. When the schematic design is finished and approved, the basic character of the structure or structures has been determined. When design development has been completed, operational functionality and appearance are fixed.

There is a diminishing school of thought that deprecates the importance of the design of physical facilities in rendering patient care; the thesis holds that personal organization, staff knowledge, and professional skills are the true determinants of successful hospital operation. Although it is true that these human factors are central and indispensable in any undertaking composed primarily of complex personal services, it is equally true that facilities can enhance or detract from such services. A functional design can promote skill, economy, conveniences, and comforts; a nonfunctional design can impede activities of all types, detract from quality of care, and raise costs to intolerable levels. As one observer has stated, a nonfunctional building is "the nemesis of any hospital striving to compete in the current climate of competition and emphasis on productivity."[10]

Historical background

Architectural design has been one of humankind's great challenges for many centuries, and it is no less so today. It is one of the means whereby humans have changed and continue to change their natural environment. As a physical reflection of rising human aspirations, unquestionably, it ranks preeminent among the so-called civilized characterizations.

Over the past century, there has been a decided evolution in architectural thought with regard to philosophical legitimacy, striking at the very heart of the purpose of design. Ruskin, in the latter part of the nineteenth century, stated, "Architecture is the art which so disposes and adorns the edifices raised by man, for whatsoever uses, that the sight of them may contribute to his mental health, power and pleasure."[11] This expression, representative of the views of the period, stressed that architecture was, in essence, an art and that the measure of its success was aesthetics. Michael Foster probably expressed a consensus of those now practicing architecture when he recently stated, "Architecture is essentially the art of reconciliation. It involves resolving specific and general demands of its users within a projected image of three-dimensional form. The design of a building is a creative, rather than a calculable process but, unlike other art forms, it is concerned with a positive search for solutions."[12] Richard Neutra also has expressed a viewpoint held by a vast number of present-day architects: "All our expensive long-term investments will be considered legitimate only if the designs have a high, provable *index of livability*. Such designs must be conceived by a profession brought up on social responsibility, skilled and intent on aiding the survival of a race. . . ."[13] Neutra's opinion voices the concern of a great designer that architecture must primarily serve human physical needs through environmental enhancement.

The evolution of hospital architecture traces a course closely similar to that of the broader field. Malcolm T. MacEachern's investigations generally reveal the transition of the hospital from a structure merely providing protection from the elements to the modern building created to serve distinct purposes of patient care and treatment.[14]

Aesthetics versus function

Over the past two decades, there have been many discussions of aesthetics and function as they relate to hospital design. Such discussions have centered on three main issues: (1) whether or not architectural aesthetics should preempt functionality; (2) the propriety of spending public funds for architectural embellishments to utilitarian structures; and (3) whether or not beauty in architecture and appropriate functionality can be achieved in a single structure.

Bradford Perkins has recognized the difficulty in reconciling functionality and aesthetics in hospitals:[15]

> Different building types generate very different design constraints. These differences must be reflected in the continual regeneration of a firm's design philosophy and process. High-technology, code-constrained and programmatic buildings such as hospitals and laboratories often present more difficult aesthetic challenges than a development office building or a luxury condominium where a different combination of a client's decision-making, program, budget and technical priorities govern.

John G. Read, some years ago, comprehensively researched the subject of aesthetics versus function in hospital design and drew the following conclusions:[16]

> It is hard to imagine a situation where function or beauty can only be obtained at the total expense of the other. Faced with this, a hearty search for alternative solutions should first be considered.
>
> However, a true balance must be kept. To sacrifice a great amount of beauty for very little function or vice versa is not wise. It would be wise, though, to favor function in borderline cases.
>
> Function should dictate the form of our hospitals—that is, a very careful analysis of function. Then, the state of beauty inherently obtained should be assessed and increased if possible. The functional analysis should thrive on objectivity, but the assessment of beauty must be subjective, for beauty, though discoverable, cannot be truly defined.
>
> Adopt a method, a formal one, which involves the attainment of useful and appropriate criteria for function and beauty. Apply it to the problem of design, but maintain the uniqueness of solution.
>
> When one considers function versus beauty, clarify the context in which these goals are being considered; is it economy, efficiency, luxury, pleasure, comfort, dependability, etc.?
>
> Certain administrative approaches to hospitals have considered (and built a good case for doing so) medical care, nursing care, supply and administration as the four basic "systems" within a hospital. The environment (one might say the architectural design) is just as much a system as any of these, affecting inputs, affecting outputs, being productive or destructive, exerting its dynamism not only in "every corner of the building," but also around the clock. As such, it should possibly receive as much attention as any of these other four systems.

We believe, after involvement in hundreds of hospital planning and design programs, that aesthetics and function are not truly at variance. Although beauty is essentially a subjective perception, a large number of beautiful designs have been effected that were also highly functional. In truth, aesthetics and function can be synergistic, with at least a part of beauty stemming from the fitness of design for purposes intended.

Traditional versus emerging concepts

Jacques Barzun, the noted philosopher, some years ago called the general hospital "one of man's most complex organized efforts to date."[17] Since Barzun's statement, great technological advances and other changes in diagnostic and treatment methodology have dramatically increased the complexity of hospital operations.

As a utilitarian structure housing the many diverse procedures necessary to implement various programs of service normally offered, the general hospital stands as a true challenge to architectural design. That a single person, through rational thinking, intuitive genius, or both, could comprehend the vast number of multifaceted considerations in the requirements of today's medical center seems hardly conceivable. Therefore, although design may reflect the labor of only one or two designers, the end product, as a conceptual mental achievement, must also represent the best thought of a number of professional consultants, as well as the technical knowledge of several hospital and medical disciplines.

Coupled with the complexity of the functions of a hospital is its dynamic nature, as exhibited in operational changes over the past two decades. It is safe to say that few hospital structures built according to the needs of 20 years ago could adequately meet today's demands without either appreciable alterations or expansion.

Thus it seems reasonable to assume that architectural design must necessarily be a multidisciplinary endeavor to ensure that the finished structure will meet current and long-term operational requirements to an optimal degree. This team approach to design directly controverts the "fountainhead" approach espoused by a school of traditional design methodology. George T. Heery has described the traditional design approach:[18]

> Traditionally, design has often been approached through the "fountainhead" theory. This specifically includes the approach employed not only by earlier-period architects but also that which has been espoused and employed by many contemporary architects on through the beginning of the 1970s. The theory is that the design of a building, group of related buildings, or other architectural elements must flow from the mind of one man. Preferably, this man is some sort of genius. The designer plays the role of the "fountainhead," and all other design and construction management disciplines have as their roles merely the support and execution of his design concept.
>
> A great deal of very bad architecture has been produced under this theory, though a great deal of poor architecture will probably always be produced with any given approach. But in an emulation of such true architectural geniuses of the twentieth century as Mies van der Rohe, Le Corbusier, Wright, and Gropius, the typical design process in many architectural firms has sometimes deteriorated to something like the following:

The program is given to a designer in the design department, who retires to his ivory tower and with soft pencil and yellow paper in hand starts the one-man process in the full expectation that he alone will come up with the right design. His main areas of attack are floor-planning, siting, and visual effect. He may consider, after some study, that he should seek a limited amount of structural or mechanical engineering advice. And, after a while, he may begin to use one or two more designers to work under his supervision, and he may even direct some research activities by others. After a design begins to take shape, which may well be several weeks or even months into the process, he may then bring in an estimator. Alas, all too often, he then starts over.

This age-old honored approach is, at best, inefficient. It is surely lacking in any real engineering integration. There is insufficient early construction cost input. Realistic time schedules for the design process are ignored, as are overall constraints that should have early identification. It is assumed, falsely, that construction management considerations can wait until later or be set in motion independently of the design process. Yet the process is a time-honored one, and he who tampers with it is said to be an insensitive poetry smasher by those who would promulgate the fountainhead approach.

Although Heery's criticisms of the traditional approach are strong, his remarks fairly represent viewpoints held among practitioners of architecture at the present time.

The federal government, through the Public Building Service of the General Services Administration (GSA), has been a prime proponent of a team approach to the design of all governmental structures and has strongly espoused the inclusion of construction-oriented individuals on the design team. Unquestionably, such individuals, whether they be members of firms engaged in general contracting or in basic construction management, can make valuable contributions to the design process.

Much criticism has been voiced regarding GSA's advocacy, primarily by architects who lean toward the "fountainhead" approach. Nevertheless, the basic good sense of requiring construction-oriented input to the design process seems to make GSA's position completely tenable.

The influence of functional planning

In the case of hospitals, however, functional complexities far outweigh physical complexities and demand an addition to the planning and design team of persons who understand not only the work processes of individual departments but those of the hospital operating as a single functional system. Architects and construction-oriented professionals acting alone may efficiently apply measures to control not only building costs but the time required for design and construction; they may also provide a building that operates efficiently as a physical structure. However, it is equally possible that they may entirely miss the mark in terms of operational functionality—and functionality, as a prime determinant of operational efficiency, is a major factor in the total life cycle cost of all hospital structures.

There is also little doubt that quality of care and treatment is directly affected by the degree to which design accommodates both inter- and intradepartmental functions. Valid comparisons have been made among operational systems and designs to accommodate them; such comparisons reveal that the time required to deliver immediate, critical care (a definite element of quality of care) can vary quite widely. Additionally, the percentage of professional time available for direct patient care has been shown to be in correlation to effective design.[19]

A new discipline called *functional planning* has emerged over the past two decades, which augurs well for the future of hospital design. Individuals possessing adequate training and experience in this field have made and are making substantial contributions to the planning and design process. Usually, such planners have backgrounds in hospital management, but many are the trained personnel of consulting firms specializing in both hospital program and facility planning.

Regardless of function-versus-aesthetics considerations, it is well-recognized that facilities should be a response to planned programs of services and systems of operation most feasible for their implementation in terms of cost and quality of care. This recognition has led to an accumulation of that body of knowledge now known as functional planning. One of the prime purposes of this text is to explain methodologies that are inherent to functional planning as a part of the total facility planning and design process.

Although functional planning of hospitals has not reached its maturity, and indeed may never do so, concepts springing from its practice are burgeoning yearly as intense study is made of alternative operational and building systems. There are even more innovative changes in operational methods and procedures on the horizon as demands for greater employee productivity are considered. All will directly depend upon architectural design for implementation; few can be brought into being without direct input to the design process by functional planners.

Granted, some worthwhile innovations will be conceptualized by hospital personnel, but most will evolve from research efforts effected by professional planners seeking to improve operational efficiencies. As in industry and most fields of technical endeavor, greatest progress can be expected from definitive programs of research rather than from the thoughts of operational personnel.

The team approach to design

The concept of hospital architecture here espoused is that its best implementation must stem from the knowledge of various professional disciplines, whose selected representatives relate constantly to the design team, both before and during design; furthermore, design must be in response to predicted demands, operational functionality, constraints of the real world, such as costs, and an optimal physical, social, and psychological environment for the various categories of building inhabitants.

The complexity of the problems involved and pertaining constraints under which any hospital is now constructed very definitely demand a team approach to design, rather than the isolated efforts of the single discipline of architecture.

Summary

Construction in the health care field, especially by hospital corporations, will remain strong in the years ahead, and the need to understand planning in its varied aspects will be an imperative for hospital officials. Essentially, planning is making decisions about future courses of action, and the several processes described in this chapter have been shown to be effective in reducing the probability of serious error when choices are made. Failure to adopt and to adhere to a specific methodology almost invariably results in a deterioration of the quality of planning.

Architectural design represents the most definitive act of planning in any building project. Accordingly, it is highly important that functionality and aesthetics become reconciled in structures that are largely utilitarian in nature. Functionality is an imperative, but there is no reason that beauty cannot accompany it, even to the extent that beauty may be sought for beauty's sake alone.

Modern-day architecture, excepting perhaps those structures designed for nonutilitarian purposes, should result from a team effort. Cost simplifications and the complexity of hospitals and most health-related structures demand that the broad knowledge inherent to a variety of disciplines be brought to bear on the design process. These considerations negate the "fountainhead" approach to design popularized some generations ago.

Although representing a new discipline, functional planning already has achieved recognition through its contributions to operational functionality and has become a key factor in hospital design. Future research in this area of the planning and design process may further enhance productivity in the health care field.

Notes

1. Owen B. Hardy, "Systematic Processes Applied to Health Care Planning," *Journal of the American College of Hospital Administrators*, Winter, 1971, p. 10.
2. Warren B. Brown and Dennis J. Moberg, *Organization Theory and Management* (New York: John Wiley & Sons, 1980), pp. 271–272.
3. John Argenti, *Systematic Corporate Planning* (Berkshire, England: Van Nostrand Reinhold (UK), 1974), pp. 11–12.
4. Robert M. Fuller, *The New Management* (New York: Macmillan, 1974), p. 81.
5. *Ibid.*, p. 156.
6. Hardy, "Systematic Processes," p. 14.
7. John Dewey, *How We Think* (Boston: D.C. Heath and Company, 1933), p. 17.
8. *Ibid.*, p. 117.
9. The General Electric Company used the approach in planning space reentry systems and later introduced it to health systems planning.
10. R. C. McWhorter, President, Hospital Corporations of America, 1984: personal communication.
11. John Ruskin, *The Seven Lamps of Architecture* (London: J. M. Dent & Sons, 1963), p. 7.
12. Michael Foster, ed., *Architectural Style, Structure and Design* (New York: Excalibur Books, 1982), p. 9.
13. Richard Neutra, *Survival through Design* (New York: Oxford University Press, 1954), pp. 4–5.

14. Malcolm T. MacEachern, *Hospital Organization and Management* (Berwyn, Ill.: Physicians Record Co., 1962), pp. 1–71.

15. Bradford Perkins, "Practice: Design Quality, a Central Architectural Management Issue," *Architectural Record*, March 1984, p. 47.

16. John G. Read, "Aesthetics versus Function As They Affect Hospital Design" (Toronto, Ontario: University of Toronto, Department of Hospital Administration, March 1965), pp. 16–17 (mimeographed).

17. Jacques Barzun, Professor of Philosophy, Columbia University, New York City, 1965: personal communication (telephone interview).

18. George T. Heery, *Time, Cost and Architecture* (New York: McGraw-Hill, 1975), pp. 71–72.

19. Chi Systems, Inc., "The Friesen No–Nursing Station Concept: Its Effects on Nurse Staffing," report of a study conducted at Scarborough Centenary Hospital, Toronto, Ontario, 1970, p. 1.

2

The Planning and Design Process

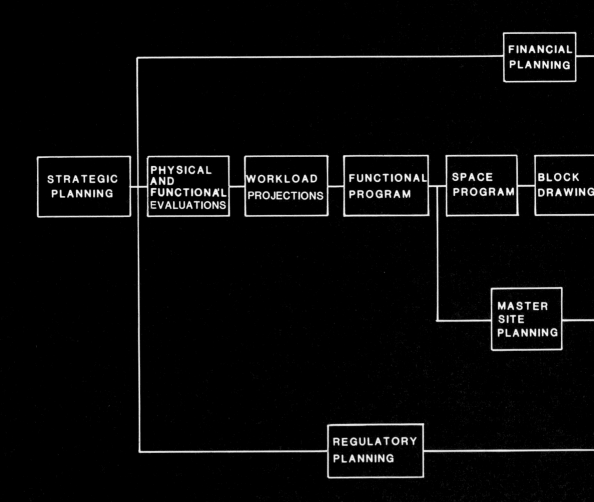

The facility planning and design process: an overview

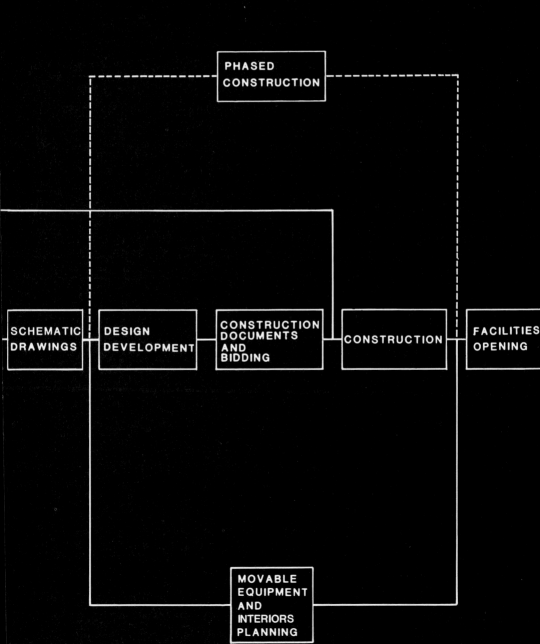

Consummation of a major hospital building program involves many people engaged in diverse but related efforts over a considerable time period. The program process comprises a significant number of interlocking steps, each of which is characterized by technical complexity. Moreover, as the cost of fixed equipment and the building fabric itself has rapidly advanced, projects of even limited scope may now cost millions of dollars. Some reduction in time requirements has been accomplished over the past 15 years, primarily through use of a design and construction methodology in which at least some phases of design and construction overlap. Nonetheless, the continuum has not been simplified; coordination has become more important, and correspondingly greater sophistication among planning team members is well recognized as a circumstantial requisite.

Consequent to the many important requirements of current facility planning, some hospitals have formalized the process either through "plans for planning" or through detailed scheduling techniques. Such planning represents a conscious effort by responsible management to visualize the work as an interrelated step-by-step process for guidance of all participants. This planning, when described narratively and presented as a graphic model, can bring order and coordination to the process, eliminate tangential and unnecessary actions, prevent hostilities among planning team members, and considerably expedite project completion. Although the efforts involved require considerable management skill, both in plan preparation and in implementation of an approved course of action, they almost invariably conserve both time and money.

No two formal plans for planning or process scheduling presentations will be similar owing to variation in time of formalization, project scope, organizational (hospital) structure and staff capabilities, and the optimal approach to planning, design, and construction. However, the planning and design process for a project of appreciable scope typically involves certain steps. Therefore, in this chapter we present a theoretical model, comprehensively configured, that embraces the classic steps in facility planning and design. An understanding of this model will be helpful to all those engaged in programs of hospital and related health care facility construction—hospital board members, hospital executives, architects, planners, and others—in formulating individual plans for a specific institution.

In terms of broad categories of activities, without designation of team members or their responsibilities, the process of hospital project planning can be depicted as a multistep or staged process. In the theoretical model presented here, these steps are as follows:

1. perception of need for a building program

2. strategic planning and feasibility assessments

3. organizing for planning, design, and construction

4. determining the planning, design, and construction approach

5. scheduling planning, design, and construction

6. opening the completed project.

Step 1: perception of need for a building program

For many years, a perceived need has been the prime stimulus for programs of hospital construction. Typically, observable facility obsolescence or inadequacies have generated the need perception. Currently, hospitals and other health care providers are viewing physical facilities as a tool to enhance ability to compete in the field, so that management increasingly considers facility improvements or expansion. Although the regulatory agencies still bridle ambitious competitiveness to a considerable extent, competition is certainly gaining as the driving force for hospital and related health care constructions. Thus, even though obsolescence and demand volumes will continue to stimulate the majority of constructions, the opportunity to increase market shares through facility enhancements will also provide initiatives.

With meaningful health care facilities planning virtually dead from the standpoint of the regulatory agencies (for reasons noted in the Preface), both the large investor-owned and nonprofit systems may pound these agencies with certificate of need (CON) applications largely tailored to gain or maintain a competitive edge and, in turn, to increase their respective market shares. Many independent hospitals will respond to the challenge; thus, an appreciable spiral of construction stemming largely from the forces of competition can be expected.

At the present time, there is little probability that logical planning based upon the concept of regionalization will occur. However, the large systems are considering facilities shown to be competitively advantageous among their geographically related hospitals. In this manner, the concepts of both regionalization and vertical integration may be implemented indirectly as outgrowths of the competitive climate.

For the foreseeable future, then, it is quite likely that private perceptions of need, some of which will originate from desires to gain competitive advantages, will stand as the first identifiable step in most facility construction programs.

Step 2: strategic planning and feasibility assessments

Active planning begins with strategic planning and feasibility assessments. The strategic planning process should include a first-level analysis for program planning. Concurrently, a debt capacity analysis should be performed to predict the broad capability of a particular hospital (or system of health care facilities) to finance construction.

Every strategic planning process should be an outflow from a comprehensively configured data base, outlined in some detail in Chapter 3. The necessity for this data base is no less important than it was in the era of regulation; indeed, most authorities regard it is as being even more important. Unwarranted and unrealistic competitive wishfulness must be put into objective perspective *before* decisions involving millions of dollars are made. Many hospitals have been reluctant to assemble an appropriate data base, through either ignorance or a reluctance to devote necessary time to the task. Such hospitals run the great risk of succumbing to competition over a period of years. The data base points up false notions and also uncovers opportunities not recognizable otherwise. The data base does not stifle leadership or boldness, but it definitely prevents hospitals from proceeding in wrong directions.

Those executives who neglect to assemble the data base at the outset should also realize that in the case of large projects, for which financing must be sought, prospective bond underwriters will require proof of programmatic and financial feasibility for construction based on *any* initiative. Even though the remaining regulatory agencies play a largely passive role, they also will require proof of feasibility. Obviously, documenting the case for a program *before* it is finally conceived makes far better sense than leaving this task until *after* it is conceived, when errors in decision making may become apparent during preparation of the required proof.

The strategic planning process should also generate a study report that defines the programmatic role of the hospital and its related system components, over at least a 10-year period, and that interprets this role broadly in terms of physical facilities, such as beds, outpatient clinics and services, and the general space requirements for departments of all types and various vertically integrated programs. Sharing of services and facilities with all components of the system should be clearly outlined. Medical personnel requirements must be carefully determined in conjunction with an analysis of the existing medical staff.

Following completion of the strategic plan and its adoption as the planning guide for the future, capital costs of implementing construction and basic financial capabilities must be determined. At this point, refined costs cannot be prepared because definitive drawings and specifications are not yet available, but to proceed further without a realistic assessment of financial capability to implement is a mistake of the first order. Despite the many horror stories of the past, architects continue to be commissioned to design facilities that cannot possibly be financed, although even a cursory examination of costs, capital assets, and borrowing capacities would reveal the nonfeasibility of the project. The outcome of proceeding without regard for financial constraints oftentimes involves a complete redesign (for a fee), additional planning fees, repetition of internal planning efforts (to the embarrassment of management), and considerable lost time, which can be costly from a number of standpoints.

In evaluating the capacity to finance a proposed project, even at this early stage, the hospital should employ a financial consulting firm to perform a debt capacity analysis or other financial assessment. Some hospitals have the capacity to perform this work internally, but the objectivity of the results is oftentimes questioned. Some prospective lenders will also examine financial documentations, as well as the statistical projections of the strategic plan, and will render an opinion relating to feasibility, but these opinions, too, are often cursory and overly optimistic owing to the desire to curry client favor. In some instances, to the regret of responsible hospital officials, a complete financial feasibility study, which must be later performed by a public accounting firm, reveals the nonfeasibility of a project judged earlier by the prospective lender to be feasible; typically, the lender then declares that the required funds would have been loaned, despite knowing all the while that the necessity would not have occurred. All factors considered, we believe that the surest and, in the long run, most economical way to proceed is to employ a reputable accounting and financial consulting firm to prepare a non-biased assessment of financial capability, usually a debt capacity analysis.

The primary criterion in evaluating financial capability is a given hospital's ability to generate cash payments to repay a required loan, with interest in full, according to a practicable time schedule. In most instances, lenders will require the hospital to have an equity of appreciable value in the completed construction. Whoever may be consulted as to financial capability will wish to examine expense and revenue statements relating to existing operations, because the best indicator of a hospital's ability to produce cash is past experience, upon which appropriate projections, with due weight given to the changed conditions resulting from a building program, can be formulated.

Thus, although at this point an accurate and detailed financial assessment is not necessary, nor even possible owing to lack of information about the precise scope of the proposed project, reliable estimates—based on reasonable assumptions, existing financial documentations, and the strategic plan—pertaining to topside budgets can be prepared. Certainly the importance of an early determination of a proposed project's financial feasibility cannot be disregarded, because continued planning should proceed only with assurance that expenditures will be within the limits of absolute constraints and that costly repetitive efforts will not be unnecessarily entailed.

Step 3: organizing for planning

If the strategic plan shows that a construction program is indicated and the financial evaluation indicates that it is feasible, the hospital must then organize to undertake the project. Too often in the past, hospitals have established contracts with architects and functional planners even before the strategic plan was completed. Certainly, there is little need to organize for physical plant planning when the feasible parameters of a project are unknown, for these may have considerable bearing upon the selection of the professional planning team.

If the strategic plan indicates facility construction, however, management must give serious account to its implementation. In many instances, officials believe that existing organizational structures can respond adequately to the exigencies of physical plant planning, design, and construction—but this is seldom the case. Failure to recognize the special needs involved often results in confusion, irreconcilable hostilities, and facilities of poor functional quality that in many instances are not related to either primary or derived demands certain to accrue, or to productivity requirements in the current climate of DRGs and competition.

Organizing for planning requires several important actions:

- development of a decision-making mechanism

- appointment of a director of planning

- organizing for internal review of planning documentations

- selection of the professional planning team

- organizing the planning team and formulating operating procedures.

Each of these actions is discussed in the following sections.

Development of a decision-making mechanism

Regardless of the quality of planning, there are a sufficient number of diverse interests related to hospital planning and construction that conflicting opinions are bound to arise. Unless channels are established through which issues may be properly directed to respective decision-making points, conflicting viewpoints may develop into serious controversies. Although the governing board represents the ultimate institutional authority, experience has shown that only those matters of considerable import should be routinely decided there. Specifically, the planning and design of major building programs impose a sufficient additional strain upon the management hierarchy that it is essential to provide a special mechanism to handle the issues directly related to these endeavors.

In major programs there are generally four levels of decision making, and it is axiomatic that decisions should be made at levels pertaining to the impact of the decision. The first level of authority is usually delegated to the director of planning, who serves as an arm of hospital administration; the building committee occupies the second level. At the third level, a separate committee with broad and diverse user representation can be organized to handle matters of significant importance and those in which controversy may arise. Of course, the governing board, at the fourth or uppermost level, must retain ultimate authority and responsibility for the building program in its entirety. The staff and line relations involved in this organizational arrangement are set forth in Figure 2–1.

The planning director's role in decision making may be relatively minor regarding substantive matters. The director's functions usually relate more to scheduling and coordinating the activities of planners, architects, engineers, construction managers, financial advisors, and other professional team members; scheduling tasks to be performed by members of the internal hierarchy; formulating appropriate reports; and seeing to it that matters for decision (beyond the first level) are channeled to appropriate points in the decision-making chain.

The building committee has traditionally served in a key decision-making role, acting exclusively upon many important matters and reporting directly to the governing board. In these instances, there have usually been only two or three levels in the chain. We believe, however, that the process can be facilitated by the interjection of the special user committee between the building committee and the governing board. The building

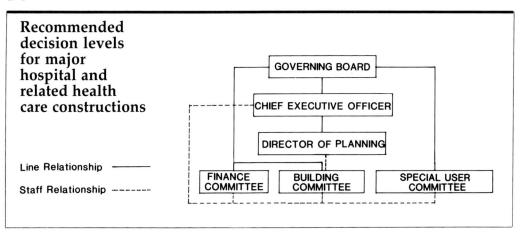

Recommended decision levels for major hospital and related health care constructions

Line Relationship ———

Staff Relationship – – – – –

GOVERNING BOARD

CHIEF EXECUTIVE OFFICER

DIRECTOR OF PLANNING

FINANCE COMMITTEE

BUILDING COMMITTEE

SPECIAL USER COMMITTEE

committee can fulfill the important function of considering a variety of highly technical matters and rendering recommendations and advice related thereto. The special user committee, rather than being a working body, has the sole function of decision making, short of the governing board's ultimate authority and responsibilities.

To the special user committee, there should be referred matters that involve the often conflicting interests of different disciplines or departments, such as medicine versus administration, surgery versus medicine, or nursing versus supply, and broad and diverse representation is critical to the acceptability of its decisions. It is patent that a physician, for example, will be more favorably inclined to accept a decision made by a committee on which physicians hold membership; likewise, nursing administration will be more placable when nursing has a deciding voice. At the same time, the presence of diverse disciplines will help to achieve necessary compromise, so that the probability of balance among departmental allocations will become greater, and "empire-building" can be more successfully avoided.

The efforts of the special user committee, in addition to reducing the overall workload of the governing board, have the effect of relieving governing board members of detailed consideration of many controversial matters that do not possess great intrinsic importance. In considering the actions and recommendations of the user group, the governing board can also be assured that a "thrashing out" has already taken place and that the board's action can be taken with a much greater awareness of probable internal repercussions.

Whatever structure is created, it should be openly published, with the authority assigned to each point in the chain clearly outlined. The vast majority of authoritative opinion leans toward written, as opposed to unwritten, management policies of all major types, and the importance of reducing to writing that policy related to planning of a large building program cannot be denied. Such a program is an undertaking that is relatively rare, even in the complete course of a manager's professional life, and those in other disciplines who must be involved in the process cannot possibly be expected to retain or agree on one-time verbalizations that may not be clear and wholly free from contradiction.

Appointment of a director of planning

A planning director is essential to the success of most large hospital building programs. Although establishing the position still is the exception rather than the rule, the practice seems to be proliferating, especially within organizations in which strategic planning possesses a high priority. Certainly there are sufficient activities generated directly by a major building program to warrant a full-time person, and in some very large programs one or two assistants can be justified.

The job of a director of planning in a large building program is a highly sensitive one. An ability to coordinate is critical. Managerial skills are more important than technical skills, although knowledge about the basics of design, economics, or functional planning is desirable. The person selected should have considerable perceptual ability, as well as a pleasant appearance and demeanor.

It is essential that a highly specific, written job description be provided. The magnitude of authority delegated to the planning director can vary widely, depending upon the situation, but for the director's protection, as well as in the hospital's best interests, this should be carefully spelled out. The level and scope of required decisions must be understood both by the director and by all others. The director's position in the table of organization and specific duties should be explained to all planning team members, medical staff leaders, and members of the management hierarchy.

Organizing for internal review of planning documentations

Internal review of planning documents and design drawings can become an extremely tedious and time-consuming process unless it is handled properly. An appropriate review mechanism embraces the decision-making mechanism, but it must be broadened to include certain groups to which no decision-making authority has been delegated. For example, certain user representatives should be asked to review documentations, assess alternatives, and submit recommendations. The decision-making authority relative to those recommendations should be retained elsewhere—as noted previously, with either the director of planning, the building committee, the special user committee, or the governing board.

The manner in which review of appropriate documentations and drawings by the medical staff is conducted will vary widely, depending upon the particular situation. Our experience over hundreds of projects, however, indicates that a conspicuous lack of regard for the concerns of the medical staff will have undesirable consequences. Rather, reviews should be scheduled on an organized basis, and recommendations should be recorded and transmitted to appropriate decision-making bodies. It is not necessary or desirable that the medical staff alone, or any department thereof, be accorded the power of approval or disapproval of any part of planning documentations. Likewise, it is not necessary to seek out hypotheses regarding needs or functional planning theories from staff members, provided competent consultants and architects have been employed. However, the medical staff voice will seldom be stifled, and when opinions are voluntarily expressed they should be received with respect. Formal recommendations stemming from scheduled reviews should be seriously considered by those to whom decision-making authority has been delegated. If a specific recommendation is rejected, the reasons therefor should be made clear.

Example documentations that should be formally reviewed by medical staff representatives, on a departmental basis, include strategic plan goals and objectives of the functional program, master site plan, block plan drawings, schematic drawings, and design development drawings.

Administrative heads of departments will ordinarily be requested to review all relevant planning documentations and drawings and to submit comments in writing to the director of planning. The director, in turn, should review the comments, hold discussions where necessary, and remit written recommendations to the appropriate decision-making body. Most points will be cleared up directly with members of the planning team, but some differences of opinion will usually have to be settled formally at an appropriate level in the decision-making chain.

In some instances, management has organized user review committees related to diagnostic and treatment elements, supporting services, inpatient nursing, administrative services, and so forth. These committees can well serve in lieu of review by individual institutional department heads, but there is little question that department heads should serve on the respective committees that will review documentations related to their department.

The finance committee of the governing board is charged with important review responsibilities, especially when appreciable capital funding is required. This body will confer frequently with the financial consultant and the investment banker and, from time to time, will make appropriate recommendations to the governing board.

Selection of the professional planning team

The competence of the professional planning team will determine, more than any other single factor, the quality and suitability of completed facilities. This team should be selected with care, according to thoughtfully formulated criteria. A complete team should possess capabilities in four specific areas:

- financial feasibility consulting

- functional planning

- architectural and engineering services

- construction management.

On large, complicated projects, each capability should be represented by an independent firm, probably serving as a separate contractor to the owner. In the case of the latter-named three, a team of firms can be formed to render services under a single contract. On smaller, less complicated projects, design and construction management can be performed by a single contractor, usually at a savings in fees, or the services of a construction manager can be eliminated, on the grounds that such services on uncomplicated projects are redundant.

The financial feasibility consultant is often viewed only as a member of the financial planning team. However, owing to the interdependence of the work efforts of all four components of the team, the inclusion here seems appropriate. In later discussions of financial planning (Chapter 5), we refer to the actual tasks performed in a financial feasibility study as being a part of financial planning.

The functions of the investment banker are discussed under financial planning (Chapter 5). We note here that if funds are to be borrowed, as is usually the case, the advice of a reliable firm is indispensable, and certainly the choice among candidates should be made with care. Selection of an investment banker should be consummated not later than at the time a professional planning team is assembled. Tentative financial advice, in many instances, will be needed earlier.

The first task involved in selecting planning team members is to assign authority for accomplishing the selection process. A special committee is usually so charged. The next step is to formulate written criteria governing the selection process. If desired, a point-scoring system can be devised for a quantitative assessment of applicants' qualifications, to allow comparison, but this is not essential. After criteria are prepared and agreed upon, the process should be organized and a time schedule constructed, culminating in signed contracts.

Although there will be some projects in which all four members of the team as designated are not contracted, we consider each in the following discussion since a majority of major projects now require the indicated skills, assigned and organized according to the dictates of the work involved.

Financial feasibility consultant

The financial feasibility consultant usually functions independently of all other members of the planning team. However, experience has proved that the danger of bias, as is conceivable when this consultant also performs either or both strategic planning and functional planning, is more imagined than real. In fact, in some instances, time and money may be saved owing to the importance assigned to financial considerations in other aspects of planning. Nonetheless, many if not most hospitals desire the independence of all four professional members of the planning team.

The financial feasibility consulting firm had best be experienced in hospital work and be able to provide in-depth talent. The firm should choose a person responsible for the project who can interface compatibly with designated hospital representatives, and whose continuity on the project can be assured. The selection committee should confirm the suitability and competence of the consultant's representative in an interview during which the proposed work is discussed. Proximity of the consultant's office to the hospital, affording ready availability for on-site consultations when needed, is of considerable importance.

Any establishment of basic criteria for selection of the financial feasibility consultant will usually qualify the "big eight" and several other large accounting firms. The use of formal criteria seemingly may eliminate some competent smaller firms that rightfully should be given consideration, depending upon local circumstances, but almost invariably is effective in weeding out firms that cannot deliver top-quality services.

Functional planning consultant

There continues to be a large number of persons who are attempting to sell their services as functional planners, either on a part-time or full-time basis. Some are retired hospital administrators; others have backgrounds in industrial engineering, architecture, or related disciplines. Many are relatively inexperienced and do not have the qualifications to advise competently on a project involving millions of dollars.

Fortunately, the American Association of Healthcare Consultants (AAHC) requires its membership to possess certain minimum qualifications related to past experience and education.[1] The roster of individuals composing this professional organization provides a ready source from which a highly competent functional planner can be selected. Hospital executives are well advised to obtain the membership listing of the AAHC, to select several firms represented, and to proceed with detailed interviews in the selection process.

Demonstrated past performance, financial stability, in-depth talent of a multidisciplinary nature, current workloads, and qualifications of the project manager to be assigned to the job are major issues to be considered in selecting a functional planning consultant. The interview selection process should also consider a planning team composed of individuals specifically named by the consulting firm. The quality of a functional planner's work will be no better than that permitted by the competence of the two or three persons with definitive work assignments, and especially to be evaluated is the project manager.

Architect

With regard to selecting an architectural and engineering (A&E) firm, the American Hospital Association has formulated excellent criteria that can be obtained upon request, obviating the need for detailed discussion here.[2] The basic criteria, however, are the same as those for other members of the planning team.

Although the practice is diminishing, a number of A&E firms have attempted to specialize in functional planning. Even when motives and objectives have been of exemplary character, however, such attempts have not been notably successful over a long period of time. Functional planning, from the beginning, almost invariably occupies a secondary role, the importance of which is lessened as key internal decisions are made, and which diminishes further over time, as the project progresses, until it is accorded only lip service.

Our assessment is that architects should rely primarily upon hospital-oriented and -educated persons who pursue functional planning independently, and we believe that hospital management is ill-advised to accept claims by A&E firms of functional planning expertise comparable in quality with that afforded by several of the firms listed by the AAHC.

Construction manager

The construction management (CM) approach began to assume major importance in the construction industry in the late 1960s and 1970s. In this approach, a specialized firm serves, to one degree or another, as the owner's agent and manager of the building process. Claimed benefits of CM have generally been as follows:

1. the control of design and construction time

2. the control of construction and other associated costs

3. the enhancement of construction quality

4. reduced problems of coordination for the owner.

The environment of the late 1960s and 1970s, involving rapid inflation, a prodigious amount of construction, and the need for fast construction schedules and well-managed construction processes, made the use
of CM nearly inevitable. Thomsen has noted:[3]

> For institutions such as schools, hospitals, universities, prisons
> and some of the bigger corporations, some versions of CM
> became the common delivery method [during the 1970s]. These
> clients were characterized by a bureaucratic process, a board or a
> staff inexperienced in the field of design and construction or in
> the need to manage a design and construction process that
> would be well documented for public or shareholder scrutiny.

At the present time, a great majority of major hospital and related
health care construction projects continues to be delivered through the
services of a CM firm, both for Thomsen's stated reasons and because the
complexity of hospital design and construction poses monumental problems of coordination. Despite the fact that CM has not lived up to the
early expectations of being a panacea, it remains the approach of choice
for most large hospital projects.

A great problem that has beset CM as a universal approach to the
building process stems from the fact that firms and individuals with marginal competence and finances have been able to enter the field. Thomsen
puts this matter in perspective: "But a construction manager required no
license as did architects and engineers. Nor did he require a successful
business organization with a strong financial statement that a general
contractor must have. Too many lightweights entered the field."[4] Thus, it
behooves hospital officials to scrutinize carefully not only the technical
qualifications and experience of prospective construction managers, but
their financial status as well.

Both the Association of General Contractors (AGC) and the American Institute of Architects (AIA) have drafted example contracts for CM
work. The AGC sample contract assumes that trade contracts are with the
CM firm and provides for a guaranteed maximum price (GMP). The AIA
example contract envisions "a professional service with prime trade
contractors under direct contract to the owner."[5]

Because major construction usually relies heavily upon borrowed
funds within a restricted debt capacity, the GMP route set forth under the
AGC example contract has become the approach of choice for hospitals.
The great desirability for establishment of a GMP usually means that the
role of the construction manager may change from one of pure coordination of trade contracts, and of technical advisor to the hospital and architect, to one closer to that of a general contractor, especially when costs

approach an overrun (above the GMP). Still, the hospital obtains early construction-oriented input into the design process, and this alone may save millions of dollars. Usually such savings cannot be pinpointed, because costly alternatives that an architect working alone might have produced are not around for comparison.

Although fees for CM services still vary quite widely, they are becoming more standardized, and some selection criteria should be considered in this regard. Criteria based on technical competence; knowledge of local availability of materials and procurement constraints; proximity of key personnel; in-depth multidisciplinary talent; financial capability and stability; and current workloads have been successfully drawn up and used in a number of situations. Although most planning directors can draft a point scoring system reflecting the selection criteria, several such systems are circulating in the field and can easily be obtained.

Selection timing and methodology
The functional planner, the architect, and the construction manager can all make valuable contributions in the early stages of a project and should be contracted at approximately the same time. Because the functional planner has the most intense involvement in the very first stages, that firm might be brought aboard first, but the other two should closely follow. If an independent financial consulting firm has been contracted to set initial budgetary limits, that firm will have already been selected. In the event that this task has been accomplished internally with or without the advice of a prospective lender, the selection of a financial consultant can possibly be deferred until such time as precise operational parameters and valid capital cost estimates are in hand. The services of this consultant, however, will be desirable at the time workload projections are made.

The selection process should be one of system and order; giving unstructured interviews on a first-come, first-served basis is to be avoided. Although the number of applicants to fill respective positions on the planning team may be limited, this is rarely the problem. Instead, on major projects, the number of applicants is usually larger than the hospital can reasonably be expected to interview, especially in the case of A&E firms. Therefore, some methodology for screening should be devised.

Rather than merely reviewing brochures and other promotional material that applicants may submit on a voluntary basis, the hospital, through its director of planning, should submit a structured questionnaire to various interested firms and, on the basis of responses received, narrow down the firms to be interviewed to a reasonable number (usually four to six). The questionnaire should obtain information about the general nature of the firm and should ascertain its capabilities and experience related directly to the type of project to be undertaken. Past client references should be checked.

The interviewing process, which should focus on those individuals to be assigned by a prospective firm to the project, ought to be structured with ample time reserved for questions (most of which should be predetermined) and answers. Public relations departments of large firms have actually devised basic "acts" that can be extremely persuasive but misleading. The give-and-take in a dialogue with those to be committed to the project can be a decided contrast to an artfully done "slide show."

Minutes should be taken of each interview, with answers to questions being carefully recorded. In most instances a later interview will be desirable to recall impressions and, in some instances, to clarify more substantive issues.

It is much less confusing to resolve the selection of one team member at a time rather than to intermingle a number of diverse interviews over an extended period. For example, architectural firms alone should be interviewed within approximately one week and a decision rendered the week thereafter.

Dilatory actions can mean only a reduced possibility of selecting the best firm; memories dim, outside pressures accrue in one way or another, and some applicants will exert continuing sales efforts, which may not be annoying but may give unfair advantage to the party with the best-subsidized marketing arm.

Some benefit may be gained in holding second interviews when two applicants seemingly have equal capabilities. Such additional interviews should be similarly structured for each party and should both clarify points covered in the original interview and raise additional points. Usually, a decision can easily be made following a second round of interviews.

Organizing the team and formulating operating procedures

Organizing the team
There are a number of ways in which the professional planning team can be organized, but two are most common, and each of them has merit under different situations. One approach involves employment of independent firms, with each reporting separately to the director of planning or another hospital official; in the other approach, the financial planner reports directly to the hospital, and the remaining three consultants are organized as a team under one of several possible arrangements.

If the hospital has a strong director of planning, whose primary job is to supervise the planning for a major building program, there may be advantages in having all members of the team report directly to this official. The use of dynamic tension becomes possible (a debatable advantage), and independent thought is assured. With the span of control involving only four firms, the planning director usually is able to coordinate the separate activities of each team member satisfactorily. This is not to imply that the separate planning groups always work at arm's length; rather, their work together is under the director's coordination.

If the director of planning is inexperienced or has other major duties, leaving less than full time to planning activities, an advantage may lie in seeking a contract with a consortium composed of the A&E, functional planning, and CM firms. Usually the architect or construction manager will be assigned a lead role, under terms of the contractual agreement. The financial feasibility consultant should continue to report directly and independently to the hospital. This arrangement relieves the hospital of coordinating efforts of independent and, unfortunately, oftentimes hostile professional planning team members. Interests of a consortium are

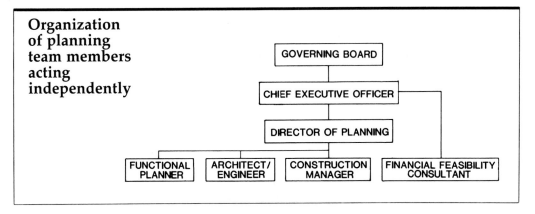

Organization of planning team members acting independently

GOVERNING BOARD

CHIEF EXECUTIVE OFFICER

DIRECTOR OF PLANNING

FUNCTIONAL PLANNER | ARCHITECT/ ENGINEER | CONSTRUCTION MANAGER | FINANCIAL FEASIBILITY CONSULTANT

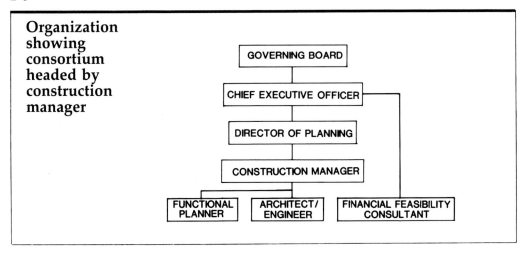

Organization showing consortium headed by construction manager

GOVERNING BOARD

CHIEF EXECUTIVE OFFICER

DIRECTOR OF PLANNING

CONSTRUCTION MANAGER

FUNCTIONAL PLANNER | ARCHITECT/ ENGINEER | FINANCIAL FEASIBILITY CONSULTANT

best served by self-coordination, but objective thought is preserved through the professional and organizational independence of each firm.

Experience has shown that a consortium as described can perform quality work, but consortium contracts continue to represent a small minority among those being executed to deliver planning, design, and construction services to hospitals throughout this continent.

Figures 2–2 and 2–3 illustrate the two basic arrangements noted.

A few hospitals have employed the services of an outside firm to coordinate activities of the named professional planning team members. If such a firm possesses knowledge of and competency in execution of the planning and design process, as described in this text, this approach certainly is legitimate. However, fees for this service have usually been substantial, and we lean toward employment of an experienced director of planning as a more reasonable approach to coordination.

Formulating operating procedures
Channels of communication among team members and the hospital should be clearly outlined, in writing, at the outset. If this is not done,

there will be a strong possibility that coordination will deteriorate as the project progresses.

When any formal correspondence is directed from one team member to another or from a team member to the director of planning, copies should be supplied to all. Beyond this, there should be a person (other than the director of planning) in the hospital to whom copies of all correspondence should be sent. This person, in most instances, should be the chairperson of the building committee, who preferably will also be a member of the governing board.

Meetings of the planning team can be called on an impromptu basis, but coordination will be best served by regularly scheduled meetings. The same advantages inherent to holding scheduled department head meetings in the hospital accrue from such meetings among members of the planning team. Early in the project, when the functional planner only is intensely involved, monthly meetings may be sufficient. When the architect becomes heavily engaged in master site planning and block and schematic drawings, weekly meetings should be chaired by the director of planning, and the chairperson of the building committee or other representatives of that committee should be present.

Step 4: determining the planning, design, and construction approach

After the professional planning and design team has been selected, the hospital should select a specific approach to project construction. This decision will materially affect the manner in which planning and design are carried out. Early determination of the optimal approach will allow the preparation of meaningful schedules and will avoid later work repetitions.

In a still valid 1975 AIA report, *Project Delivery Approaches*, an overview of delivery methods states, "Once the project is underway, it is often too late to change approaches (for example, once construction documents have begun, it is too late to easily break the construction contract into separate 'packages' in order to meet conditions in the market-place)."[6]

Our experience on a host of projects indicates that a definitive approach to planning, design and construction must be selected *no later* than after the completion of schematic drawings, or repetitive work will be necessitated. However, in order to prepare appropriate and meaningful schedules to guide the work of each planning and design team member, as well as to achieve a coordinated approach to financing, an approach should be determined *before* facility planning and design activities are undertaken.

A decision in this regard should be made by the hospital with advice from the professional planning team. Each approach should be carefully considered. A brief discussion of the currently leading approaches follows.

Traditional design and construction approach

The "Standard Form of Agreement Between Owner and Architect," AIA Document B141, states, "The architect shall prepare from the approved Design Development Documents, for approval by the Owner, Drawings and Specifications for the construction of the entire project including the necessary bidding information, and shall assist in the preparation of bidding forms, the Conditions of the Contract, and the form of Agreement between the Owner and the Contractor."[7] Thus, one bid package for the entire project is prepared, and in most instances, one contract is awarded to a single general contractor, who will subcontract major portions of the work to other construction firms. Construction does not start until the preparation of all design and contract documents has been finished. This approach is the *traditional design and construction approach*.

In the event that a construction manager has not been employed, or that the CM contract does not provide for coordination of work by the several trades required on site, the general contractor assumes this responsibility. Otherwise, of course, the construction manager is in control of the construction and is obligated to provide sufficient personnel at the project site for coordination of the work of contractors with activities and responsibilities of the owner and architect.

The AIA report *Project Delivery Approaches* states that the traditional approach is applicable where clearly defined linear phases are required for purposes of financing or by the selected approach; where the complexity or uniqueness of the project dictates that design details be fully developed before construction is begun; where the owner puts a premium on maintaining conventional roles and relationships and ways of doing things; where cost and time are not overriding concerns; and where there is some timidity about abandoning traditional ways of doing things.[8]

Our experience indicates that this construction approach is still highly advantageous for projects in which design and construction are not highly complex and in which only simple phasing of construction activities is required. This approach is also attractive for projects not requiring detailed scheduling in order to continue ongoing hospital operations. Usually, but not necessarily, the traditional approach is applicable to small projects, because these generally are not as complex as are large projects; however, a very large project that is comparatively straightforward may benefit by this approach, from the standpoints of both time and money. The subsiding of inflation has also made the traditional approach somewhat more attractive, both for the hospital and for contractors.

Phased construction methodology

After approval of schematic design drawings and outline specifications, the A&E firm can prepare construction documents for bidding on initial contracts under the *phased construction* (fast-track) *approach*. The sequencing of contracts may vary somewhat, as do the contents of each, from project to project, but to some extent the order is the same, because hospital buildings possess similar components and systems that can be put together in a single optimal way from the standpoint of efficiency in construction. For this reason, we have elected to set forth here a sequencing of contracts extracted from a master schedule of construction that was prepared for one of the largest projects in North America—the Erie

County Medical Center in Buffalo, New York, completed in 1977.[9] The order shown—which is based on the CPM (critical path method) scheduling technique—and the work involved under each contract represent a somewhat standard approach at the present time.

Contract No. 1—General

Excavations, concrete foundations, structural steel, metal deck, concrete slabs (not on grade), stairways, parking, water lines, sanitary and storm sewers, slab on grade (mechanical plant).

Contract No. 2—General

Precast siding, windows-panels-glazing-caulking, aluminum louvers, roofing–flashing–sheet metal work, sky domes, exterior doors (mechanical plant), miscellaneous masonry.

Contract No. 3—General

Elevators, escalator, dumbwaiter, ACT [automatic cart transportation] system, block shaftways (stairs and elev.), fireproofing, doors and door bucks (stairways and mech. plant), main catwalks, insulation (ext. walls), temporary heat and power, toilet partitions–glass, glazing-paint-lockers-benches (mech. plant).

Contract No. 4—Plumbing

Roof drains, conductors, plumbing fixtures, water tanks, oil tanks, fire storage tank.

Contract No. 5—Heating, Ventilation, and Air Conditioning (HVAC)

Large air handling units, boiler, other equipment.

Contract No. 6—Electrical

Power substation, power house, temporary light and power distribution.

Contract No. 7—General

Interior partitions-finishes-hardware, built-in equipment including large lab, morgue ceilings, glass and glazing (interior), vacuum cleaning system, aluminum entrance doors and frames, pneumatic tubes.

Contract No. 7B

Site work, landscaping.

Contract No. 8—Plumbing

Interior drains, hot and cold water, gases, natural gas, lavatories complete, equipment piping, equipment connections.

Contract No. 9—HVAC

Air handling, ducts, temperature control, insulation, induction units, radiation, equipment connections (morgue).

Contract No. 10—Electrical

All lighting, panels, feeders, low voltage transformers, fire alarms, power supply, equipment power, clocks, equipment connections, site lighting.

Contract No. 11—Separate Contracts

A. Laundry
B. Sterilization
C. Kitchen Equipment
D. Laboratory Equipment
E. Destructors
F. X-ray, Cobalt, etc.
G. Communications Systems
H. Computers

Separate bid documents (construction drawings and specifications) are prepared for each bid package, bids are solicited, contracts are awarded, and construction is commenced all in accord with a master schedule—usually based on PERT (program evaluation and review technique) or CPM (critical path method)—prepared by the construction manager and approved by the hospital. The construction manager or the architect, depending upon contract provisions, will hold responsibility for determining appropriate bidders, submitting bid documents to them, and evaluating and awarding bids, all subject to hospital approval.

Fast, successful construction depends upon many factors, two of which are the qualifications of successful bidders and the experience and capabilities of the construction manager. Unless expert coordination and supervision of the multiple independently contracted activities are exercised on site, chaos can result. Some of the disillusionment with CM has resulted from such situations; the key to avoiding similar problems, of course, is selection of a CM firm with a solid track record of success in staying on a predetermined time schedule and within a projected budget.

The great theoretical advantage of phased construction lies in the saving of time. While planning and design continue, construction can begin. It also has a generally unspoken advantage in the hospital field, where decision making can be unbelievably slow and where impasses among power groups can prevent any definitive actions except those of immediate urgency. Thus an early construction commitment forces later actions to keep the project alive and proceeding.

Figure 2–4 is a familiar presentation of the time savings possible under phased construction.

Other approaches

Several alternative approaches to construction have been developed over the past several years, all of which claim to lower costs or to shorten the planning, design, and construction period.

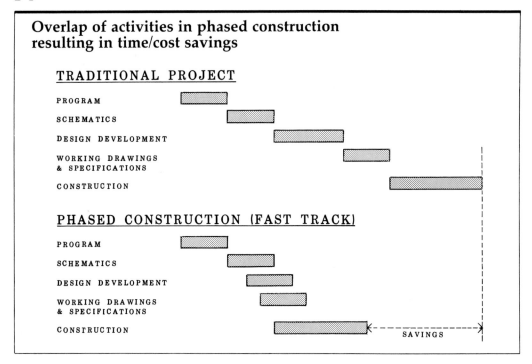

**Overlap of activities in phased construction
resulting in time/cost savings**

TRADITIONAL PROJECT

PROGRAM

SCHEMATICS

DESIGN DEVELOPMENT

WORKING DRAWINGS
& SPECIFICATIONS

CONSTRUCTION

PHASED CONSTRUCTION (FAST TRACK)

PROGRAM

SCHEMATICS

DESIGN DEVELOPMENT

WORKING DRAWINGS
& SPECIFICATIONS

CONSTRUCTION

SAVINGS

One such approach, the *turnkey* or *package deal* approach, offers at the outset a predetermined, all-inclusive price for the completed construction. The developer, who provides all planning, design, and construction services, guarantees that the building will meet code requirements, but usually little more. Quality may be sacrificed in the developer's desire to achieve a profit margin of undefined proportions, depending upon a number of factors. Owing to the poor quality evidenced in a number of projects built under this approach, it has apparently fallen into disfavor.

The *design/build* (D/B) approach features contracting by the hospital with a single firm to accomplish both design and construction for a stipulated contract price. This price may or may not be guaranteed at the outset, but it is all-inclusive. Usually, as under the CM method of project delivery, a guaranteed price is established during the course of the design development phase.

Two phases are normally identified under D/B. The first phase is devoted to planning and design, with the hospital having the option, upon completion, either to shelve the project or to purchase the documents developed and to proceed with competitive bidding for construction. The second phase, of course, involves construction of the facilities as planned and designed.

D/B has gained some favor, but the quality of the finished hospital is no better than that allowed by the knowledge of a single D/B contractor, and the probability that competency will be exhibited in all required disciplines may be small. Furthermore, the checks and balances that occur among planning team members are diminished, so there is a possibility for a contractor who is less than completely honest to take advantage of a hospital whose executives and board members are inexperienced—as is often the case. The importance of this matter is discussed in the following section.

The *rationalized-traditional* approach has been shown to provide some cost reductions and has been utilized primarily in construction undertaken by the large investor-owned systems. Standardized programming, design, and construction methods are employed through close cooperation among the architect, general contractor, and hospital officials. Great interior similarity among a number of hospitals built will be evidenced, but sacrifice of quality is not necessarily attempted in order to reduce costs. Cost reductions, which may not be as large as originally claimed, have been obtained through standard construction approaches, large purchases of similar items, and constant employment (assuring stability) of the same design and construction groups, who usually work at less-than-standard fees.

A warning: claims of savings versus true costs

Some contractors have made extravagant claims of savings under the approaches they employ. On close examination, however, such savings may not actually exist—at least not to the extent and in the manner stated. As an example, turnkey or D/B contractors may claim that they can build a hospital with a given number of beds for about half the cost already estimated by an independent architect or construction manager. This may, in fact, be true, but the resulting construction will not in any sense compare with that contemplated by the independent firms. Whereas the turnkey or D/B contractor may claim that stated savings will come from standard construction approaches, mass purchasing, and advanced technical know-how, the savings will, in fact, come from fewer gross square feet per bed—accruing to a *reduced total square footage* of construction in the project—coupled with a *reduced quality* of construction.

The most reliable and reputable construction and architectural firms in the United States agree that the total cost of any hospital project is determined almost entirely by four factors:

1. the total number of square feet constructed

2. the nature of the construction

3. construction quality

4. time spent in design and construction.

Simultaneous manipulation of two of these factors—the total number of square feet of construction and construction quality—by a contractor can result in variation in construction cost of, say, a 200-bed hospital by as much as 100 percent. Moreover, there is no reason to believe that turnkey or D/B has any appreciable advantages regarding the other two factors cited, especially when a phased design and construction approach is undertaken under supervision of a responsible CM firm, of which there are now many in the nation.

The figures showing how the cost of a typical 200-bed hospital can vary by simultaneous manipulation of the two factors cited are displayed in Figure 2–5.

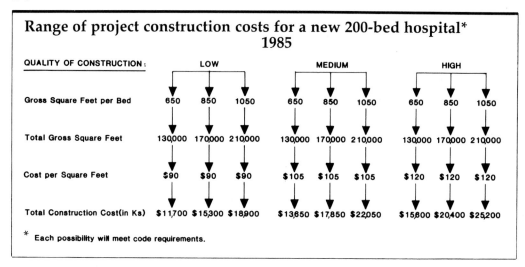

Range of project construction costs for a new 200-bed hospital*
1985

QUALITY OF CONSTRUCTION:	LOW			MEDIUM			HIGH		
Gross Square Feet per Bed	650	850	1050	650	850	1050	650	850	1050
Total Gross Square Feet	130,000	170,000	210,000	130,000	170,000	210,000	130,000	170,000	210,000
Cost per Square Feet	$90	$90	$90	$105	$105	$105	$120	$120	$120
Total Construction Cost(in Ks)	$11,700	$15,300	$18,900	$13,650	$17,850	$22,050	$15,600	$20,400	$25,200

* Each possibility will meet code requirements.

A few turnkey and D/B firms also make offers to perform all planning and design work free, as an incentive for the hospital to award them the contract. (Similar proposals were offered by some architectural firms during the 1950s.) Preying upon the wishful thinking of those who are always searching for something free, these contractors gain a foothold that may be difficult to dislodge when disillusionment occurs. It is well to keep in mind that no professional work is ever free: the cost may not be direct, but it always goes to somebody, in some manner. Good ethics dictates that cost should always go to the organization—in this case, a hospital—for which the services were performed. Nonetheless, it is doubtful that such gullibility will be eradicated in the foreseeable future.

These remarks should not be construed to derogate the intrinsic worth of the turnkey and D/B approaches. We merely note that the opportunity exists in these approaches, more so than in some of the others, for ulterior motives to be exercised by the single developer or contractor involved—to the detriment of the hospital.

Step 5: scheduling, planning, design, and construction

Required planning activities vary quite widely among facility construction projects, depending upon the nature of the project, resources in hand, and information already obtained at the time perceived needs occur. Such activities can conceivably range in scope from the simple formulation of a room program (a listing and description of all rooms to be constructed) to a complete continuum of planning studies, as described later in this section. Necessary design work, in reality, varies little, except in quantity, although the approaches to executing design vary, as has been outlined earlier. Also, from time to time one or more of the phases to be described here are omitted, usually to the detriment of the completed facility. In their roles as decision makers, hospital officials must carefully analyze specific situations, determine activities to be undertaken, and chart an appropriate course of action.

We now describe the various activities that should usually be performed in the course of a major project. The listing has been arranged in a desirable chronological order of performance but is based in some instances merely upon need for the output of one activity as input for another, prior to completion. Where work can be performed concurrently, this is so stated.

Obviously, the entire flow of work as described can be outlined through the use of either the PERT or the CPM scheduling technique. Schedulers frequently utilize one or the other since the concept of network scheduling was originally developed to speed and order the work of special purpose or "one-time through" projects involving diverse and complex activities.

Figure 2–6 graphically displays an example schedule of the activities described, shows assignments among team members, and relates reviews and approvals by the hospital as the process progresses. In addition, a highly simplified critical path network, unrelated to time, is displayed at the beginning of following chapters to show relationships among the several work phases as each is discussed.

Activities of the Professional Planning and Design Team

1. Strategic Planning

   Primary Responsibility: Hospital consultant. Oftentimes, the firm employed will also have capabilities related to functional planning. However, the strategic plan should be a stand-alone contract to preclude biased conclusions that might lead to unneeded facility construction work.

   Description: May take the form of a regional survey, community survey, or program study and plan for a single hospital. (Previously discussed under Step 2: Strategic Planning and Feasibility Assessments; see also Chapter 3.)

   Concurrent Activities: Facility planning work should await completion of this study, although portions of the physical and functional evaluation can be undertaken in some instances.

2. Feasibility Evaluation (usually a debt capacity analysis)

   Primary Responsibility: Can be accomplished internally if the hospital possesses the capability. May be accomplished by an investment banker or independent financial consulting firm.

   Description: Usually, examination of existing financial documentations to determine cash available for capital funding, cash generation capability, and net equity for the purpose of estimating borrowing capabilities. (Previously discussed under Step 2: Strategic Planning and Feasibility Assessments.)

   Concurrent Activities: Portions of the physical and functional evaluations can be performed.

Activities of the
professional planning team

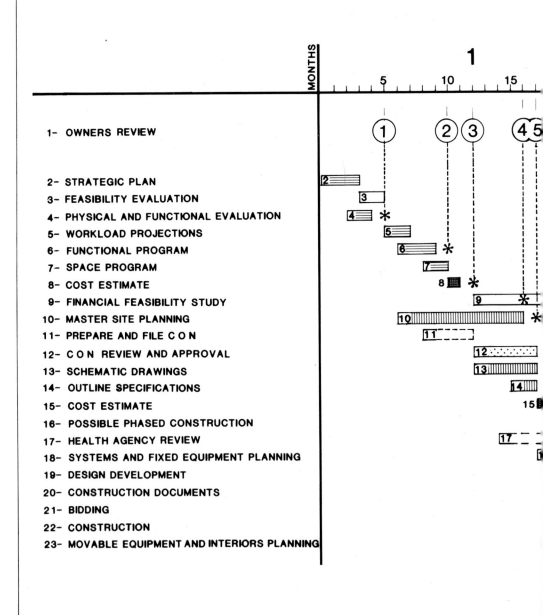

1- OWNERS REVIEW

2- STRATEGIC PLAN
3- FEASIBILITY EVALUATION
4- PHYSICAL AND FUNCTIONAL EVALUATION
5- WORKLOAD PROJECTIONS
6- FUNCTIONAL PROGRAM
7- SPACE PROGRAM
8- COST ESTIMATE
9- FINANCIAL FEASIBILITY STUDY
10- MASTER SITE PLANNING
11- PREPARE AND FILE C O N
12- C O N REVIEW AND APPROVAL
13- SCHEMATIC DRAWINGS
14- OUTLINE SPECIFICATIONS
15- COST ESTIMATE
16- POSSIBLE PHASED CONSTRUCTION
17- HEALTH AGENCY REVIEW
18- SYSTEMS AND FIXED EQUIPMENT PLANNING
19- DESIGN DEVELOPMENT
20- CONSTRUCTION DOCUMENTS
21- BIDDING
22- CONSTRUCTION
23- MOVABLE EQUIPMENT AND INTERIORS PLANNING

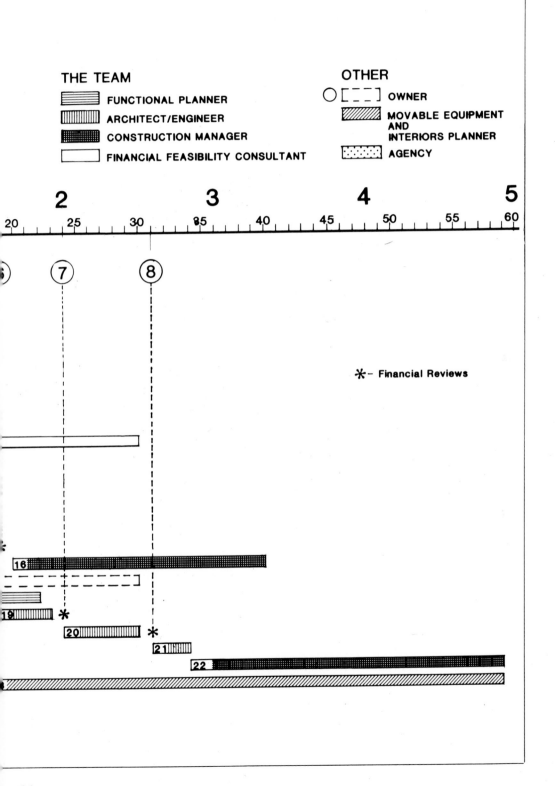

THE TEAM

FUNCTIONAL PLANNER
ARCHITECT/ENGINEER
CONSTRUCTION MANAGER
FINANCIAL FEASIBILITY CONSULTANT

OTHER

○ [_ _ _] OWNER
MOVABLE EQUIPMENT AND INTERIORS PLANNER
AGENCY

2   3   4   5

20   25   30   35   40   45   50   55   60

⑦   ⑧

✳ – Financial Reviews

16

19
20
21
22

3. Physical Evaluation of Existing Facilities

Primary Responsibility: Architect, or functional planner with A&E capabilities.

Description: This is a study to determine the degree of physical obsolescence of existing facilities, to identify major code violations and physical problems, and to project future usability.

Concurrent Activities: Work on the functional evaluation can proceed simultaneously; in most instances, the physical and functional evaluations can be conducted in a single study.

4. Functional Evaluation of Existing Facilities

Primary Responsibility: Functional planner.

Description: This is a study to define functional problems that detract from operational efficiency, quality of patient care, and convenience of building inhabitants; to evaluate traffic flows and physical relationships; to determine space insufficiencies in terms of current requirements; to study need for modernization, alterations, and expansion, according to strategic plan findings; and to note possible alternative future uses of the structure as a whole, as well as of various departmental areas.

Concurrent Activities: Physical evaluation.

5. Review and Acceptance of Evaluations

Primary Responsibility: Hospital officials.

Description: The physical and functional evaluations should be read and studied by the director of planning and all members of the building committee, and by others as indicated. The director of planning should prepare a written commentary for the building committee, which should approve, formulate exceptions, or reject the studies. Recommendations should be passed on to the chief executive officer, who will personally review them and secure action by the governing board.

Concurrent Activities: Workload projections can be started.

6. Preparation of Workload Projections

Primary Responsibility: Functional planner, advised by financial consultant.

Description: Historical workloads (e.g., laboratory tests, x-ray examinations, surgical operations) are linked to applicable units of primary demand (outpatient visits, admissions, and patient days), and a historical pattern in utilization indexes is established. Both utilization indexes and the units of primary demand are then extended to desired future years, although primary demand figures usually will have already been extended in the strategic plan. Projected indexes are applied to forecasted primary demand figures to obtain estimated workloads. All calculations are reviewed with appropriate department heads to identify abnormal deviations in historical data, to ascertain changes in operational methods, and to address the possibility of certain unique events that could affect the extensions of past trends. These projections form the basis for functional programming, revenue projections, and staffing estimates.

Concurrent Activities: The functional planner can determine and formulate concepts of operation for the proposed project, according to previous study findings. These concepts will be incorporated in the functional program.

7. Functional Programming

   Primary Responsibility: Functional planner.

   Description: Using approved recommendations and findings of the strategic plan, findings of physical and functional evaluations, and workload projections, the functional planner formulates recommendations for operational concepts, the detailed room composition of the project, required phasing, alterations, internal and external traffic flows, interdepartmental relationships, and operating systems. The resulting single document sets the basic character and scope of the project.

   Concurrent Activities: Site selection and site evaluation (see activity 14) can proceed and extend through activity 9.

8. Review and Acceptance of Functional Program

   Primary Responsibility: Hospital officials.

   Description: The director of planning, the building committee, the users, the medical staff committees, and the governing board (or designated committee) should review workload projections and the functional program. The director of planning should coordinate the review and submit final recommendations to the chief executive officer, who will also review and then obtain appropriate action from the governing board. The usual output is an approved document with addenda reflecting hospital amendments.

   Concurrent Activities: Assuming that changes will not drastically affect the scope of the project, the functional planner can proceed with net space programming. The architect can continue site selection and evaluation work.

9. Space Programming

   Primary Responsibility: Functional planner or architect, or both.

   Description: Based upon the functional program, as amended and approved by the hospital, a room-by-room listing is made of all areas in the proposed project. Net square footage is assigned to each space, and totals accumulated for every department or functional entity. Using the net figures, appropriate calculations are then made to set gross totals for each department or functional entity, as well as the total for the entire project.

Concurrent Activities: The financial consultant can proceed with expense and income projections, which should be based upon workload projections and projected staffing patterns. Site planning can proceed.

10. Preparation of Cost Estimate

Primary Responsibility: Construction manager.

Description: Based upon the functional program, space program, and findings of site planning work, plus recorded cost experiences per square foot for similar facility components in the local geographical area, an initial cost estimate can be made.

Concurrent Activities: The financial consultant can proceed with the feasibility study, and the architect can proceed with master site planning.

11. Review and Acceptance of Space Program and Cost Estimate

Primary Responsibility: Hospital officials.

Description: The director of planning, building committee, users, medical staff committees, and the governing board (or designated committees) should review the space program. The director of planning should coordinate the review and submit final recommendations to the chief executive officer, who will then review and obtain appropriate action from the governing board. All reviews should be made in consideration of the cost estimate.

Concurrent Activities: Block plan drawings (see activity 14) can be prepared as site planning continues. Financial feasibility work can proceed.

12. Financial Feasibility Study

Primary Responsibility: Financial consultant.

Description: Tentative findings of the financial feasibility study should be prepared and reported. The report should be based upon the project cost and projected revenue and expenses.

Concurrent Activities: Master site planning can continue, and early schematic drawings can be started by the architect. (See Chapter 5 regarding decision to continue with such drawings prior to CON approval.) The investment banker can identify the best manner of financing the project if commercial borrowing is required.

13. Review and Acceptance of Financial Feasibility Study Findings

Primary Responsibility: Hospital officials.

Description: The finance committee should review findings as submitted by the financial consultant and formulate recommendations to the governing board. The governing board must make relevant decisions and publish instructions based thereon.

Concurrent Activities: Master site planning (activity 14), schematic drawings (activity 17), and analysis of financing methods can all move forward. Initial steps toward filing a CON application (activity 16), such as filing the letter of intent and making early contacts with regulatory agency personnel, should be taken.

14. Master Site Planning

Primary Responsibility: Architect, advised by functional planner.

Description: The preparation of a master site plan can be completed. Typically, four tasks may have been involved: (1) site selection; (2) site evaluation; (3) block plan drawings; and (4) preparing design drawings and specifications for the master plan. Site selection entails a qualitative comparison of possible site choices and the selection of one; site evaluation involves soil test borings, determination of availability of required utilities, and evaluation of other characteristics of a site already selected. Block plan drawings are single-line drawings of gross areas only, denoting relationships of departments, internal vertical and horizontal traffic flows, external traffic flows (both pedestrian and vehicular), and expansion requirements. A master site plan represents an architectural delineation of programmed facilities as situated on the site, usually at 1 inch = 40' or larger scale. The master site plan should project the ultimate development of the site.

Concurrent Activities: Schematic drawings (activity 17) and any necessary financial feasibility study refinements can all proceed, if indicated. The investment banker can begin preparation of the official statement for bonds to be offered. Preparation of the CON application (activity 16) should be ongoing.

15. Review and Acceptance of Master Site Plan

Primary Responsibility: Hospital officials.

Description: The director of planning, building committee, governing board, the chief executive officer, and, in some instances, an appropriate committee of the medical staff should review the work performed under master site planning. Final recommendations, coordinated by the director of planning, should be transmitted to the chief executive officer for board approval.

Concurrent Activities: A continuation of work on schematic drawings and matters related to financing is appropriate. Continuing work on CON application.

16. Preparation and Filing of CON Application

Primary Responsibility: Hospital officials.

Description: The director of planning, guided by the chief executive officer, and possibly assisted by a hospital consultant, should complete the CON application. All the previous work related to the strategic plan, financial analyses, facility evaluations, functional planning, space programming, and A&E site drawings, including block plan drawings, should be reported, at least in summary form, in this application. The form prescribed by the applicable agency should be followed, but with the information that has already been generated, the strongest case possible can be made for the project.

Concurrent Activities: If a decision is indicated to proceed with schematic drawings (see Chapter 5 related to this matter), such design work should proceed. Financial planning should also continue.

17. Preparation of Schematic Drawings, Elevations, Sections, Details

Primary Responsibility: Architect, advised by functional planner and construction manager.

Description: Schematic drawings should be single-line, beginning at ¹⁄₁₆″ scale and developing into ⅛″ scale, that reflect all rooms, corridors, and mechanical spaces, level by level. Door openings are shown, but most other details are omitted. Planned future additions should be shown. Elevations and other drawings should reflect general disposition of materials and outline typical construction systems.

Concurrent Activities: Financial work and preparation of outline specifications (activity 18). CON application review. A decision by the health systems agency (HSA) or other appropriate agency should be in hand *before* schematics are completed.

18. Preparation of Outline (Summary) Specifications

Primary Responsibility: Architect, guided by construction manager.

Description: The purposes of these specifications are (1) to establish direction for contract document specifications and (2) to allow an accurate cost estimate. Site work; structural system; exterior materials; interior materials; conveying systems; plumbing and fire protection; electrical systems and requirements; fixtures, furnishings and equipment (all fixed); and all other items that are significant in determining the design and cost of the project must be described at a level of detail required for cost estimating.

Concurrent Activities: Possible work by the financial consultant and investment banker. Necessary reviews of CON application.

19. Agency Review of Schematic Design

Primary Responsibility: Appropriate agency of state health department and A&E firm.

Description: The requirements for agency reviews vary from state to state and the necessary reviews must be determined by hospital officials during early planning. However, the completion of schematic drawings and outline specifications represents a certain point of review. We have not described any other review but have merely made this notation as a reminder that such reviews must be met as required by individual state regulations. Some adjustments in design, based on state standards and applicable codes, may be required.

Concurrent Activities: Systems and fixed equipment planning (activity 22), design development drawings (activity 23), and preparations for marketing of bonds. Environmental data sheets can be prepared.

20. Preparation of Cost Estimate

   Primary Responsibility: Construction manager.

   Description: With schematic drawings and outline specifications in hand, the construction manager will be able to produce a highly accurate cost estimate. This estimate should be formally prepared and submitted to the owner.

   Concurrent Activities: Functional review of schematic drawings can proceed among hospital committees and officials. As necessary, further work by the financial consultant and investment banker.

21. Hospital Review and Acceptance of Schematic Drawings, Outline Specifications, and Cost Estimate

   (Assumes that CON application has been approved and that stipulated changes, if any, have already been incorporated into the drawings.)

   Primary Responsibility: Hospital officials, advised by the functional planner, architect, and construction manager.

   Description: All parties who have review responsibilities should examine the relevant area of interest on the schematic drawings. The functional planner and the architect should be available for explanations when reviews are accomplished. After necessary changes and compromises at lower echelons, drawings are submitted to the chief executive officer for review and for governing board consideration and approval. The governing board, with schematic drawings, outline specifications, and completed cost estimate in hand, can authorize proceeding with design development drawings and preparation of contract drawings and specifications for initial site work and early general contracts if phased construction (see under Step 4: Determining the Planning, Design, and Construction Approach) is contemplated.

   Concurrent Activities: Plans for procurement of funds for construction should be completed at this point if phased construction is to be undertaken. A guaranteed maximum price (GMP) is sometimes obtained at this point from or by the construction manager. If a GMP is obtained, this figure can be used in completing the financial feasibility study. The functional planner can finish the preparation of environmental data sheets.

22. Systems and Fixed Equipment Planning

   Primary Responsibility: Architect, advised and assisted by functional planner and construction manager.

   Description: Planning of systems and fixed equipment to include medical gases, housekeeping vacuum, pneumatic tube systems, other transport systems, diagnostic and therapeutic x-ray equipment, supply processing and distribution systems, data processing, trash disposal, laundry, major specialized lighting, dietary system, casework, specialized plumbing fixtures and communication systems. Can be carried out largely by the functional planner, advised by the architect and construction manager. Preparation of formal documents is the responsibility of the architect.

Concurrent Activities: Full-scale design development work can proceed, and construction documents for initial bid packages can be prepared in the case of a phased construction program.

23. Preparation of Design Development Drawings

Primary Responsibility: Architect, advised by functional planner and construction manager.

Description: Drawings at ⅛" or ¼" scale of all areas to be constructed are prepared. Fixed equipment, major movable equipment, and items of furniture are shown, together with interior elevations of all specialized rooms.

Concurrent Activities: Preparation of construction documents (activity 25) can proceed, and first bid packages readied in phased construction methodology. Most GMPs are obtained at this point under phased construction if the owner must have complete assurance of total cost. In these instances, the financial feasibility study is completed, and final plans for funding the construction must be prepared. Movable equipment and interiors planning (activity 29) should begin.

24. Review and Acceptance of Design Development Drawings

Primary Responsibility: Hospital officials.

Description: Again, all categories of persons with review responsibilities should carefully audit these drawings in sessions with the functional planner, the architect, and the construction manager. Exceptions that cannot be resolved by compromise should be referred to the special user committee for decision and recommendations to the governing board. The planning director should coordinate all reviews and finally submit drawings, comments, and recommended actions to the chief executive officer for review and for governing board disposition.

Concurrent Activities: Initial bids can be awarded and construction started under a program of phased construction. Succeeding bid packages can be readied and work on all remaining construction documents started. Movable equipment and interiors planning is carried forward.

25. Preparation of Construction Documents

Primary Responsibility: Architect, advised by the construction manager and functional planner.

Description: Preparation of working drawings, specifications, and conditions of the contract. Under phased construction, these three elements are prepared for each separate contract; under conventional construction, they are prepared for every aspect of the total work.

Concurrent Activities: Bidding (activity 27) requirements and the form of agreement can be prepared. Movable equipment and interiors planning can proceed. Costing and budget refinements by the construction manager can be carried forward.

26. Review and Acceptance of Construction Documents

Primary Responsibility: Hospital officials, advised by the architect, construction manager, and functional planner.

Description: Hospital officials should carefully examine all construction documents under both phased and traditional approaches to ascertain a level of acceptable quality and to see that owner directives have been followed. Acceptance and exceptions should be signified in writing.

Concurrent Activities: Preparation for bidding should be completed. Final cost estimates should be submitted to the hospital. Movable equipment and interiors planning proceeds.

27. Bidding

Primary Responsibility: Architect, assisted by the construction manager.

Description: Invitations to bid, instructions to bidders, and the bid form are prepared, and prebid activities (evaluating and ascertaining competent bidders) undertaken. Invitations to bid are mailed to prospective bidders. Contract documents are delivered to interested bidders. Prebid conferences are held, and bids prepared by bidders. Bids are opened and reviewed, and a contract is awarded. This process is followed under both phased and conventional construction methodologies.

Concurrent Activities: Completion of plans for funding. Movable equipment and interiors planning proceeds.

28. Construction

Primary Responsibility: Construction manager, or general contractor, or separate specialized contractors, as specified. Work is monitored by the architect.

Description: Preconstruction conferences are held, and the construction of the project is undertaken and carried forward to completion. As is implicit in all these descriptions, construction may be implemented either by a phased or traditional methodology.

Concurrent Activities: Movable equipment and interiors planning is completed. Hospital officials schedule opening activities, plan for staff, and undertake employee orientations. In employee orientations, the functional planner should play a definitive role.

29. Movable Equipment and Interiors Planning

Primary Responsibility: Movable equipment planner or interior decorator. May be one or two respective firms on large projects. Movable equipment planning may be accomplished internally on small projects, and the architect may perform interiors planning.

Description: This planning, started in design development, is finished during construction. Installation of movable equipment, of course, must be planned as a part of opening, together with completion of interiors planning (e.g., completion of signage programs).

Concurrent Activities: Design development, the review process, preparation of construction documents, bidding, and construction are all undertaken and finished during the planning of movable equipment and interiors.

Obviously, the preceding listing represents a highlighting of key activities only. A host of additional activities, primarily related to financing, cost estimating and control, and regulatory agency approvals could have been included, but our purpose here has been to give emphasis to planning and design activities. (See Step 6 in Chapter 5, "Establishing Construction Costs and Determining Feasibility," for additional points in the process when cost estimating is often accomplished.)

Step 6: opening the completed project

The activities required prior to and at opening will vary according to the scope of the project—that is, whether a totally new hospital, a complete replacement hospital, the nucleus for a planned replacement hospital, a major expansion, or a minor expansion is involved. Our comments, both here and in Chapter 12, are concerned primarily with the first four kinds of projects; readers can, however, make inferences regarding activities that may apply to less extensive projects from the remarks here set forth.

Certainly, the ease and efficiency with which a completed project is opened has a great influence on employee morale, the quality of patient care and comfort, and the image of the hospital within the community it serves. The effect of an unsuccessful opening cannot be measured accurately, but our experience has shown that mistakes made in getting operations under way sometimes detract from operational results for more than two years. Thus, the importance of a well-planned and well-executed opening must be underscored.

Scheduling activities

The great number of activities to be accomplished both prior to and after opening indicates that a detailed master schedule should be prepared by hospital management. Both PERT and CPM are proven techniques. Also, within the context of the schedule, checklists should be formulated on a continuing basis.

Input to this schedule must be contributed by the architect, construction manager, functional planner, the medical staff, most department heads, and a number of others, such as vendors and utilities providers.

Owing to the usual necessity to hire key staff members, and to provide for proper orientation at an early date, many major projects require the formulation of an activity schedule one full year prior to opening. Of course, refinements must be made on a continuing basis up to and past the actual opening date.

Hiring and organizing staff

In the case of a completely new facility, the governing board's first action in the early planning stage, following a decision to build, should be to engage an administrative head for the new facility if the position does not already exist. An assistant should be employed as soon as possible thereafter to serve as director of planning. Recruiting and forming the nucleus of a medical staff, if not already accomplished through physician participation in the decision to build, is a very early imperative. Schedules should be established for the employment of other key personnel—chief engineer, director of personnel, director of nursing, materials manager, and other department heads—in a logical sequence geared to the need for their orientation to and participation in preparation for opening the new facility.

In the case of replacement or major expansion of an existing facility, these persons and groups should be kept informed from the beginning of planning; their ranks should be supplemented as necessary to staff and open the new facility and to perform their functions in the transition and opening periods. Schedules for employing supervisory and lower-level employees must be established, and the necessary activities carried out sequentially as training and opening dates near. Supplementary medical staff positions should be filled.

From the first, in all instances, good management dictates that a table of organization be thoughtfully prepared and published. It should reflect a structure anticipated to be used for the foreseeable future after opening, if possible, and it should be tailored to accommodate the operational concepts and systems around which the project has been designed.

Organizational strategy is a complex subject, too detailed for discussion here. However, it should be noted that basic responsibility for opening a department should rest directly with the respective department head. Assistance can be provided from several sources, and coordinated scheduling should be accomplished for all elements to be geared, but no derogation of the principle that the department head must be responsible for actual opening and start-up should be allowed.

Orientation and training

During the planning and design process, board members, the chief executive officer, medical staff, and the director of planning will have participated in decision making on concepts, systems, and patient care functional principles to be established and incorporated in a new facility and will have become familiar with any departures from tradition. In projects involving existing facilities, an even broader participation may be expected. In both cases, where the project is a major one, at no later than a year to nine months prior to opening, orientation programs conducted by members of the medical staff, the director of nursing, the materials manager or chief engineer (or both), and other key personnel should begin. Visits to other hospitals successfully utilizing similar concepts and systems can be arranged. As supervisory personnel are employed (according to schedule in the case of a replacement or expansion project), carefully planned orientation programs for these personnel should be conducted in preparation for their training of other departmental employees. Training curricula should be established and training programs scheduled to assure that before opening occurs, personnel at all levels have a thorough understanding of their functions and the procedures to be followed in performing their tasks.

Preparing documentation

The preparation of policy manuals, procedure manuals for each department, equipment manuals, preventive maintenance programs, spare parts inventories, requisitioning procedures, and all other documentations to be used in the new facility should be initiated as early in design and construction as warranted by their nature and should be completed in advance of the sequential need therefor, if possible.

This is a massive but vital undertaking. It is related to the various processes of management and should not be neglected in any type of project with major scope.

Controlling the opening process

The classic management control process should be applied throughout opening activities. There can be no substitute for measuring results by objective criteria and taking corrective action as necessary.

An integral part of control is reporting, which can be either verbal or in writing. In either case, it should be on a scheduled basis.

After an opening schedule has been prepared, review sessions should be held as frequently as required. These may progress from biweekly to weekly and even to daily as the time of opening draws near. Such sessions are beneficial in adjusting the activity schedule and checklists and in making decisions in light of new information. They provide a mechanism by which key persons involved in the opening can receive direct orientation from each other and whereby the single person in charge can control progress.

Systems and equipment testing and operational shakedown

As construction of various departmental and patient care areas is completed and equipment is installed, all systems and equipment must be carefully checked for conformance to specifications and trouble-free operation. Respective department heads ought to conduct trial runs of operations within their departments under conditions conforming as closely as possible to "real life." It is particularly important that interfaces of functions between and among departments be coordinated to assure that established procedures are followed and that a smooth flow of interdepartmental activities, persons, and materials has become routine as opening day nears. Volunteer groups can be involved, as well as hospital staff. In the case of a replacement hospital or major expansion, careful scheduling of shakedown operations will be required to assure that functions in the existing plant are not unduly interrupted.

Opening and follow-up

As opening time draws near, reviews will be intensified, and the activities checklist will be verified at shorter intervals. Preparations to receive or transfer patients will be completed. Medical staff will increase participation. Community relations programs should be pursued, and planning for opening day ceremonies completed.

Many projects are opened in a single day; some extend their openings over several days or several weeks or even months. In any event, either the structure as a whole or specific sections should be given official acceptance only when all specifications and performance standards are found to be in conformance with contractual requirements.

Close operational monitoring will be required of supervisory personnel, the functional planner, architect, and construction manager, as well as suppliers of major equipment items. Such monitoring should continue as long as is necessary (perhaps several weeks in some instances) to assure that all systems are operating efficiently and that all functions can be carried on with no more than predictable difficulty. The chief executive officer possesses the responsibility to see that this is done.

Follow-up opening should extend formally to the end of the guarantee upon the structure itself and most items of major equipment. This is usually at one year. If the opening is successful, however, operations should have "settled" within a period of three to six months, and the opening can be considered complete.

Summary

The structuring of a process to guide planning, design, and construction efforts is only the first task management faces when any large health care building project is contemplated. There are six main phases which then can be broken down into a broader number of work components. These phases are:

1. perception of need for building program

2. strategic planning and feasibility assessments

3. organizing for planning, design, and construction

4. determining the planning, design, and construction approach

5. scheduling planning, design, and construction

6. opening the completed project.

After realizing, by one means or another, that a building program may be a consideration in providing solutions to the future of the health care institution (Step 1 in our theoretical model), the active planning, design, and construction phases (Steps 2 through 6) become matters of great importance and concern to management. In the following chapters, we outline a process for accomplishing the entire work and describe specific ways for dealing with each phase. Chapter 2 merely provides an overview of the various phases outlined; it is a prelude to the process we have recommended, and discussions related to the defined steps of the process start with Chapter 3.

The detailed listing in this chapter of the 29 discrete activities typically required in the course of a planning, design, and construction project can be used by hospital officials as a checklist to monitor the progress of the ongoing project. Effective measures for establishing management control are presented in Chapter 15.

Opening a major project can be an extremely tedious event, and our remarks here are meant merely to point out the great importance of a successful opening. More detailed information about this matter is contained in Chapter 12.

Notes

1. American Association of Hospital Consultants, "By-Laws as Amended January 7, 1974" (Washington, D.C.: 1974), pp. 1–5 (mimeographed).
2. *Selection of Architects for Health Facility Projects* (Chicago: American Hospital Association, 1975).
3. Charles B. Thomsen, "Construction Management: What's Happened To It? Is It Still Valid?" *Architectural Record*, March 1984, p. 39.
4. *Ibid*.
5. *Ibid*.
6. Andrea O. Dean, "Pros and Cons of Various Project Delivery Approaches, Traditional and Otherwise," *AIA Journal*, February 1976, p. 48, quoting Davis D. Haviland, *Project Delivery Approaches* (Washington, D.C.: American Institute of Architects, 1975).
7. *Standard Form of Agreement Between Owners and Architects*, AIA Document B141 (Washington, D.C.: American Institute of Architects, 1974), p. 3.
8. Dean, "Pros and Cons," quoting Haviland, *Project Delivery Approaches*, AIA, p. 48.
9. Used by Erie County (New York) Department of Public Works; CPM Master Schedule of Construction for Erie County Medical Center, mid 1970s.

3

The Planning and Design Process

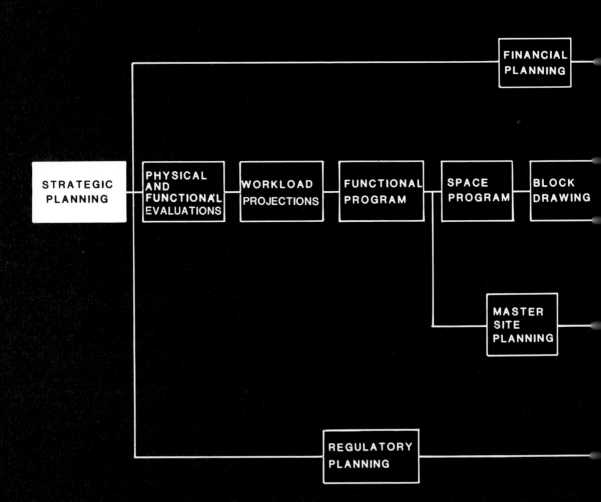

Strategic Planning

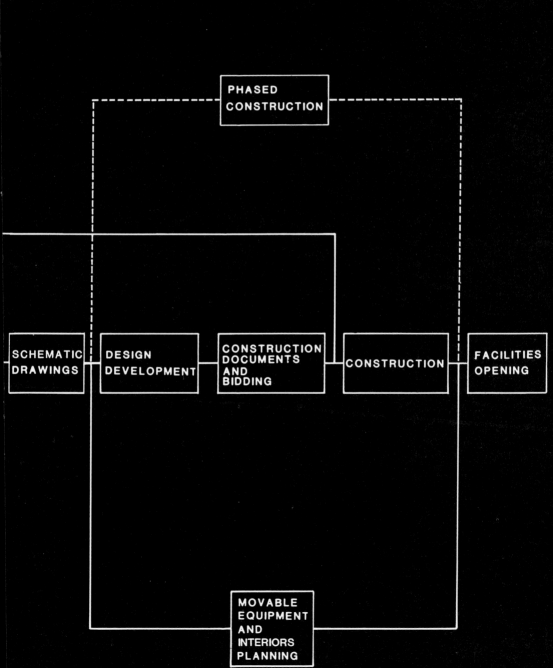

The critical role of strategic planning has now been recognized by executives throughout the health care field. Not all hospitals and other health care institutions have performed strategic planning effectively, but its importance is no longer challenged. Moreover, the necessity to base programmatic provisions upon provable strategic decision making will be increasingly accentuated in the immediate years ahead. The current dynamic health care delivery environment, as well as prospective reimbursement by diagnosis-related groups (DRGs), will require that the hospital chart its future by carefully made strategic decisions, taking into account not only projected programmatic demand but detailed financial forecasts.

There has been considerable confusion over the years regarding the appropriate term for such goal-oriented planning. Various terms, each with its own implications of scope and purpose, have been in common usage: role and program planning, long-range planning (which can apply to either program or facility planning), marketing, and strategic planning. Because the term strategic planning has recently gained wide favor, we have chosen it for use throughout this book. From the standpoint of the practical executive, however, terminology is not highly important. *Results achieved* should be the basic criterion of any goal-oriented plan that results in an implementing action. For our purposes here, certainly the choice of a specific term is not critical. Through appropriate planning by whatever name, valid programmatic actions have been determined by health care institutions. What *is* highly pertinent here is the proposition that facility planning must be a response to logically conceived and thoroughly accomplished planning for those programmatic actions that an institution intends to implement.

Nonetheless, we have elected to set forth commonly accepted definitions for these terms:

- *role and program planning*—planning by a health care institution that specifies a mission and defines a role within the context of a specific area's or region's total health care delivery system and further determines the programs of service that will be implemented to fulfill the role. Such planning usually suggests programmatic actions extending over a 5- to 20-year period.

- *long-range planning*—that planning or decision-making process undertaken by a health care institution that defines a role and mission, establishes goals, and allocates resources for a period of up to 15 to 20 years. This planning may or may not provide complete direction for development of all services to be offered. (This definition ignores the connotation of this term as used in facility planning; see Chapter 7 for a discussion of implications in that regard.)

- *marketing*—as defined by MacStravic, "the design and management of exchange relationships with important publics";[1] by Kotler, "the analysis, planning, implementation, and control of carefully formulated programs designed to bring about voluntary exchange of values with target markets for the purposes of achieving organizational objectives."[2] Although the term marketing may imply a shorter time period than that suggested by the other terms here defined, in our opinion it includes strategic planning and also facility planning when required. Considerable financial planning and organizational planning may be involved as well.

- *strategic planning*—as defined by Brandt, planning that "deals with market-positioning issues and directions beyond the current budgeting cycle";[3] by Linneman, planning that "involves looking into the future and deciding what the basic thrust of your business ought to be . . . [which] results in a strategy that, over time, brings about fundamental changes in your business."[4]

In considering the scope of strategic planning from the standpoint of hospitals specifically, Domanico has stated:[5]

> Strategic planning encompasses the existing hospital practice of facility and program planning, and also includes the hospital mission identification, goal setting, market strategy, image building, community relations, [assembling] a comprehensive planning data base, assessment of prime competitors, present and future medical staff development, fund development, [and] cooperative and political planning. Strategic planning must be highly integrated into existing planning and operating functions. Implementation of a strategic plan will prioritize investment opportunities and promote long-range hospital growth and development in [the] face of regulatory impediments and potential competitor and consumer interest group opposition.

We find the broader scope of the strategic planning process as described by Domanico most useful for our purposes here.

Because strategic planning involves a variety of planning activities, as listed by Domanico, they must be ordered into a process. An ordered process allows responsibilities to be assigned appropriately throughout the organization and also produces rational interrelationships among decisions validly reached. In this chapter we describe a generic process that we have used in assisting a host of hospitals. Figure 3–1 provides a graphic representation of the process which is composed of a series of simple steps; we discuss each step separately in following sections.

It should be noted that the generic process we have adopted can also be used for either program planning, long-range planning, or marketing, as defined previously.

A rapidly vanishing argument among management theorists holds that strategic planning, which is very definitely inclusive of program planning, can be effectively done—and perhaps even *should* be done—in disregard of a hospital's existing physical facility. Clearly, this is not possible, as any experienced executive knows and as the initiate manager learns early on. Any service or program undertaken by a hospital or other health care institution requires space—most often, specially adapted space. The presence or absence of appropriate space influences strategic decisions in many ways, and the decision to provide appropriate space for a particular program as the result of an implementing action is often the most important decision reached in a given strategy formulation.

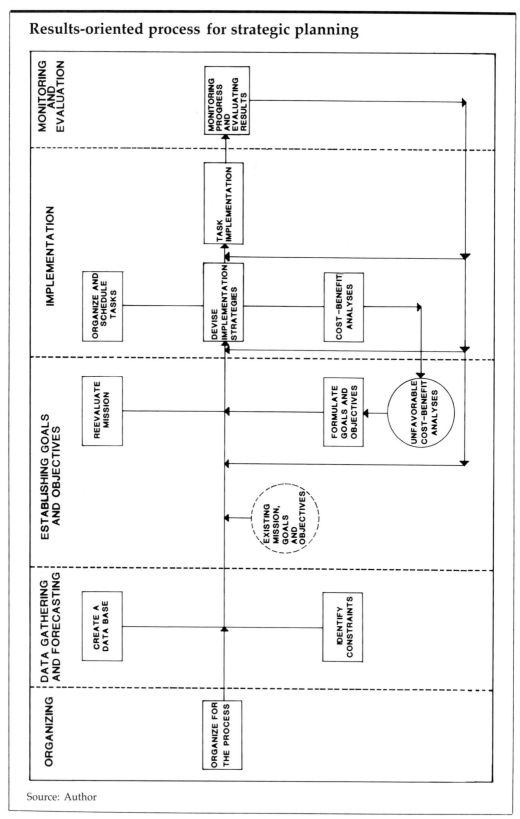

Results-oriented process for strategic planning

Source: Author

Certainly a great deal of ill-advised construction has occurred in the health care field. This fact, however, in no way negates the proposition that facilities are and always will be a matter of proper concern when strategic planning is undertaken. We suggest that some strategic planners' disavowance of the importance of facilities stems from the psychological tendency to deny the significance of an area of intellectual expertise in which one possesses little or no competence!

Organizing for strategic planning

In the atmosphere of competition within which most hospitals are now forced to operate, employment of a full-time strategic planner has assumed greater significance than ever before. The title of such a person is not of great importance, but many hospitals have recently created a position entitled "Director of Marketing," even though the major time commitment actually involves tasks inherent purely to strategic planning. This title does recognize, however, that marketing is inclusive of strategic planning, as we have previously noted. Even so, facility planning should result directly from strategic planning in all instances. Regardless of the various ways in which the accumulation of data and its conversion to information may be accomplished, a single person must be assigned the responsibility for strategic planning, and that person should report directly to the chief executive officer of the hospital, who of course reports directly to the governing board.

In many instances, the board may wish to appoint a strategic planning committee to advise, assist, and express approval or disapproval of strategic actions proposed by the person or persons involved in strategic planning. Desirably, this committee should be small (from five to seven members) and should represent the board, the medical staff, and management. Board members should include those who have strong community interests. Meetings should be held no less frequently than once every two months.

We have worked with many such committees throughout the nation in assisting hospitals to prepare an initial formal strategic plan and have found them to be extremely useful. In addition to assistance in shaping an action plan, they provide a means whereby the actual leadership of the hospital follows a decision process that later can be explained to the full board, when plan approval for implementation is sought. Our interface with this committee has involved making periodic progress reports relating to the various stages of the process, as outlined in Figure 3–1.

Data gathering and forecasting

Creating a data base stands as absolutely essential in the formulation of any sound strategic plan. Many hospitals have not achieved successful results from strategic planning simply because of a failure to recognize the need for an appropriate data base or to a reluctance to expend the money and time necessary to assemble it. "Quick and dirty" answers, based on statistics of a like nature, have been sought. In all instances, however, an appropriate data base stands as a necessity to formulating sound decisions related to programs of action and facility planning itself.

The integral parts of a data base, as regarded by most of the major management consulting firms, are set forth in the following sections. The current emphasis upon marketing has required that the perceptions of consumers and key "publics" regarding the hospital be ascertained through various types of surveys to discover the attitudinal climate in which the institution may be operating. Such surveys, although not directly a part of a strategic planning data base, are quite useful. For our purposes, they have been considered a recently added aspect.

Patient origin study

Through the patient origin study, the hospital determines precisely the location and size of its geographical service area and the degree of its dependence upon each part thereof. (See Figure 3–2.)

3–2

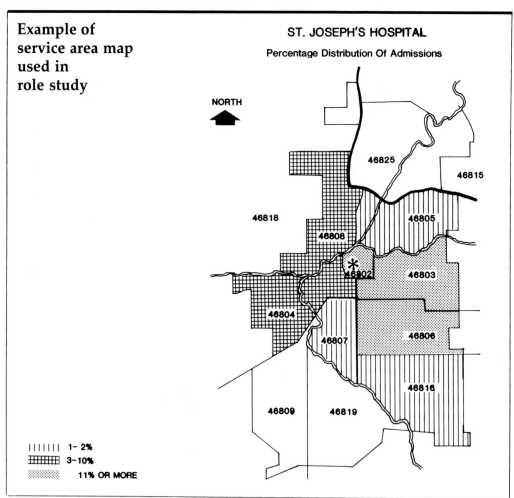

Example of service area map used in role study

ST. JOSEPH'S HOSPITAL

Percentage Distribution Of Admissions

NORTH

46825

46815

46818

46805

46808

46802

46803

46804

46807

46806

46816

46809

46819

||||||| 1– 2%

▦▦▦▦ 3–10%

░░░ 11% OR MORE

A 20 percent random or systematic sampling of discharges—or admissions—for a current three-month period is satisfactory for assuring validity and reliability. The discharges should be recorded by zip code (preferable in urban areas) or by county or other geographical or governmental entity in which accurate population numbers are routinely recorded in censuses and reliable estimates.

The hospital's total discharges should be allocated by number and percentage to specific geographical areas. A *primary* service area, defined as one in which 70 percent or more of admissions originate, should be identified. A *secondary* area, in which an additional 15 percent or more originate, should also be identified. Remaining small percentages can be lumped together as "other," except with reference to those areas in which the hospital has an interest in business expansion; these data should be "broken out" for specific attention.

The origin of emergency and ambulatory care visits should be determined by the same statistical methodology as that used for inpatients. Emergency and ambulatory care patient origins are usually found in a much smaller area than that for inpatients, but both primary and secondary areas should be identified.

Patient origin study data can be broken down by specific services, such as psychiatry, respiratory therapy, and other services in which the hospital may have a specific business interest. Only the inpatient and emergency room studies are usually undertaken.

Patient destination analysis

The patient destination analysis yields information about out-referrals with a potential for admission to existing or contemplated vertically integrated programs of the hospital, such as long-term nursing or home care. The study should record discharge diagnoses and group them according to the following categories: home; nursing home (by name); other place of congregate living (by name); referral hospital (by name); and expired.

As an example of the benefit of such studies, one of us recently assisted three horizontally related hospitals in strategic planning. In this case, the discharges from the three institutions proved to be sufficient to maintain a 90 percent occupancy rate in a 100-bed nursing home.

Market share analysis

Market share is determined by dividing all admissions to all hospitals that originate in a specific geographical area into the admissions of the study hospital originating from the same area. Ideally, the calculations should identify the share of each hospital involved so that the intensity of competition can be ascertained. Over time, market shares will allow evaluations of the competitiveness of each hospital. Emergency and ambulatory care market shares can also be determined, but the market shares of discharges retain greater importance.

Service area population studies: current analysis and projections

For an accurate service area population study, the 1970 and 1980 censuses should be used, together with a 1975 estimate (if available), as well as a current reliable estimate. These figures must correlate with the specific geographical areas identified in the patient origin and market analysis studies. Since the census does not record by zip code area, census tract or other populations may have to be assigned to the zip code areas. In many areas, public agencies or certain private firms have already done this. It may be necessary to overlay a zip code map with a transparency of a census tract map in order to transfer the population figures to the proper zip code areas.

Three distinct segments of the population should be identified:

1. residents 14 years of age and under

2. female residents of age 15 through 44

3. residents 65 and older.

Totals should be obtained for each category. The 14-and-under analysis provides information about opportunities for pediatric services. The analysis for females 15 through 44 is oriented toward obstetrics and gynecological services, and the data for the 65-and-older group provide a base for geriatric program considerations and information about increased admission rates.

The analyses as outlined will allow trends to be ascertained and reflected in trend lines. Growth percentages can also be determined for the time periods used.

Projections of population for both the primary and secondary service areas should be made for 5- and 10-year periods from the time of analysis and for any year of specific interest to the study hospital. Projections for these target years should be obtained from reliable sources, if possible, or they can be formulated by applying curve-fitting techniques or straight-line extrapolations to past trends. In any case, the hospital should ascertain beforehand that the projections obtained or formulated will be acceptable to the governmental agency with approval authority for any facility project that may be later determined as desirable and feasible.

Although historical trends and projections should always be determined for primary and secondary service areas, they can also be prepared for specific geographical areas in which the hospital desires to increase its market share.

Use rates and area demand

Before any valid quantified justification can be established for a specific hospital program, use rates must be determined and area demand projected.

By dividing the population, *in thousands*, of a given geographical area (the primary, secondary, or other specific service area of interest) into the total discharges generated from the area, the number of discharges per 1000 population can be determined. The use rate of a given hospital can be calculated by dividing the population of its primary service area, for example, in thousands, into the discharges that were obtained from the area. Of course, the same year must be used with regard to discharges obtained and population figures used.

Obviously, a trend in use rates would be evident even if only two years were used—for example, 1980 and the current study year.

Although desirable, establishing a trend is not absolutely necessary. However, establishing a use rate for the most recent year in which a patient origin study was performed, and for which reliable population figures are available, is essential.

Establishing and projecting use rates for emergency and ambulatory care visits should be accomplished in the same manner and for the same periods as those used for inpatients.

By making certain assumptions about the competition, the current health care delivery trends referenced to discharges, and the current intentions of the study hospital, and by noting any historical trend in market shares and use rates, a use rate (discharges per 1000 population) can be estimated for future 5- and 10-year periods and for any other target year desired. This use rate can then be multiplied by the projected population, in thousands, for each of the same years. Thus, an intelligent estimate can be made of the *number of discharges that the hospital might reasonably expect* for these years. These projections, of course, are figures of prime concern.

The use rate for each service area being studied and the number of total discharges for each area should also be determined. When multiplied by the respective projected population in thousands for the target years, the *extent of the total area demand* can be determined. This figure is also of prime concern because it allows executives of the study hospital to make decisions about market saturation, about the nature and extent of competitive strategic moves, and, not least, about programmatic needs.

It is obvious that use rates can be projected for specific services, such as medical, surgical, pediatrics, obstetrics, and psychiatry, as desired. In the case of obstetrics, however, the number of births can be more validly projected by employing birth rates that have been recorded over a past 3- to 5-year period. Such separate projections should probably be accomplished for most hospitals with a capacity of 150 beds or more.

A use rate for emergency and ambulatory care visits should also be accomplished in the same manner as that outlined for inpatient discharges.

Projections

The trend in lengths of stay must be established by service if projections of discharges have also been made by service. At the least, a trend should be established for obstetrics separate from all other services. Ideally, lengths of stay should be determined for each competing hospital, and certainly, respective service area trends must be analyzed and projected in order to compute the total extent of projected area demand referenced to patient days of care.

By multiplying respective projected discharges by correlated projected lengths of stay, patient days for the selected target years can be obtained. A division of the patient days so obtained by 365 days will yield a daily average census for the separate service areas being studied.

The gross number of beds needed by the study hospital can be roughly determined by dividing 80 to 85 percent into the census figure obtained for the entire hospital. The total number of beds needed in each service area can be obtained by dividing 80 to 85 percent into the calculated daily census for the area under consideration.

If the projections, for either the study hospital or the service area, or both, have been accomplished by service, then the number of beds should also be calculated by service. It is more accurate and more desirable to make calculations by service, of course.

In making calculations by service, most professional planners use the following occupancy rates to calculate bed requirements for an individual hospital:

- medical and surgical   85 percent

- pediatrics   75 percent

- obstetrics   70 percent

- psychiatry   90 percent

Of course, total beds needed by the hospital can then be determined by adding projected figures for all services. Most planners merely separate special care beds from the separate service projections, as a percentage of the total, although special algorithms, not presented here, have been developed for this purpose.

The total beds projected for the respective service areas can also be determined by adding the results of individual service calculations, if area census projections have been performed by service.

Implications of the projections

The number of beds existing in the respective service areas, by service or by total, as the case may be, should be recorded and displayed in tabular form. These numbers should be compared with the numbers projected as needed by the methodology outlined under preceding headings. Either surpluses or deficiencies should be established for all projected target years.

Another table showing all existing beds and beds approved for construction added to that total should also be prepared. Comparisons of these numbers with the numbers projected will provide realistic estimates for the target years and will allow hospital executives to make informed decisions relating to future overbeddings or needs for growth, by location. Considerations regarding vertically or horizontally integrated services can also be explored with this basic information. For example, a projected surplus of beds may give rise to considerations of converting acute care beds to other uses. Projected bed deficiencies usually motivate management to consider expansions or to undertake vertically integrated programs that will either reduce lengths of stay or disallow the necessity to hospitalize certain categories of patients.

In the case of projected emergency and ambulatory care visits, the gross need for individual examination space can be determined by dividing 3000 annual visits (a typical caseload) into the total projections. The sufficiency of treatment capabilities can be determined by comparing the figure obtained with the number of available treatment spaces in the emergency ambulatory care suite. More refined methodologies for calculating treatment spaces do exist, and can be used, if indicated.

Figure 3–3 records the basic methodology involved in calculating needs as has been explained in preceding pages.

Medical staff analysis

The importance of a thorough medical staff analysis, as well as an area-wide study of physician sufficiency, cannot be overestimated inasmuch as all business volumes, both inpatient and outpatient, depend upon physician services, except with regard to a few wellness-health promotion-type programs. Simplistically, provided that a sufficient area population is present, all problems referenced to the business volumes of an individual hospital can be related to either or both of two situations: (1) there is not a sufficient number of physicians on the staff overall or in some specialties (a very common problem, which is often either overlooked or ignored) and (2) those physicians who are on the staff are sending appreciable numbers of their patients, possibly both inpatients and outpatients, to other health care facilities, for a variety of reasons. The medical staff analysis is designed to give information about these situations currently and to project future problems, so that remedial actions can be taken.

The record of each physician's utilization of the hospital should be accumulated over a 3-year preceding period in terms of discharges, patient days, average length of stay, and such other statistical and financial data as may be indicated.

In addition to the usual identification data (e.g., age, specialty), an analysis should be made of office locations by zip codes. Also, the percentage of each physician's total practice that the study hospital has obtained must be trended for a 2- or 3-year period.

The following basic information should be generated from the physician data:

1. physician distribution by age and specialty

2. physician distribution by staff tenure and specialty

3. discharges by age and specialty

4. discharges by tenure and specialty

5. patient days by age and specialty

6. physician office distribution by distance from hospital and by zip code

7. profile of top 15 (or 20) admitting physicians, including age, years of tenure, board certification, office zip code, number of discharges, number of patient days, and average length of stay

8. staff membership category by specialty (active, associate, courtesy, and honorary)

9. distribution of each physician's total discharges by hospital.

Algorithm for estimating future outpatient visits and bed requirements

3

A.
CALCULATE ADMISSIONS AND OUTPATIENT VISITS PER 1000 POPULATION FOR THE PREVIOUS 5–10 YEAR PERIOD

B.
PERFORM TREND ANALYSES ON INDICES DEVELOPED IN "A" ABOVE

C.
PREDICT INDICES FOR YEARS CORRESPONDING TO THOSE OF POPULATION PROJECTIONS, BASED ON TRENDS DEVELOPED IN "B", OTHER MORE CURRENT DATA AND INFORMED OPINION ABOUT THE FUTURE OF HEALTH CARE DELIVERY

D.
MULTIPLY POPULATION IN 1000's BY PREDICTED INDICES TO OBTAIN NUMBER OF FUTURE ADMISSIONS AND OUTPATIENT VISITS ✳

1

PERFORM PATIENT ORIGIN STUDY FOR INPATIENTS AND OUTPATIENTS TO IDENTIFY HOSPITAL'S SERVICE AREA

2

ESTABLISH HISTORICAL POPULATION GROWTH IN SERVICE AREA AND MAKE PROJECTIONS FOR 5 AND 10 YEAR PERIODS

✳ 1 /

CALCULATION OF OP VISITS ENDS HERE

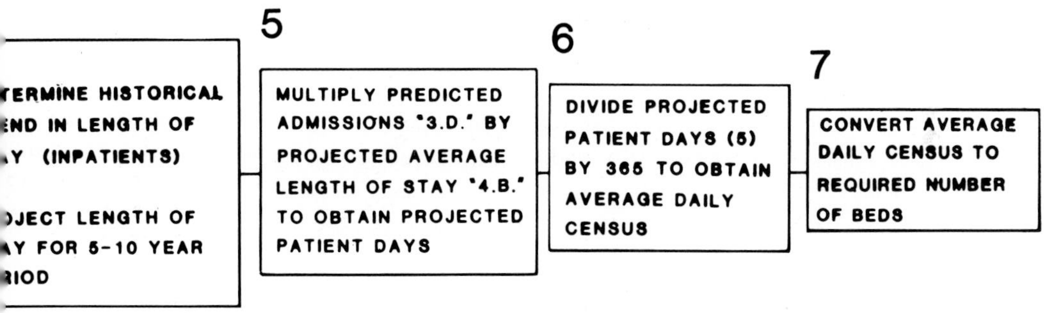

4

ERMINE HISTORICAL
END IN LENGTH OF
Y (INPATIENTS)

OJECT LENGTH OF
AY FOR 5-10 YEAR
RIOD

5

MULTIPLY PREDICTED
ADMISSIONS "3.D." BY
PROJECTED AVERAGE
LENGTH OF STAY "4.B."
TO OBTAIN PROJECTED
PATIENT DAYS

6

DIVIDE PROJECTED
PATIENT DAYS (5)
BY 365 TO OBTAIN
AVERAGE DAILY
CENSUS

7

CONVERT AVERAGE
DAILY CENSUS TO
REQUIRED NUMBER
OF BEDS

Physician sufficiency ought to be determined for every service area studied (primary, secondary, and other), by calculating the number of physicians per unit of population. The number, by specialty, practicing in each area of interest should be compared with averages throughout the United States and as recommended by the American Medical Association and the Graduate Medical Education National Advisory Council. This comparison will reveal any gross deficiencies or surpluses.

Hospital executives should be informed about each of the following items through the analyses of the physician data:

- concentrations of older doctors (whose productive lives are limited) among specific specialties

- deficiencies in numbers within specialties

- disproportionate numbers of admissions and patient days by a few doctors

- disproportionate numbers of admissions and patient days by older doctors

- proportion of physicians' total hospital admissions (majority, all, or only a token number) received by the study hospital

- time-distance relationships of physicians' offices to the hospital, listed as percentages of physicians (e.g., percent near, percent far)

- staff turnover, indicating stability or instability

- whether the hospital serves as an overflow or as a primary facility to its medical staff

- whether the staff as a whole can be classified as "young" or "old"

- staff quality, as indicated by the presence of a broad array of specialties or by the lack of needed specialties

- a disproportionate balance in numbers available in different specialties

- the sufficiency or insufficiency of primary care physicians to support adequately the specialists on the staff through referrals

- the sufficiency or insufficiency of physicians, area-wide, based on ratios of number of specialists to population unit

- the adequacy of staff numbers to support expansions, in the event the need has been revealed by the primary demand analysis and projections.

Physical plant inventory

The purpose of the physical plant inventory is to allow a comparison of facility capacities with the requirements of patient care demand, both inpatient and outpatient, that will be predicted as a part of the data base. This inventory will allow intelligent decisions about conversions to other uses versus the need for expansions, or about the character of additions that may be indicated to accommodate recent changes in modes of health care delivery, especially those related to outpatients. The many constraints exerted by the existing physical facilities upon strategic planning are well known and need not be further reviewed here.

Data to be accumulated as a part of this inventory are as follows:

1. bed numbers, categorized by service and by type of accommodation (e.g., private, semiprivate)

2. bed numbers, both licensed and in operation (by service)

3. bassinet capacity of all types of nurseries

4. number of labor beds, delivery rooms, birthing rooms, and postpartum recovery beds

5. number of major and minor operating rooms available and in use

6. number of cystoscopic rooms in use

7. capacity of postoperative recovery rooms

8. number of major and minor operating rooms devoted exclusively to outpatient surgery

9. number of parking spaces available by classification of use

10. number of acres in hospital site

11. total number of gross square feet (GSF) per bed.

The sufficiency or insufficiency of the physical facilities can easily be determined following the completion of all projections of utilization.

Utilization data

In the formulation of a utilization data base, the totals for discharges, emergency visits, and other ambulatory care visits should be regarded as *primary demand* figures. They have the nature of independent variables. Other recorded utilization figures can be classified as *derived demand* figures, because they have the nature of dependent variables.

A complete utilization data base typically records statistics for a 3-year complete period and for the year to date if the recording occurs 6 months or beyond in the current year. The current-year figures are merely extrapolated to obtain a fourth year for better trend analysis. Utilization data for the following are recorded with reference to *primary* demand:

- discharges

- patient days

- average daily census

- average length of stay

- deliveries

- live births

- newborn days

- average newborn census (by type of nursery)

- emergency visits

- nonemergency ambulatory care visits

- clinic visits (by type of clinic)

When indicated, the data can be broken down according to major services or specialties.

In a typical large acute care hospital, the following data should be recorded to reflect derived demand utilization:

- surgical operations

- cystoscopies

- x-ray examinations

- x-ray treatments

- EKGs

- EEGs

- stress tests

- ultrasound tests

- physical therapy visits

- occupational therapy visits

- laboratory tests (anatomical, clinical)

- pulmonary function procedures

- respiratory therapy treatments

- pharmacy prescriptions filled

- nuclear medicine scans

In all instances, outpatient data should be separated from that for inpatients.

Of course, data should also be recorded for all special services offered by the hospital, such as open heart surgery, cardiac catheterization, angioplasty, computed tomography (CT), wellness and health promotion programs, and home care programs.

Analysis of utilization

With the utilization data for a 3-year period having been assembled, trends are immediately apparent. Where the trends are proceeding in an unfavorable direction, the hospital executive and administrative staff should be able to ascertain the reasons for the trend and begin to think about taking some measures of remedial action. Where trends are favorable, conclusions can also be reached, and lessons may be drawn from the favorable causes for application elsewhere.

With regard to the relationship between primary demand and derived demand, it can easily be seen that all derived demand flows from primary demand. Not only should simple, direct trend lines be noted from the figures as assembled, but the relationship between primary demand and derived demand, in terms of a ratio, should be noted. For example, with the figures assembled as outlined in the utilization data base, it is a very easy matter to determine the number of inpatient x-ray examinations *per discharge*, simply by dividing the total admissions into the number of total inpatient x-ray examinations. When this is done for the four yearly periods specified, a trend will be apparent. It may be observed that the total number of x-ray examinations is *up*, while the number per admissions is *down*. Such important findings may be detected in several other instances of derived demand. Of course, if the trends in these ratios are unfavorable or out of character with regional or national trends, the reasons should be detected so that remedial action can be taken.

Utilization projections

Generally, an executive and the administrative staff will have gained some idea of space, equipment, and personnel needs by department or service from the expressions of department heads or specialty physicians. With the data base as outlined, calculations can easily be made to project total departmental utilizations for the target years for which discharges have been projected. Simply stated, a figure can be projected for any departmental utilization *per discharge* on the basis of trends, established as outlined in preceding paragraphs. By multiplying the projected ratio by projected discharges, the *total utilization* for any department can be calculated.

The specific methodologies for calculating these utilizations (workloads) of each department are outlined in Chapter 7. It should be recognized that one of the basic reasons for performing these projections is to obtain realistic information for judging certain situations and problems that routinely arise over issues of space, equipment, and personnel; without such information, judgment may be improperly based on opinion or, sometimes, on unwarranted desires. Such analyses cannot relieve an executive of what may prove to be a purely political choice, but they do supply some factual information for use in making an optimal decision.

Certainly, in the case of large additions to hospitals, departmental utilizations should be projected, and the methodology as outlined is the correct one. This will allow easy predictions of space and equipment needs.

Area health service inventory

The study hospital should inventory the services offered by all competing providers of health care, including outreach programs and facilities. This inventory should be complete and considerably detailed.

Such recordings are necessary for evaluating the desired range and depth of services covered in a *proposed* strategic program. For this evaluation, the administrator not only must know what the competition is doing but also should be able to predict the probability of approval by governmental regulatory agencies.

A large spread sheet, listing various services in a vertical left-hand column and the names of the competing health care providers horizontally across the top of the sheet, should be prepared. If the provider (usually an acute care hospital) offers the service, a checkmark can be placed at the intersection of the service and the provider columns. With this spread sheet prepared, the administrator can tell at a glance who has what and can make some intelligent judgments about what might successfully be undertaken and also, for services will low utilization, about what might best be discontinued, in view of DRG implications.

The annual "Guide Issue" of the *Journal of the American Hospital Association* is a usual source for ascertaining a competing hospital's programs, as well as records of approvals and rejections by regulatory agencies. Of course, such information can also be obtained directly through inquiry.

Industry and large business inventory

By zip code, an inventory of major industrial and business firms operating in the primary and secondary service areas should be prepared. Such inventories are useful in considering "preferred provider" plans for delivering care and in public relations work.

Strategy maps

To enhance perceptions about competition and its strength and to identify specific opportunities for growth, certain area maps, prepared with input from the data base, are invaluable. Such strategy maps often allow the chief executive officer and administrative staff to grasp situations that go unrecognized in statistical presentations. At the least, strategy maps give added meaning to statistical implications. (See Figure 3–2 for a sample map.)

Three specific service area maps are considered necessary:

1. a zip code map (or other map of the service area) depicting patient origin boundaries, overlaid by the primary road system, with current and projected populations noted within each zip code or other designated area, together with the percentage of discharges from each obtained by the hospital, as well as the locations of all area hospitals

2. a similar map, showing current and projected populations by zip code or other patient origin area, together with the numbers of physicians, categorized as either primary or referral, officed within each area

3. a map of the same region showing the locations of nursing homes, urgent care facilities, mental health facilities, and any other type of provider facility of interest.

These maps should be large and should be wall-mounted inside the management suite in an area where discussions can be held.

Revenue and expense analyses

For at least a 3-year period, separate revenue and expense analyses should be performed on accounts for Medicare, Medicaid, Blue Cross, commercial insurance carriers (as a whole or by separate carriers, as indicated), and any other revenue source that may be of interest, such as local government payments for charity. These analyses will allow executives to compare profitability by source and evaluate the hospital's dependency upon each. The results should be tabulated according to total revenues received, discharges and patient days, and percentages of totals.

Increasingly, strategic planning may depend upon DRG information. Profitability per DRG will probably become a primary basis upon which hospital strategies will be formed. Therefore, an analysis of income and expense related to DRGs should be studied as this information accumulates in physicians' records and in the hospital's financial and medical records departments.

The issues involved have been well stated by Zuckerman: "Under DRG reimbursement, profit or loss from service charges is a distinct possibility, and hospitals must carefully consider the financial consequences of all proposed initiatives. Financial simulation has become a key technique. DRGs signal the end of planning in isolation from finance."[6]

Identification of constraints

A goal-oriented strategic plan must be formulated not only with reference to an appropriate data base but also in terms of real constraints. Thus, it is necessary to assess realistically the institution's current financial limitations before setting goals and objectives. Time and personnel constraints also must be recognized when the scope and character of goals and objectives are determined. As already mentioned, physical facilities may pose very real constraints; their assessment is covered in succeeding chapters.

Some of the financial indicators that should be determined to identify constraints and capabilities are as follows: liquidity ratios, including current "acid test" collection period, and average payment period; capital structure ratios, including long-term debt to fixed asset, long-term debt to equity, times interest earned, debt service coverage, and cash flow to total debt; and profitability ratios, including mark-up, deductible, operating margins, nonoperating revenue contribution, and return on assets. In fact, these ratios as well as certain activity ratios should be routinely calculated (but seldom are) for use in routine management decision making.[7]

Those analyses that pertain purely to facility planning are discussed in some detail in Chapter 5.

Establishing goals and objectives

At this point in the process, the institution has performed a rather comprehensive self-analysis and an analysis of its operating environment. The questions "Where have we been?" and "Where are we now?" should have been answered. Some insight into probable future direction, based on the previously performed projections or predictions of trends, has also been ascertained.

The governing board and administrative officials now are ready to formulate some very important decisions that relate directly to the institution's future viability, vitality, image, and service orientations. These decisions typically involve responses to such questions as the following: "Now that we understand who we are, where we are, and where we seem to be going, what must we do in order to control our future? What should we do to serve our clientele better and at the same time assure institutional strength? In the case of identified pessimistic trends, what can we do to change them? How can we overcome threatening competition? Should our basic mission be changed? Should our image be altered or enhanced in the eyes of our several publics, and, if so, how do we go about it? Should our product mix be revised? What will constitute a program of action as opposed to reaction? Are our facilities adequate?"

Answers to these questions should be expressed in the form of goals and objectives—the next step in the process. In some instances, however, the institutional mission itself should be reevaluated. As modes of delivery change and technology advances, management may find that delivery can take several forms in a single institution, and one cannot truthfully say that current forms will never be replaced by more innovative ones. Generally, a *mission statement* describes the overall philosophy and purposes of the institution. *Goals* then express more specifically the areas in which development, change, and enhancement are sought. Goals also outline general targets to be achieved in specified areas within the context of the institutional mission. *Objectives* designate quantified targets to be attained, actions to be consummated, or points of progress to be reached within a specific time frame in achievement of the established goals.

For purposes related to controlling implementation tasks, emphasis should be placed upon quantifying objectives. For example, it is far better to frame an objective that states "Increase outpatient surgery by 20 percent during the period January 1, 1984 to June 30, 1985" than it is to say merely "We hope to increase our outpatient surgery during 1984 and the first half of 1985."

Goals and objectives sometimes relate to a very broad range of results that institutional executives may wish to achieve. Empirical observations made over a wide range of strategic efforts, all based on a structured process, reveal, however, that certain categories of goals and objectives typically are evidenced. Those observed most frequently are discussed following.

Increases in utilization through the satisfaction of unmet needs or demands.   Oftentimes, gaps in available area services that the institution can fill, either by recruiting new medical specialists or by initiating a new service, are identified. Thus the needs of the marketplace are met by the institution. On occasion utilization is also increased by responding to a well-recognized market demand that the institution had not previously attempted to satisfy. In such instances, actions taken may, again, involve the recruitment of additional medical specialists and the expansion or strengthening of existing services. From a strategic planning standpoint, the institution attempts to equate product volume with customer demand.

Increases in utilization by obtaining greater shares of area admissions and outpatient visits.   Some theoreticians raise the point that actions in this area occasion costly competition. However, competition has also been proved to promote services of a better quality. In any event, it must be recognized that competing for a given market, in one form or another, has been and will continue to be one means used by institutions to maintain strength. The means employed may entail image enhancement; meeting the needs and desires of medical staff members, both individually and collectively; offering personalized patient care; and introducing unique services designed to serve as promotional activity. Market segmentation usually assists achievement in this particular category.

Keeping facility changes (expansions and modernizations) in pace with programmatic and service developments. Although it is true that an institution can spend too much on facilities (a fact that has been brought very forcefully to everyone's attention over the past decade), it is also true, as has already been pointed out, that successful planning cannot be conducted with the somewhat naive attitude that facilities are not important. Certainly, when you can obtain a private room with a good shower in most fourth-rate motels in this nation, you surely should be able to do as well in a health care institution. In addition, it is true that some of the functional monstrosities in which hospitals, particularly, are forced to give care are costing their patients an ignored but untold amount of money.

Mergers and acquisitions. Probably the investor-owned chains have exploited these actions to best advantage, to the extent that antitrust laws will permit. The idea is to acquire the competing institution and combine its capacity in a new operation. Alternatively, two or more not-for-profit hospitals may merge voluntarily to gain synergistic effects and to allow orderly progress in the absence of what is, oftentimes, internecine competition. This category of goals and objectives has been noted very often in strategic planning.

Associations. Many types of associations exist at the present time, several of which are in essence "shared service" corporations. Others are created for special purposes, such as the massing of capital for development and the elimination of competitive impediments. This category has particularly been noted in long-range plans tailored to satisfy regulatory requirements, but associations have been observed as well in strategic planning and marketing activities.

Providing satellite care facilities. Some large medical centers are building satellite hospitals in order to satisfy area needs and also to serve as feeder hospitals providing tertiary care patients to the central facility. Many community-type hospitals, as well as medical centers, are providing ambulatory care facilities of one type or another to provide new or more ancillary services and to generate referral patients to the sponsoring institution. In other instances, physician office buildings are provided in areas where few physicians are practicing in order to respond to known demand. "Surgicenters" constitute another example. With the addition of such facilities, product distribution is enhanced, and increased consumer utilization of the institutions' services is made more likely. This category has been observed in marketing studies as well as in various types of planning studies including strategic planning.

Contract service agreements. Many large hospitals are now offering contract services of a broad variety to smaller institutions, for a profit. At the same time, the larger organization hopes to increase its own utilization through creation of either formal or informal patient referral channels. In addition, the relationship allows the larger organization to "keep an eye on" the status of the smaller partner in the event an acquisition or merger might prove profitable.

Building institutional systems.   Many larger hospitals are now bent on creating multiunit hospital systems. Some hospitals have banded together to form such a system and have included other types of institutions in the system if the relationship may prove to be beneficial from a standpoint of either direct profit or patient referral. These systems are ostensibly created to bring better services at lower costs to health care consumers.

Levels of financial capabilities.   Not infrequently are levels of financial capabilities, for either operations or capital funding, included among the goals and objectives of a results-oriented planning or marketing process. Operating ratio, net take-down, debt ratio, ratio of total accounts receivable to average daily charges, and net profit, for example, all involve the setting of quantified targets. In fact, investor-owned hospital systems very frequently establish such targets in their strategic planning activities.

Educational activities.   Most health care institutions have aspirations of an educational nature. The establishment of specific programs and of relationships with various types of schools is often included among stated goals and objectives. This category is aimed directly at one of the most important of an institution's publics—the employee body.

Others.   Less frequently observed goals and objectives are those related to indexes of patient satisfaction; indexes of the quality of patient care (e.g., reduction in infection rates); research activities; and employee-patient ratios.

Implementation

Following formulation of goals and objectives, their attainment becomes the next stage of the process. This is accomplished through carefully devised implementation strategies composed of definitive tasks to be performed. At this point, management may begin to involve many members of the personnel body. All classic management processes are usually brought into play in order to carry out the planning or marketing strategies. Certainly strong leadership must be exercised by top executives in order to unite the several categories of departmental employees behind the specified institutional goals and applicable objectives.

Implementation, being action-oriented, involves establishing priorities among defined tasks and the preparation of a time schedule for task execution. For this purpose, a typical Gant chart is satisfactory. In addition, assignment of responsibility and delegation of authority, allocation of resources, and the formulation of a system for feedback must be accomplished.

From an academic standpoint, some difficulties usually arise regarding the proper designation of objectives as objectives and implementing tasks as tasks. Oftentimes, tasks may be regarded as objectives. As a point of interest but no great importance, in general, an objective is target-oriented, and a task is action-oriented in the attainment of an objective. Regardless of designations, what *is* important is a program of planned action that accomplishes beneficial results for the institution.

Insofar as is possible, tasks should be geared directly to the attainment of a specific goal or objective. However, in a comprehensive, complex process, objectives may relate to more than one goal, and tasks may relate to more than one objective.

In the event that a facility planning project evolves from a strategic planning study, its implementation should follow the process outlined in subsequent chapters.

Monitoring and evaluation

As implementation moves forward through the efforts of those to whom tasks are assigned, progress must be monitored by the feedback system devised at the time implementation tasks were formulated. Checks must be made regarding difficulties encountered in order that they can be resolved. Certainly management control must be exercised to assure that schedules are met, budgets observed, and priorities respected. Without proper control, it is safe to say that the implementation activity will either fail or only partly succeed, and that efforts expended up to this point in the process will accrue largely to institutional expense, rather than institutional success.

Effective control can best be obtained through scheduled written reports, supplemented by discussions with those involved in the task implementation. The skillful manager will exercise supervision in a personal, helpful manner, but the controls should be geared impersonally to specific targets and schedules.

The monitoring and control process can guide implementation tasks to a successful conclusion, but the final step in the total process, graphically displayed in Figure 3–4, relates to an evaluation of results as they are achieved. Have they accomplished the goals and objectives established earlier? If not, why not? If they have, has accomplishment resulted in apparent benefits to the relevant population (e.g., patients, physicians) as planned? Has accomplishment proved to be as beneficial to the institution as was originally envisioned? Should other goals and objectives be adopted in view of changed circumstances? These questions and others are usually asked when results are reviewed.

In many instances, iterative actions will be taken, either to continue the work as started or to change it in character or scope. Seldom is monitoring a one-time-through process, terminating with the completion of all specified tasks; rather, it then assumes an ongoing status. Exceptions, of course, are those tasks related to certain objectives that have a distinct end, such as the acquisition of a satellite facility.

Regarding monitoring as it pertains to facility planning projects, Chapter 15 more fully addresses this topic.

Evaluating results of strategic planning

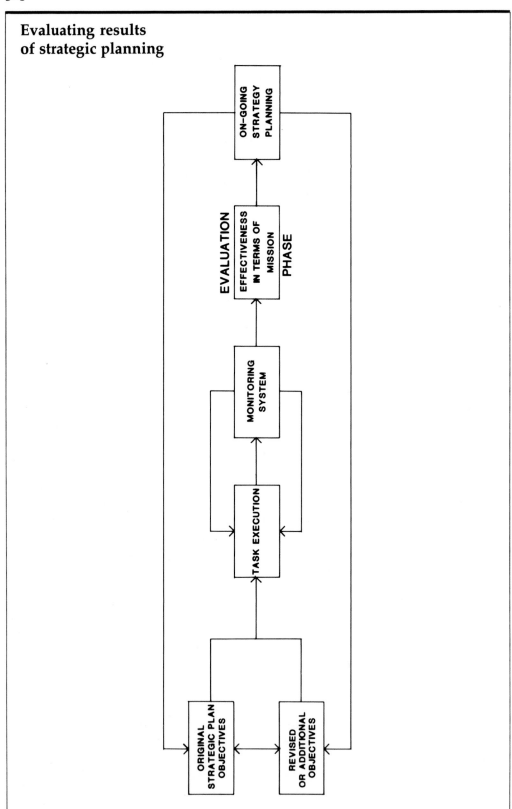

Summary

The quantifications of projected or predicted patient care demands, both primary and derived, serve as the primary basis for facility planning. These quantifications should be a major output in any comprehensive strategic plan.

A strategic planning process starts with planning to execute the process itself. An organizational framework must be determined and put in place, and a timetable devised for carrying forward the planning steps, or tasks. It is imperative that a comprehensive data and information base be assembled as the first basic planning task, or succeeding tasks may produce erroneous conclusions. The identification of constraints should be carried forward concurrently with the creation of the data and information base, and some planners regard identified constraints as an integral part of this base.

After appropriate information is in hand, hospital decision makers are ready to formulate goals and objectives; to reevaluate the very purpose of the hospital, if necessary; and, in essence, to chart the future of the institution for a coming 5-year period, with a directional course also being set for a 10-year period and possibly for a 15- to 20-year period. Cost-benefit analyses may have to be performed to order the goals and objectives on a priority basis, according to their desirability.

An implementation phase follows the formulation of goals and objectives. Without implementation, any planning process remains a futile endeavor. Implementation involves the fixing of responsibility for task execution and assigning authority commensurate with needs for success. All implementation must be scheduled as to time, also.

When implementation is undertaken, monitoring and control measures should be instituted to assure that an orderly completion of tasks occurs.

Strategic planning had best be carried forward on an ongoing basis, even in community hospitals with beds numbering as few as 150. If this is not possible, competent outside planning consultants can be contracted, with periodic updates being performed, preferably on an annual basis.

Notes

1. Robin E. Scott MacStravic, "The Relationship between Planning and Marketing," in Lee F. Block, ed., *Marketing for Hospitals in Hard Times* (Chicago: Teach'em, Inc., 1981), p. 2.
2. Philip Kotler, *Marketing for Non-Profit Organizations* (Englewood Cliffs, NJ: Prentice-Hall, 1975), p. 5.
3. Steve C. Brandt, *Strategic Planning in Emerging Companies* (Reading, MA: Addison-Wesley, 1981), p. 4.
4. Robert E. Linneman, *Shirt-Sleeved Approach to Long-Range Planning* (Englewood Cliffs, NJ: Prentice-Hall, 1980), p. 4.
5. Lee Domanico, "Strategic Planning: Vital for Long-Range Development," *Hospital and Health Services Administration* (Summer 1981): 26.
6. Alan J. Zuckerman, "The Impact of DRG Reimbursement on Strategic Planning," *ACHA Journal* 29 (July/August 1984): 44.
7. William O. Cleverly, "Financial Ratios: Summary Indicators for Management Decision Making," *Hospital and Health Services Administration* 26 (Special Issue 1, 1981): 26–47.

4

The Planning and Design Process

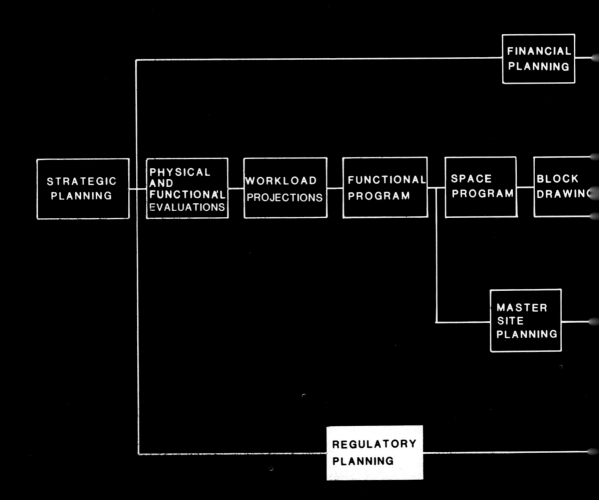

Regulatory planning

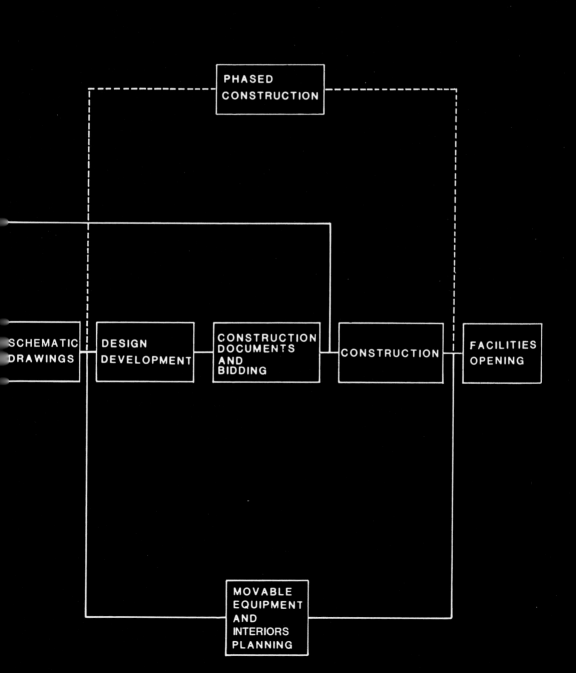

Although regulations governing the type and scope of hospital and related health care facility constructions have eased considerably in years immediately past, hospital executives still must comply with those existing in their respective states. To do so, careful planning, properly meshed with other steps in the overall facility planning and design process, must be undertaken. Generally, the certificate of need (CON) review process must be pursued, with filing through still-existing health systems agencies (HSAs) or directly with state health planning and development agencies (SHPDAs).

Historical background

The federal attitude toward regulatory planning has undergone considerable change over several decades. Hospital constructions were encouraged and, indeed, substantially subsidized from 1949 through the period 1965–1970. Owing to advancing construction costs and a realization that the country was nearing the saturation point with regard to the number of hospital beds, most federal funds for construction had dried up by 1968. Indeed, many prognosticators foresaw an overbuilding of hospital beds in the early 1960s, and the realization of a need to allocate beds and other services appropriately was expressed by passage in 1966 of the Comprehensive Health Planning and Public Health Services Amendment (PL 89-749). Regional planning was the undergirding philosophy of this legislation, and it was warmly endorsed by the American Hospital Association and by most authorities in the health care field.

As hospital costs skyrocketed in the early 1970s, federal planners came to believe that these increases were being fueled by the overbuilding of hospital and related health care facilities. Regional health care planning, implying planning for the delivery of all necessary health care services to residents of a designated geographical area, seemed to be the solution to problems relating to both cost and distribution of facilities.

Accordingly, Congress first enacted the Social Security Amendment of 1972 (PL 92-603), which required specific planning by hospitals, extended care facilities, and home health agencies in order to receive Medicare payments. This law required approval of plans by state (a) agencies and local (b) agencies that had been created under PL 89-749. Section 1122 of PL 92-603 stipulated that health care facilities would not be reimbursed under Medicare for interest and return on equity capital, or for depreciation, related to capital expenditures ruled as unnecessary by the state agencies (the so-called (a) agencies), which usually relied upon the local agencies (the (b) agencies) to make factual determination of necessity.

Owing to the required diversity of membership of the local agencies, decision making related primarily to approval of proposed constructions became extremely slow and tedious. Many providers came to view these organizations as not only a hindrance to progress but also a threat to self-interest. Thus, a schism, which later expanded, was started between governmental planners and providers.

With hospital costs continuing to far outpace the consumer price index, at the behest of federal planners and not withstanding the caution of some providers concerning the dangers of regulation, Congress passed the National Health Planning and Resources Development Act (PL 93-641) in late 1974, which was signed into law on January 4, 1975. Regional health planning constituted the very heart of this act.

Although planning for health services and the provision of resources was the true and stated purpose of PL 93-641, its implementation soon revealed that regulations and, indeed, restraint of development of services and attendant physical facilities by providers actually resulted. Thus, at this point, the pendulum of federal policy had swung to its farthest point away from the program of active support begun in 1949 with subsidization of health care construction. The schism that had appeared between regulators and providers under PL 92-603 became a near chasm.

PL 93-641 effected the creation of 204 HSAs, whose respective territorial jurisdictions blanketed the nation. The HSAs replaced the local agencies created under PL 89-749 (the (b) agencies). A single agency in each state—the SHPDA—was also legislated under PL 93-641 and replaced the state agencies created under PL 89-749 (the (a) agencies).

By 1980, annual federal funding of the HSAs amounted to $119.4 million, with additional nonfederal funding bringing the total to $126.2 million.[1] When President Reagan took office, considerable evidence indicated that the regulatory functions of the HSAs and SHPDAs, as contrasted with their planning functions, were not efficacious in controlling hospital and other health care costs. The need to resolve the conflict between these agencies and the providers, coupled with the opportunity for streamlining the federal bureaucracy as well as for budget cuts, provided additional incentive to eliminate or reduce federal funding under PL 93-641. In response to these factors, federal funding was greatly reduced—to $35.5 million by 1983.[2]

Current status

Despite the severe reduction of federal funds, there are now about 130 HSAs still in operation, and their survival has been possible by procurement of additional funding from the state, industry, local government, and other sources, plus a reduction in their respective budgets.[3] These remaining agencies have largely relinquished their adversary role in interactions with providers. However, their planning role has become largely nonexistent owing to reduced budgets, and project approvals and disapprovals have become increasingly politically motivated.

Health planning under PL 93-641 has been abolished in some three or four states, and in approximately eight others it lapses by a specified "sunset date" unless that date is extended by the state legislature.[4] In the remaining states, SHPDAs remain in place, and filings for approval of specific constructions must be made to these agencies, either directly in those areas not served by an HSA or through the relevant HSA. Filing requirements vary on a state-by-state basis, but some uniformity does exist in most states, owing to the "carry-over" of protocols developed at the peak of implementation of PL 93-641.

The federal government has now concentrated on the encouragement of marketplace competition to reduce the cost of health care delivery. The failure of regulations as implemented under PL 93-641 to effect cost reductions has been generally accepted, although regulatory advocates still abound. Those who favor regulation generally believe that an orderly development of regional planning can occur only with appropriate controls. Also, a substantial number believe that the failure of PL 93-641 was due to the insufficient authority assigned to the implementing planners and regulators. Whether the degree of regulation will increase or decrease is now a matter of conjecture and may depend upon the results achieved with the current emphasis on competition as a means to reduce health care costs.

Although the time frame may vary slightly from state to state, the typical period necessary to obtain approval of a CON application is about 180 days in those states still served by HSAs. In states in which applications are filed directly with an SHPDA, this period, for the most part, has not been substantially decreased.

Capital projects for which a CON application must be filed are no longer uniformly defined throughout the nation, although ceilings on expenditures for projects not requiring review have generally been raised in concert with federal directives. Pennsylvania, for example, has raised its ceiling to $714,000, and Illinois also has a limit set at $714,000.[5] Even though proposed capital expenditures may not exceed a state's established ceiling, the project usually must be reviewed if the cost of major medical equipment or the annual operating expense, or both, of a new service exceeds specified outlays. Such outlays in most states are considerably less than those set for capital expenditures. Furthermore, any project that changes the bed capacity of the hospital usually must be reviewed, and in many states review is required for any new service regardless of new equipment or operating costs.

Each state provides rather severe penalties for proceeding with a reviewable construction project in the absence of an approved CON. These penalties too, vary, but any federal or state payments for care under Medicare or Medicaid are uniformly denied. Clearly, the need still exists to obtain CON approval for major construction projects requiring a defined planning and design process.

CON criteria

Approval of a CON application is always based upon conformance of the proposed project to specified criteria established by the applicable agency (or agencies). These criteria were nearly uniformly standard throughout the nation until federal funding of the HSAs was drastically reduced, and indeed, philosophical intent of the criteria still remains essentially similar from state to state.

Each of the agencies involved in project review carefully compares applicable facts about a given project, submitted in the CON application, with each criterion and bases recommendation for approval (in the case of the HSAs) or actual approval (in the case of the SHPDAs) upon the degree of conformance of these facts to the several criteria. A typical set of criteria, as currently published by the Pennsylvania SHPDA, follows:[6]

Section 707. Criteria for review of applications for certificates of need or amendments.

(a) An application for a certificate of need shall be recommended, approved, and issued when the application substantially meets the requirements listed below; provided that each decision, except in circumstances which pose a threat to public health, shall be consistent with the State health plan.

    (1) The relationship of the application with the applicable health systems plan and annual implementation plan has been considered.

    (2) The services are compatible to the long-range development plan (if any) of the applicant.

    (3) There is a need by the population served or to be served by the services.

    (4) There is no appropriate, less costly, or more effective alternative method of providing the services available.

    (5) The service or facility is economically feasible, considering anticipated volume of care, the capability of the service area to meet reasonable charges for the service or facility, and the availability of financing.

    (6) The proposed service or facility is financially feasible on both an intermediate and long-term basis and the impact on cost of and charges for providing services by the applicant is appropriate.

    (7) The proposed service or facility is compatible with the existing health care system in the area.

    (8) The service or facility is justified by community need and within the financial capabilities of the institution both on an intermediate and long-term basis and will not have an inappropriate, adverse impact on the overall cost of providing health services in the area.

    (9) There are available resources (including health manpower, management personnel, and funds for capital and operating needs) to the applicant for the provision of the services proposed to be provided, and there is no greater need for alternative uses for such resources for the provision of other health services. The effect on the clinical needs of health professional training programs in the medical service area, the extent to which health professional schools in the medical service area will have access to the services for training purposes and the extent to which the proposed service will be accessible to all residents of the area to be served by such services have been considered.

    (10) The proposed service or facility will have available to it appropriate ancillary and support services and an appropriate organizational relationship to such services.

(11) The proposed services are consistent with the special needs and circumstances of those entities which provide services or resources both within and without the health service area in which the proposed services are to be located, including medical and other health professional schools, multidisciplinary clinics, and specialty centers.

(12) The special needs and circumstances of health maintenance organizations shall be considered to the extent required by Federal law and regulation now or hereafter enacted or adopted.

(13) The proposed services are not incompatible with any biomedical or behavioral research projects designed for national need for which local conditions offer special advantages.

(14) Consideration of the need and availability in the community for services and facilities for allopathic and osteopathic physicians and their patients; and the religious orientation of the facility and the religious needs of the community to be served. This provision is not intended to create duplicative systems of care.

(15) The factors which affect the effect of competition on the supply of health services being reviewed, with particular reference to the existence and the capacity of market conditions in advancing the purposes of quality assurance, cost containment and responsiveness to consumer preferences, and the existence and capacity of utilization review programs and other public and private cost control measures to give effect to consumer preferences and to establish appropriate incentives for capital allocations, have been considered.

(16) Improvements or innovations in the financing and delivery of health services which foster competition and serve to promote quality assurance, cost effectiveness, and responsiveness to consumer preferences have been given preference.

(17) The efficiency and appropriateness of the use of existing services and facilities similar to those proposed has been considered.

(18) In the case of existing services for facilities, the quality of care provided by services or facilities in the past has been considered.

(19) The contribution of the proposed new institutional health service in meeting the health-related needs of members of medically underserved groups has been considered in written findings.

(20) The special circumstances of applications with respect to the need for conserving energy have been considered.

(b) If the application is for a proposed service or facility which includes a construction project, a certificate of need shall be recommended, approved and issued when the provisions of subsection (a) are (found) satisfied, and:

(1) the costs and methods of proposed construction including the costs and methods of energy provision are appropriate; and

(2) the impact on the costs of providing health services by the applicant resulting from the construction is found to be appropriate, and the impact on the costs and charges to the public of providing health services by other persons is found to be not inappropriate.

(c) Whenever new Institutional health services for inpatients are proposed, a finding shall be made in writing by the reviewing authority:

(1) as to the efficiency and appropriateness of the existing use of the inpatient facilities similar to those proposed;

(2) as to the capital and operating costs, efficiency and appropriateness of the proposed new service and its potential impact on patient charges;

(3) that less costly alternatives which are more efficient and more appropriate to such inpatient service are not available and the development of such alternatives has been studied and found not practicable;

(4) that existing inpatient facilities providing inpatient services similar to those proposed are being used in an appropriate and efficient manner;

(5) that in the case of new construction, alternatives to new construction such as modernization or sharing arrangements have been considered and have been implemented to the maximum extent practicable;

(6) that patients will experience serious problems in terms of cost, availability, accessibility, or such other problems as are identified by the reviewing agency in obtaining inpatient care of the type proposed in the absence of the proposed new service; and

(7) that in the case of a proposal for the addition of beds for the provision of skilled nursing or intermediate care services, the addition will be consistent with the plans of the agency, if any, that is responsible for the provision and financing of long-term care services.

A certificate of need shall be issued for inpatient services when the provisions of subsections (a) and (b) are satisfied and the findings of this subsection can be made.

(d) Notwithstanding the provisions of subsections (a), (b), and (c), applications for projects described in subsection (e) shall be approved unless the department finds that the facility or service with respect to such expenditure as proposed is not needed or that the project is not consistent with the State health plan. An application made under this subsection shall be approved only to the extent required to overcome the conditions described in subsection (e).

(e) Subject to the provisions of subsection (d), subsections (a), (b), and (c) shall not apply to capital expenditures required to:

(1) Eliminate or prevent imminent safety hazards as safety codes or regulations.
(2) Comply with State licensure standards.
(3) Comply with accreditation standards, compliance with which is required to receive reimbursement or payments under Title XVIII and [Title] XIX of the Federal Social Security Act.

It should be noted that in this document, encouragement of competition, as currently emphasized, has been specified as one aspect upon which approval will be granted.

CON review process

All the approving agencies order the project review process into a series of steps, ending with the issue of an approved CON, provided established criteria have been met. Each agency publishes its individual review protocol, which can be obtained promptly by oral or written request.

Although variations do exist from area to area, a representative sample of review steps is set forth in the following sections, with discussions as appropriate.

Step 1: notification of intent letter

An initial contact with the appropriate reviewing agency should be made in order to determine its procedures and criteria and to obtain whatever pertinent demographic and other health systems data that may be availble. Hospital executives must then file a "Notification of Intent" letter so as to provide prior notification to the agency that a CON application will be filed. Most agencies urge that applicants allow a minimum of 30 days to elapse after filing of the Notification of Intent letter before filing the CON application.

The Notification of Intent letter, typically, should state the location of the project, why it is needed, its estimated cost, and how it ties in with the long-range plans of the applicant. A general description of the project should also be set forth, together with the estimated date of filing of the CON application.

After receipt of the Notification of Intent letter, agency personnel schedule a meeting with the prospective applicant to gain greater information about the proposed application and to impart, in some detail, project review policy and process and to provide whatever data resources it possesses that may be useful in the particular instance. Forms for filing the CON are furnished to the applicant at this time.

Step 2: preparing and filing the application

Most forms provided by reviewing agencies are quite detailed and somewhat complex. In all instances, the information that the applicant must provide relates to the criteria established by the agency, to which conformance must be made. That is, the application must prove conformance to the criteria.

A hospital has no choice but to put together the required information in the form prescribed. This process can take weeks in the case of a major construction project and can consume considerable time on the part of the financial and planning departments, as well as that of outside consultants and architects.

Owing to both the complexity of a major CON application and its volume, an example is not provided here. However, hospital executives who have not filed applications previously would be advised to procure not only the appropriate forms from the reviewing agency itself but a copy of a completed *successful* application from an area hospital. Many hospitals seek outside consulting assistance in preparing their applications, and this service is available from most of the recognized financial and planning consulting firms.

Step 3: review of the application for completeness

After receiving the CON application, the agency usually takes 15 to 25 days to review it and to determine whether it is complete or whether additional information must be provided. If additional information is required, a time period is specified—usually about 45 days—for filing. Failure to file within the specified time usually results in an assumption that the application has been withdrawn without prejudice toward future repeat of the process.

If the agency (or agencies) involved deems that the application is complete, the hospital will be so notified, and subsequent changes can be made only upon agency discretion.

Step 4: substantive review

Review of the application for approval or denial of a proposed major construction project involves an analysis of it referenced to conformance to established criteria by the appropriate agency staff; the establishing of a specific review schedule; notification in writing to the applicant of the schedule and specifically of the date of a public hearing regarding the application; notification in writing to all affected parties, and particularly to all competitors and potential competitors; notification to the public in a news publication of general circulation; the holding of a public hearing, usually chaired by the chairperson of a project review committee; separate review by the project review committee, composed of appointed members of the HSA or SHPDA board, as the case may be (the review meeting also is open to the public); and remittance to the agency's board of directors of the project review committee's recommendations.

Step 5: action by the agency's board of directors

Each HSA has a board of directors whose membership is mandated under federal law. These boards receive the recommendations resulting from the review process and take action as deemed appropriate. A board reviews recommendations at regularly scheduled public meetings and in its decision process considers established review criteria, the specific recommendation(s), and the "fit" of the applicant's project with the area's evolving health care delivery system.

The board notifies the applicant, the SHPDA, and other interested parties of its actions, usually within 10 days.

Where there is no HSA, the SHPDA both performs the review function and directly exercises the authority for approval or denial of an application. Even where HSAs are still in existence, the SHPDAs possess the authority for final approval through their respective decision-making processes.

SHPDAs interfacing with individual applicants, in either the presence or the absence of an HSA, make their respective decisions regarding an application through their own decision-making processes and give written notification to all concerned parties.

Step 6: appeals

In case of a denial of an application, an applicant has an appeals option, which can vary from state to state. However, a right to an appeal through the court system exists in all states. Thus, after pursuing a rather lengthy review process through the established agency (or agencies) in a given area, if a hospital's CON application is denied, management must decide whether the project should be abandoned or whether the lengthy and, in most cases, expensive appeals process should be undertaken, which also could be fruitless. A hospital should make such a decision on the basis of many factors, particularly the quality of its legal counsel, the past history of the relevant court or other appellate body, and the effect of an appeal upon the future relations between the hospital and the respective regulatory agency.

Dealing with the agencies

Many tactics have been employed by hospitals throughout the nation in seeking CON approval from respective regulatory agencies. The tactics used have generally stemmed from the attitudes of hospital executives toward the agencies or specific personnel employed by them. Overall, it can be stated that an attitude of honest forthrightness has undergirded the most successful tactics. Arrogance has proved to be the most defeating attitude and may be followed closely by obsequious cooperation.

Certainly, regulations are always frustrating, and hospital executives in many localities have had sufficient cause to chafe under the unyielding and sometimes rather self-important attitudes of agency personnel intent on reigning in expanding hospitals. In some instances, agency personnel have even assumed authority beyond the scope of PL 93-641; the Satterfield and other amendments were enacted specifically to prevent such excesses.

In retrospect, however, few can deny that hospitals have overbuilt in terms of needs nation-wide. Conversely, few would also deny that there have been many hospitals whose officials have pursued logical strategic and facility planning processes, only to see needed construction or other projects either disapproved or unnecessarily delayed. At the present time, both sides are apparently achieving greater objectivity and tolerance, and those hospitals that are carefully preparing objective plans and attempting to improve a regional health care system through programs of vertical or horizontal integration seem to be achieving a much greater degree of success with CON applications.

Officials of a small percentage of hospitals have employed a tactic of gamesmanship in dealing with the regulatory agencies. Because in the late 1970s and early 1980s a number of HSAs attempted to reduce the extent of most construction projects in one way or another, some hospital officials submitted CON applications for projects considerably in excess of what was either needed or desired. The motivating idea alleged that cutbacks would reduce the project to a level of need, but not further; cutbacks would give the HSA staff credibility in the eyes of bureaucratic officials in Washington and local HSA boards, and the hospital would obtain its true objectives at the same time. Although there is nothing illegal about such ploys, they do not equate with a standard of forthright honesty, which we believe is the standard that will endure the test of time better than any other.

Generally, we have found the following points useful in dealing successfully with the regulatory agencies:

1. The hospital must institute and carry forward a rather rigorous strategic planning process under its own initiative. Since this function is a basic role of management, the individual health care corporation cannot allow an outside agency to perform its planning, nor can it allow strategic planning to remain undone. This is especially true as competition among providers becomes increasingly keen. When any CON application is submitted, it should be based on logical conclusions derived from the analysis of a comprehensive data and information base. It should also be compatible with formulated long-range hospital goals.

2. If a construction project is included in activities proposed in the CON application, stated need should be based not only on the conclusions of the strategic planning process but on an analysis of and planning for the hospital's physical plant, as is discussed in Chapters 5, 6, 7, and 8 of this text. If this evaluation is done by competent planners, there is small likelihood that agency staff will possess grounds for refutation or will advance counter proposals.

3. If submission of both diagrams and schematic drawings of proposed construction is required, these should be derived from consideration of all major design alternatives. In the application, each alternative considered and discarded should be briefly described, and the reasons for rejection stated.

4. Agency staff members should be treated with consideration and respect. At the same time, ploys of patronization should be avoided. No known erroneous information should ever be knowingly submitted to an agency.

5. Every hospital will do well to keep studiously abreast of what relevant agencies are doing, the data and information they are using in decision making, and all new directions they are receiving from the federal government. Conversely, hospital officials should maintain a dialogue with agency personnel about general aims and intents of the hospital. Especially, forthcoming CON applications should be dis-

cussed generally with agency personnel as soon as possible, in keeping with strategic tactics as they may relate to other providers. It is well to keep in mind, however, that all information submitted to agency personnel is public information, by law.

6. *Before* preparation of a CON application begins, in early discussions with agency officials, the following should be ascertained through friendly, informal discussions *at the office of the agency*:

   - Most agencies have adopted methodologies regarding calculations of bed needs, the need for services, and the need for space to house certain services. Generally, such methodologies outlined in this text are those used by the agencies. However, hospital officials should always apprise themselves of the relevant agency's expectations about calculations, which should then be performed in the prescribed manner. Other methodologies may be presented and used to develop an argument or strategy in the application, but to ignore an agency's favored algorithm usually results in a return or disapproval of the application.

   - Most agencies have adopted population projections that they consider correct. Hospital officials are advised to use these figures, although other projections can be cited and used in alternate calculations if they possess apparent validity.

   - Under regulations formulated at the federal level, a number of standards have been set, usually per unit of population or per patient, for the provision of certain services. Although arguments can be developed for exceptions, these standards cannot be ignored.

   - Owing to a lack of funds, in many cases the agency has not updated its health systems plan (HSP) and correlating annual implementation plan (AIP), as published several years ago when funds were sufficient. However, hospital officials should always determine the status of these documents and the expected degree of conformance to their provisions, especially to those of the HSP. Hospitals, of course, should not accept any HSP as "the law," but knowledge of provisions contained therein will allow a better CON application.

7. In preparing and presenting a CON application, hospital officials should assume that both agency staff and review board members may not understand hospital operations and many specific hospital project details. The written application should contain full explanations, and verbal presentations should be made at a level to accommodate variations in expertise among review officials. In this regard, the specific background of each review official should be ascertained well in advance of both written and verbal presentations.

8. Each hospital should designate a single contact for all agency officials and make that person known to each agency involved. Likewise,

hospitals should ascertain a single agency staff person with whom contact will be routinely made.

9. For verbal presentations to reviewers, one highly articulate hospital official should be designated to handle the presentation. Although outside consultants may be called upon to present specific points of information, "hired guns" should be avoided for the main presentation features, if possible. Review boards are particularly impressed by sincerity, clarity of presentation in detail, and apparent belief in the application being reviewed.

10. In major projects, legal counsel *versed in CON law* should be employed to review all schedules; the circumstances of the submitted application; the application itself; and, especially, any competing applications or possible objections on the part of competitors. Counsel should be specifically charged with the responsibility for developing all protocol in consonance with the law. Such counsel should review proposed presentations, be allowed to make suggestions, and be in attendance during the presentation itself.

CON law has become quite complicated owing to court decisions, specific interpretations promulgated by federal implementations, and a number of amendments to the original federal enactment. Hospital officials should realize that local attorneys probably are not capable of advising on major projects and that consultation should be sought from an attorney specializing in CON law.

Other considerations

In major projects, some hospitals have spent huge sums of money in project development *before* receiving CON approval. In a few instances, these expenditures have been necessary to submit the CON application; in others, hospital officials have simply forged ahead with work beyond that necessary for CON filing, in anticipation of approval of the application.

In the first instance, the funds necessary to develop an application should be projected, and if the total is in excess of that specified by the applicable agency, an application may have to be developed for expending the development funds themselves. This matter should be clarified before starting a major project.

In the second instance, some risks are involved, and we have seen a number of projects in which redesign fees had to be paid to architects because the project approved by the agencies was considerably different from that already designed by the architect. In a few cases, the hospital had given the architect authorization to proceed through design development and into working drawings, with the result that a redesign fee amounting to as much as 80 percent of the total A&E fee was required. In most cases, however, the design process had evolved only to the conclusion of schematic drawings. Even so, approximately 15 percent of the A&E fee was required to be paid again for redesign.

Block diagrams are usually required for filing an application for a construction project. In many instances, several months may elapse before the hospital receives an approval of its project with authorization to proceed. During this time there is little for the hospital to do in its planning and design process, and seemingly, time is being wasted, with a chance that project momentum will be lost and inflation will exact an exorbitant toll. Thus, hospital officials face a dilemma: whether to wait for CON approval, or to proceed and run the risk of having to pay additional fees for both planning and design if the CON application is disapproved outright or if the project is radically altered by the nature of the approval received.

No clean-cut answer can be given regarding the dilemma cited. Certainly, before huge planning and design fees are authorized, it seems that informal sounding of agency staff should be made after some time is allowed (possibly three weeks to a month) for staff review. A favorable response, supported by a knowledge of obvious need, will usually warrant a decision to proceed. If approval is unlikely, however, the career of a hospital chief executive may be saved by a decision to wait. In any event, before a decision is made to proceed, a full disclosure of the risks involved should be provided to the hospital's governing board.

Summary

Regulatory planning has come to be a complicated process, requiring detailed attention by hospital executives. In most states, regulatory agencies still exist, despite the severe reduction in federal support for health planning, and CON approval must be obtained to pursue most construction projects of appreciable scope, as well as many others unrelated to construction.

CON applications are generally quite complex and require specific information about the hospital and its proposed project, so that a decision can be made regarding the conformance of the project to established health care planning criteria, which usually are a part of state laws. At the present time, the national emphasis upon competition among providers has been injected into the criteria.

The regulatory agencies have promulgated a distinct process in each state composed of a series of steps or events for filing, review, and approval or disapproval of a CON application. In any applicable project, this process must be carried out according to a time schedule that meshes with the overall planning and design process relating to the whole of project development.

Although some distinct accommodations are now occurring between hospitals and the regulatory agencies, each hospital seeking CON approval will do well to establish an articulated policy in dealing with the agencies. Hospital officials must base their CON strategy on pertinent factual information, desirably obtained through a formal strategic planning process. If a construction project is the subject of the application, rather detailed facility planning will also be required, as outlined in the several chapters of this text.

Cordial and frequent communications should be established between hospital and agency officials, if possible, so that each can be apprised of the other's activities. However, hospital officials must keep in mind that all information received by agency personnel becomes available for public knowledge, by law.

Some pitfalls exist in the expenditure of funds for development of major projects, prior to the receipt of authorization to proceed from the agencies. Hospitals should be acutely aware of the pitfalls and avoid them, in consistency with prudent judgment.

Notes

1. Robert Lauber and Jeanne Parks, *Historical Study of HSA Federal and Non-Federal Funding Support.* Operations Section 1, Local Planning Agency Branch, Division of Planning Assistance and Assessment, Office of Health Planning, Bureau of Health Maintenance Organizations and Resources Development, Rockville, MD, February 1984, p. 3.

2. *Ibid.*

3. *Ibid.*, p. 7.

4. Karen Hunt, "If the Feds Don't Kill Health Planning . . .," *Medical Economics,* November 14, 1983, p. 99.

5. Robert G. Pavlich, Director, State Health Planning and Development Agency, Harrisburg, PA, and Ray Passeri, Executive Secretary of Illinois State Health Facilities Planning Board, Springfield, IL, 1984: personal communication (telephone interviews).

6. Health Care Facilities Act of Pennsylvania, Section 707, 1980.

5

The Planning and Design Process

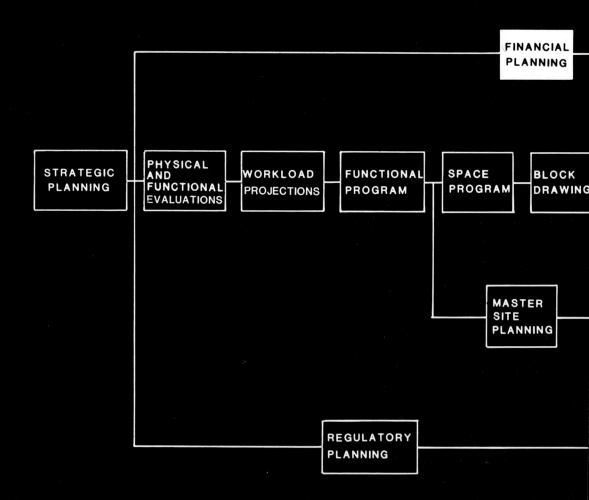

FINANCIAL
PLANNING

STRATEGIC
PLANNING

PHYSICAL
AND
FUNCTIONAL
EVALUATIONS

WORKLOAD
PROJECTIONS

FUNCTIONAL
PROGRAM

SPACE
PROGRAM

BLOCK
DRAWING

MASTER
SITE
PLANNING

REGULATORY
PLANNING

Financial planning

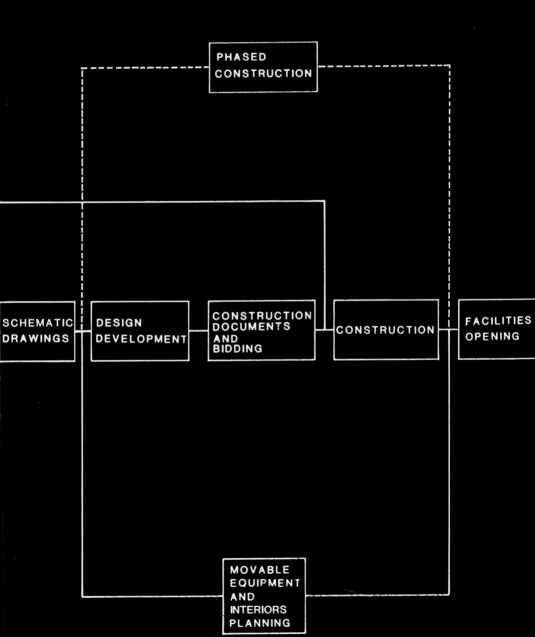

O ver the past decade, financial planning has assumed greater importance and a higher level of complexity than ever before. This has occurred for a number of reasons, particularly the great increase in the cost of construction itself and rapidly rising interest rates. At present the reality of prospective pricing of hospital services is a cause of great concern not only to hospitals but to the debt and equity markets as well. Thus it seems certain that hospital decision makers will give even greater emphasis to expert financial analysis for capital projects in the years ahead.[1] Indeed, a hospital's ability to raise capital may well be the factor upon which its future depends, and certainly this ability will be the primary factor in determining the basic quality and scope of most major construction projects.

Although there are differences of opinion about the availability of capital during immediately ensuing years, the consensus seems to be that even though hospitals will have to provide better proof of credit worthiness, those that can do so will have adequate access to needed money for construction. Corporate reorganizations, mergers, joint ventures, and other techniques will, in fact, allow hospitals access to a broader variety of capital markets than that previously possible.[2]

Methods of financing

Unless the debt capacity for the hospital industry is reached (which is not considered likely) or government regulations restrict access, the tax-exempt bond market will probably be the preferred source of funds for hospital construction in the foreseeable future. Hospitals reported the sale of $1.3 billion in tax-exempt bonds issued in 1974.[3] By 1980, this figure had risen to $3.56 billion, and by 1983, to $9.55 billion.[4] However, the broader variety of capital markets available for access may stem the rise in tax-exempt bond issues, especially where small projects and vertically integrated projects are being considered. The investor-owned systems, of course, will continue to procure their equity and debt directly from commercial sources in one way or another.

Philanthropy will undoubtedly continue to decline, but private endowments may provide the impetus and part of the equity a hospital needs to undertake major construction. Participation in capital formation by all segments of government may completely dry up. Specifically, mortgages on facilities, funded depreciation, and true liens on gross revenues, alone or in combination, promise to constitute the methods by which most constructions will be financed in the decade ahead.

Major purpose

Because this text relates more directly to functional planning and design, we do not provide detailed explanations of the various methods of

---

Note: This chapter was written with substantial assistance from David F. Shanahan, Partner in the firm of Ernst & Whinney (Chicago office).

financing construction costs, from either qualitative or quantitative standpoints. Our primary concern here is the general implications of financing from standpoints of scheduling and management control. Because of the anticipated increased importance of financial planning, it will be imperative that this process be done both expertly and in necessary detail. Moreover, it should be done promptly and according to a published schedule that will accommodate the activities of the other planning team members, as well as those of hospital officials. Task assignments of the investment banker, the financial feasibility consultant, and legal counsel should be programmed in the same manner as for those of the functional planner, architect, and construction manager.

Because we believe the largest single source of capital funding will be through issues of tax-exempt bonds, we have elected to base our discussion on this method. The reader is directed to other literature, which is plentiful, regarding alternative methods of capital financing.

Steps in financial planning

After the strategic planning process has indicated that a major construction project (relative to the individual hospital) should be undertaken, the financial planning tasks necessary to bring the project to fruition should be identified. These tasks may vary in both nature and scope, depending upon situational factors, but it is usually wiser to establish financial feasibility through a thorough and completely unbiased process, by using skilled, experienced personnel, than it is to undertake a marginally sufficient effort.

Step 1: initial activities

The first step in financial planning should be to select both an investment banker and an outside financial consultant (usually a reputable, nationally known accounting and consulting firm). These members of the financial planning team need not be selected simultaneously, but since the investment banker receives no remuneration unless and until the bonds are sold, there is no reason to delay this firm's engagement.

A few hospitals may elect to establish debt capacity through early study by internal personnel. This approach always has its hazards, especially when marginal feasibility of a project is a concern. In smaller projects for which easy financing is obvious, internal work may be acceptable, but even in such cases, the broader experience of an outside consultant may be the better bargain; positioning for the future *after* financing a small project—which many times does not occur to internal personnel—may be a key issue that should be raised.

Although bond counsel may have no responsibilities while debt capacity is being established, there is usually no reason to delay this engagement. With each member of the financial planning team aboard, time commitments can be established and then fulfilled in a more orderly manner and with a greater degree of certainty.

A timetable for the performance of financial planning tasks should be prepared. This schedule should be separate from, but chronologically related to, that of the overall project schedule (as explained in Chapter 2). It should be formally expressed and based upon agreements with each party involved. At present the most common methods for formulating such timetables are the critical path method (CPM) scheduling technique and the use of simple Gant charts.

Hospital management, advised by the investment banker, financial feasibility consultant, and bond counsel, should put together this schedule, and it should be approved first by the finance committee and then by the full governing board.

Step 2: productivity (workload) projections

In the event that workload projections were not prepared during the strategic planning effort, they should be performed at this time by either the functional planner or the financial feasibility consultant. If they have already been prepared by the functional planner, they must be reviewed and verified by the feasibility consultant for accuracy and reasonableness. These projections (discussed more fully in Chapter 7), together with the primary demand figures projected in the strategic plan (DRG-categorized admissions and patient day and ambulatory care visits) form the basis not only for revenue projections, staffing estimates (linked to payroll costs), and various other parts of the financial feasibility study but for the functional program and the space program.

Step 3: debt capacity analysis

A preliminary analysis should be performed to assess the amount of debt the hospital will be able to incur, according to current and anticipated equity and current and anticipated status of certain financial rates and indicators. This analysis, called a *debt capacity analysis,* allows the hospital to establish a viable project budget. It is intended as a tool for hospital decision making relative to the nature and scope of the project to be undertaken; it is not intended to be used to obtain financing. However, some portion of this analysis may later be incorporated into the formal financial feasibility presentation used in obtaining bond ratings and project funding.

A debt capacity analysis does exactly what its name implies—it determines probable debt capacity on the basis of the hospital's several aspects of financial strengths and potential financial alternatives. A *financial feasibility study,* on the other hand, is an analysis of a specifically proposed project under a specific method of financing for that project; it may involve the preparation of financial projections or, under certain circumstances, the preparation of a financial forecast. A *financial forecast* is an estimate of the most probable financial position, results of operation, and changes in financial position for one or more future periods; it is used to assure to the best extent possible that the scope and nature of the finally designed project will in fact be financially feasible.

The nature of a debt capacity analysis may vary, depending upon individual situations, the quality of strategic planning, and the quality of financial records the hospital has been keeping. A typical analysis, however, contains the following:

1. a listing of potential financing alternatives and the requirements associated with each

2. a comparison of financing alternatives, stating advantages and disadvantages of each

3. an examination of the independent financial values inherent to the hospital's past and current situations

4. an analysis of certain financial ratios indicative of liquidity, profitability, capital structure, and activity

5. a comparison of key ratios and indicators, with averages and medians, commonly used in the field of capital financing

6. a statement of assumed sources and use of funds for different debt levels, under at least two alternative methods of financing, projected for the first and second years of operation. These statements must make some basic assumption about the contemplated construction in terms of its ability to handle projected demand levels; cost of construction is assumed as a part of the different debt levels compared. Specifically, the following should be determined:

   • approximate debt service per patient day

   • approximate incremental increase in depreciation and interest expense per patient day

   • approximate charge rate per unit of service (in the past, per patient day; in the future, prospective pricing per DRG, probably) needed to obtain the targeted annual debt service coverage.

7. an assessment of implications of alternative debt levels in terms of effect on patient service charges and costs, and especially with reference to existing and proposed Medicare, Medicaid, and Blue Cross cost reimbursement limitations. For each alternative level of debt, the following parameters should be estimated:

   • additional gross revenue per patient needed, if any, to maintain financial feasibility of the project

   • cash flow generation

   • debt service coverage ratio

   • the amount of money available for construction and other costs of the project

   • approximate debt service per patient day and possible other units of service.

These items should be presented, in summary form, for use by hospital executives and board members in a schedule entitled "Comparison of Impact of Alternative Levels of Debt Financing."

Step 4: selecting a financing method and setting a topside project budget

On the basis of the strategic plan and the debt capacity analysis, a topside construction budget and a total project budget should be established. In some cases, if the capabilities and condition of existing facilities have already been assessed through performance of physical and functional evaluations, it is conceivable that a precise project budget could be established in this step. In addition, the hospital governing board, in its subjective judgment, may wish to establish a specific project budget at this point. However, we believe that it is best merely to set *outside limits* of capital expenditures and to allow projection of needs and design itself to establish construction and total project costs within the outside limits, prior to setting the final terms of a project budget.

At the same time, on the basis of the debt capacity analysis, a financing method should be selected. (For our purpose here, we have assumed an issue of tax-exempt bonds.) During this step legal (bond) counsel should begin study of applicable laws and legal proceedings necessitated by the tax-exempt issue. Counsel should also gain familiarity with all previous board proceedings and the nature and scope of the project envisioned.

Step 5: securing CON approval

The process of obtaining regulatory approval is discussed in some detail in Chapter 4, and although this step is not actually a part of financing, we list it here owing to its important relationship to financial and other planning.

At the time the CON application is filed, the cost of the project will have been estimated; therefore, the proposed financing of the project can be set out in some detail. The following extract from a 1980 CON application shows typical requests for financial information by an HSA:[5]

> . . . Current statement of financial resources . . . to include an audited balance sheet and profit and loss statement (including notes) of the previous fiscal year's operations.

> A monthly cash flow statement for the last 12 months and projected for the 24 months from the completion of the project.

> Document the financial feasibility . . . and that it can be accomplished without unreasonable charges . . . to include a projection of income and expense on a pro-forma basis for the first two years of operation after completion of the project.

> Document the availability of resources (including . . . funds for capital and operating needs).

> Document that the proposed project can be adequately staffed to include specific manpower requirements by . . . proposed salary. . . .

> . . . The costs and methods of the proposed construction, including the costs . . . and the probable impact . . . on the costs

of providing health services by the person [hospital] proposing the project.

Provide a statement of the total cost of the project, to include the cost of studies, surveys, designs, plans, specifications, fees, construction, equipment, land, and interest during construction. Such statement . . . should take into consideration such factors as inflation and actual costs of other like projects within the area.

It can be seen that the debt capacity analysis already performed is a ready source of the information required under the CON application. Other required information not produced in the debt capacity analysis must be prepared at this time.

When the CON application is filed, block diagrams by the project architect usually must be included as a part of the submission, along with a cost estimate of the proposed project, based on these drawings. Some of the regulatory agencies—improperly, we believe—are requesting that schematic drawings also be filed. This occasions an expenditure by the hospital (15 percent of the total cost of all A&E work) that could well be avoided.

Step 6: establishing construction costs and determining feasibility

Construction costs can be estimated with some degree of accuracy at various points in the course of a major project:

1. on completion of a space program by the functional planner or architect

2. on completion of block diagrams and a tentative site plan (usually submitted with the CON application)

3. on completion of schematic drawings and outline specifications

4. on completion of design development drawings and, for the most part, specifications

5. when bids are taken, if a traditional construction approach is pursued. Of course, total project costs are absolutely set at this time, except for movable equipment and some work by minor contractors at opening.

Under phased construction a guaranteed maximum price (GMP) for construction can be obtained under several methods after schematic drawings and outline specifications have been completed. However, in most current programs, determination of a GMP is delayed until completion of design development drawings.

In the case of all cost estimates, the investment banker uses the latest refined estimates of net revenue prepared by the financial feasibility consultant to compare requirements of a debt retirement schedule, which is formulated on the basis of the cost estimates as well as complete development financing costs. A rather conservative interest rate and bond issue maturity data—typically at 30 years from the date of issuance—are used in preparing this schedule.

Thus, from all standpoints, refinements of estimates and projections are ongoing, with the beginning cue provided by the financial feasibility consultant's initial estimate of the debt capacity of the hospital. As work progress is made by one party, refined and expanded figures' allow greater accuracy by others—to assure, finally, that amounts allowed for construction costs and capital funding are as close as possible.

Most investment bankers have regarded a proposed project as being feasible when estimated net revenues allow a minimum coverage of 1.5 times the first year's debt service and 1.8 to 2.0 times that for the second and third years of operation. These leverage ratios have been lowered over the past decade with greater dependence on debt service cash flow generating from recognition by third-party payors of depreciation and interest expense.

Step 7: formalizing documentations

Documentations prepared by the financial feasibility consultant, investment banker, and legal (bond) counsel must await completion until project construction costs are known. If phased construction is undertaken, a GMP can represent the figure on which the preparation of these documentations in final form will be based. If a traditional construction approach is undertaken, the favored bids will make up this figure.

It is *essential* that the various options in choice of a construction approach be considered early, and a decision made with regard thereto, so that the work of the investment banker, financial feasibility consultant, and legal (bond) counsel can be scheduled accordingly. It is highly desirable that all documentations relative to financing be completed as early as possible after a GMP is in hand, or after bids are taken in the case of a traditional approach. If scheduling has been properly done, at the time a construction cost is guaranteed the financial feasibility study should be substantially completed; leases and the bond trust indenture should require only minor revisions, and the official statement (essentially, a prospectus prepared in connection with the bond offering) should require relatively small additions.

Step 8: obtaining the funds and starting construction

When the investment banker has firm construction costs in hand, the official statement can be completed after its review and approval by the governing board. The investment banker then releases the statement to prospective buyers and the rating agencies. After obtaining necessary ratings, the investment banker determines an appropriate interest rate and discounted points and makes a final commitment to purchase the bonds.

When the bonds are sold and with funds in hand, construction contracts can be signed. In the case of phased (fast-track) construction, only initial contracts are signed, but under the traditional approach, the general contract can be let for the entire work. Plans for the investment of unused funds at highest obtainable rates should also be carried out during periods for which such funds are not committed for contractual payments.

Example of scheduling of financial planning

We have prepared an example of a financial planning schedule geared to a design and construction schedule, which is set forth in Figure 5–1. Although individual schedules must be prepared for each project, the example shown emphasizes that complexity of the activities requires a *formal schedule* that should be established at the very beginning of any major project and continuously refined as the entire process proceeds.

From the start of financial planning (following completion of a strategic plan and a decision of the governing board to embark upon a program of facility planning and design) to the sale of bonds, considerable variations in elapsed time may be evidenced from project to project. The example schedule shows a period of 14 months. However, some projects will require less than a year, depending upon the project scope, the time required for preparation of programming and design documents, and the time required for executing the steps of the financial planning process.

At the start of each project, as the schedules of planning, design, and financial team members are being put together, the critical time requirements of specific tasks will become evident, and the effect that those requirements will have on the work of other parties will be clearly seen. Adjustments will be required both initially and as planning progresses, but it should be remembered that quality work by all parties necessitates adequate time for task performance.

The intent of scheduling, then, is not to subject the various contracted parties to excessively demanding time deadlines but rather to attain certain objectives: (1) the elimination of wasted time; (2) coordination of the tasks of independent team members into a single, efficient process; and (3) establishment of effective management (hospital) control over the work of each party. The attainment of these objectives leads to a major goal—cost containment.

Tasks of team members[6]

The nature and scope of the work required of each member of the financial planning team should be clearly outlined at the start of the financial planning tasks (outlined previously under Steps in Financial Planning). Such clarification is essential to avoid overlap of duties and to ensure a clear understanding of individual responsibilities by all concerned.

The tasks of the investment banker, financial feasibility consultant, and legal (bond) counsel are generally specified in rather detailed agreements. The part (if any) played by the strategic or functional planner in the process must also be established. Although we list here the preparation of productivity statistics (workload projections) as a duty of the financial feasibility consultant, such projections are in many, if not most,

Example of financial planning model, typical tax-exempt bond financing process

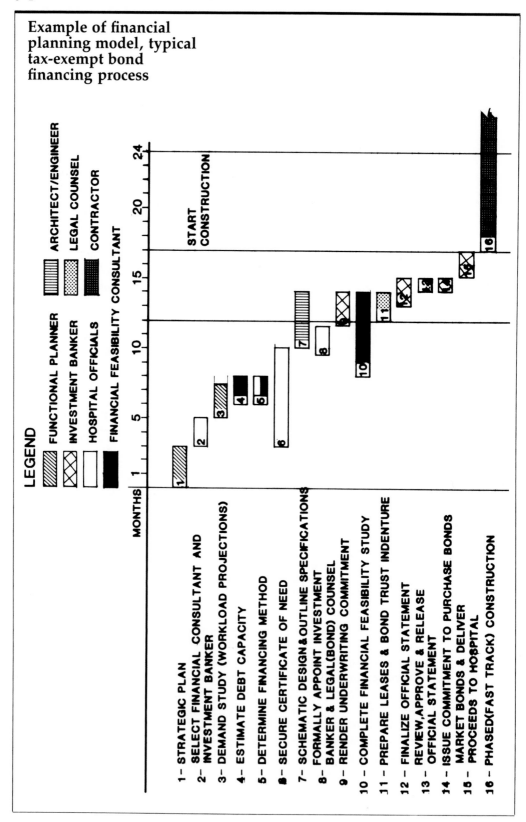

instances performed by the strategic or functional planner. Our experience indicates that financial planners working alone may adopt a too-conservative approach to workload projections, and that other planners have a tendency to be too liberal. The best approach, we believe, is for the strategic or functional planner to prepare such projections and for the financial planner to review and verify these figures for accuracy and reasonableness. In any event, these projections must be realistic, and the financial planner must be satisfied that they are so, because both cost and revenue projections rest squarely on the future-demand units the hospital is expected to receive.

The following listings of duties of the investment banker, financial feasibility consultant, and legal (bond) counsel are intended to be comprehensive, and the individual characteristics of a project may not require the level of effort indicated. The timing of completion of duties that *are* required, however, must be coordinated by hospital management so as to position the hospital into the money market competitively. Early completion is usually most desirable (to the extent possible) since the hospital can be more selective about when it chooses to make market entry.

Investment banker

Some hospitals rely more heavily than do others upon an investment banker in early stages of a project. Our preference is to rely upon the investment banker only for advice in early stages, with the financial feasibility consultant performing the gathering and manipulation of financial information and data. The following list of tasks reflects that preference:

1. surveys the hospital's debt structure and financial resources to determine borrowing capacity for future capital financing requirements

2. reviews all pertinent financial statistics and economic data, such as debt retirement schedule, tax rates, and overlapping debt, that would affect or reflect on the issuer's ability and willingness to repay its obligations

3. advises on the time and method of marketing; terms of bond issues, including maturity schedule; interest payment dates; call features; and bidding limitations

4. prepares an overall financing plan detailing the recommended approach and probable timetable

5. prepares, in cooperation with bond counsel, an official statement, notice of sale, and bid form and distributes same to all prospective underwriters and investors where applicable

6. assists the issuer in getting local public acceptance and support of the proposed financing

7. keeps in constant contact with the rating services to ensure that they evaluate the credit properly

8. supervises the printing, signing, and delivery of debt instruments

9. advises on investments of debt proceeds.

Financial feasibility consultant

Perhaps the best description of the financial feasibility consultant's scope of duties is the listing of statements, schedules, and functions required to be performed. These statements, schedules, and functions are as follows:

1. an analysis of debt capacity (and alternative financing methods), more fully described in preceding pages

2. an assessment of the medical staff's support for the project

3. an analysis of current hospital utilization

4. an analysis of the social and economic characteristics of the hospital's service area

5. an assessment of the hospital's competition in its service area

6. productivity statistics by revenue-producing centers over the five previous fiscal years

7. schedule showing effect of refinancing current outstanding indebtedness on total project cost and forecasted operating expenses

8. a schedule showing the amount of research dollars obtained in the five previous fiscal years, compared with the direct expenditures incurred and to be incurred by such research projects, highlighting therein the amount of dollars the hospital has to underwrite internally toward such research projects

9. the hospital's full-time equivalent employees per occupied bed and per revenue-producing and nonrevenue-producing departments for the five previous fiscal years, including therein the assumptions as to salary and wage increase projections

10. key financial ratios, particularly those highlighting the hospital's pricing strategies as they affect balance sheets:

  - *liquidity ratios*—reflect the hospital's ability to meet its short-term liabilities

  - *leverage ratios*—reflect the hospital's ability to satisfy long-term debt requirements

  - *composition ratios*—reflect how total assets are divided among the various asset categories; measure the quality of asset distribution sufficient to impress potential investors with the hospital's management of these assets

- *activity ratios*—measure the extent assets are used to operate the hospital; sometimes referred to as "turnover" ratios

- *profitability (earnings) ratios*—measure profit in terms of both patient revenues and total assets, thus testing hospital management's ability to maintain and sustain the fiscal integrity of the income statement and, more important, the balance sheet.

11. construction fund drive projections

12. source and applications of construction funds

13. historical audited financial statements for the past five years

14. forecasted financial and statistical summaries for the construction period and two fiscal years after completion

15. forecasted statements of revenues and expenses for the construction period and two fiscal years after completion

16. forecasted statement of changes in cash and short-term debt for the construction period and two fiscal years after completion

17. forecasted balance sheets for the construction period and two fiscal years after completion

18. forecasted statements of changes in fund balances for the construction period and two fiscal years after completion

19. notes and assumptions of the forecasted financial statements

20. debt service chart—use of funded depreciation interest, and so forth

21. analysis of equity versus debt (historical and forecasted)

22. an assessment of the sensitivity of the financial forecast to a change in critical variables such as regulation of reimbursement, utilization, interest rates, and major pending projects.

Legal (bond) counsel

The scope of duties performed by the legal (bond) counsel varies considerably, as does that of the investment banker, depending on the nature of the issue, its size, and the standing of the issues. Legal counsel generally provides the following major services:

1. examines the applicable law(s) under which the financing is proposed

2. reviews the bond proceedings, board resolutions, ordinances, election documents, if any, and any other documents to determine whether counsel can render an approving opinion on the validity of the issue

3. in cooperation with legislators, public officials, underwriters, and investors, may be required to engage in drafting legislation, including constitutional amendments; devising new methods of financing; or creating new public instrumentalities

4. prepares trust indentures, board resolutions, ordinances, contracts, and other documents required for the investor's acceptance of the debt instrument

5. cooperates with the financial feasibility consultant and the investment banker in adoption of a plan of financing and associated timetables to secure the most suitable financing from a legal point of view

6. prepares appropriate course of action in connection with any litigation to resolve legal questions; may prepare or assist in the preparation of pleadings, briefs, and other litigation papers and may be required to appear in court

7. "dots the i's and crosses the t's"—searches and meticulously examines laws, legal instruments, and proceedings as required to satisfy the legality of the proceedings and the validity of the debt issue and also to minimize the risk of litigation on the debt instruments following their issue

8. secures for the record an appropriate statement from authorized officials of third-party payors, area-wide planning agencies, and other agencies as required to state that the financing method meets the "reasonableness criteria" of third-party regulations—thus assuring the investor and the hospital that the debt service will be recognized as a fully allowable cost under the regulations and as projected in the financial feasibility study.

Summary

The increasing importance of financial planning under prospective pricing is obvious. Therefore, more so than ever, experts will be required to perform financial planning tasks. The duties of these specialists must be properly identified and scheduled so as to assure an orderly conduct of their work and the overall planning and design process.

Although credit worthiness will require better proof than in past years, there will be adequate capital from a broader variety of sources for hospital and related health care construction in the decade ahead. We believe that tax-exempt bond issues will continue to dominate as the source of choice for most nonprofit or government-related health care providers. The investor-owned systems will continue to rely directly upon the commercial market for debt and equity financing.

The principal tasks involved in financial planning (assuming an issue of tax-exempt bonds) are

1. selection of financial planning team members (investment banker, financial feasibility consultant, and legal (bond) counsel) and preparation of a schedule for their individual and combined efforts

2. preparation of a debt capacity analysis

3. selecting a financing method and setting a topside budget

4. preparing schedules and statements to secure CON approval

5. preparing a formal financial feasibility study, composed of a broad variety of statements and schedules proving the feasibility of the specifically proposed project

6. issuing an official statement, obtaining a bond rating, and selling the bonds.

The specific tasks performed by each member of the financial planning team are complex and highly specialized. These tasks should be itemized at the outset of a project to preclude, to the extent possible, conflicts and overlaps.

Notes

1. Neil E. Bennett and Bruce W. Fisher, "Looking Back, Looking Forward," *Hospitals,* April 1, 1983, p. 88.
2. Jo Ellen Mistarz, "Capital Outlook," *Hospitals,* March 16, 1984, p. 64, quoting Judson T. Bergman.
3. "Hospital Tax-Exempt Bond Sales Skyrocket in 1974" (editorial), *Hospitals,* April 1, 1975, p. 31.
4. Mistarz, "Capital Outlook," *Hospitals,* March 16, 1984, p. 61, quoting *Bond Buyer.*
5. *Certificate of Need Criteria.* 1980. Health Systems Agency of Northeast Florida, Area 3, Inc.
6. Task listings were originally provided by Richard J. Oszustowicz for the first edition of this book and have subsequently been revised by David F. Shanahan and the authors.

6

The Planning and Design Process

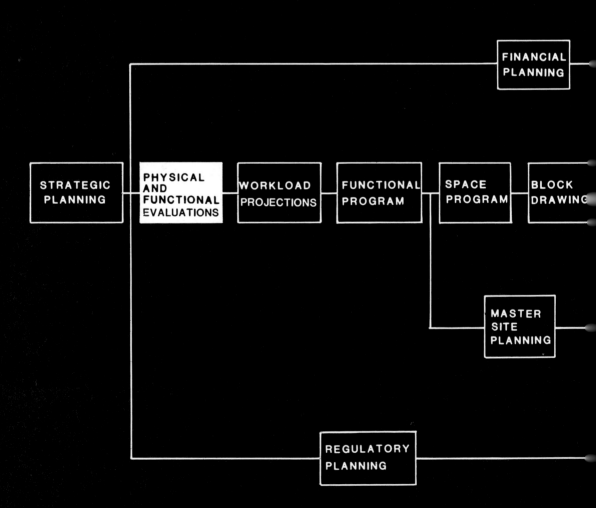

Physical and functional evaluations

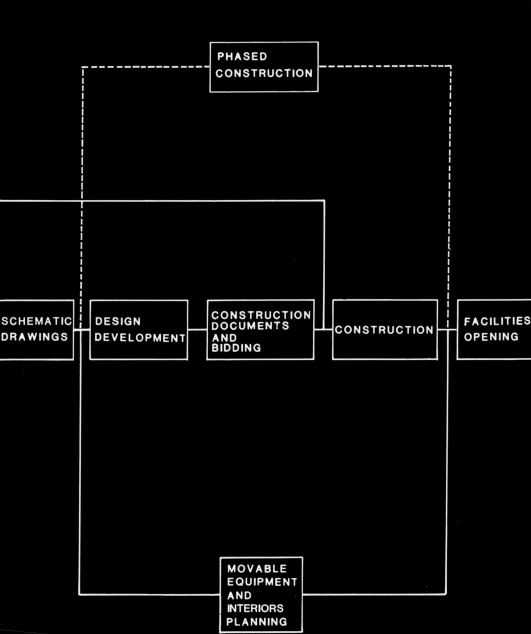

Many programs of expansion, alterations, or replacement require that existing facilities be evaluated from both physical and functional standpoints. When an existing structure is relatively new and the envisioned project is merely an extension of a preconceived long-range facility plan, such work may be superfluous. However, it has been only during the past 15 years that the great importance of long-range master site planning, flexibility, and expansibility has come into wide recognition. Older hospitals, generally, must be seriously studied with regard to their future usability when appreciable facility changes are considered.

Existing facilities often constitute a resource whose value and best future use may well be subject to considerable debate. Thus, performance of objective evaluations by outside professionals who are cognizant of the state of the art, insofar as functionality and building standards are concerned, and who know or have been apprised of the long-term programmatic future of the individual institution, establishes a sound and necessary base for all further planning. Even where a plant, to an objective eye, is totally obsolete and should be razed, there may still be a need for a methodical recording of all obsolescent features. Not infrequently, decision makers who approve razing are called to task by persons whose emotional attachments, lack of foresight, conservative views, or misguided intentions take precedence over a logical viewpoint. At such times, it is far better to be supplied with professionally documented evidence than to rely upon expressions of personal opinion.

Since establishment of the regulatory agencies, hospitals have had to provide positive proof of the need to spend large sums for any significant program of alterations, modernization, or expansion. In every instance, such proof can be derived from thorough physical and functional evaluations. Thus, not only are the findings of such evaluations important from the standpoint of early decision making, but they can serve as later proof of need when the CON application is filed.

In a simple analogy, the physical and functional evaluations in the facility planning process can be viewed as corresponding to preparations for an extended road trip. Before the trip begins, the condition of the trip vehicle should be considered in relation to the envisioned travel demands, and then it should be determined whether to trade for a new automobile, if a competent mechanic so advises, or to have an extensive overhaul accomplished or perhaps only to replace the spark plugs and tires. Whether any of these actions can be accomplished, of course, will depend on how much money is available for repair or replacement. Similarly, after the strategic plan has indicated the type and scope of a hospital's projected programs for future years, an existing facility's capability to support the programs should be evaluated and decisions made as indicated. In each instance, decisions depend upon future demands, present resources (which for a hospital may include plant, personnel, community support, and so on), and availability of funds to implement a course of action.

Although we have intentionally separated our discussion here into two parts to distinguish physical from functional features, some authorities merely undertake a so-called rating that does not attempt to differentiate between the two types of characteristics. For example, some 20 years ago, as authorized under Hill-Harris Act amendments, teams from the various Hill-Burton state agencies individually inspected hospitals throughout the nation and made evaluations based upon a "plant rating" checklist.[1] This checklist made no attempt to classify items as physical or functional, and it proved to be effective to the extent that it established a uniform method for classifying hospital facilities as either "conforming" or "nonconforming."

More recently, in 1984, the Office of Health Facilities of the U.S. Department of Health and Human Services (DHHS) published a *Plant Survey Form*[2] that purports to inventory the condition of existing facilities for comparison with identified need to aid in hospital planning and budgeting.

The question arises as to whether either the Hill-Harris plant rating technique or the *Hospital Plant Survey*, or another similarly constructed technique, can be used as a substitute for physical and functional evaluations as discussed here. We believe that the four checklists that were utilized in the Hill-Harris technique (Parts A and B as an evaluation of complete buildings; Part C as a measure of conforming and nonconforming beds in individual nursing units; and Part D as a measure of selected but essential service departments)[3] together could logically substitute for a physical evaluation. Also, the *Hospital Plant Survey* could be so used. However, although these lists may be fairly thorough in considering physical features, they are deficient in considering the basic functionality of a plant.

There is no substitute for the work of a qualified professional consultant who seeks greater detail in findings, who knows the expected growth and role of the institution, who conceptualizes possible alternative future uses or disposition of the facilities, and who will make specific recommendations as to alterations, additions, renovations, or razing within the context of a long-range plan. Thus, although plant rating findings as described can perhaps serve as a substitute for the findings of a physical evaluation as contemplated here, they would need to be interpreted in terms of the hospital's future facility requirements. Moreover, in considering the functional efficiency of a plant, the rating technique does not seem to be satisfactory. Conformity and optimal functionality are not synonymous, especially when the future is being planned.

There is a clear distinction between the kinds of work involved in physical and functional evaluations, and findings of each study apply to different aspects of a hospital's buildings. In order to formulate recommendations as to the disposition or future use of a structure, however, the separate findings should be considered together. Ideally, a single set of general recommendations should be prepared by the evaluators working in consort. We and our associates have found this to be a practical approach leading to the complete satisfaction of hospital management, in hundreds of instances.

Physical evaluation

The basic purposes of a physical evaluation are as follows:

1. to identify physical plant problems and deficiencies that detract from efficient building operations, including energy consumption

2. to determine physical plant characteristics that do not conform to current minimum standards and codes, or that otherwise detract from the safety and comfort of building inhabitants

3. to estimate degrees of obsolescence for various areas of the plant

4. to assess serviceability of the plant in meeting future programmatic objectives of the hospital

5. to provide a basis for recommendations as to possible alternative actions, such as specific modernization activities, expansions (as indicated by the worth of the existing plant), change to other uses, gradual phasing from patient care, or razing.

The methodology used in performing a physical evaluation is to examine drawings, specifications, and the plant itself and then to compare findings with applicable reference standards. Although codes and regulations are generally becoming more stringent, the DHHS has recently published *Guidelines for Construction and Equipment of Hospital and Medical Facilities*, which sets forth standards that currently serve as valid minimum criteria.[4] In addition, each state publishes a document, mostly derived from the aforementioned federal document and usually entitled *Rules and Regulations for Hospitals*, that is relevant within its jurisdiction. Cities and counties also publish codes, ordinances, and regulations that are locally applicable, but the cited federal and state documents, plus their lists of referenced codes and standards, contain ample criteria for evaluative comparison purposes. As indicated, records of "down time" for various systems can be kept by the chief engineer, to provide clues to potential sources of trouble.

A competently accomplished physical evaluation surveys the building with regard to the whole and each section or part. All physical systems are considered. Findings are recorded in the form of deviations from standards or problems created by the observed deviations. Most physical evaluations have a negative character reflected throughout the text, but conclusions drawn are based on the degree of seriousness of the findings and may indicate that problems noted are relatively inconsequential. Recommendations should be formulated on the basis of the findings in relation to the expected future role of the hospital.

Although there are a number of formats that can be used to effect the evaluation using the methodology described, one that has been widely used divides the work effort and report findings into 10 basic parts,[5] as follows:

- site characteristics and parking

- building characteristics and condition

- fire safety

- plumbing systems

- medical gas systems

- electrical systems

- heating, ventilization, and air conditioning (HVAC)

- transportation systems

- disposal systems (trash, garbage)

- energy efficiency.

These divisions can be construed to encompass all physical characteristics of any hospital structure; therefore, the listing can serve as a definitive outline and guide to the evaluation study. From this broad outline, further divisions are made to allow an orderly, systematic work effort, leaving small chance for gross omissions and erroneous arrangement of subject matter. As a result, the evaluation can lead to valid findings as an input to the planning process.

Site characteristics and parking

A site selection and evaluation process is described in Chapter 9, and the reader is referred to those pages. Suffice it to say here that a physical evaluation of an existing plant with reference to site characteristics and parking should evaluate the site as to the adequacy of its size for current and expected usage; problems related to configuration, topography, drainage, erosion, vegetation, views, noises, odors, and prevailing winds; restraints of use such as easements, restrictions, and zoning; and the availability of sufficient access routes to the population the hospital serves or should be serving.

Off-street parking ought to be assessed for conformance with applicable local codes and ordinances, and the number of spaces available versus needs as actually evidenced should be noted. The condition of parking facilities must be examined with regard to such factors as lighting, need for repairs, appropriateness of layout, and accessibility both from site entrances and from the hospital building itself.

Safety hazards, if any, require identification and investigation. Examples are steep inclines, flooding possibilities, lack of proper lighting, condition of roadways, absence of appropriate signs, lack of pedestrian safety precautions, and the like.

Building characteristics and condition

The condition and obsolescence of the fabric of the building also must receive attention. Beyond a description of the building, which should include information regarding dates of construction of the original plant and any additions, together with a general assessment of the obsolescence of each part, the several specific structural elements are considered.

Foundations, the structural frame, roof, insulation, walls and partitions, materials and finishes, building orientation and sun control, hazards (structural, not life safety), and capabilities of future expansion are all assessed to an appropriate degree. Provisions to withstand natural disasters, such as earthquakes and hurricanes, must be evaluated in comparison with applicable design requirements.

Some evaluators merely report findings narratively (albeit from a professional viewpoint), and others have devised quantified scales for point-by-point rating. If the person actually making the evaluation is experienced and professionally competent, we do not believe that point ratings are necessary. However, if the task has been delegated to a person with minimal experience in this regard, a definitive, quantified checklist is desirable.

Fire safety

The *Code for Safety to Life from Fire in Buildings and Structures* contains the reference standards by which fire safety features must be compared.[6]

This portion of the evaluation can be roughly divided into ten categories of building characteristics, as follows:

1. fire resistivity of the structure (e.g., corridor walls, doors, glass)

2. smoke barriers

3. interior finishes (e.g., paints, wall and floor tile)

4. exits (e.g., adequate positioning, width, designation, construction, direction of door swings, barrier-free access)

5. corridor widths, fire alarm systems, and fire-extinguishing system (sprinklers, hoses, extinguishers)

6. chutes, shafts, and chases

7. fire doors

8. elevators (emergency controls)

9. hazardous features of high-probability fire-originating areas (e.g., kitchen, laundry, trash collection and disposal areas), storage for flammables and potentially explosive materials

10. emergency movement routes and other observable characteristics.

Plumbing systems

Few older hospitals possess adequate plumbing systems, and many of these hospitals exhibit numerous irregularities from code requirements. Moreover, many relatively new hospitals do not meet all requirements, apparently as a result of inadequate inspection at the site during construction or lack of appropriate agency control over the quality of drawings and specifications.

Consideration of plumbing systems should extend to building and site water supply (adequacy), distribution throughout the buildings, hot water supply, steam lines, water treatment, fixtures of all types, sewage system, disposals, and the like.

Medical gas systems

Over the past 15 years, standards regarding the provision of piped medical gases (construed also to include vacuum) have been broadened to include many additional patient care areas, and new gases have been added to the list of requirements.

For each gas required to be piped, the evaluator should consider the supply and storage system, distribution to required areas, zoning, controls and alarms, condition of lines and valves, proper venting, and any conditions that may impair effective operation or present potential safety hazards.

Electrical systems

Evaluation of electrical systems usually includes not only the basic electrical service system and its various components and characteristics but also hospital-owned communications systems, the telephone system, dictating system, emergency power system, and doctors' registry system.

Appraisal of the electrical system begins with determination of the type of service to the site and a comparison with features desirable from the standpoint of adequacy and reliability in case of power failures. Two separate sources are usually regarded as needed, with automatic throw-over to the secondary (back-up) system. The secondary distribution system is evaluated in terms of economics (cost effectiveness) and adaptability.

General lighting throughout the facility should be sampled as to foot-candles at work levels, which should be compared with applicable standards.

Both the sufficiency of numbers of outlets and their characteristics with regard to type and location are considered in terms of codes and needs.

Nurse call systems in patient diagnostic and treatment areas, both routine and emergency, are evaluated in comparison with state-of-the-art equipment and with regard to actual condition. Code requirements must be considered.

Modernity of the telephone system, paging system, television system (both closed-circuit and public-patient), data processing system, and doctors' registry is noted along with an appropriate opinion regarding physical condition. The dictating system is accorded the same observations.

A few other systems, such as a bed status system or other data transmittal system, may be in place in some hospitals, and these must be at least cursorily evaluated.

Of considerable importance is the standby capability of the emergency generator. Many older systems still in use fall far short of code requirements, especially with regard to extent of service and throwovers allowing completely uninterrupted service.

Heating, ventilation, and air conditioning (HVAC)

In considering environmental control systems, not only should code requirements be taken into account, but adequacy of the systems in terms of basic comfort for building inhabitants and protection against air-borne contaminants.

Most older hospitals possess totally inadequate systems, and those built in phases on a patchwork basis seldom meet standards that would be considered satisfactory in any other environment. Infrequently, however, one does encounter a structure erected over the past few years that has not been satisfactorily planned from the standpoint of human comfort.

The evaluation of HVAC systems should consider the following as a minimum:

1. boiler type, capacities, accessories, controls and emergency capabilities

2. distribution system

3. thermal and acoustical insulation

4. ventilation system

5. air-conditioning system (including requirements for special areas)

6. humidity controls

7. filters

8. thermostats (temperature control)

9. air pressure (positive, negative, and equal), room air changes, and exhausting

10. special controls, especially those relating to energy conservation.

Transportation systems

Transportation systems include those committed to both human and supply transportation.

Elevators are evaluated as to age, number, type, speed, loading capabilities, controls, size, and door widths. Essentially the same characteristics are evaluated for dumbwaiters and tray conveyors.

The state of the art for pneumatic tubes has vastly improved over the past few years, but many systems that are virtually obsolete are still in evidence. Some can be brought up to satisfactory standards, and some cannot. Such factors must be determined in the evaluation process.

Other systems installed in some hospitals, such as belt conveyors and automatic supply transportation devices, require appraisal in terms of obsolescence and basic physical condition. Large pneumatic tube systems for the transport of linen are in this category. In some instances, such systems commonly transport both linen and trash (bagged).

In recent years, environmental standards have changed greatly, thus altering the status of many hospital systems, especially in the case of incinerators. Instances of nonconformity are to be determined and noted.

Disposal (trash and garbage) systems

Many systems are in use for handling trash and garbage, from basic manual systems with high-risk factors for contamination to highly automated closed systems. The appropriateness of such systems must be evaluated in terms of economy in handling, probability for contamination, safety, and code conformance. Obsolescence and unsightliness should also be noted.

Energy efficiency

Evaluation of the HVAC systems will cover equipment responsible for approximately 60 percent of the total energy consumption in a typical hospital or other related health care facility. The remaining 40 percent is consumed, on the average, by lighting and miscellaneous electrical (15 percent); laundry (12 percent); food services (7 percent); medical equipment (4 percent); and miscellaneous (2 percent).[7] Each of these areas must be considered from the standpoint of energy efficiency. Typically, an energy survey and audit should be performed and indexes of efficiency established.

Although many hospitals will logically decide to proceed further than an energy survey and audit, the costs required to "retrofit" an obsolescent plant in terms of energy conservation should not be considered solely within the context of energy savings, unless a desirable payback from such projects can be achieved almost immediately, and *before* other major alterations, additions, or changes in building usage can be accomplished. The thought here is that major retrofit projects should be considered within the context of all changes to be undertaken. Specifically, the following should be accomplished in evaluation of energy efficiency:

1. examination of the adequacy of energy management control systems

2. historical review of energy usage to ascertain BTU usage per square foot per year at the building line

3. survey of insulation features

4. review of the efficiency of HVAC equipment.

Functional evaluation

Whereas the physical evaluation is concerned solely with physical, "measurable" characteristics of the hospital plant, the functional evaluation is concerned with functional features—that is, factors that affect the facility's ability to serve as an efficient workshop for personnel and as a supportive environment for both personnel and patients. There is no sharp line of distinction between the physical and functional aspects. In a broad sense, however, the physical side is concerned with what the building and its habiliments are made of, and the functional side considers how they are or can be used. Thus, the functional evaluation purports to measure to some degree the plant's adaptability to current and expected future functions, the operational efficiencies allowed or inefficiencies caused, and the comfort or discomfort of building inhabitants, related to the environment afforded. Its emphasis is on people and processes rather than physical mechanisms.

Specifically, four basic objectives attach to the functional evaluation:

1. identification of deterrents to operational effectiveness and efficiency that stem from functional deficiencies exhibited by the existing site and buildings

2. determination of functional features that do not conform to current minimum standards (as specified in applicable state and federal publications)

3. appraisal of the plant's layout from the standpoints of flexibility and expansibility, in relation to future programmatic objectives

4. formulation of recommendations relating to aspects of future plant use or disposition, as outlined under Physical Evaluation (i.e., modernization activities, expansions, change to other uses, gradual phasing from patient care, or razing).

Basic concepts of functionality

The methodology used in performing a functional evaluation involves a comparison of functional features to adopted criteria. As in the physical evaluation, the DHHS *Guidelines for Construction and Equipment of Hospital and Medical Facilities*[8] and pertinent state rules and regulations form the basis for the criteria. However, beyond codes and regulations there are a number of functional concepts widely recognized among hospital consultants, administrators, and architects that can also be established as standards against which functional attributes can be measured. Some of the more commonly used concepts are noted in the following discussion.

Holistic perspective of operational processes
Diagnosis, care, and treatment of patients require the services and resources of all hospital departments. No single department should be a self-contained entity, and many operations extend across all departmental lines. Increasingly, a health care facility on a single site is being viewed as an open system, with departmental functions regarded as parts of a whole. In our view, there has never been any sound reason for why this should not be so.

Current operational processes definitely require a holistic perspective in plant planning, and efficiency is enhanced when the total hospital operation is a single system, as opposed to a conglomerate of independent kingdoms.

Interdepartmental relationships
People move from one functional area to another in a hospital and spend considerable time in doing so. Supplies, equipment, and hard-copy data and information are transported from place to place, both automatically and manually, and appreciable time consumption is thus occasioned. These various types of traffic flow, weighted as to volume, frequency, importance, and critical need, establish relative degrees of functional relationships among departments; these relationships, in turn, indicate

relative degrees of desirability for physical closeness. Unquestionably, physical plant layout, based on a holistic perspective, should provide physical proximities among departments that reduce total volumes and distances of pedestrian traffic and expedite transport of things that must be moved. The accomplishment of these goals will increase efficiency and help to raise the quality of patient care.

"Form follows function"

In pursuing a holistic approach to health care facility planning, inter-departmental relationships will determine basic architectural layout and form of the building, taking into consideration pertinent constraints. Individual departmental design should add to the efficiency of functions to be performed in the accomplishment of an assigned mission. The sizes and shapes of respective rooms should be specifically planned to accommodate functions to be performed therein, equipment requirements, and numbers and types of occupants.

Expansibility

When expansions are considered, the future worth of a hospital plant is definitely enhanced by its expansibility. Capital costs in expanding will be directly affected, and future operational costs will be affected by the degree of functionality possible to achieve in the expanded facility. Thus, original design should have anticipated both costs of future additions and their functionality.

Flexibility

Flexibility involves the degree of efficiency by which space and equipment can be changed from the accommodation of one function to another. Obviously, capital costs will be affected by the ease with which this can be done, and the functionality of altered areas will affect operational costs.

Automation

The concept of automation revolves around efficiency in operations and conveniences to human beings. For tasks primarily involving personalized services, however, each application of automation must be carefully considered, in terms of not only efficiency but also its effect upon the human environment.

Automation in hospitals has been proved to be efficient and environmentally acceptable in areas of data processing, supply processing and distribution, mass movement of people, research, and laboratory applications. The advantages or disadvantages of automation in individual situations must be considered in accomplishing evaluations from a functional standpoint.

Separation of clean and soiled

Infection control and the prevention of cross-contamination begin with the basic layout of a hospital and extend into departmental design and individual space development. Routes and storage points of soiled supplies should be definitively separated from those of clean; mixing of dirty and aseptic personnel traffic should be prevented; and cleaning of dirty instruments, equipment and supplies ought to be isolated from clean processing areas. In short, proper sorting of traffic, storage, and processing should be evidenced by the design of the existing facilities.

Privacy
Factors indicating that privacy for the patient should be available in bedrooms, emergency rooms, examination rooms, and most other diagnostic and treatment spaces are numerous and well-documented.

It is true that certain patients desire constant surveillance by hospital personnel; it is equally true that after this condition is satisfied they prefer seclusion, at their option, from other patients. Although most patients desire staff association and, during periods of long convalescence, social contacts with other patients, availability of privacy when it is desired and needed should be clearly evidenced. Patient privacy is justified merely from humanitarian aspects and in consideration of personal dignity, but it also reduces cross-infections and raises quality of care and affords a better environment for communication between patient and staff members.

Patterns of circulation
Corridor schemes and vertical circulation should facilitate optimal travel times and distances, directness, avoidance of congestion, and simplicity. As a general premise, the mission of a person entering the building at each entrance should be anticipated, and the corresponding route of travel inside the building made as short and direct as possible.

To an optimal degree in individual situations, the following types of internal traffic should be sorted and separated by design:

1. emergency traffic from all other traffic

2. inpatient from outpatient

3. visitor from patient

4. supply from pedestrian (excepting transport personnel)

5. soiled from clean

6. entering personnel from other traffic

7. entering doctors from other traffic

8. traffic with one department from that with another (intradepartmental)

9. special traffic (e.g., operating suite traffic) from other traffic.

Cul-de-sac design and administrative control center
Departments or functional entities in a hospital should not be penetrated by interdepartmental traffic. Each department should be integral to itself insofar as pedestrian traffic is concerned and should, in effect, represent a cul-de-sac design, excepting emergency exits.

Classically, intradepartmental traffic is admitted to the relevant department by way of an administrative control center (ACC).[9] The ACC should have positive control over all entering and exiting traffic. It should serve as a reception point and provide for direct view of waiting spaces for visitors and patients. As a communications center, the ACC should receive most incoming calls and be connected via the communications system, as required, to other functional spaces in the department.

This concept is particularly applicable to nursing units. No unit should have interdepartmental traffic passing through it.

Balance

Objectives in terms of patient care, education, and research should be priority rated, and physical facility provisions should be related thereto. Although the prime objective of an institution may be education and research rather than patient care, the protection, comfort, and convenience of the patient cannot be disregarded. Social changes alone have made obsolete the wards of yesteryear with their "gang" toilets and showers. It cannot be expected that patients should be denied, in this age of affluence, amenities lesser than those found in their homes and in the average motel or hotel.

Performing the functional evaluation

Actual survey work includes various tasks that, when completed, yield meaningful findings upon which to base recommendations. A logical format that we have used to good advantage is set forth here.

Tabulation of functional deficiencies

Experienced evaluators usually use a preconstructed checklist, pursue a methodical inspection of the plant itself on a department-by-department basis, and perform an analysis of a set of "as-is" architectural drawings in order to tabulate functional deficiencies. The checklist used indicates specific features for which a comparison should be made with adopted criteria.

Space analysis

The net space devoted to functions by department is ascertained and compared with that needed as estimated from current and projected workloads and recognized indexes of utilization.

The total net space of the hospital, along with the total gross space, is determined, and the net-to-gross ratio is calculated. Modern plants, efficiently designed, will exhibit a ratio of 60 percent or higher.

The gross square footage per bed is also determined, but the significance of this indicator promises to be reduced as greater proportional provisions are made for ambulatory care. The gross area per bed per nursing unit or floor should remain as a valid indicator of space sufficiency, however.

Analysis of pedestrian, supply, and vehicular traffic patterns

Routes of internal pedestrian traffic by type (inpatient, outpatient, visitor, personnel, physician, student, and various other types) are methodically traced and evaluated in terms of adopted criteria, such as directness, degrees of separation, or distances.

Supply traffic, both clean and soiled, including trash, is traced to note deviations from ideal separations and also to note route efficiency.

Vehicular traffic on the site is evaluated in terms of convenience to patrons and basic rationality.

Departmental relationships
A theoretical closeness matrix for the department or functional entities actually in operation within the hospital should be prepared, to show quantifications of optimum desirability for closeness among the units according to functional relationships. A similar matrix should be prepared to quantify the actual relationships in existence. The differences throughout should be noted and quantified. Of course, wide differences indicate poor relationships and a plant with low degree of functionality.

Systems analysis
Several systems that are greatly desirable from a cost-benefit standpoint are entirely absent in many existing hospitals. Furthermore, those in existence may not provide the functionality of which such a system is capable owing to minimal provisions or irrational installation features.

The systems that should be evaluated from these standpoints are medical gases (including vacuum); data processing; supply processing; supply transport; housekeeping vacuum, communications (including nurse call, both routine and emergency); pneumatic tube; dietary; and trash disposal.

Equipment evaluation
Fixed equipment and major movable equipment of all types should be studied from a functional standpoint. The absence of automated and other features that would occasion operational savings, optimal quality of care, and patient and personnel convenience should be tabulated as appropriate.

Recommendations

Physical and functional evaluators prepare recommendations of actions to be taken regarding existing facilities based on findings of the two evaluations and on the planned strategies of the hospital in future years. Those who have prepared the physical and functional evaluations must be intimately acquainted with strategic plans already developed in order to prepare valid recommendations relating to any future changes in physical facilities—both site and plant.

Recommendations so developed should be at a *general* level of detail only. Ultimate detail will be prepared in the later functional and space programs.

Although the two evaluations as described are usually definitive, and formulated recommendations based upon them are most often patently valid, in some instances further cost-benefit studies may be required. If they are, the evaluations performed can be used as bases, and cost-benefit analyses can be accomplished in the manner outlined in Chapter 13.

Findings and conclusions related to major deviations from established criteria are summarized. Recommendations are then formulated, addressed to the following areas of concern:

1. Whether the hospital should relocate to a new facility on the existing site or to a new site or should modernize or expand at the existing site should be forthrightly stated along with the reasons therefor.

2. If a conclusion is reached that a relocation should be accomplished, recommendations should outline possible alternative uses of the existing facilities, based upon their adaptability and worth. If relocation is to be accomplished at the same site, site placement of new facilities (and phasing of construction if indicated) should be delineated in conceptual diagrams showing their relationship to existing facilities.

    If a recommendation is made that existing facilities should be altered, modernized, or expanded, construction required to accomplish a first phase should be briefly explained. How future phasing could be implemented should also be generally explained and graphically delineated.

3. Site requirements should be set forth. Parameters of the new site, if relocation thereto is recommended, should be summarily outlined.

    When findings indicate a program of expansion at the existing site, a site acquisition schedule designating specific parcels of land should be drawn up, if such is indicated. When construction of new facilities on the existing site is warranted, a similar schedule must also be considered.

4. If recommendations specify alterations, modernization, or expansion, a schedule of recommended alterations should be formulated and priority rated. Alternative placements of needed additions should be suggested. How added areas could be tied in to existing facilities should be explained and graphically outlined (an example is shown in Figure 6–1).

    A schedule of modernization work, related to systems improvement, elimination of hazards, renovation to remove obsolete features, and plant upgrading in general, should be prepared and priority rated.

5. The disposition of major existing fixed equipment, in terms of obsolescence, will necessitate consideration under each alternative suggestion for basic facility change.

6. A closeness matrix can be prepared at this time to validate any conceptual plan for expansions and other needs related to interdepartmental relationships. This matrix allows a comparison with the previously prepared theoretical matrix showing optimal desirabilities for closeness among departments or functional entities. Ideally, however, departmental locations throughout should be considered in the later functional program.

7. Other recommendations may be required as indicated in each situation.

**Example of conceptual
phasing alternative
proposed at
conclusion of
physical and
functional
evaluations**

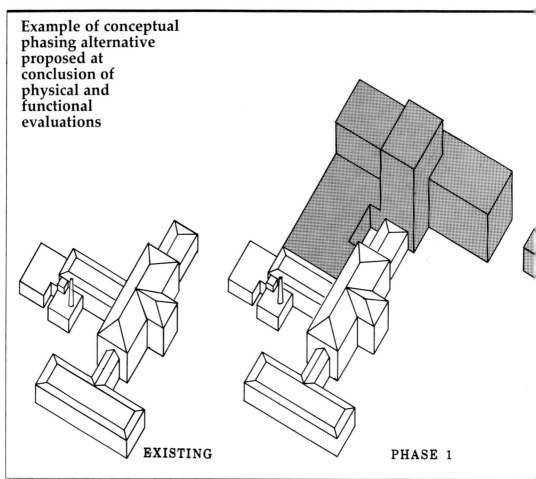

EXISTING   PHASE 1

In summary, recommendations should outline the broad aspects of alternatives that will allow the hospital to replace its facilities or to expand, upgrade, or renew. Each alternative, as formulated, should be feasible, should increase plant efficiency, and should reduce levels of obsolescence.

In subsequent functional programming, the functional planner will recommend and describe in detail specific actions for facility development.

Summary

Physical and functional evaluations reveal the true worth of an existing physical plant when strategies for the future are being considered. These evaluations also determine how new constructions should be related to old and identify the type and extent of feasible alterations and modernizations, if any, for each department or functional entity. No valid judgments regarding the disposition of existing facilities can, in fact, be made

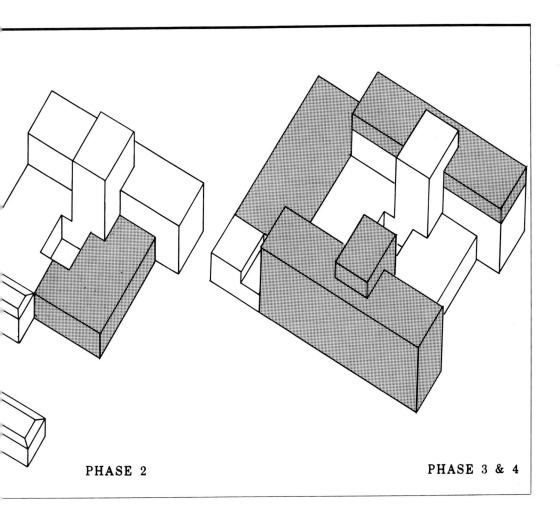

PHASE 2   PHASE 3 & 4

without the information generated by these evaluations. The regulatory agencies have long recognized the importance of appropriate appraisals of existing facilities when considering expansions and other facility changes, and the hospital CON application can be substantially bolstered by information from professionally accomplished physical and functional evaluations.

The physical evaluation embraces ten basic areas of investigation. These are:

1. site characteristics and parking

2. building characteristics and conditions

3. fire safety

4. plumbing systems

5. medical gas systems

6. electrical systems

7. HVAC

8. transportation systems

9. disposal systems (trash, garbage)

10. energy efficiency.

Criteria by which evaluations are made are set forth in various publications by regulatory agencies of appropriate jurisdiction and standards known to the hospital field.

A functional evaluation determines how efficient the physical plant is in accommodating the functions transpiring in it and also measures to some degree the protection, comfort, and convenience afforded to building occupants, not the least of whom are the patients.

Again, findings and conclusions are reached by comparing criteria to plant characteristics. Criteria are obtained primarily from standards published by federal and state governments, but are also formulated from state-of-the-art concepts of optimal building arrangements and operational processes.

From the findings of both evaluations, obtained by comparing criteria to plant features, the primary problems of an existing plant can be objectively and factually stated. Then, broad recommendations can be formulated as to site requirements; the type and extent of feasible alterations, expansions, or modernizations; the phasing of future facility changes; whether or not contemplated expansions should conform to the character of the existing facilities, or vice versa; whether or not the hospital should relocate (as indicated by the condition of the existing plant and site) or rebuild at the same site; and what disposition should be made of existing facilities in case a change in use is indicated.

Notes

1. "Hill-Burton Introduces Plant Rating Technique" (editorial), *The Modern Hospital* 104, no. 3 (March 1965): 100–103.
2. *Plant Survey Form*. (Rockville, MD: Department of Health and Human Services Offices of Health Facilities, 1984) (internal publication).
3. "Hill-Burton Introduces Plant Rating Technique," p. 103.
4. *Guidelines for Construction and Equipment of Hospital and Medical Facilities*. Department of Health and Human Services. Pub. No. (HRS–M–HF) 84–1A (Rockville, MD: DHHS Office of Health Facilities, 1984).
5. Methodology originally developed by Friesen International, Inc., and later refined by Lawrence P. Lammers, AIA.
6. National Fire Protection Association, Inc., *Code for Safety to Life from Fire in Buildings and Structures*, NFPA Pub. No. 101–1981 (Quincy, MA: National Fire Protection Association, Inc., 1981), pp. 101-1–101-202.
7. Estimated by Heery Energy Consultants, Inc., Atlanta, GA, 1984.
8. *Guidelines for Construction and Equipment of Hospital and Medical Facilities*. Department of Health and Human Services.
9. This term was originated by Friesen International, Inc., Washington, DC.

7

The Planning and Design Process

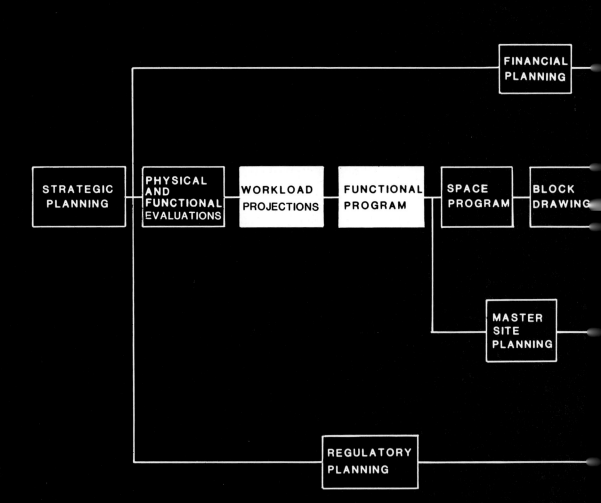

Workload projections and the functional program

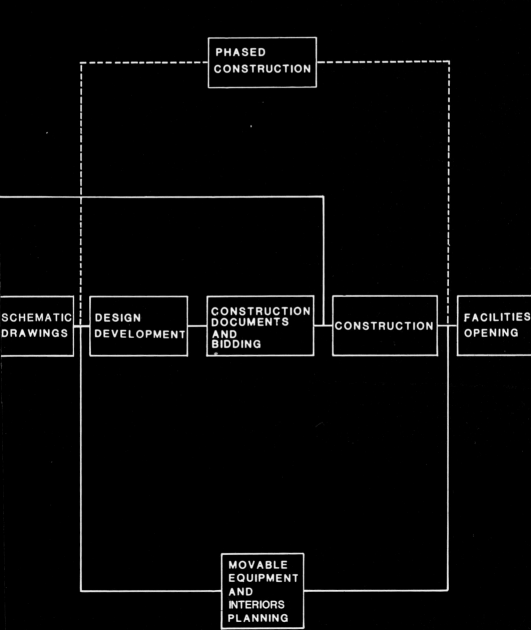

The critical importance of workload projections has already been cited. Together with admissions and patient days by service, plus categorized outpatient visits (all determined in the strategic plan or as updated thereafter), they form the basic utilization data required for the financial feasibility study. As well, they are prime determinants of space provisions as programmed by the functional planner. These projections must be objectively and competently accomplished, because, in reality, they represent commitments on the part of the governing board that go far beyond financial considerations.

For example, acknowledging that approved projections of censuses, outpatient visits, and workloads will be the basic determinants of rooms and usable space that the hospital will provide for all inpatient care and diagnostic and treatment departments, the governing board is making, in effect, a quantified commitment to the hospital's service area in terms of highly important health care services. On the one hand, unrealistically high projections can cause serious problems in financing; on the other hand, too low projections can cause inconveniences, management problems, and downright inferior care for years to come by reason of crowding, overloaded equipment, and unreasonable queuing of patients. In addition, it must be remembered that not all health care costs appear in accounting statements of providers; some of them are incurred directly by patients and their families through inconvenience and lost time resulting, for example, from poor hospital planning and management. Thus the necessity to estimate correctly hospital workloads in future years draws sharply into focus.

Making the estimates

There is no magic about making workload projections, but we believe that only an objective, independent outsider with a mature professional background should make them. Professional common sense, some mathematical and statistical ability, and a determination to attack the work from an objective problem-solving standpoint, rather than in support of a preconceived opinion, seem to be the primary ingredients involved in making correct estimates.

There are three prime parameters projected in the strategic plan that are used in estimating future workloads as dependent variables (derived demand) flowing from them. Trends in the historical relationship between the two are analyzed and projected for future years. The projected relationship is then applied to the appropriate projected independent variable to ascertain the numerical value of the workload or dependent variable.

It should also be pointed out that the formulation of statistical projections, though absolutely necessary, is only the starting point in determining future workloads. For example, the historical relationships between some procedures and admissions may not constitute a valid base for estimations. Cases in point are chest x-ray examinations and certain laboratory tests sometimes performed upon admission. In these instances, by administrative decision alone (dictated, of course, by clinical considerations), future workloads can be altered considerably. Instituting a new service, such as the creation of a primary care center staffed with full-time physicians, can generate additional workloads not possible to predict on the basis of in-house historical activity (because none previously existed); thus, the estimator must look to other hospitals that have already undergone similar experiences. Addition to the medical staff of a new specialist will oftentimes substantially alter past trends, as can the departure of a key specialist; in these instances the practice volume of a single staff member has to be considered.

At the present time, certainly all straight-line projections of past utilizations must be questioned. With health care cost reductions being effected chiefly through reduced utilizations, both primary and derived demand projections must be evaluated in terms of a national trend that began only in 1984. Moreover, just *where* the downward trend will stop remains to be seen, although it will almost certainly not extend below the levels of the mid to late 1960s.

Although procedures can begin with statistical calculations, the estimator should hold conferences with every hospital department head and ascertain any operational change or other factor, past or future, that has affected or will affect departmental utilization. Finally, the estimator should make adjustments according to the current national and regional trends. These adjustments should then be discussed with both the director of planning (if any) and the chief executive officer. Every situation proves to be unique, and as we have pointed out, objective problem solving is an important part of the process.

In the case of a new hospital, of course, the estimator must rely exclusively on local, state, and national utilization statistics, tempered with current trends, as bases for indexes adopted.

A few consultants and architects make claims of having computerized the projection of workloads. Since the calculations involved are so simple and because each situation seems to possess unique considerations, we can regard these claims only as "sales gimmicks." As in the case of space programming, we believe that if computerized models are followed completely and without extensive adjustments, the procedure can yield highly invalid results.

The projected departmental workloads commonly calculated for a typical community hospital are listed in Exhibit 7–1. As in this example, such projections should designate the workload unit and the parameter used as the independent variable from which the workload unit (representing the dependent variable) flows. Of course, calculations can also be made for various special services, such as ENT examination rooms, certain cardiology rooms, ophthalmology examination spaces, and dental rooms, as indicated for the particular hospital.

In each instance, the projections should be made for a minimum of 5 years, and most authorities believe that a 10- to 15-year outlook should be formulated. Obviously, the longer the projected time, the more the validity will decrease. Nevertheless, not recognizing the importance of long-term trends in these basic activities is a mistake of the first order.

As noted in Exhibit 7–1, visits to the emergency–ambulatory care suite, projected in the strategic plan along with inpatient activity, are regarded as workloads also, but they are converted as an independent variable directly into activity spaces or work stations. Supply processing

Exhibit 7–1

Projected workloads commonly calculated for a typical community hospital

Department or functional entity	Workload Unit (dependent variable)	Parameter of Utilization (independent variable)
Laboratory	Tests by functional section (e.g., hematology, chemistry, microbiology)	Admissions, outpatient visits
Blood Bank	Tests and transfusions (by type)	Admissions, outpatient visits
Respiratory Therapy	Days of treatment and number of treatments, by type	Patient days, outpatient visits
Pulmonary Functions	Procedures or tests, by type	Admissions, outpatient visits
Pharmacy	Prescriptions, requisitions	Admissions, outpatient visits
Physical Therapy	Treatments, by type	Admissions or patient days, outpatient visits
Occupational Therapy	Visits or treatment, by type	Admissions or patient days, outpatient visits
EKG	Tests	Admissions, outpatient visits
EEG	Tests	Admissions, outpatient visits
Nuclear Medicine	Imaging and scanning procedures, by type; in vitro assays, by type	Admissions, outpatient visits
Diagnostic Radiology	Examinations, by type (e.g., GI series, colon, gallbladder, IVPs, chest) and sometimes by location (e.g., main department, emergency suite, and clinics)	Admissions, outpatient visits
Therapeutic Radiology	Visits and treatments (deep and superficial)	Admissions, outpatient visits
Surgery	Surgical procedures (urological procedures separately)	Admissions and number of physicians with surgical privileges

Note: Outpatient surgery should be treated as an independent variable and projected on the basis of population or cases per surgeon.

Delivery and Birthing Rooms	Deliveries	Number of FTE obstetricians (also area birthrate and other factors)
Laundry	Pounds	Patient days
Dietary	Meals	Inpatient census, employee complement, students and physicians
Medical Records	Categorized processing functions related to patient records	Admissions, outpatient visits
Admitting and Registration	Admissions, preadmissions, and outpatient registrations (as applicable)	Admissions, outpatient visits
Business Office	Claim forms processed, discharges processed, statements issued, credit settlements, accounts posted (as applicable)	Admissions or discharges, outpatient visits
Social Service	Counseling sessions or visits	Admissions, outpatient visits
Autopsy Suite		
Morgue	Deaths	Admissions, DOAs
Autopsy Room	Autopsies	Admissions, DOAs

and distributing (SPD) is not listed because of the number of workload units involved, and also because the workload units, in part, flow from other dependent variables (e.g., surgical operations). Further comments about SPD are contained in subsequent pages in this chapter.

To summarize our discussion on workloads, the methodology involves the following steps:

1. Relate historical workloads to admissions, patient days, or emergency-ambulatory care visits, as applicable. In some instances, ratios of historical workloads to admitting physicians are determined.

2. Analyze trends in the utilization indexes so formulated.

3. Extend the utilization indexes to the same years used for the parameter forecasts (admissions, patient days, emergency–ambulatory care visits), and make appropriate qualitative adjustments.

4. Apply the indexes as extended to respective parameter forecasts to obtain the estimated workloads. Evaluate the projections in terms of current national trends referenced to DRGs and prospective pricing.

The functional program

Relevance to the facility planning process

In the course of the facility planning process, functional programming stands as one of the most important planning activities. After hospital approval, a functional program becomes a major policy document. As such, it serves as a guide for the architect and construction manager, a constant reference for hospital officials, and the source from which the functional planner will formulate a space program. It also gives indications to the financial consultant regarding staffing patterns, and finally, the hospital will use it in drafting procedures for the operation of the facilities when opened.

The functional program, prepared by either staff members or consultants specializing in the facility planning, bridges the gap between those who are intimately acquainted with detailed operational requirements and the architect who will accomplish the design. More and more, in recent years, its preparation has been by hospital consultants who, through experience, study, and research, have come to be specialists in what is known as functional planning.

Simply stated, functional planning of hospital facilities relates to those efforts before design that determine operational concepts and specify functions (in terms of procedures, required equipment, and numbers and categories of space users) that will take place in the spaces of a proposed structure, both individually and collectively. However, the scope of functional planning duties has now been extended to include actual descriptions of facilities, in narrative or graphic form, that deal with interdepartmental and intradepartmental relationships, traffic flows of all types, and methods for obtaining flexibility and expansibility—all of which were once considered the province of the design architect.

Not only does the functional program represent a definitive plan, but it serves as a control mechanism for all members of the professional planning team, plus the several categories of users represented in the hospital. Certainly the functional program can be amended as the project work proceeds, but it cannot be peremptorily or capriciously changed by individual parties to the planning; it stands as an approved policy statement of the governing board and, as such, requires governing board approval for appreciable modifications. The term "functional program," though now nearly universally recognized, is not uniformly used throughout the consulting and architectural world. The terms "master program," "master facilities plan," and "long-range facilities plan" are still in common usage, but they generally refer to a facilities plan that is, in essence, closely similar to what we describe here as a functional program.

Formulating the functional program

There are three basic types of proposed construction projects for which a functional program is usually formulated, each of which affects the approach to preparing required documentations. These are

1. relatively minor additions and modernizations that are not of sufficient scope to warrant changes in existing operational concepts but are extensive enough to require formal planning

2. major additions and modernizations sufficient in scope to warrant changes in basic concepts of operation, if desirable

3. construction of a new or replacement hospital.

In all three types of proposed projects, determination of activity space requirements can be undertaken on the basis of projected workloads, and the methodology employed will be essentially the same. With regard to the philosophical and conceptual nature of the project, however, there will be decided variations, depending directly upon into which of the three categories a given project falls. We first discuss activity space determinations and then describe methods for converting workloads to appropriate parameters for use in the functional program. Finally, we set forth relevant comments for each of the three types of proposed constructions.

Activity space determinations
Workloads, for all three types of proposed constructions previously noted, can only be translated directly into *activity spaces* or *work stations*, in the respective departments or functional entities. Rooms that are additionally required to support the activity spaces or work stations must be programmed not only in consideration of the volume of workloads but upon the following four bases:

1. personnel or physician requirements (which can vary considerably, as in the case of surgeons' locker space: 20 surgeons may perform the same volume of surgery in one hospital as that accomplished by 50 in another)

2. concepts of operation (as in the case of a single-corridored operating suite utilizing an in-suite supply processing system, as compared with a triple-corridored suite operating under a centralized supply processing system)

3. educational requirements (determined by an institution's educational role, as reflected by numbers and types of students, instructors, curricula, instructional scheduling, and equipment needs)

4. research requirements (determined by the volume and type of research, numbers of researchers, research subjects including animals, and equipment needs).

In some instances, the square footage of an activity space itself may be affected directly by code requirements or the specific desires of the hospital decision makers. For example, current regulations allow a general operating room to be programmed at a minimum of 360 square feet. Most consultants recommend 400 sq. ft., and some hospitals dictate space in excess of 400 sq. ft., depending upon a number of factors. Also, specific equipment items envisioned to be utilized in accomplishing some workloads and their respective capacities will directly affect not only the size of an activity space but the number of such spaces as well.

As noted earlier, an additional factor that has a major effect on the programming of both activity spaces and support spaces is the trend of growth in workloads. Usually, estimations are made for a period of time in the future, beginning with completion of a construction project. For a major project, an average planning and construction time is approximately 5 years, although the span may vary widely, depending upon the scope and complexity of the project. Professional planners of competent stature will also project for an additional 5 years and, on many occasions, for 10 years. If, for example, workloads indicate that six operating rooms will be required upon completion of an expansion project (first 5-year projections) and that two additional rooms will be needed at the end of 10 years (second 5-year projections), with one of the two being required at approximately the midpoint of the second 5-year period, considerable economic justification could be established for providing either one or both rooms initially. As well, predictable inconveniences and ill will might be avoided. The same reasoning could be used in programming some of the surgical support spaces, especially those internally located and not easily expanded.

Case study of operating room requirements: An example of the methodology for calculating activity rooms in a department can be demonstrated by an actual case study for an operating suite.[1] Some changes have been made in the actual study for the purpose of clarifying some problems that occur with a great deal of frequency.

In the strategic plan, the number of inpatient surgical procedures was calculated using three different methodologies: (1) utilization by medical staff surgeons of the existing surgical suite; (2) population-based demand; and (3) medical-surgical services utilization trends. These three methodologies yielded the 4-year projected net inpatient case utilization of the suite, disregarding open heart work, which was justified on other bases as a new service. From these figures were subtracted the number of cystoscopy and endoscopy patients (calculated separately to determine the unique needs involved); Saturday and Sunday patients (a restricted schedule was planned for Saturday and emergencies-only for Sunday); and 3 PM to 7 AM patients on Monday through Friday (no elective case would be scheduled after 3 PM). Thus we obtained, under each methodology used to project the workload, the number of inpatient operations that would be performed during the hours of regular scheduling. To these figures we added 500 outpatient operations estimated to be performed in the inpatient suite; this estimate was based on judgments by surgeons that they should be performed there rather than in a separately planned outpatient surgical center to be located on hospital grounds (clinical considerations related to the rise of emergency situations). These calculations are summarized in Table 7–1.

The study hospital wanted to initiate open heart work, and justification (through calculations not included here) could be provided for one room.

It is important to remember that the actual period to be considered in the calculation of operating rooms required is the *hours of regular scheduling*; if the suite is sized to accommodate all scheduled cases, it can accommodate all other cases as well. In our example suite, the number of hours to be available for regularly scheduled cases was 7.5 during each day over the 5-day work week, Monday through Friday. The number of annual days during which full scheduling would occur was set at 255.

Table 7–1

Inpatient surgery projections based on alternate methodologies

| | Method | | |
Steps in calculation	1 Physician demand	2 Population- based	3 Medical-surgical utilization
1. Total inpatient procedures*	12,650	10,786	11,002
2. Exclude cystoscopy-endoscopy patients†	− 2,840	− 2,438	− 2,484
3. Exclude Saturday-Sunday patients†	− 938	− 805	− 821
4. Exclude 3 PM–7 AM patients†	− 1,284	− 1,102	− 1,123
	7,588	6,441	6,574
5. Add outpatient surgery assumed as inpatient	500	500	500
Projected inpatient procedures during scheduled hours††	8,088	6,941	7,074

*Consultant's projections.

†Estimates based upon six-week sample of operating room utilization.

††Excludes cystoscopy, endoscopy, and open heart; includes gynecology and 500 outpatients.

We reviewed the operating room schedule over a 6-week period and found that the average length of operations (including the 500 outpatient operations) was 1.86 hours and that the average turn-around time between operations was 0.58 hour. Thus, one operation could be performed during a period of 2.44 hours.

The following list summarizes our calculations to determine the number of operations that could be performed in one room per year:

1. operating room capacity (in hours) per room
   a. annual days available = 255
   b. hours per day = 7.5
   c. hours available per year (a × b) = 1912

2. operating room capacity (in operations) per room
   a. hours available per year = 1912
   b. hours per patient = 2.44
   c. capacity in patients per year per room = 783.6 (a ÷ b)

We then calculated the number of rooms required under each of the three methodologies cited. Projected workloads were divided by each room's capacity to determine a raw number of operating rooms required. This number was rounded to the next larger whole number, and an additional room was added to allow for unscheduled (emergency) cases that might require immediate availability of an operating room. The projected total rooms needed (excluding cystoscopy and endoscopy) was calculated to be between 10 and 12. Our final calculations, as described, are presented in Table 7–2.

Table 7–2

Projected total operating rooms based on alternate methodologies

| | Method | | |
| | 1 | 2 | 3 |
Steps in calculation	Physician demand	Population-based	Medical-surgical utilization
1. Projected 1988 inpatient surgical workload (open heart not included)	8088	6941	7074
2. Operating room capacity (each room)	783.6	783.6	783.6
3. Raw number of rooms needed (1 ÷ 2)	10.32	8.85	9.03
4. Rounded rooms needed	11	9	10
5. Additional room for emergency	1	1	1
Total general inpatient operating rooms needed	12	10	11

Table 7–3

Room assignments for 13-room operating suite

No. of rooms	Room dedication	Room dimensions (in feet)
1	Open heart	22 × 26
1	Neurosurgery	22 × 26
1	Orthopedic	22 × 26
1	Optional use, plus open heart back-up	22 × 26
1	Orthopedic	20 × 20
1	Ophthalmology	20 × 20
1	ENT (ear, nose, and throat)	20 × 20
6	General surgery	20 × 20

We adopted the mid-range figure of 11 rooms needed as a base point. However, because of the necessity in this instance to dedicate certain rooms—one for open heart, and another as a back-up room for open heart work—a total of 13 rooms was actually recommended. (Several additional simple calculations were required by the HSA for final approval of the 13-room suite.) The room assignments, excluding cystoscopy and endoscopy, of the recommended suite are summarized in Table 7–3.

With regard to remaining spaces in this suite, we programmed them on the basis of the following: the operational concepts adopted (a triple-corridored suite to separate soiled and clean traffic, the case-cart supply system, and remote supply processing); the surgical and nursing staffs, by number involved; other patient requirements (e.g., patient holding and recovery, urological and endoscopy procedures); and certain administrative functions necessary to operations. Quantifications were possible to validate the need for most spaces additional to the procedure rooms themselves.

Converting workloads to activity rooms, work stations, or equipment items
Because of diverse functional requirements involved in projecting workloads of the various departments (previously noted), one basic methodology cannot be used to translate the several workload volumes into spaces. Additionally, there is more than one way to accomplish each of the translations. Therefore, although other acceptable methodologies exist, we have elected to present here those methods of calculating that we ourselves have used extensively and that have proved to be satisfactory.

Clinical laboratory, blood bank, and in vitro assays: The object is to translate projected workload volumes to space for work stations in each laboratory division that will be occupied by one technician working a calculated number of scheduled hours over a 1-year period. Thus, after projection of the annual number of total tests in a division (the workload) that will be performed during scheduled hours and determination of the number of tests that one technician can accomplish while working all the scheduled hours, the number of work stations can be calculated by simply dividing the single-technician tests into the total tests. It is important to note that tests performed in other-than-scheduled hours are not a factor and must be separated from the total workload (just as in the operating suite example); these tests can certainly be accomplished adequately if sufficient space is provided for the scheduled workload. Although standard technician workloads for all laboratory divisions on both an hourly basis and an annual basis (for standard scheduled hours) are now available, in existing laboratories a historical annual workload for a single technician can easily be determined. This figure, or another derived from various sources, can be subjectively adjusted by assuming future increased or decreased efficiency based on a number of factors.

Technicians require different amounts of space (including that provided for equipment) in the several laboratory divisions, but these requirements have also been fairly well standardized. In each instance, the number of technicians needed in a division during scheduled hours is multiplied by space provisions for each to obtain total space. If the laboratory is large enough to require one or more offices per division, such space is provided solely on the basis of staffing. The basis for programming other spaces throughout the laboratory—such as cold rooms, balance rooms, storage, accounting, specimen receipt and accession, executive offices, classrooms, and so on—may vary but should always include function, personnel, and equipment in one way or another.

Blood bank and in vitro assay space calculations are similarly accomplished.

Diagnostic radiology: The object is to translate projected workloads to number of items of diagnostic equipment that will be located in respective rooms, some of which vary in size.

The different types of equipment (and thus, rooms) relate to needs for work such as gastrointestinal (GI) and fluoroscopic, colon fluoroscopy, intravenous pyelography, neuroradiology, CT scanning, angiography, chest radiography, nuclear imaging, mammography, and tomography; workloads are grouped to be performed on equipment most accommodative or most preferred by the radiologist.

The following formula can be used for the translation in the case of general radiographic rooms:

$$GRR = \frac{PAE}{DY \times SHD \times ERH}$$

where GRR = number of general radiographic rooms
PAE = projected annual examinations
DY = number of days per year the rooms are available for examinations
SHD = scheduled hours of operation per day
ERH = examinations per room per hour.

Remaining departmental rooms are programmed on the bases of support, administrative, and educational needs, which embrace a variety of functions that do not lend readily to quantifications. Film processing and storage are exceptions, however.

Respiratory therapy: Days of treatment and number of inpatient treatments are related to inpatient bed areas of one type or another, and no calculations are required insofar as activity spaces are required. (Treatments are carried out usually in the patient's room.)

The object as regards projected outpatient visits is to translate them into numbers of patient treatment stations, which vary in size. A suitable formula, similar to that for radiology, is as follows:

$$TS = \frac{PAT}{DY \times SHD \times TSH}$$

where TS = number of treatment stations
PAT = projected annual treatments
DY = number of days per year the stations are available
SHD = scheduled hours of operation per day
TSH = treatments per station per hour.

Other spaces in a department of respiratory therapy must be programmed in relation to staffing; equipment cleaning, repair, and storage; administrative requirements; and educational needs. These spaces, of course, form the vast majority of the total needed. Although these spaces seldom relate directly to inpatient utilization, owing to the unique nature of each hospital, most qualified planners have historical figures of average net square feet per bed in general hospitals, which are useful in determining the reasonableness of total space figures established directly from the bases set out here.

Pulmonary functions, EKG, and EEG: In each instance the object is to translate projected workloads to numbers of test rooms, some of which vary in size. Pulmonary functions and cardiology sometimes house two equipment items in one room, for which adjustments may be required. The formula is the same as that for respiratory therapy, with the substitution of test rooms (TR) for treatment stations (TS).

Each of these three functional entities will require a number of support spaces related to staff or patient needs, equipment cleaning and storage, and administration. In some instances, there may be requirements for teaching and research space.

Pharmacy: The object is to translate volumes of projected prescriptions and requisitions filled into activity space in the drug distribution area. Other required spaces must be calculated on other bases. The *Unit Dose Primer*, published by the American Society of Hospital Pharmacists, is a useful document that clarifies functions inherent to either a centralized or a decentralized pharmacy dispensing and distribution system (unit doses).[2] *Planning for Hospital Pharmacies*, published in 1974 by DHEW, is still a valid guide for deriving work-station staffing patterns and work volumes.[3]

Since space requirements vary quite widely, depending upon the operational system adopted (e.g., unit dosage versus traditional), we do not set forth here any methodology for determining space needs. However, we believe the best approach is to assign an annual workload to a pharmacist or technician (which can be determined on a historical basis) and divide that workload into the total projected annual workload to determine the personnel number required. By assigning each person a standard square-footage work space in the distribution area and multiplying that by the number of personnel required, total space in the distribution area can be obtained.

Physical therapy: Currently there are fairly definitive industry standards regarding the number of treatment modalities, by type, that one therapist can perform. Calculations should translate projected annual treatments, by type, into a therapist staffing pattern and the staffing pattern into patient treatment stations or rooms. Other spaces must be programmed on bases such as staff and supply requirements, or educational needs.

Alternatively, the same formula outlined for respiratory therapy outpatient treatments is an acceptable approach for determining space needs for physical therapy treatment stations.

Occupational therapy: Calculations involve converting projected patient visits and treatments, by type, into patient activity spaces and treatment stations, respectively. Calculations are similar to those for physical therapy.

Therapeutic radiology: Calculations should aim to convert projected annual visits into office and examination space, and annual treatments (superficial and deep) into equipment items that will usually be housed in separate rooms of different sizes.

Office and examination space can be calculated according to projected daily work volumes, average length of time of visits and examinations, and scheduled hours, but the calculations must be correlated with the number of therapists and their scheduled work hours.

Rooms required for therapy can be determined by using a formula similar to that for general radiographic rooms.

Delivery and Birthing Rooms: The object is to translate numbers of projected deliveries into delivery or birthing room requirements. Since these procedures are not scheduled, and because rooms must be available on a 24-hour basis, some considerable down-time is inevitable among the rooms provided. The respective proportions of births to be accomplished in traditional delivery rooms and in birthing rooms should be determined and separate numbers projected on an annual basis.

The projected number of deliveries to be accomplished in delivery rooms on a daily basis should be divided by a "thumb-rule" factor of either 3 or 4 to determine the number of rooms to be provided. (A figure of 3 deliveries per day is used to project up to three rooms; 4 deliveries per day, to project four or more rooms.)

The number of birthing rooms to be provided will depend upon the projected daily deliveries to be accomplished in birthing rooms and the hospital's policy on the time to be spent in the room by mother, infant, and family members. With the assumption that the entire patient day is spent in a birthing room, the projected annual birthing room deliveries are multiplied by the average length of stay to determine patient days in birthing rooms. This number can then be divided by 365 to determine an average census; the number so obtained is then divided by an occupancy rate of 50 percent to determine birthing rooms needed.

If hospital policy stipulates that no more than, say, three to four hours can be spent in a birthing room, after which the patient is transferred to regular accommodations, birthing room requirements can be calculated in the same manner as for delivery rooms.

It should be noted that when a hospital provides both delivery and birthing rooms, hospital policy should provide for flexibility in use between the two categories to prevent huge space allocations to areas of low use intensity.

Space needs for labor rooms, postpartum recovery areas, and doctors' sleep areas can all be determined quantitatively by simple calculations, after certain hospital policies are established. Remaining support areas must be programmed on bases related to staffing, operational concepts adopted, or number of activity spaces determined as outlined.

Laundry: Calculations are accomplished to convert projected daily pounds of linen for processing (classified by type) to selected items of equipment, chosen according to peak daily volumes, equipment capacities, and a weekly operational schedule. Space can be determined only after equipment selected is tentatively laid out in a functional manner. Processing equipment requirements determine space needs in sorting and washing areas, and in clean-linen processing rooms only. Space in clean-linen and pack-preparation rooms must be determined on the basis of shelf requirements and work stations for preparing packs, both of which will depend upon hospital policies in the use of linen and adopted inventory levels.

Dietary: Projected number of meals prepared and served by type per unit of time, usually annually, converts to specific equipment needs based upon the food system selected (traditional, cook-chill, ready or convenience); scheduling is also an integral factor. Precise space requirements in processing and distribution areas can be determined only after required equipment has been laid out in a rational manner, accounting for various work stations and staging and assembly activities.

Staff dining area is determined by peak seatings of patrons, on the basis of projected meals served at one sitting, usually at noon.

Areas relating to needs for refrigeration, patient tray assembly, storage, cleaning, administration, education, and other support functions are programmed on a variety of bases. Usually, although hospital personnel and the functional planner may tentatively program the dietary department, an experienced dietary consultant should review the program prior to the completion of schematic drawings. Since most A&E firms actually employ a dietary consultant to prepare both schematic and design development drawings of dietary, this approach will occasion no extra expenditures by the hospital.

Dietary is the single department for which we believe a specialized consultant other than the functional planner is required in facility planning. Despite the presence of this specialist, we have observed both overprogramming and underprogramming in a number of hospitals. The functional planner has a distinct responsibility to see that such does not occur. Control over processing, holding, and distribution space can be exercised by means of historical allocations in efficient departments on the basis of both net and gross square feet per inpatient bed. The functional planner can calculate staff dining space independently on the basis of the number of sittings at the room meal and in consideration of the number of patrons attending the sitting.

Engineering suite: Theoretically, activity spaces in this suite can be programmed on the basis of workloads envisioned to be accomplished within each division of the department. However, we believe that a more realistic approach is to program on the basis of a staffing pattern and historical allocations of space to the various divisions of the shop area.

Medical records: Required activity spaces or stations can be calculated directly from categorized workloads and annual scheduled hours of work. From these figures a staffing pattern can be determined for each functional area, with an allocation of space for each staff member. Required shelf space in a current-records storage area can be calculated on the basis of the total number of records envisioned to be retained in the department before being sent to central archives. Thus, shelf space needs depend upon the length of retention and the number of records for the individual hospital that can be contained in each 12 inches (or other measurement unit) of shelf space.

Various types of supporting spaces will be required, depending upon staffing and physician needs. Infrequently, some educational and research space will be necessary.

Centralized supply processing and distribution (SPD): Programming for this area is probably the most complex of all hospital departments. Generally, no hospital should attempt to program an SPD department without the assistance of an experienced functional planner. In brief, however, categorized workloads can be quantified, on the basis of the operational concepts adopted, and these workloads can be converted into equipment and personnel needs, which form bases for required activity spaces. It is critical that before any quantified determinations are made, both the physical and functional relationships of the SPD department with other departments should be decided, notably, those with the operating suite, obstetrical suite, inpatient bed areas, dietary, and laundry. After this, workloads can be calculated, followed by necessary conversion to activity spaces or work stations. Supporting spaces can then be programmed on the basis of the procedures involved in each functional area, the staffing pattern, administrative needs, and the dictates of certain fixed and movable processing and distribution equipment.

Admitting suite: All functions assigned to the admitting suite can be quantified, the quantification converted to numbers of personnel needed, and personnel numbers further converted to work stations, which can be specifically sized to accommodate anticipated numbers of occupants with necessary furniture and other equipment. Some support spaces, depending on functional needs of the admitting system employed, will be required.

Business office: All business office functions can be quantified, except for some necessary support functions, and the quantifications converted to the need for specialized personnel during a scheduled 8-hour work period, usually on either a 5- or 6-day work week basis. The personnel requirements can then be converted to space needs based on the functions performed.

Social service: The object is to convert projected social service visits into numbers of offices for social service workers. This can be done by converting a standard daily workload for a social worker into a yearly workload and dividing that figure into projected total visits. Some support spaces may be necessary, depending upon the size of the department and the services provided to patients and their families.

Autopsy suite: Projected deaths are converted to morgue capacity in bodies by calculating peak daily loads. Thus, projected annual deaths divided by 365 equals daily deaths. By assuming that each body will remain in the morgue for an average of 12 hours and that twice the average daily deaths should be a peak capacity, a morgue capacity can be provided equal to the projected peak of daily deaths.

The autopsy room's capacity in tables can be determined by calculating the projected daily workload (annual projection divided by the number of days autopsies will be performed), multiplying the daily workload by the time it takes to perform one autopsy, and dividing that figure by daily hours autopsies will be performed (usually about 8).

Emergency–ambulatory care suite: The object is to translate projected visits, by type, into activity rooms or patient treatment stations, equipped as needed for the respective types of visits. Usually, types of visits are categorized as follows: trauma, orthopedic, cardiac resuscitation, medical emergency, ophthalmology, ENT (ear, nose, and throat), pediatric, and routine adult examinations and treatment. Increasingly, psychiatric visits are also being given account.

In each of these categories, calculations should be based on the peak 3-hour period of the day, determined by survey, rather than upon a 24-hour workload, even though the entire suite may be open for that period of time.

After the survey is accomplished, the percentage of the total average daily workload that the peak 3-hour workload represents is applied to the projected workload. The following formula can be used:

$$ER = \frac{PAV \times PPP}{3 \times 365 \times ERH}$$

where ER = examination rooms required
PAV = projected annual visits
PPP = percentage of daily visits represented by 3-hour peak period
3 = 3 hours
365 = days in year
ERH = examinations that can be accomplished in one room per hour

Various "thumb-rule" factors have been used in specifying the number of visits that one room in each of the visit categories can accommodate annually. These factors range in value from 3000 visits per room or work station to 5000. Obviously, greater accuracy than this is desirable; therefore, use of the methodology presented here is recommended.

A variety of support spaces are required in addition to the primary activity spaces, some of which—such as x-ray—can be determined on the basis of workload. Others must be programmed on the basis of staffing, patient needs, and administrative requirements.

Use of activity space calculations
Exclusive of bed area, activity space determinations (as in preceding example) constitute less than half of the actual net usable space programmed in today's general acute care hospital. The remaining areas are composed of (1) space that is supportive of the activity spaces, (2) educational space, and (3) research space. However, the activity spaces form the nucleus for all programming. These are the spaces that drive the need for all others; the activities performed in them, by volume and type, drive the need for all staff and equipment. Although educational and research space allocations can vary quite widely under identical conditions (equal workloads and resulting activity allocations), even here activity volumes exert limiting constraints.

With calculations of activity spaces in hand, the programmer is ready to give detailed consideration to concepts of operations, educational and research requirements, and all spaces supportive to the activity spaces.

Minor addition or modernization projects
Since operational concepts of a hospital become fixed upon completion of construction, it is seldom feasible to reorient them in the course of a functional program of minor additions or modernization. Although no blanket statements can be made to this effect, the basic inflexibility of bricks, mortar, concrete, and steel usually means that problems sealed into the structure at the outset will continue to limit efficient operations until razing. Although professionally accomplished cost-benefit studies can determine the feasibility of most alternatives that may be formulated regarding any such system or other major building characteristic, our experience indicates that in the absence of major additions, only rarely will drastic building changes result in operational savings over the remaining useful life of a building sufficient to justify capital costs involved.

Usually, regardless of advances in state-of-the-art operational concepts, a minor addition will be completely compromised by an existing structure, owing to both economic factors and the necessity to achieve operational uniformity.

Consider the case of adding 40 beds to an existing 400-bed facility constructed in the early 1960s. There is great likelihood that the original structure possesses nursing-station-type nursing units of about 30 beds each; decentralized supply processing and distribution (which cannot be called a system); a hot-and-cold-food distribution system; a labor progress and delivery suite at the third level; and a single-corridored operating suite at the fourth or fifth level. Most physicians and many employees probably enter the hospital at the emergency entrance, and supplies are incoming at possibly four different entrances. Even if the administrator and governing board were aware of the existence of new and innovative concepts that would be a decided improvement over all the features mentioned, it is doubtful that the cost of changes to implement them can be justified. Thus, for the 40-bed addition, inclusion of any new system therein can hardly be justified, excepting perhaps an advanced nurse-call system—which would then differ radically from other call systems found throughout the existing structure.

We have reached the conclusion that, except in unique instances where there are obvious reasons for performing cost-benefit studies, it is better to accept the basic premise that minor additions and alterations do not justify major changes throughout a large structure. Of course, in some cases, appreciable modernizations may occur simultaneously with a minor addition. The installation of piped gases, pneumatic tube systems, more efficient air-conditioning systems, major "retrofits" to accomplish energy conservation, and other changes of comparable magnitude may be consummated at the time of a minor addition merely from the standpoint of upgrading, with no appreciable influence exerted by the addition.

Although it may seem regrettable to perpetuate the past by building something that is operationally out-of-date from the moment of opening, relatively small additions frequently are forced into this category, owing to the compromising influences of the larger structures to which they are appended.

The placement of a small addition sometimes becomes a matter of considerable concern, more from the standpoint of master site planning and long-range facility planning than from operational considerations. In many cases, for example, a minor addition has been tacked onto a larger structure in the exact site location in which a later major addition should have been placed. Such instances are the result of poor planning or, to be more accurate, *no* planning.

Major expansion or modernization projects
As contrasted with minor addition or modernization projects, larger projects must be addressed from a different conceptual perspective. Although each situation will be unique in many respects, size of the addition and obsolescence of an existing structure usually speak strongly against perpetuation of obsolete building characteristics and outmoded operational systems. That such perpetuation has been effected, however, is all too plain in hundreds of hospitals on this continent. Local circumstances, usually related to penchants for seeking simple, immediate, low-cost solutions and plain lack of foresight have ensured that many major projects were obsolete upon opening.

We discuss several considerations of expansion and modernizations in Chapter 13 (under Alternative Programs of Modernization or Expansion). In that chapter we note that a number of cost-benefit studies are usually needed to justify various operational and building systems selected for both new and existing areas. Changes to newer operational concepts and incorporation of latest state-of-the-art building systems often not only are cost-effective but also upgrade quality of care and treatment, but the feasibility of such changes should be proved before decisions are made.

In the life of hospital structures, there usually comes a time when a major addition should take the character of a nucleus for a new plant, rather than adapt to the old. If this is not done, and additions continue to conform to old structures and existing operations, a new addition can literally be compromised by a structure built 50 years ago. At some point the chain of compromise should be broken. Although this alternative can be considered in the performance of cost-benefit studies, special attention should be given this method of plant regeneration from philosophical, conceptual, and operational standpoints.

Thus, prior to formulating details of the functional program for governing board approval, concepts that are to be included in the expanded plant must be justified and defined.

The importance of concept definition at the outset of functional programming is great, for as has been repeatedly stated, adopted concepts and workloads, plus teaching and research requirements, are the prime determinants of space needs.

Functional programming for major additions and modernizations is very similar to that performed for new structures, except that detailed descriptions of uses of existing facilities will be required. Regardless of the initial inclinations of hospital officials, it is incumbent upon the functional planner, as a professional, to advise as to the most feasible combination of concepts for a particular hospital. By no means should the process be one in which the client simply chooses "wants" or dictates preconceived notions. The functional planner ought to have full opportunity to present pertinent information and related recommendations, for the worth of specialists is in their better knowledge and greater informational depth with regard to the area about which consultative advice is sought.

After deliberation, the hospital should select the operational concepts around which programming will be written, and the functional planner can begin work, provided that sufficient details regarding educational and research programs have been developed in the strategic plan. If not, some further data gathering may be required in order to program classrooms, other educational spaces, and research facilities.

In contrast with new hospital construction and minor additions, major alterations usually entail a sequence of construction phasing (geared to continuing operational and transition requirements), which can be determined by the functional planner, provided in-house A&E support is available, or provided the hospital-appointed A&E firm lends assistance with regard to feasibility. Whereas phasing was once the exclusive province of the independent, hospital-appointed A&E firm, functional planners are increasingly employing one or more architects to validate their ideas regarding the feasibility of such things as phasing and operational concepts.

The format of the functional program for major addition and modernization projects can take a variety of forms, so long as the way the hospital is meant to operate in the interim and upon completion is adequately described for all concerned, and necessary information is included for space programming and various aspects of the work of other members of the planning team. Additional comments about format are set forth later in the chapter under Presentation and Format.

New hospital projects
A new hospital project can be construed to mean the total replacement of an existing facility or building of a new plant for a newly created organization. Hospitals are sometimes completely rebuilt at an existing site, with perhaps only a connecting link to existing obsolete facilities, which are converted to other uses. In other instances, a new plant is constructed,

and the existing one is completely razed. Of course, some hospitals have followed the inner-city exodus to suburbs and have completely relocated, disposing of the old plant in one way or another.

Functional programming for a new hospital, whatever the facility's origin, is in many respects much simpler than that for a major expansion and modernization project. Certainly, conceptual constraints are fewer, and chances of providing a highly cost-effective structure in terms of functionality and advanced state-of-the-art operational systems are somewhat greater. At the same time, however, because constraints are fewer, feasible alternatives are oftentimes more numerous.

Resolving operational concepts: As in the case of a major program of additions and modernization, before active functional programming for a new hospital begins, decisions have to be made regarding a number of operational concepts, and it is the responsibility of the functional planner to bring those that are appropriate to the attention of hospital officials for resolution of matters requiring decision.

This resolution can be accomplished in a number of ways, and a few functional planners have engaged in "selling" hospital officials upon concepts strongly espoused. Another approach is to review various feasible alternatives with the hospital, set forth comparative data regarding each, and allow decision-making processes to proceed to logical conclusions. The latter approach has the best chance of proving ultimately successful in that greater numbers of the hospital family are allowed to participate in the decision making.

In a sense, both of these processes are akin to an inductive thought process or, narrowly, the formulation and testing of hypotheses. After favored alternatives have been chosen, the further planning approach is a deductive process: that is, subsequent decisions are made in consideration of accepted bases.

To determine major operational concepts at the outset is clearly a logical, efficient, and time-saving approach. Many major concepts cut across all departmental lines and exert operational and design influences throughout the structure. Indeed, it is not possible to program a hospital that will operate as a total, coordinated system without first having determined operational concepts. To program solely from the standpoint of a departmental basis using a so-called "building-block" approach can result only in a group of separately operating departmental "kingdoms," as it were, with duplication of many spaces and functions throughout the structure.

Some of the concepts that usually require deliberation and decision making among hospital officials are as follows:

- all single-patient rooms versus some mix of singles and doubles, or of singles, doubles, and four-bed wards

- an integrated, centralized SPD system versus the traditional "central supply" concept (which in reality features multiple processing points and oftentimes multiple receiving points)

- automation of supply distribution versus manual distribution

- "no nursing station" nursing units versus those with nursing stations (each with implications as to size of units)

- team or primary nursing care versus functional nursing care

- combined surgical and obstetrical suite versus separate suites

- triple-corridored operating units versus single-corridored suite (departmental concept only)

- ready foods versus convenience foods versus cook-chill versus traditional dietary systems

- in-house laundry versus outside processing

- unit-dose drug-dispensing system versus variations of the unit-dose system versus traditional systems

- fully automated data processing versus various degrees of automation

- functional bloc layout of emergency–ambulatory care suite versus traditional layout (departmental concept only)

- staff corridor concept in radiology versus traditional concept (departmental concept only)

- open bay concept in laboratory layout versus segregated service concept (departmental concept only)

- nuclear medicine as a separate service versus a division of radiology versus a division of pathology versus imaging as a part of radiology and in vitro assays as a part of pathology.

Teaching hospitals require an even greater definition of operational concepts. In addition to those receiving consideration in community-type hospitals, the following are often debated:

- complete decentralization of clinical research spaces by department versus centralized clinical research space, flexibly allocated

- floor laboratories versus a centralized teaching laboratory

- flexibly used ambulatory care areas versus completely segregated clinics, by service

- complete decentralization of faculty offices versus centralized grouping of a selected percentage

- floor pharmacies versus a centralized service only.

Presentation and format

The functional program's best presentation will be in a manner and format understandable by all parties requiring orientation as to its contents. Because there will be many individuals of a variety of disciplines who will need to refer to it over a period of years, there is little question but that narrative and graphic descriptions are best suited to this purpose. Mere listings of numbers and types of things and people will not suffice; rather, a combination of the printed word and graphic displays will ensure best comprehension by the broadest number of readers. Figures 7–1 and 7–2 are examples of such graphic displays that can be incorporated into a functional program.

Among the functional program's several purposes, one is to record the operational rationale of the hospital as a whole and each of its departments; broad, basic descriptions of both intradepartmental and interdepartmental procedural aspects must be presented, for there is little hope that appropriate reflections of functions can be depicted in drawings unless the designer understands them. Furthermore, a mere understanding of what transpires in each individual room of the hospital will not suffice, nor will a comprehension of the work of each individual department. It is only when a totality of understanding occurs—about room functions, departmental functions, and those of the hospital as a whole—that appropriate design can be executed.

Additionally, if the hospital is to operate properly when it is opened, those who work therein must also possess a complete understanding of procedural aspects. As we have noted previously, form should follow function in design (but not to the point where flexibility is unreasonably limited). Once the building is finished and opened, however, functions follow form. In many cases, extremely serious operational problems have developed after opening because executives who assisted in planning the hospital around innovative concepts were no longer employed at opening. Appropriate orientation was not given those who followed; consequently, attempts were made to operate the hospital in traditional fashion with costly, unsatisfactory results.

Some designers voice displeasure regarding the study required to understand the functional program in all its aspects, but it is far better for hospital officials to endure expressions of this displeasure for a few weeks or months than to occasion half a lifetime of suffering and inconveniences for building inhabitants through a design resulting from a lack of knowledge about how the hospital is to operate, both as a whole and with regard to each of its elements.

A logical and highly satisfactory format for presenting the functional program is to set forth its philosophical bases in initial pages, followed by somewhat detailed discussions of concepts flowing from them that have interdepartmental implications. From these discussions should come a holistic perspective of the hospital as an operational system.

The various departments and separate functional entities can then be grouped by similarity of purpose, such as inpatient nursing services, diagnostic and treatment services, administrative services, supporting services, and auxiliary services. Within the groupings, separate discussions of each department and functional entity can be set forth under basic headings, as outlined in the following listing.

1. *historical utilization.* Here the actual workloads of the department or functional entity, separated as to utilization parameter as indicated (typically, admissions or patient days and outpatient visits) and cate-

Example of flow diagram used in definition of a concept for supply processing and distribution

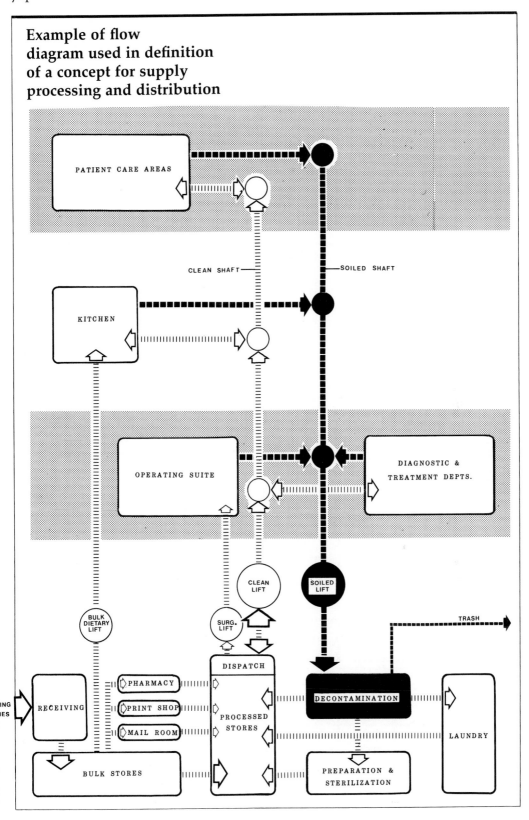

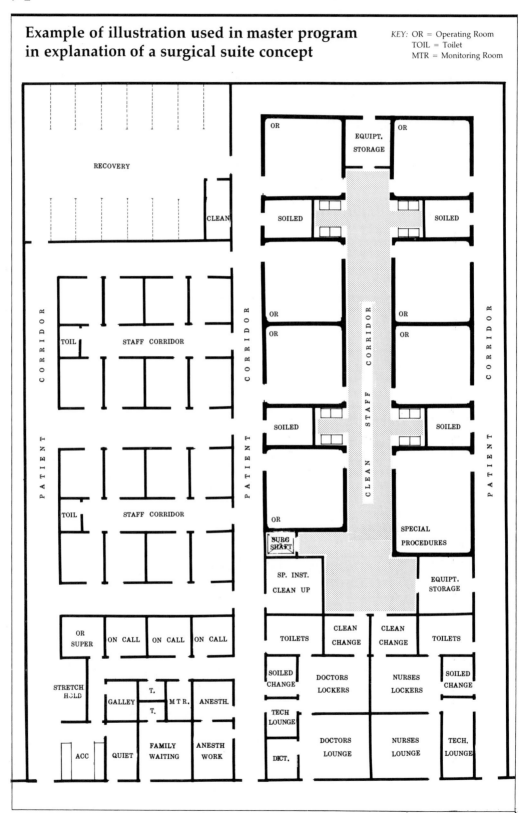

Example of illustration used in master program in explanation of a surgical suite concept

KEY: OR = Operating Room
TOIL = Toilet
MTR = Monitoring Room

gorized according to departmental divisions or functional areas, should be set forth for a preceding 3-year period. The ratio of the workloads to the applicable parameter should be shown under each year's figures.

2. *projected utilization.* Under this heading the projected primary demand utilization parameter for targeted years should be first set forth. Directly under these figures should be shown the projected ratio between calculated workloads and the primary demand utilization parameter. On the next line is shown the workload used in activity space calculations (obtained by multiplying the ratio figure by the primary demand projection). Some explanatory notes may necessarily follow since there are usually some unique circumstances involved in each projection. For example, currently, subjective adjustments based on recent national trends should be explained.

3. *programmed activity spaces.* The number and type of activity or work station spaces required to accomplish the calculated workloads are set forth here, categorized by function or departmental division if necessary. The exact manner in which calculations have been made should be demonstrated.

4. *description of functions and facilities.* Here the functional planner describes the basic procedural functions involved in some detail and provides a complete listing of all rooms in the department, including both activity spaces and supporting spaces (which actually include all other spaces, regardless of their functional purpose). The listing of rooms can be set forth under a number of formats and one extensive study on space programming by a reputable planning firm has suggested a division among activity spaces, support spaces and administrative spaces.[4] We do not recommend this approach, however, for two reasons: first, the division between administrative spaces and support spaces is artificial, and many rooms could be subsumed under either heading; second, the arbitrary division handicaps interested departmental staff, physicians, and others who may be attempting to check groupings of functional areas or divisions for completeness.

Our best judgment is that all spaces should be set forth in a straightforward listing, and if groupings are indicated, they should be done according to general function or purpose. For example, in the department of radiology we have usually formed groupings for general radiology; special procedures (all spaces related to invasive cardiovascular and other special rooms); nuclear medicine; ultrasound; CT scanning; and other supporting spaces. Under this format, respective divisional personnel can quickly determine whether all required spaces have been given account; in addition, it is much easier to explain intradepartmental relationships, both functional and physical, if spaces are listed under functional groupings.

Each room or space is described in terms of functions transpiring therein (in many instances the room's name designation is sufficient); types and numbers and persons using the room; and equipment for carrying out functions, both fixed and major movable, when such equipment affects sizing of the space.

The room listing and the information pertaining thereto should be presented in tabular form.

5. *functional relationships and physical proximities.* The functional planner uses this heading to outline functional relations transpiring with other departments and generally weight the desirability for physical closeness to them. Although a matrix detailing ideal physical closeness throughout the hospital is prepared later in the planning process, it is advisable that this matrix be preceded by narrative discussions and diagrams illustrating possibilities for achieving acceptable proximities.

6. *flexibility and future expansion.* This final departmental heading devotes discussion to the best means for achieving flexibility in the particular area, the probability of future expansion and the order of its magnitude, and how expansion would best be accounted for in design and carried out when required. Graphics are used as appropriate.

Final pages of the functional program are devoted to discussions of building systems that affect various aspects of functionality or flexibility and expansion.

The functional program for a typical community hospital usually results in a 150- to 250-page typed document, interspersed with graphic drawings. For a major teaching hospital, multivolume documentations are often required.

Budget responsibility

Although a formal space program has not been performed at this point, the functional planner will have been compelled to definitively determine space implications of the functional program. It is the functional planner's responsibility to know and provide assurances that the recommended state-of-the-art systems, together with required gross total space, can be brought within budget limits established at the time. Unquestionably, the functional planner must consult with both the hospital-appointed A&E firm and construction manager during preparation of the functional program, and discuss total space implications with both of these professionals before final submission to the hospital.

Review and approval

Upon completion of the functional program, the functional planner delivers copies to the director of planning (or person filling that role), whose responsibility it is to distribute copies to other members of the professional planning team; the building committee; user committees as appropriate (including those of the medical staff); the executive staff; and members of the governing board.

The director of planning coordinates the reviews and the discourse that transpire with the various members of the functional planning consultant firm and, finally, brings the documentations, which may include addenda, to the chief executive officer for appropriate action and board approval.

After approval, the functional program becomes a major policy document of the hospital, capable of being substantially changed only by board authority.

Summary

Workload projections drive the need for departmental personnel, equipment, and space, except in the case of the management suite. They are derived from historical ratios between workloads, as a dependent variable, and primary demand parameters, an independent variable; when this ratio is multiplied by primary demand parameters (admissions, patient days or outpatient visits) already projected in the strategic plan, the workloads are obtained. At the present time, owing to the advent of DRGs and prospective pricing for admissions, subjective judgment may alter extrapolations of this ratio, as well as projections of primary demand, as previously noted.

After projected workloads have been converted to departmental activity space requirements, all other supporting spaces must be programmed on the basis of a variety of factors. In many instances the need for such spaces can be justified on quantified bases, but some are determined by requirements for supervisory personnel, storage, equipment, and patient and staff amenities. Educational and research needs, if any, must be given account. Operational concepts adopted also exert an influence.

There are three basic types of proposed constructions for which a functional program should be prepared:

1. minor addition or modernization projects

2. major expansion or modernization projects

3. new or replacement hospital projects.

In minor additions and modernizations, functional efficiency of the plan can seldom be improved owing to the fixed nature of operational systems already built in; thus, the addition is compromised in terms of current state-of-the-art from opening day. In major expansions and modernizations, the opportunity usually exists to start the nucleus of a new plant by bringing the "old" into conformance with the "new," rather than vice versa. Consideration can be given to converting the whole into a modern state-of-the-art plant. When new or replacement hospitals are started, hospital officials, led by the functional planner, have the opportunity to provide a highly cost-effective facility that responds to the needs of modern care and treatment.

As to presentation of the functional program, a minor program can be outlined very briefly, but major programs and new hospitals require rather voluminous documentations. Such documentations should start not at the department level by a building-block approach but by viewing the hospital as a total operational and physical whole that operates as a system and into which each department is appropriately fitted. Philosophical bases and the operational concept flowing from them should be first determined and outlined so as to describe a grand scheme of operation. Departmental programming then follows, and is presented under six basic headings:

1. historical utilization

2. projected utilization

3. programmed activity spaces

4. description of functions and facilities (which sets forth a complete room program containing all primary activity spaces plus those required for supporting functions)

5. functional relationships and physical proximities

6. flexibility and future expansion.

The final pages of the functional program should be devoted to brief discussions of building systems.

Although the functional program is a documentation separate from a space program, the space program must be prepared in concert with the functional program, for the functional planner possesses the responsibility to ensure that the functional program does not exceed budget figures already established.

After necessary reviews by hospital officials and approval, the functional program represents a major policy document to be used as a guide for all members of the planning team. Additionally, it will be used as a guide for staffing and operating the facility when it is opened.

Notes

1. Example has been based upon Owen B. Hardy's work for an Ernst & Whinney project.
2. Marc R. Summerfield, *Unit Dose Primer* (Bethesda, MD: American Society of Hospital Pharmacists, 1983).
3. *Planning for Hospital Pharmacies.* Department of Health, Education, and Welfare Pub. No. (HRA)74-4003, 1974.
4. A multivolume publication, e.g., *Evaluation and Space Programming Methodology for Pharmacy.* (Chi Systems, Inc., 1981); other volumes (1981–1983) are available for various other departments.

8

The Planning and Design Process

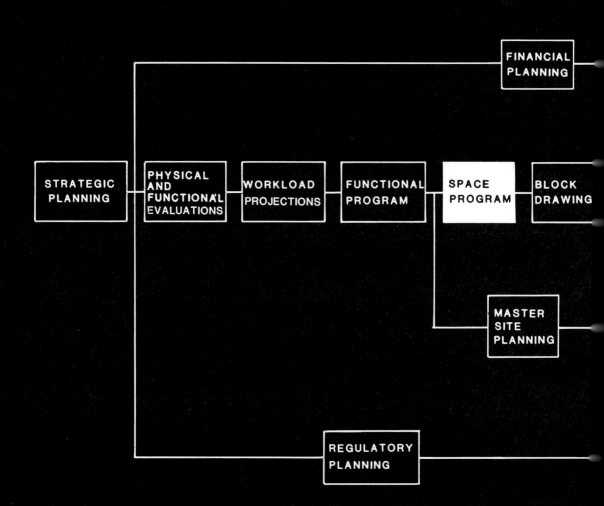

Space programming

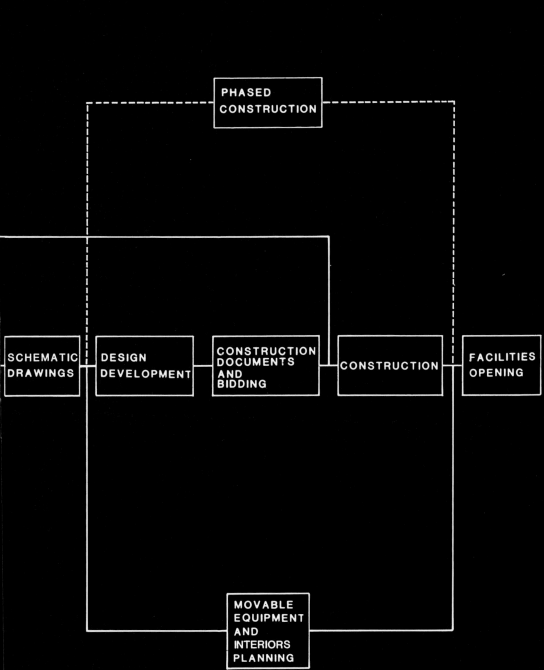

Definitions

A *room program* is a listing of every room or area in a proposed construction to which an operational function is assigned. It is a direct derivative of the functional program, wherein each room named is discussed with regard to function, functional relationships, and major environmental characteristics. Rooms in the listing usually follow the order of the functional program and are grouped by department or functional entity.

A *departmental net space program* is a room program coupled with an assignment of square feet of space for each room or other functional area in a department or separate functional entity. A departmental *gross space program* is obtained when net space is converted to gross space, most commonly by applying empirical conversion factors to net spaces by department or functional entity. *Hospital gross space* is space that cannot be assigned to a specific department, such as that for interdepartmental circulation, mechanical chases, central elevator core and penthouse, and certain exit stairways. Adding the net space totals for all departments and separate functional entities gives the *total net space* for the hospital. Adding the gross space totals for all departments plus the hospital gross space gives the *total gross space* for the hospital. The *hospital net-to-gross ratio* is the total gross space divided into the total net space.

Responsibility

Because the functional planner must develop a room program and a tentative space program during preparation of the functional program in order to assure budget conformance, it is logical that this consultant should retain responsibility for at least formal net space programming. The architect should provide conversion factors in order to formulate a gross space program; thus, the final gross program should be the responsibility of the A&E firm. This firm, however, should be called upon to respect certain ratios of net to gross space, at both the department and complete-hospital level, that are recognized in the field today.

Traditionally, architects have prepared space programs derived directly from functional programs developed by functional planners or hospital officials. In many instances, architects have simply constructed a space program in the absence of a functional program (a certain start to a bad design), and all too often designers have undertaken their work in the absence of both a functional program and a space program! With increasing knowledge on the part of both hospital officials and architects, however, detailed, explanatory functional programs are being prepared by experienced functional planners, followed by appropriate net and gross space programs, all before the beginning of design.

Purposes

Space programming serves several major purposes:

1. *guidance to designers.* Every functional space to be included in the hospital, by department or functional entity, is listed, along with the net square feet to be assigned to each.

2. *assurance for users.* The methodical listing of every room and respective assigned square footages provides all department heads assurance that agreed-upon rooms and spaces will appear in the design from the start, and that omissions of vital functional areas and wrong space allocations will be prevented.

3. *control by hospital executives.* A space program represents a control mechanism over design from the standpoints of project cost and conformance to management intentions regarding rooms and departmental sizings, as well as the basic character of the entire hospital.

4. *early information for other members of the professional planning team.* The financial consultant can proceed with firm expense and income projections, based upon workload projections, and can project staffing patterns; the construction manager receives information regarding totals of different types of spaces necessary for preparing a first definitive cost estimate.

Programming considerations

A number of considerations are involved in assigning space to an individual room or area, and such considerations may vary for different rooms throughout the hospital. It is true that a design for an individual space (including assigning dimensions and net square feet thereto) can be accomplished if the architect knows (1) what is to be done in the space; (2) who will be doing it; and (3) what equipment and environment are needed.[1] However, different architects with the same information outlined under this so-called "rule of three" may reach various conclusions regarding dimensions and space necessary for a room. For example, of the various architects we have dealt with, some believed that an 8' × 10' configuration would suffice for an examination and treatment room in an outpatient department. Others held the opinion that 10' × 12' is the proper assignment; still others advocated 10' × 15' (largely based on bay sizing), whereas a few espoused the need for a 12' × 14' space. It is easy to note that the smallest space—8' × 10'—totals 80 square feet, and the largest—12' × 14'—totals 168 square feet, or over twice the smallest amount. Thus, leaving perceptions of information contained in the "rule of three" for the architect alone to interpret in design is a debatable practice.

We hasten to add, however, that *design achieved* is the final determinant of all space allocations. Although guidelines can be delivered to the design architect and controls can be placed upon design activities, the space finally allocated will be that placed within graphical lines on design sheets. In all instances, no incentive should be removed from the design architect to achieve innovative, efficient design solutions to accommodate specific functions and combinations of functions. However, the design architect should not be the only or final arbiter of the appropriateness of proposed space allocations.

State and federal regulations affect space assignments in a number of instances. For example, most states stipulate minimum square footage requirements for spaces assigned to operating rooms, delivery rooms, nursery bassinets, beds in both private and multibed rooms, pediatric cribs, patrons in dining areas, central storage areas, and certain specified examination-treatment rooms. Such minimum standards have long appeared in federal guidelines and are currently published by the Department of Health and Human Services in *Guidelines for Construction and Equipment of Hospital and Medical Facilities.*[2] Therefore, simply for new construction to be licensed for operation, minimum space assignments for a number of functions have to be met.

Budgets influence space assignments. It is often the case that hospital owners would like large private rooms, with a net space of up to 160 square feet. Large rooms (the cited 12′ × 14′) may be functionally desirable in the outpatient department, and radiologists can advance good reasoning as to the functional requirements for an 18′ × 20′ radiography-fluoroscopy room. In fact, however, each of these rooms can support their designated functions in smaller spaces. When budgets are restricted, space assignments to individual rooms are usually at their functional minimum. When budgets are unrestricted, assignments can be made optimally or even liberally.

In some instances, hospital officials will dictate square footage allocations regardless of functional requirements, thereby causing changes from normal space assignments. For example, some radiological special procedures rooms in certain community hospitals may be much larger than those supporting heavy usage in some of the nation's most noted medical centers, solely because the radiologist in a community hospital usually possesses considerable power. The HSAs, however, have certainly curbed excessive tendencies in this regard, and the competitive environment in which hospitals may operate in the years ahead will curb them even more.

In projects involving modernization and expansion, space assignments may not equate with a functional optimum owing to the restrictive inflexibility of the original configuration of external and internal walls, chases, columns, spacings, and so on.

Finally, it may be best, if future expansion has been forecasted to occur in a relatively short time, to provide more space in a few internally locked-in areas than will be needed upon completion of a planning project. For example, if an admitting area clearly must be expanded in a validly forecasted expansion (to occur five or six years following completion of the project being planned), it is usually more economical to include the space initially unless there is an easy avenue of expansion indicated in design. The functional planner, through experience, will be able to identify such areas and can make appropriate provisions if not precluded by a restrictive budget.

Plainly, space programming is not a science, nor is it an art to be practiced by a talented designer working in seclusion; neither is it a chore to be resolved through manipulations of pat formulas. Rather, it is a methodical task requiring consideration of a broad number of factors that will differ in specific situations.

Methodology

The functional planner will accomplish a final listing of rooms and assign net spaces during preparation of the functional program according to workloads and the activity spaces required to accommodate them, adopted operational concepts, educational requirements, research requirements, and expected need for various support spaces. On completion of the first draft of the functional program, the accumulated gross totals for departmentally grouped space listings are then calculated with the use of conversion factors, either obtained from the architect or based upon the functional planner's experiences. In the event a topside budget has been set and if the total estimated cost is clearly over budget, the functional planner must then determine how best to make reductions. Of course, if the topside budget is not restrictive, the most feasible program in terms of expected functional requirements should be developed.

There are two basic ways to reduce a space program in the event a budget is exceeded: (1) entire rooms, or entire departments or functional entities, can be removed from the functional program, or (2) space assignments to some individual rooms can be reduced. A combination of these two approaches, based upon the functional planner's knowledge of the various priorities involved, is most commonly employed.

In reducing space programs by as little as 5 to 10 percent, the logical approach, usually, is to reduce numbers of support rooms and some space assignments across the board. This approach will seldom be intolerably detrimental to the overall program. If a required reduction is in excess of 10 percent, elimination of some activity spaces may be required. However, as stated, there is no sure approach that can be applied in every situation; therefore, the functional planner should carefully consider all the factors involved in specific situations and should seek opinions and advice from other members of the professional planning team, as well as from appropriate members of the hospital executive staff.

Examples of space programming procedures

Perhaps the best way to illustrate the methodology for formulating a space program is to provide some examples of documentations actually accomplished. Exhibit 8–1 shows how net spaces were assigned to rooms

Exhibit 8–1

Example of net space assignments to surgical suite rooms

This space program was formulated upon the assumptions that design will incorporate the triple-corridor concept, thereby affording a positive separation of all types of clean and soiled traffic, and that all supply processing will be accomplished remotely, with clean supplies being delivered to the surgical suite by automated means on a case-cart basis.

Functional Category	Room Designation	Criteria for Space Assignment	No. of Rooms	Unit Space (NSF)	Room Totals	Suite or Department Totals
Administrative and Lounge and Change Areas	1. Administrative Control Center	Space for two clerks working at 24-in.-wide sitting-height counter approximately 16 ft. long. Equipment includes three straight chairs, 17″ × 19″; two file cabinets, 15″ × 24″; OR status board; OR scheduling board; communications console; cathode ray tube and 4-in. pneumatic tube station	1	140	140	
	2. Office, Operating Room (OR) Supervisor	Furniture for supervisor and two seated guests	1	100	100	
	3. Office, OR Coordinator or Assistant Supervisor	Furniture for coordinator and one seated guest	1	80	80	
	4. Office, OR Secretary	Space for typing desk and chair; file cabinet, 15″ × 24″; and chair for one seated guest	1	80	80	
	5. Office, Anesthesiologists (accessible to outsiders)	Furniture for one anesthesiologist and two seated guests	1	100	100	
	6. Conference-Classroom, capacity of 12	Space for bookcase, 14″ × 60″; and 12 persons seated at conference table in straight chairs with arms; allow 20 NSF per person	1	250	250	

Administrative and Lounge and Change Areas (continued)

7. Surgeons' Lounge	Space for peaks of 15 physicians at 15 NSF each	1	225	225
8. Doctors' Charting and Dictating Areas	Open 4'×4' cubicles, each with built-in 20-inch counter and one straight chair, 17"×19"	4	16	64
9. Male Doctors' Locker Room	Space for 80 lockers (provides for 15 percent growth); each locker 12"×16"×72"; four sitting benches, each 16"×60"	1	320	320
10. Clean Change Room, Male Doctors	Space for three doctors simultaneously donning scrub suits and shoe covers; to contain one 25"×53" mobile exchange cart and three straight chairs, 17"×19"	1	60	60
11. Soiled Change Room, All Male Personnel	Space for three persons simultaneously removing soiled scrub suits or coats and shoe covers; to contain two soiled-linen hampers, 31"×31", and three straight chairs, 17"×19"	1	60	60
12. Toilet and Shower Area, Male Doctors	Space for three showers, each 3'×3'; two urinals, 12 NSF each; two water closets, 16 NSF each, and two lavatories, 12 NSF each	1	140	140
13. Female Nurses' and Doctors' Lounge	Space for peaks of 15 persons at 15 NSF each	1	225	225
14. Female Nurses' and Doctors' Charting and Dictating Areas	Open 4'×4' cubicles, each with built-in 20-inch counter and one straight chair, 17"×19"	1	16	16
15. Female Lockers (Nurses and Doctors)	Space for 70 lockers, each 12"×16"×72", and four sitting benches, each 16"×60"	1	300	300

Exhibit 8–1 continued

Functional Category	Room Designation	Criteria for Space Assignment	No. of Rooms	Unit Space (NSF)	Room Totals	Suite or Department Totals
Administrative and Lounge and Change Areas (continued)	16. Clean Change Room, Female	Space for three persons simultaneously donning scrub dresses and clean shoe covers; to contain one mobile exchange cart, 25″×53″, holding clean scrub dresses and shoe covers, and three straight chairs, each 17″×19″	1	60	60	
	17. Soiled Change Room, Female	Space for three persons simultaneously removing soiled scrub dresses or coats and shoe covers; to contain two soiled linen hampers, 31″×31″, and three straight chairs, 17″×19″	1	60	60	
	18. Toilet and Showers, Female	Space for three showers, each 3′×3′; three water closets, 16 NSF each; and three lavatories, each 12 NSF	1	120	120	
	19. Locker Room, Male Nursing Assistants	Space for 14 lockers (4 more than needed for present staff, to allow for students and growth); each locker 12″×16″×72″; one sitting bench, 16″×60″	1	80	80	
	20. Clean Change Room, Male Nursing Assistants	Space for two persons donning scrub suits and clean shoe covers simultaneously; to contain one 25″×53″ mobile exchange cart and two straight chairs, 17″×19″	1	40	40	
	21. Toilet and Shower, Male Nursing Assistants	Space for one shower, 3′×3′; one water closet, 16 NSF; one urinal, 12 NSF; and one lavatory, 12 NSF	1	50	50	

Category	Item	Description	Qty		
	22. Coffee and Refreshment Room (serving all lounges)	Space for standing-height counter, 24″×72″; to contain 12″×12″ sink and equipment as follows: coffee-maker, microwave oven, undercounter refrigerator, and cold-drink dispenser, 18″×30″	1	50	50
Family Waiting Areas	23. Family Waiting Area, serving Surgical Suite	Space for peaks of 26 persons (based on current average of 22), 15 NSF each	1	400	400
	24. Toilet, Male, serving Waiting Area	Water closet for handicapped, 24″×36″; urinal, 12 NSF; and lavatory for handicapped, 12 NSF; provide 4-ft. clearance in front of each fixture and 5-ft. turning radius in room	1	50	50
	25. Toilet, Female, serving waiting area	Water closet for handicapped, 24″×36″, and lavatory for handicapped, 12 NSF; provide 4-ft. clearance in front of each fixture and 5-ft. wheelchair turning radius in room	1	50	50
	26. Telephone Booths, serving Waiting Area	Enclosed type to assure privacy, 36″×36″	2	9	18
	27. Doctors' Consultation Room (with families after surgery)	Space for two lounge chairs, 31″×35″; two straight chairs with arms, 22″×22″; one lamp table, 18″×28″; one center table, 18″×48″	1	100	100
Patient Holding Area	28. Holding and Preparation Room	Space for peaks of 16 patients queueing for 13 operating rooms, two cystoscopic rooms, and one endoscopic room; space for 16 stretchers, maximum of 35″×80″; Allow 3 ft. between stretchers and 1½ ft. from headwall; assume 6-ft.	1	1250	1250

Exhibit 8-1 continued

Functional Category	Room Designation	Criteria for Space Assignment	No. of Rooms	Unit Space (NSF)	Room Totals	Suite or Department Totals
		aisle between two rows of eight stretchers each and 160 NSF for supplies and nurse and doctor desk work at entrance end of room; assume room of approximately 56' × 22'4" = 1250 NSF (see attached diagrams for suggested layout [not provided here])				
	29. Soiled Alcove	To contain flushing rim sink, 22"×25"; mop service basin, 24"×26"; and two 25"×53" mobile carts; recommend 60 NSF	1	60	60	
	30. Stretcher Holding Alcove	On peripheral corridor, space for two wheeled stretchers, each 31"×77"	1	42	42	
Cystoscopy and Endoscopy	31. Cystoscopy Room	Minimum clear area of 250 NSF, exclusive of fixed cabinets and built-in shelves; allow 38 NSF for cabinetry and shelves; room to be 16'×18'	1	288	288	
	32. Cystoscopy Room	Special functions room requiring space provisions for newly developed combined x-ray and cystoscopic table equipment; see equipment specifications attached [not provided here]	1	360	360	
	33. Endoscopy Room	Space provided exceeds current requirements, but size at 16'×18' for future flexibility	1	288	288	

Cystoscopy and
Endoscopy (continued)

No.	Room	Description	Qty	NSF	Total
34.	Scrub Area or Alcoves serving Cystoscopy and Endoscopy	Space for two knee-operated scrub sinks, each 22″×28″, and two persons scrubbing simultaneously; may or may not be located together; each to be 40 NSF	2	40	80
35.	Clean Work and Supply Storage Area serving Cystoscopy and Endoscopy	For storage of supplies and sterile liquids on mobile carts, sterilizing, and clean supply preparations: space for six mobile carts, each 25″×53″; one standing-height work counter, 24″×8′, with cabinetry underneath; one cabinet-type flash sterilizer, approx. 30′×51″; various stands, stools, and IV apparatus; two warming cabinets, each 28″×30″; lavatory	1	260	260
36.	Soiled Holding Room, serving Cystoscopy and Endoscopy	For holding all soiled supplies and wastes on carts awaiting pick up by central personnel: to contain flushing rim sink, 22″×25″; hand-washing lavatory; work counter, 24″×60″; and space for holding eight case carts, 24″×36″, and three soiled-supply pick-up carts, each 25″×53″	1	100	100
37.	Film Processing Room	Equipment manufacturer recommends 60 NSF	1	60	60
38.	Toilets serving Cystoscopy and Endoscopy	Water closet and lavatory, plus grab bars; joins procedure room	3	24	72
39.	Dressing and Prep Room serving Cystoscopy and Endoscopy	Space for two straight chairs, 17″×19″; one prep stretcher, 30″×79″; one utility table, 16″×20″; three clothes lockers, each 12″×16″×72″; and lavatory	1	80	80
40.	Toilet adjoining Dressing and Prep Room	Water closet, lavatory, and grab bars	1	24	24

Exhibit 8-1 continued

Functional Category	Room Designation	Criteria for Space Assignment	No. of Rooms	Unit Space (NSF)	Room Totals	Suite or Department Totals
General and Special Operating Rooms	41. Operating Room dedicated to Cardiac Surgery	ICHD report of the cardiac surgery panel recommends optimum size of 22' × 26'	1	572	572	
	42. Operating Room dedicated to Neurosurgery	Dimensions of 22' × 26' specified by chief of neurosurgery	1	572	572	
	43. Operating Room dedicated to Orthopedic Surgery	Dimensions of 22' × 26' specified by chief of orthopedic surgery	1	572	572	
	44. Operating Room, optional use, to serve as back-up for Cardiac Surgery	Same as for dedicated cardiac surgery room (see Item 41); dimensions of 22' × 26'	1	572	572	
	45. Operating Room dedicated to Neurosurgery	Decision of surgical staff to size at 400 NSF rather than required minimum of 360 NSF; dimensions of 20' × 20'	1	400	400	
	46. Operating Room dedicated to Orthopedic Surgery	Decision of surgical staff to size at 400 NSF rather than required minimum of 360 NSF; dimensions of 20' × 40'	1	400	400	
	47. Operating Room dedicated to Ophthalmologic Surgery	Decision of surgical staff to size at 400 NSF rather than required minimum of 360 NSF; dimensions of 20' × 20'	1	400	400	
	48. Operating Room dedicated to ENT Surgery	Decision of surgical staff to size at 400 NSF rather than required minimum of 360 NSF; dimensions of 20' × 20'	1	400	400	
	49. Operating Room, General Surgery	Decision of surgical staff to size at 400 NSF rather than required minimum of 360 NSF; dimensions of 20' × 20'	5	400	2000	

Rooms To Accommodate Support Functions for Operating Rooms (Supply and Other Functions)

No.	Room	Specifications	Count	NSF	Total
50.	X-ray Control Booths	Equipment manufacturers' specifications	8	20	160
51.	Clean Supply and Equipment Room serving the Cardiac Surgery and Optional-Use Operating Rooms	Space to house three extracorporeal pumps, each 3' × 5'; oxygenators; cardiotomy reservoirs; shelving for packs; three mobile carts, each 18" × 30"; and drug prep area with shelving, rubber-lined sink, and refrigerator	1	260	260
52.	Equipment Cleaning and Maintenance Room serving the Cardiac Surgery and Optional-Use Operating Rooms	3' × 16' shelving for tubing; 5' × 2' work counter with double sinks; desk, 30" × 60"; file cabinet, 15" × 24"; and free floor work area of 40 NSF	1	140	140
53.	Blood Gas Laboratory, not included in Operating Room Program; use Laboratory in adjoining ICU				
54.	Scrub Areas, each serving two Operating Rooms (nine sized at 400 NSF and neurosurgery room at 572 NSF)	Located between every two operating rooms; space for four knee-operated scrub sinks, each 22" × 28", and four persons scrubbing simultaneously; recommend 8' × 10' (see attached diagram for typical layout [not provided])	5	80	400
55.	Scrub Areas serving rooms dedicated to Cardiac Surgery, Orthopedic Surgery, and Optional Use (all sized at 572 NSF)	Located in alcove adjoining room door on clean corridor side; space for three knee-operated scrub sinks, each 22" × 28", and three persons scrubbing simultaneously; recommend 5' × 10'	3	50	150

Exhibit 8-1 continued

Functional Category	Room Designation	Criteria for Space Assignment	No. of Rooms	Unit Space (NSF)	Room Totals	Suite or Department Totals
Rooms To Accommodate Support Functions for Operating Rooms (continued)	56. Orthopedic Supply Storage Room	Located adjacent to dedicated orthopedic rooms on clean corridor side; stores splints, plaster, pins, special attachments, and tables; recommend 8' × 10'	1	80	80	
	57. Substerile Rooms, each serving two Operating Rooms (nine sized at 400 NSF and neurosurgery room at 572 NSF)	Located between every two operating rooms, back to back with scrub areas; space for flash sterilizer, 16" × 16" × 76"; warming cabinet, 24" × 20" × 74"; standing-height work counter, 24" × 48", with 12" × 12" sink; recommend 6' × 10' (see attached diagram for typical layout [not provided])	5	60	300	
	58. Soiled Holding Rooms, each serving two Operating Rooms (nine sized at 400 NSF and neurosurgery room at 572 NSF)	Located between every two operating rooms, back to back with substerile room; to contain flushing-rim sink, 22" × 25"; mop service basin, 24" × 24", space for storing six 24" × 25" and two 25" × 53" mobile carts; recommend 6' × 10'; opens to peripheral corridor only (see attached diagram for suggested layout [not provided])	5	60	300	
	59. Soiled Holding Room, serving Cardiac Surgery, Optional Use, and Largest Dedicated Orthopedic Operating Room	Located on peripheral corridor close to served rooms; to contain space for flushing-rim sink, 22" × 25"; mop service basin, 24" × 24", and space for eight 25" × 53" mobile carts; recommend 8' × 10' (see attached diagram for suggested layout [not provided])	1	80	80	

No.	Room	Description	Qty	NSF	NSF
	Rooms To Accommodate Support Functions for Operating Rooms (continued)				
60.	Film Processing Room, serving Dedicated Orthopedic and other Operating Rooms	Opens to clean corridor with pass box capability from both dedicated orthopedic rooms; equipment manufacturer recommends 60 NSF	1	60	60
61.	Storage Alcove, Mobile x-ray Unit	For holding one mobile x-ray unit, 27"×70"×78"	1	24	24
62.	Large Clean-Equipment Storage Room, serving all Operating Rooms	Opens to both clean and peripheral corridors; storage for various apparatus (e.g., hyper- or hypothermia units, accessories to tables, instrument stands and tables); may be two rooms, each at 250 NSF depending upon design	1	500	500
63.	Anesthesia Work Room	Space for a 30'×16' standing-height work counter with double-basin sink, cabinetry underneath, and wall-hung cabinetry above; refrigerator, 36"×42"; five mobile supply-storage carts, each 25"×51"; ten anesthetic machines, each 30"×36"; ten anesthetists' stands, each 15"×15"; working and circulation space for four persons	1	400	400
64.	Gas Storage Room, serving Anesthesia Work Room	For storage of flammable gases and liquids; vented to outside; opens to anesthesia work room; recommend 30 NSF	1	30	30
65.	Special Instrument Processing Room (for processing fragile instruments and equipment and doctor-owned equipment)	Two sections: soiled section opens to peripheral corridor, clean section opens to clean corridor; soiled section to contain triple-basin sink mounted in 30"×10' stainless steel counter; mobile sonic cleaner, 24"×30'; space for four supply carts, each 25"×53" (see attached diagram for layout [not provided])	1	300	300

Exhibit 8–1 continued

Functional Category	Room Designation	Criteria for Space Assignment	No. of Rooms	Unit Space (NSF)	Room Totals	Suite or Department Totals
	66. Secured Supply Storage Room	Contained in clean-supply core; for access of supervisory nursing personnel only: for highly valuable supplies; suggest 60 NSF	1	60	60	
	67. Clean Supply Core, serving all rooms (sometimes called "center staff corridor")	Minimum width of 14 ft. at any point; to remain inviolate to patient and soiled traffic of all types; provides circulation for all clean staff and supplies to all operating rooms; storage of all case carts and back-up supply carts, access for all clean supplies delivered from supply center via automatic lift device; estimate 3,000 NSF in addition to secured storage room (see conceptual diagram attached as to alternate corridor arrangements of entire suite [not provided])	1	3000	3000	
Postoperative Recovery	68. Open Bay Patient Area	For post-anesthesia recovery of maximum of 22 surgical patients on stretchers 36″ × 86″; provide head-to-wall orientation of stretchers, with gases, suction, emergency call, and blood pressure cuff wall-mounted for each patient; IV track in ceiling; provide 14-in. shelf along head wall 30-in. high as continuous work counter; minimum of 3½ ft. between stretchers and 8-ft. aisle. Total area to be 24′ × 86′, or 2,064 NSF less 200 NSF for nurse charting and work area	1	1864	1864	

No.	Space	Description	Qty	NSF	Total
69.	Isolation Recovery Rooms	Isolation rooms for recovering infectious patients: provide for in-and-out patient flow independent of main recovery room, nurse access from Recovery Room, and vision from Recovery Room; allow 120 NSF of clear bed space, to contain wrist-blade-controlled lavatory in standing-height work counter, 24″ × 48″	2	135	270
70.	Nurse Charting and Work Area	Space for charting, forms execution, and communications, centrally located to open area: provide 20 linear feet of 24-in. wide sit-down counter, pullout drawers underneath; two 4-drawer file cabinets, 15″ × 24″; and six straight chairs, each 17″ × 19″; space for pneumatic tube station	1	200	200
71.	Medications Preparation Alcove	Space for three nurses preparing medications at self-contained medicine work station, 20′D × 60″W × 80″H; recommend 60 NSF	1	60	60
72.	Clean Supply Room	For storing clean supplies used in recovery: space for two supply carts, each 25″ × 53″; two linen carts, 25″ × 50″; one wrist-blade-controlled lavatory; and miscellaneous clean items of equipment (e.g., heat lamps)	1	140	140

Exhibit 8-1 continued

Functional Category	Room Designation	Criteria for Space Assignment	No. of Rooms	Unit Space (NSF)	Room Totals	Suite or Department Totals
Postoperative Recovery (continued)	73. Soiled Supply Room	For temporary holding of soiled supplies awaiting pick-up by decontamination personnel: allow for pick-up flow from corridor side only; space for flushing rim clinical sink, 22″ × 25″; mop service basin, 24″ × 24″; three wire carts for soiled pick-up, each 25″W × 50″L × 58″H, and miscellaneous janitor equipment; wall-mounted shelves, 12″ × 8′	1	100	100	
	74. Utility Room, Soiled, serving Isolation Rooms	Provide for direct access from isolation rooms; to contain flushing rim sink, 22″ × 25″, and counter, 24″ × 50″, with 18″ × 18″ s/s washbasin	1	30	30	
	75. Nurses' Lounge and Toilet	Provide one water closet and lavatory, plus lounge space for three	1	80	80	
	76. Patient Toilet (for outpatients)	Design for handicapped; to contain one water closet, 24″ × 36″, and one lavatory, 12 NSF	1	50	50	
Consultant's Monitoring	77. Physiologic Monitoring Room, serving all Operating Rooms	Locate at periphery of surgical suite; to contain physiological data read-out devices and CCTV monitor; table and straight chairs to accommodate four consultants simultaneously	1	200	200	
						21,328

named and described in terms of their functions in the functional program. In this example, the surgical suite is part of "Diagnostic and Treatment Services" and is the same suite for which workloads were forecasted and numbers of operating rooms calculated in Chapter 7.[3]

In specifying the criteria for space assignment (the third column in Exhibit 8–1), wording should be brief but sufficiently detailed to designate functions, equipment that may have a bearing on the space assignment, and numbers of hospital users involved in the function, if those numbers affect the space assignment.

Many functional planners set forth no criteria for space assignments in the formulation of net space programs, or if they do, they provide statements so brief as to be nearly meaningless. After engaging in space programming for nearly 15 years, we believe that its quality is improved with increased comprehension by hospital officials of the rationale utilized in the entire effort. Therefore, our best judgment is that the criteria for space assignments should be described briefly but in sufficient detail that hospital officials can understand why the specific assignment was made.

It should be remembered that the purpose of a space program is not to provide determinants for numbers or types of spaces. Such information appropriately belongs in the functional program and is only summarily noted in the space program. The function of the space program is to formulate net space assignments to predetermined individual rooms and then to accumulate totals by department and service.

In pursuing any space program, there will be hospital officials who disagree with some of its provisions. Most commonly, those with strong departmental orientations find that their space assignments are undersized or that rooms they believe should be included have been omitted from respective departmental groupings. Suffice it to say that no hospital can be all things to all people. If every department were to be configured and sized according to ideals described in various publications, gross square footages undoubtedly would be so great as to be totally impractical. Thus, in functional programming and subsequently in space programming, not only do departmental priorities have to be weighed, but the effects of various departmental provisions upon the financial feasibility of the hospital as a whole must be carefully considered.

Space program summary

On completion of the programming of net spaces, the functional planner should provide a summary of this work. Again, in order to lend best understanding, we provide a summary for an actual hospital,[4] presented in Exhibit 8–2. This example shows net square feet (NSF) and departmental gross square feet (DGSF) for each major service area. The example institution—a complete replacement hospital, opened in 1984, at a new site—was programmed for 309 beds, an average patient stay of 7.3 days, and approximately 13,000 admissions annually. The "Diagnostic and Treatment Services" includes both a Level 2 obstetrical department and a surgical suite containing provisions for open heart work. (We point out specifically, however, that this hospital is not the same as that used for

Exhibit 8–2

Space program summary

Service no.	Service	NSF	DGSF
1.0	Administrative Services	20,653	26,331
2.0	Diagnostic and Treatment Services	50,758	78,808
3.0	Supporting Services	42,279	52,898
4.0	Auxiliary Services	3,580	10,454*
5.0	Nursing Services	82,436	139,456†
	Total	199,706	307,947

Notes:

1. Excluding 6,000 GSF in the power plant (a building gross figure, rather than departmental gross), the departmental net-to-gross ratio is 66 percent ($199,706 \div 307,947 = 0.66$).

2. Building gross square feet (BGSF)—interdepartmental corridors, central elevators and penthouse, exit stairways, central HVAC equipment, central electrical service, and all other gross space not assigned to departments—should approximate 10 percent of total space. Thus, 90 percent of $x = 307,947$.

   $x = 335,497$ GSF for total hospital

   335,497 GSF for hospital − 307,947 DGSF = 33,550 BGSF

3. The hospital net-to-gross ratio should be 60 percent (199,706 NSF ÷ 335,497 GSF = 0.595 or 0.60).

*Gross figure includes power plant (6,000 GSF).

†This figure includes the Special Services suite, which is not included under Diagnostic and Treatment Services.

the detailed listing of operating suite spaces.) There were no provisions for separate pediatric and psychiatric services—an HSA dictate. In the final stages of planning, obstetrics was deleted as a service owing to interhospital negotiations, and the opened facility contains only 289 beds, with vertical expansion potential to approximately 390 beds. We have not shown, in the example, the deletion of the obstetrical service.

This hospital features four major concepts, all of which appreciably alter the character of a space program when contrasted with that for a traditional hospital:

1. a centralized supply processing and distribution center that serves the entire hospital

2. a ready-foods dietary system, providing on-site preparation and freezing of foods, with "end-heating" of trays in microwave units on the patient floors

3. patient-oriented nursing units, characterized by the omission of nursing stations

4. a triple-corridored operating suite to achieve the case-cart method of providing supplies and instruments for most operations.

We have grouped the various departments and functional entities under five major services: Administrative, Diagnostic and Treatment, Supporting, Nursing, and Auxiliary. No individual rule governs the grouping of departments or functional entities by service, however. For example, the main lobby could reasonably be designated as supporting space rather than administrative space. Recognizing this fact, functional planners can, and do, arrange functional programs and, subsequently, space programs in various ways without appreciable effect upon the validity and success of the total program. Although no system of grouping can resolve all conflicting opinions about where a given service should be placed, it is far better to provide some groupings than to set forth, for example, a single alphabetical listing. Generally, the example groupings do have some affinities among their respective services with regard to purpose, location, and net-to-gross conversion factors. As a consequence of all these factors, we believe that ease of comprehension of both the functional program and the space program is facilitated by groupings closely similar to those we adopted for this hospital.

Owing to increasing space requirements for building gross square feet (BGSF) related to more sophisticated equipment and a trend toward higher proportions of space allocated to departments with high net-to-gross conversion factors, hospital net-to-gross ratios have been decreasing. In effect, it is now somewhat difficult to achieve a 60 percent figure in many efficiently designed facilities. In our example, however, the A&E firm was able to achieve a 60 percent ratio, and we regard it as a highly efficient design.

We stress that the net-to-gross ratio as calculated at this point is merely a prediction of what the A&E firm should be able to achieve in design. The design itself is the only true measure of a net-to-gross ratio. For example, a poor design might easily turn the net space program as is shown into a building of 360,000 GSF or more, and implications of this fact are fully discussed in Chapter 14.

If, indeed, a design for the example space program were to produce a building of 360,000 GSF, a net-to-gross ratio of 55.5 percent would be obtained. Since a net-to-gross ratio of 60 percent is achievable under ordinary circumstances, the designer should return to the drawing board to eliminate about 30,000 GSF; this reduction, at $100 per square foot in today's market, would result in a savings of $3,000,000.

Example conversion of departmental net space to gross space

As we have stated previously, the architect most commonly performs the conversion of net spaces to gross spaces, and if the responsibility has been so fixed, the functional planner relies upon the architect's expertise in this work. In some instances the architect, especially when inexperienced in hospital construction, will rely quite heavily upon the functional planner for guidance.

Regardless of who performs the conversion of net spaces to gross space, the entire work should then be submitted to hospital officials. Judgments should be made within the context of total information regarding the space programs. If officials make decisions either to reduce the program or to add to it, they should do so through consideration of all its aspects.

We have elected here to show how the departmental net spaces for our example institution were converted to departmental gross spaces. Exhibit 8–3 provides this information.[5]

Other net-to-gross conversion methodologies

The methodology and various conversion factors presented in this chapter have been empirically developed, from drawings of capable architects and engineers throughout the world, and we regard the procedure as being sound. Many planners and architects use a similar approach to the task. Others, however, employ approaches unique to their respective experiences.

In the early 1970s, we worked with a noted architectural firm in Canada[6] that used the following approach: First, a small percentage (usually 5 to 10 percent) for minor internal corridors and wall thicknesses was added to the departmental net square footage assignment. Then, to the totals as accumulated for services (e.g., administrative, diagnostic and treatment, supporting) an additional percentage—ranging from 20 to 30 percent—was added for interdepartmental corridors, vertical elements, HVAC spaces, and exterior walls. The methodology proved to be sound, for when totals were accumulated, a reasonable net-to-gross ratio was obtained.

Some planners and architects use the easy approach of making a conversion based simply on the total net square footage figure accumulated upon conclusion of net space programming. (Had we employed such a methodology in producing the gross area of 335,497 square feet for our example institution, we would have multiplied the net area of 199,706 square feet by 1.68.) We do not believe that such a simplistic approach should be pursued. By contrast, the conversion by department or functional entity allows comparison of the designer's space allocations in block diagramming (the prelude to schematic drawings) for each area with the converted figure as obtained. If the gross space design allocations for departments and the space program gross square footage allocation do not closely match, the designer should be forewarned about the difficulty to be encountered in providing the required net spaces within the gross space design allocations when schematic drawings are undertaken. Adjustments had thus best be made immediately.

Exhibit 8–3

Conversion of departmental net space allocations to gross space

Service	Item no.	Department or functional entity	NSF	Conversion factor	DGSF
Administrative	1.1	Main Lobby	1,973	1.25	2,466
	1.2	Communications Center (Switchboard)	475	1.25	594
	1.3	Gift Shop	800	1.25	1,000
	1.4	Admitting Suite	765	1.33	1,017
	1.5	Physicians' Entrance and Lounge	500	1.25	625
	1.6	Management Suite	2,440	1.33	3,245
	1.7	Nursing Administration	1,060	1.33	1,410
	1.8	Medical Records	3,180	1.25	3,975
	1.9	Personnel Administration	1,020	1.25	1,275
	1.10	Security	345	1.25	431
	1.11	Medical and General Library	1,440	1.25	1,800
	1.12	Social Work Department	500	1.33	665
	1.13	Acounting and Business Office (excludes Mailroom)	4,485	1.25	5,606
	1.14	Data Processing	750	1.33	998
	1.15	Central Purchasing	520	1.33	692
	1.16	Public Relations	400	1.33	532
		Total	20,653		26,331
Diagnostic and Treatment	2.1	Emergency–Ambulatory Care Center	4,384	1.5	6,576
	2.2	Diagnostic Radiology, Nuclear Medicine, and Ultrasound	11,979	1.5	17,969
	2.3	Surgical Operating Suite and Cystoscopic Rooms	14,309	1.75	25,041
	2.4	Clinical Laboratory	10,619	1.33	14,123
	2.5	Morgue and Autopsy	665	1.33	884
	2.6	Delivery and Labor Progress Suite	4,045	1.75	7,079
	2.7	Rehabilitation Medicine	3,667	1.5	5,501
	2.8	Gastroenterology and Endoscopic Suite	1,090	1.5	1,635
	2.9	Special Services: EEG, EMG, Critical Care Monitoring, Noninvasive Diagnostic Cardiology, Respiratory Therapy, Pulmonary Functions, Cardiac Rehabilitation	4,735*	1.5	7,103*
		Total	50,758		78,808

Exhibit 8-3 continued

Service	Item no.	Department or functional entity	NSF	Conversion factor	DGSF
Supporting	3.1	Supply Processing and Distribution Center	13,425	1.25	16,781
	3.2	Print Shop	440	1.25	550
	3.3	Pharmacy	1,995	1.25	2,494
	3.4	Volunteers' Suite	440	1.33	585
	3.5	Housekeeping Suite	800	1.25	1,000
	3.6	Maintenance and Engineering	3,940	1.25	4,925
	3.7	Food Service (Dietary)	11,380	1.25	14,225
	3.8	Central Archives	800	1.25	1,000
	3.9	Mail Room	120	1.25	150
	3.10	Laundry	3,720	1.25	4,650
	3.11	Personnel Facilities (central lockers, lounges, time clocks, etc.)	960	1.25	1,200
	3.12	Learning Resources Center	4,079	1.25	5,099
	3.13	Employee Health Unit	180	1.33	239
		Total	42,279		52,898
Auxiliary	4.1	Central On-call Facility for Residents and Full-time Staff	740	1.33	984
	4.2	Snack Vending Area	960	1.25	1,200
	4.3	Pastoral Care and Chaplain	480	1.25	600
	4.4	Helipad		—	
	4.5	Power plant (net figure shown is for work space only; total figure assumes entire boiler plant)	320	—	6,320†
	4.6	Grounds Maintenance and Equipment Storage	600	1.25	750
	4.7	Clean and Soiled Supply Rooms	480	1.25	600
		Total	3,580		10,454
Nursing		*Chassis*			
	5.1	Surgical Intensive Care	3,270	1.7	5,559
		1st Bed Level			
	5.2	Cardiac Care Unit (CCU) and Medical Intensive Care Unit (MICU)	3,830	1.7	6,511

		NSF		GSF
5.3	Noninvasive Cardiology and Special Services	4,735		7,364††
5.4	Coronary Care Step-down Unit (21 beds)	4,527	1.7	7,696
5.5	Medical-Surgical Patient Unit (20 beds)	4,332	1.7	7,364
	Management and Nursing Administration (accounted for under Administrative Services)			
5.6	Core spaces	2,045	1.7	3,477
	2nd Bed Level			
5.7	Orthopedic Unit (21 beds)	4,527	1.7	7,696
5.8	Medical-Surgical Unit (Intermediate Surgical) (20 beds)	4,332	1.7	7,364
5.9	Medical-Surgical Unit (21 beds)	4,527	1.7	7,696
5.10	Obstetrical Unit (20 beds)	4,332	1.7	7,364
5.11	Nurseries	1,628	1.7	2,768
5.12	Core spaces	1,965	1.7	3,341
	3d Bed Level			
5.13	All spaces	19,193	1.7	32,628
	4th Bed Level			
5.14	All spaces	19,193	1.7	32,628
	Total	82,436		139,456
	Totals for all spaces:	199,706		307,947

*Not included in total. Service will be located on lowest bed level.

†6,000 GSF for boiler plant not to be included in total DGSF for hospital.

††4,735 NSF is presumed to be placed in 7,364 GSF—the gross space contained in a normal 20-bed team zone.

Summary

Space programming stands as a step of critical importance in predesign planning work. Experienced functional planners are usually charged with the formulation of a net space program, and architects either convert the net space figures to gross space or advise the functional planners in this conversion.

The creation of a net space program occurs by assigning square footage figures to numbers and types of rooms to be included in respective departments, based on justifications established in the functional program document. Space assignments are based on a number of factors, the most important of which are related directly to optimal functional use. Others include budget considerations, owner dictates, state regulations, and the restrictions of existing building confines.

In addition to providing direction for design, both net and gross space programs give management a distinct control over the cost and character of the building project.

A carefully prepared functional program and a space program, as companion documents, allow management to settle many important aspects of a project without the trial-and-error process oftentimes encountered in design. Accordingly, project expenses are usually far less.

Notes

1. E. Todd Wheeler, *Hospital Design and Function* (New York: McGraw-Hill, 1964), pp. 23, 155, 201, 206.
2. *Guidelines for Construction and Equipment of Hospital and Medical Facilities.* Department of Health and Human Services Pub. No. (HRS-M-HF) 1984-1A (Rockville, MD: DHHS Office of Health Facilities, 1984).
3. Based on Owen B. Hardy's work for an Ernst & Whinney project.
4. Ibid.
5. Ibid.
6. The firm was Bregman & Hamann, Architects, Engineers, Planners, in Toronto, Canada.

9

The Planning and Design Process

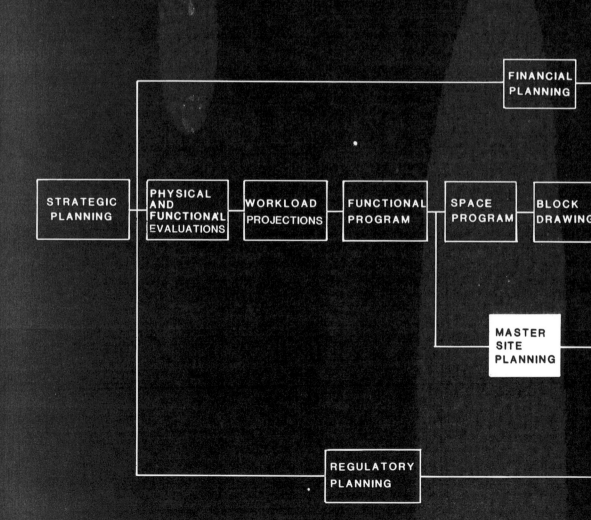

Master site planning: a long-range perspective

```
                    ┌─────────────────┐
        ┌ ─ ─ ─ ─ ─ ┤ PHASED          ├ ─ ─ ─ ─ ─ ─ ─ ┐
        ╎           │ CONSTRUCTION    │               ╎
        ╎           └─────────────────┘               ╎
        ╎                                             ╎
        ╎                                             ╎
```

| SCHEMATIC DRAWINGS | DESIGN DEVELOPMENT | CONSTRUCTION DOCUMENTS AND BIDDING | CONSTRUCTION | FACILITIES OPENING |

MOVABLE EQUIPMENT AND INTERIORS PLANNING

Past, present, and future

The physical facilities of most hospitals on this continent have been constructed with a life expectancy in excess of 40 years. Many structures 60 years old are still being utilized, and a few constructed prior to the turn of the century continue in operation. However, use of most older buildings has been at great cost, from both capital and operational standpoints, because hospital planners, historically, have been short-sighted. North America is replete with examples of hospitals possessing boxed-in departments; outer walls set to property lines or roadways, thus precluding design freedom in expansion; and electrical, mechanical, and structural systems that cannot be expanded or economically altered. Not only have structures been designed with a short-range perspective, but in many instances, site selection and other components of master site planning have been carried out with little attention to what the future may hold and with less than optimal regard for the best interests of future users.

It is probably true that the untrained human mind has great difficulty in perceiving the required scope of site and facility planning. However, because today's building requirements literally dictate structures that will be capable of physically supporting health care functions for more than 40 years into the future, it is obligatory for planners to look beyond normal program planning for a 10-year period; certainly, it is unreasonable to hold that the first 10 years of a 40-year period will be more important than the remaining 30. Although those who follow must assume complete responsibility for their own actions, health care planners should realize that for any proposed construction, the commitments involved will extend over many years and, for better or worse, will affect the lives of vast multitudes in future generations. To fulfill the responsibility owed by every generation to succeeding ones, site planning should account not only for the expansion of structures and proper parking and traffic flows but for siting of replacement structures. Too often, hospitals have been forced to relocate for the sole reason that insufficient building space was available for replacing obsolete structures.

In looking to the future, it seems unlikely that coming years will be any less dynamic than have been the past two decades. Technology will continue to advance, and patterns of health care delivery will change in response to a number of factors, not the least of which will be legislative enactments and the competitive forces of the marketplace. Thus it behooves planners and management to look beyond immediate project needs and to plan definitively for future phases that can be validly forecasted. Provisions for flexibility of site use and expansibility of structures should be incorporated into all site planning to a feasible degree.

Master site planning defined

Master site planning has been defined in various ways, even by those whose professional orientation is in landscape architecture, urban planning, or civil engineering. Most authorities agree, however, on the basic activities encompassed—that is, site selection, analysis, and the development of drawings visually portraying buildings and uses of all parts of the site. However, most definitions have two major deficiencies: (1) failure to stipulate that site planning should extend well beyond initially envisioned construction and (2) failure to recognize that the functional character and configuration of specific buildings govern site planning to a great extent. It is true that adjustments can be made in building design in consideration of site characteristics, but it is equally true that a functional hospital design, for example, cannot always fully accommodate adjustments to site characteristics, and in fact, there are many sites for which complete adjustment would prohibit building functionality to the extent that the sites should not be used.

Accordingly, we have formulated a broader and more specific definition addressing these concerns. In our definition, master site planning for a hospital has four components:

1. the rational selection of a site to accommodate in a functional manner all construction envisioned for a 15- to 20-year future period

2. the evaluation of a selected site in terms of topography, drainage, adequacy of utilities, soil conditions, design grading, required fill dirt, natural features, aesthetics, restrictions, easements, existing structures, and environmental impact of necessary site work

3. presentation in visual form (block plan drawings) of the phased design of the site to reflect vehicular and pedestrian traffic flows, parking, building configuration and placement, and organization and character of green space, as well as other landscape details

4. preparation of construction documents to contract for site work required under the proposed project.

Site selection

A systematic and objective methodology should be utilized in site selection to ascertain the desirability of a site for hospital usage from many standpoints, including those related to building expansibility and plant regeneration. The professional knowledge required in site selection pertains to architecture, engineering, and hospital planning. The process involved requires careful accounting for each of the nonfinancial attributes, as well as analysis of site acquisition costs.

The most valid methodology in this regard was recently published by the American Hospital Association.[1] This methodology, devised by James Lifton and Owen B. Hardy, essentially describes a cost-benefit analysis, quantified in such a manner that two or more sites can be compared in terms of both quality and costs. Quality is reflected through various site attributes that very definitely affect use of the site for location and operation of a hospital. The assignment of values to these attributes is accomplished subjectively to a great extent, but when analysis is done by knowledgeable senior consultants, the validity of results can be assured. Costs include acquisition cost of an acreage determined to be large enough to accommodate the hospital and its projected growth over a period of time, supplemented by the cost of multilevel parking, if required, and all other costs necessary to bring the site to a condition of "ready to build."

Site quality

Nonfinancial factors reflecting site quality include the following:[2]

1. proximity of the site to patients in a properly identified service area

2. site size and usable acreage

3. major road access

4. proximity to medical staff offices

5. site configuration and orientation

6. proximity to other hospitals and health care delivery facilities or organizations

7. easements and restrictions

8. direct access

9. zoning

10. accessibility to public transportation

11. proximity to medical staff residences

12. amenities, such as views, noise levels, and environmental air quality (e.g., industry-generated odors)

13. proximity to personnel

14. environmental impact on surrounding areas

15. availability of fire and police protection.

It can be seen that if aspects of several of the factors noted are sufficiently negative or detrimental a site could be arbitrarily disqualified without further consideration; the methodology outlined gives account to this fact.

Through a process of factor analysis, each site is scored in terms of a range of points assigned to each of the nonfinancial factors. The total number of points for each site considered is used in ranking the sites and in relating the individual scores to "ready-to-build" costs at respective sites.

This methodology can be used not only for the siting of hospitals but for a number of other related health care delivery facilities and, notably, primary care facilities.[3]

Site relationship to service area and site size
Although all of the factors as outlined in the described methodology are obviously important, we believe that two deserve some emphasis. These are (1) the relationship of the site to patients within an identified area in terms of travel time thereto and (2) site size.

Existing densities of population within a service area should be determined, and densities over a 15- to 20-year period should be projected. Travel time from centers of high population density in the primary service area should be checked, plus travel time to outer fringes of that service area.

Generally speaking, a hospital that has a role of providing emergency care, other elements of primary care, and secondary care should be located so as to occasion a travel time of no more than 25 minutes for all persons residing in its primary service area. Within the primary area, it should be located closest to the bulk of the population served.

Certainly, it is important to consider the location of other hospitals in the area. Overlapping of primary service areas should be avoided when possible, and a location should be selected that does not provide a great amount of unnecessary "double coverage" of either primary or secondary care. However, in a few unique instances, proposed facilities of less than full service coverage may actually be complemented by existing facilities.

Although examples of wrong locations of hospitals in relationship to patients are evidenced throughout the continent, certainly the mistake most frequently seen pertains to site size. Too often in the past a group of well-meaning citizens has procured a site half as large as is desirable and has committed the community to building a hospital thereon, with the assurance of serious economic and functional restraints in future years. Proper planning should dictate that determinations be made as to the number of acres needed for the development of all structures to be located on the site, both initially and ultimately, as well as for ample parking, circulation, and suitable landscaping. If the number of acres ultimately needed cannot be obtained initially, there ought to be some assurance that acquisition can be accomplished when desired.

The reasoning described preceding applies not only to new hospital constructions (located where a hospital has not previously existed), but to replacement hospitals as well. In some instances, the size of an existing site may be and should be a prime factor in making a decision to rebuild and relocate. Many inadequate urban sites can now be sold for commercial purposes at a handsome price; funds so obtained can then be applied to the cost of an optimally sized site.

Many so-called authorities in the past have stipulated that for a certain-size hospital a specific number of acres is required, and figures have been quoted in the range of 25 to 75 acres. We are convinced that such "thumb rules" are totally invalid owing to the host of factors involved in specific situations. For example, in a fairly dense urban area, a rational analysis will reveal that it is better to design buildings to cover minimum site, while still retaining functionality, and to provide multi-level parking, rather than to consume a vast expanse of space with on-grade parking. In surburban or rural areas, it is usually better to provide at least a horizontally oriented grouping of diagnostic treatment services, and some designs can afford an offset bed tower, located on grade. Thus, the required acreage can vary quite widely, and the appropriate site size can be determined only after analysis.

Comparative site costs

Comparison of costs related to prospective sites has oftentimes been based simply upon acquisition cost. In some instances, after selecting a site and obtaining an option to purchase, or after actual purchase, hospital officials have discovered that one or more of the other costs in bringing the site to a "ready-to-build" state brings the total to a sum far above that for a rejected site that had a higher price tag for acquisition. Such situations can be avoided by appropriate prior investigation of all site-related costs that will be encountered in constructing the envisioned hospital.

Costs that should be given careful account in site selection can be subsumed under either (1) site acquisition or (2) site preparation. *Acquisition costs* include a base purchase price for a primary parcel, plus the cost of options for other parcels and the cost of additional parcels themselves. Acquisition-related costs, such as expenditures to vacate leases, must be given account. Conversely, proceeds from the sale of excess site parts must be subtracted from a purchase price.

Preparation costs typically include expenditure for demolition of existing structures; grading and fill; drainage systems and protection against ground water; unusual footings and foundations; ready-to-use utilities (sewer, electricity, water, and gas); and miscellaneous, such as shared costs for improving access roads.[4]

Obviously, the costs as enumerated cannot be determined by mere visual inspection of the site. Only competent professionals can perform the investigations required, and most A&E firms possess the required capabilities.

Weighing site quality and costs

After quantitatively scoring each site under consideration with reference to site quality (nonfinancial factors) and accumulating costs as outlined, a rational decision can be made regarding the selection of a single site. For evaluation, there will be, on the one hand, a total point-scoring for each site, related to nonfinancial attributes; on the other, there will be respective figures of total costs that are site-related. Direct, factual, and logical comparisons can then be made in order to choose the best site. In this manner, the effects of bias, intuitive opinions, and personal interests are held to a minimum, and the responsibility owed by every hospital governing board to the community it serves is then properly discharged.

Site evaluation

Site evaluation occurs both in the site selection process, as outlined herein, and also after ownership of a selected site has been vested in the hospital. In most instances, detailed site evaluation from primarily a physical standpoint is performed when decisions have already been made to proceed with hospital construction, and expansions and replacements form the majority of these cases. Thus, if a decision has been made to construct on a selected site, evaluation of some of the nonfinancial factors important in actual site selection becomes unnecessary. Relationships to populations to be served, offices of medical staff members, and residences of personnel will have been definitively determined and will require no evaluation. As well, major road access, accessibility to public transportation, zoning, and surrounding neighborhoods are factors that will require little or no attention.

Site attributes that still have to be evaluated in terms of their effect on building design and location and site planning are direct site access; site size and configuration; easements; restrictions; views, noise levels, and air quality; prevailing winds; availability of fire protection; energy conservation; and environmental impact of the proposed construction upon the neighborhood.

Although costs must always be determined with regard to factors involved in evaluative processes, when evaluation is performed for a site already selected for construction, the primary objective is to determine the most feasible method for accomplishing necessary site work, rather than merely to determine costs (as outlined under Site Selection).

If an already selected site is being evaluated, acquisition cost no longer needs to be considered, but the adequacy of utilities—water, sewerage, electricity, and natural gas—remains as a prime factor for investigation. Soil analyses, test borings, and determinations related to site grading, needed fill dirt, drainage, and protection against ground water all have to be accomplished. As stated, rather than merely a cost determination, the evaluative process becomes one of how best to make necessary site provisions in terms of actual needs.

Physical factors

A detailed topographical map, usually scaled at 1 inch = 40 feet, is necessary in site evaluation work, and if such has not been prepared prior to the decision to build, a civil engineer must be employed to perform the necessary work. Substantive information shown on this map should include the following:

1. all natural features—streams, lakes, woods, swamps, rock features, and so forth

2. all manmade features—buildings, easements, storm drainage and sewerage, driveways, parking areas, ramps, walls, curbs, fire hydrants, water lines, electric lines, telephone lines, gas lines, poles and light standards

3. property lines and names of adjoining owners

4. basement and first-floor elevations of all buildings

5. contours, shown in intervals of no more than 5 feet

6. elevations, shown as a grid system with intervals of 50 feet.

The topographical map provides the basis for various analyses required to bring the site to a "ready-to-build" state and for site design, including drainage systems; grading, parking, traffic, circulation systems, and the provision of green space and other aesthetic features.[5]

In addition to the topographical map, soils of the site should be tested for later use by horticulturists. The water table must be checked in order to determine the treatment of basement areas. Test borings must be performed in order to determine requirements for footings.

With regard to test borings, it is well to observe that throughout the continent, radical differences in subsurface findings occur within very short distances. In sites in Canada, Georgia, and Illinois, for example, we have noted rock formations sufficient to support large multilevel buildings within 100 yards of apparently similar terrain where extensive pilings would have been required to support such structures. Thus, subsurface conditions may be completely unpredictable without appropriate analysis.

In many instances, the hospital-appointed A&E firm will perform analyses related to energy conservation, such as identification of vegetation and land forms, seasonal temperatures and direction of the sun rays, prevailing winds, and underground water. Building orientation, use of glass, underground construction, and feasible installation of heat pumps all have assumed great importance with the increased cost of energy sources.[6]

Environmental factors

In recent years, the environmental impact of any construction upon the life and habits of people in surrounding areas and upon values of adjoining properties must be taken into serious account. In fact, in planning any major hospital construction project, environmental impact statements must be prepared and filed with appropriate governmental agencies before proceeding with construction. It is well to hold meetings with adjacent property owners early in the planning process to gain an understanding of their thoughts about the envisioned construction and to correct any misconceptions, and also to ascertain any developments that they may be contemplating.

Presence of noisy roadways, airports, and racetracks and a variety of off-site nuisances that may affect site or building planning must be taken into account.

Zoning regulations, code regulations, and restrictions have to be analyzed to determine whether changes or waivers are indicated, or whether compliance will adversely affect normal operations, future growth, and strategic plan fulfillment.

In state and provincial capital areas, national capital areas, certain historic site locations, or other localities subject to covenants or other regulations, various provisions that affect architectural style and design may exist. These provisions must be ascertained from appropriate commissions to see whether they affect the type of buildings to be site-located or whether site design itself will be affected. Both Washington, D.C., and Ottawa, Canada, for example, have provisions that must be taken into definite account when hospital designs are prepared. Many newer municipalities also have architectural review boards or similar bodies from which approvals must be obtained.

Aesthetic factors

Site aesthetics are highly important and should be protected and enhanced to the extent possible. Natural features should be carefully evaluated and preserved if possible; views should be studied from the standpoints of building location, orientation, and configuration; green space and objects of beautification must be carefully planned to avoid objectionable, harsh, or uninteresting appearances.

Although functionality of both site and buildings is the quality that stands paramount in all hospital design, certainly functionality without aesthetics, and especially site aesthetics, would be a sterile goal. Careful study and treatment of aesthetic factors related to a site will assure a pleasing environment—which, it should be noted, can provide therapeutic relief for both patients and family members at times when needs are greatest.

Block plan drawings

Block plan drawings are sometimes omitted by the design architect. This is a mistake. Not only do block plans afford a simple means for testing internal building arrangement to secure best functionality, but they constitute the best design approach to testing various site schemes.

After completion of space programming, the functional planner should prepare a closeness matrix (discussed more fully in Chapter 10) for guidance of the A&E designer. With the matrix as a guide, the designer should then allocate the departmental gross areas to building levels and produce drawings that show interdepartmental corridors, elevators, and the properly related block departmental areas. No individual rooms need be delineated. Alternative designs can be produced in relatively short time for use in studying all interdepartmental traffic flows and relationships among departments. Usually, these drawings are executed in $\frac{1}{16}$-inch scale (1 inch = 16 feet) and then reduced to the scale of the site plan (typically, 1 inch = 40 feet) for use in its development.

Tentative building designs are tested against the site plan from the standpoints of expansion, traffic flows, building entrances, parking, views, energy conservation, and a number of others factors outlined later in the chapter under Preparing the Master Site Plan. Finally, the best design as it relates to internal functionality and integration into a total plan for the site is identified.

Even at this early stage of design, models are useful to demonstrate alternative plans for building forms and siting. There is one danger in modeling at this state: hospital officials may become engrossed with their preference for external aesthetics to the detriment of judging best internal functionality. It is probably wise that designs be evaluated from drawings only until selections are narrowed to no more than the best two or three designs. Then, models can be made without risk of aesthetics becoming the dominant factor in the selection process.

Preparing the master site plan

As block plan drawings are being developed, structuring a site plan and presenting it in a scaled drawing can proceed. Actual formulation of a site plan includes the following:

1. determining specific locations of buildings and parking areas

2. designing circulation systems, both pedestrian and vehicular

3. designing a drainage system, both surface and subsurface

4. developing a plan for site grading

5. integrating the site from the standpoint of total functionality

6. creating aesthetic appeal and enhancing functionality through proper planning of landscape details.

Of course, planning utilities must be undertaken in connection with formulation of the site plan, but such work also relates to the A&E's design of the building itself and is not discussed here.

Formulation of the site plan as it relates to construction will require various tasks to be carried out in initial phases. In performing these tasks, the site planner must keep clearly in mind flexibility of site use, planned or unplanned additions to structures, and the erection of additional buildings on the site at some future date.

In following sections we discuss each aspect of formulating the site plan.

Determining building locations

A thorough site evaluation will have revealed the various factors that are site-related and that will affect building location. Other than site factors, the unique nature of a hospital and the best operational functionality must be considered. Multistructure complexes present special problems: each building should have an appropriate functional relationship with others, and external access points and an intrasite circulation system must be considered.

In determining optimal building locations, the site planner should adhere to certain basic principles:

1. Each building on the site should be able to expand independently of every other building, to its maximum expected growth. Moreover, all site-planned buildings should be so placed that their maximum growth will not be impeded by property lines, easements, roadways, or other rights-of-way. Seemingly, such expansion regarding building locations would be self-evident, but there are literally hundreds of examples on this continent in which gross violations are apparent, and in which a correct placement would have been possible without additional cost. Buildings were simply site-located without thought of the future.

2. Site planning must consider relationships between proposed vehicle parking areas and building locations. Ideally, categorized parking areas should be related directly to building entrances assigned to specific categories of hospital users (e.g., visitors, physicians, emergency vehicles). It follows that building location should allow the location of parking so that appropriate relationships with respective building entrances can be established. This principle is given further elaboration in the following section.

3. Views for inpatients must be considered in determining building location.

4. A variety of site-related factors—such as noise levels, air quality, prevailing winds, easements, restrictions, site configuration, site access, topography, drainage, soil conditions, and vegetation and land forms—should be considered in determining building locations. To allow site-related factors to dictate building location, however, in disregard of possible effects upon building functionality and total site functionality, is a mistake.

5. Existing buildings on a site and their placement in relationship to site access points, as well as their future functional relationship to proposed buildings, will influence placement of proposed buildings. It should be kept in mind, however, that obsolescence of existing buildings diminishes their importance and future functional worth. Therefore, although it cannot be stated conclusively that the old should be adapted to the new, rather than vice versa, this principle must be considered when site locations of new buildings are considered. In many instances, a major building project should be considered the nucleus for regeneration of a new hospital, and building location should be considered from that standpoint.

6. The long-term future of the hospital, as outlined in a 15- to 20-year outlook derived from the strategic plan, should be reflected in facilities located on the site plan, whether or not they will be constructed as a part of the immediate project. To plan on the assumption that the project under way will be the "last" or the "only" construction is a mistake of the first order.

Figure 9–1 depicts a site plan for a typical community hospital, reflecting consideration of those principles just discussed that are amenable to graphical interpretation. Figure 9–2 is an example of long-range site planning showing phased development.

Designing circulation systems

There are seven basic categories of traffic entering and exiting the hospital site:

1. visitors

2. inpatients

3. outpatients

4. emergency vehicles

5. personnel and students in various health professions

6. physicians and medical students

7. supply and repair.

9–1

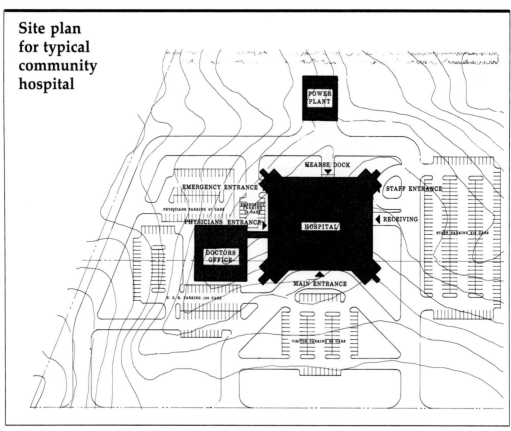

Site plan for typical community hospital

Examples of the phases of a long-range master site plan

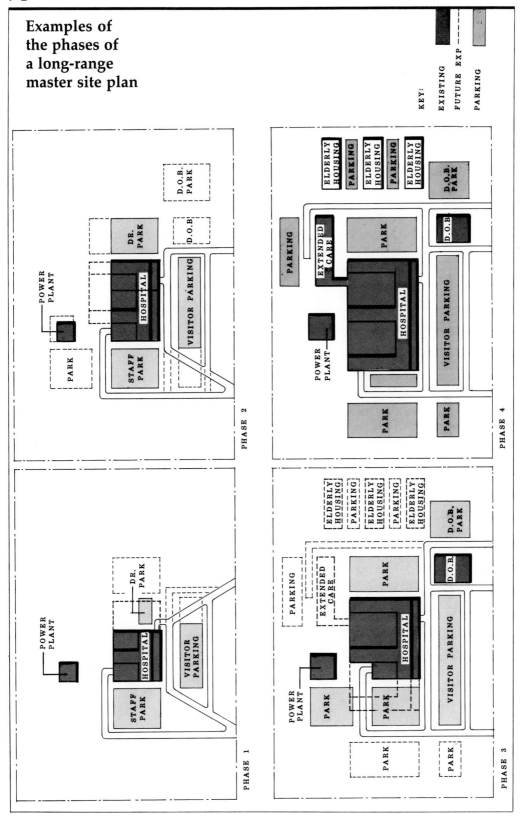

These flows should be separated and channeled to parking areas oriented directly to the entrances specified for use by each category. Particularly, emergency vehicles should not have to flow through or be deterred by other traffic; supply traffic should be separated from (and possibly circumvent) other traffic; and physicians should be assured easy and quick access to their exclusive parking lot. Depending upon the size of the hospital, site configuration, and numbers of persons expected to compose each category, there may be as few as four basic entrances or as many as seven for a single structure. In every instance, parking should be related directly to respective entrances.

The theory that people can "walk around the building" to get from parking to an entrance is based on false reasoning. Understandably, hospital visitors, personnel, and other users wish to come into the entrance nearest their assigned parking, and the site plan should so allow. If this is not done, unauthorized entry or the need for constant policing will be the result, both of which are undesirable.

Figures 9–3 and 9–4 conceptually illustrate solutions to the principles just discussed. Figure 9–5 shows one architect's solution for a specific project in Florida.

In some situations, highly restricted sites in urban areas force the design of a "grand entrance" for use by all building entrants, with the exception of supply and emergency traffic. Although this may represent the only and best solution, a "grand entrance" concept produces congestion and needlessly long internal traffic distances to destinations for some traffic categories. It also defeats traffic control and produces confusion in "finding the way" to destinations. Certainly, the grand entrance concept simplifies site planning, but it is detrimental to functionality.

External entrances determine, to some extent, internal design. Each building entrant has an ascertainable destination inside the building. As a

9–3

Bubble diagram
of parking
relationships

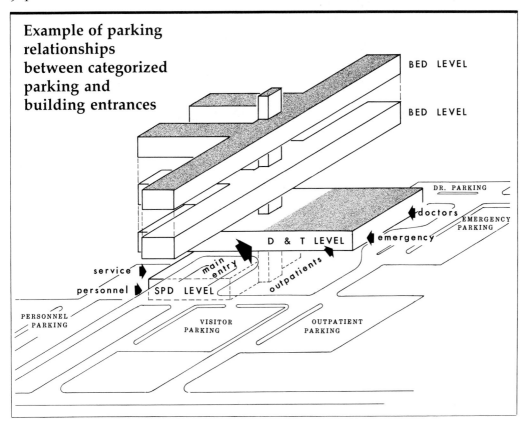

Example of parking relationships between categorized parking and building entrances

BED LEVEL

BED LEVEL

DR. PARKING

doctors

EMERGENCY PARKING

D & T LEVEL

emergency

service

main entry

outpatients

personnel

SPD LEVEL

PERSONNEL PARKING

VISITOR PARKING

OUTPATIENT PARKING

Aerial photograph showing hospital and related parking

Medical Center Hospital, Largo, Florida. Peter Marich, AIA, Architect.

general premise, *the mission of a person entering the building at a respective entrance should be anticipated and the route of travel required by that mission inside the building made as short and direct as possible.* Needed services should be immediately at hand once the building is entered. If this premise of functionality and efficiency is followed, geometry will preclude the "grand entrance" and will literally dictate four to seven basic outside entrances, as mentioned previously.

As a corollary, the location of external entrances will also govern location of related parking areas, as well as roadway linkages necessary for ingress and egress.

Superfluous multiple entrances defeat control and thus should not be allowed. We have noted as many as 25 entrances to a single structure. In such a situation, there is no possibility of rational internal or external traffic patterns, traffic control, or security.

Traffic occasioned by one category of traffic should not flow past the entrance provided for another. We have seen proposals for ambulance and hearse traffic to flow directly past the main entrance!

The number of parking spaces provided for each category of entrants must, at a minimum, conform to local ordinances. The architect, however, should be charged to perform a detailed study, quantifying the actual number needed on valid bases. In some instances, a study by a traffic engineering consultant may be indicated.

Future growth of the hospital will probably require expansion of parking. It is imperative that additional parking be given account on the site plan along with expansion of buildings.

The size of parking spaces should be checked, and 300 square feet per vehicle is regarded as a minimum. The width of driveways must also be checked for current and future adequacy.

Distances and routes from farthest parking spaces to respective entrances should be considered. The configuration of parking areas can often be changed to shorten these distances and mitigate circuitous routes.

In multiple building complexes, site traffic and parking should be separated and sorted in consideration of the entrants to each building. In other words, parking for each building must be considered separately. Also, in some complexes the circulation system must often be planned on the basis of primary and secondary vehicular arteries. *Primary arteries* serve multiple flows, and *secondary arteries* serve flows related to specific buildings.

Hospitals are somewhat distinct in that many site visitors are either sick or old, or both. Moreover, employees and physicians are often forced to respond to emergency situations, when time is vital. Thus, pedestrian ways had best be made short and direct.

Drainage systems

The design of a drainage system, consideration of factors related to energy conservation, determination of building location, planning a circulation system, and site grading must be considered as interrelated factors, each of which will influence the other. Among them, owing to the importance of building functionality and the overriding concern to locate buildings properly on the site, determination of building locations usually assumes a degree of precedence. However, in unique circumstances, one or more of the other factors may exert the dominant influence. If site-related factors force a planning solution that is unacceptable from a functional standpoint, the site should not be used.

Storm drainage. Storm drainage systems are needed to control surface runoff and must be designed so that the greatest intensity or duration of rainfall expected does not result in flooding of the hospital building or grounds. As a general rule, a storm drainage system should afford positive flow of water directly away from site buildings.

Subsurface drainage. Subsurface drainage systems are necessary in many areas owing to low soil permeability and the presence of a high water table in low areas. They must be used in some cases to prevent frost heaving. Understandably, a hospital site should be kept in a stable, flood-free, and bog-free condition at all times.

Developing a plan for site grading

Site grading is the means whereby the physical form of the site can be developed to accommodate building location, site drainage, and patterns of circulation; increase functionality of the site and allow best functionality of buildings; integrate the site into an operational whole; and enhance site aesthetics. Developing a grading plan involves a testing of tentative building locations and circulation arteries on a topographical map against tentative spot evaluations that will be used to create a drainage system, shown on the same map. Consideration of requirements from both standpoints will determine the grading plan.

In most instances, especially in the case of hospitals with a single, primary structure, it is advantageous to allow building entry at two levels. Thus all supply, personnel, and routine physician entrances can be located at the lowest level, with visitor, outpatient, inpatient, and emergency patient entrances located at the level above. This arrangement greatly reduces requirements for elevators and assists in creating a highly functional building and site plan as well. Because portions of the building are placed underground, energy is conserved. Site grading is usually required to afford the arrangement as described, although minimal work may be necessary where contours are accommodating.

Very definitely, site grading should be employed to afford best individual building functionality and functionality of the site as a whole. The cost of initial site grading is only a single factor in determining its extent; life cycle costs of site work weighed against benefits should constitute the approach in fixing budgets for site grading.

Topsoil should be stockpiled and conserved in rough grading for use in finished grading. This procedure will allow green space to be appropriately developed when the project is finished.

Site integration

Integrating the site from the standpoint of total functionality implies that site and building should operate as a system. The interplay of design considerations among those pertaining to buildings and to the site itself should yield an operating whole. Thus the site should not be designed separately and apart from buildings; rather, the two should be related one to the other in design.

Certainly, site design should not be exercised as an afterthought. The functionality of buildings directly depends upon site design—which, in reality, should be an extension of the building design.

We specifically indicate in Chapter 2 that master site planning (site selection or evaluation) may begin during functional programming. This opinion is based on our strong belief that the basic size and configuration of programmed buildings, as well as functions that are to take place therein, must be understood by the site planner before preliminary design work can be completed.

Planning landscape details

Landscape details are most often governed by budgetary considerations, but an experienced and skilled site planner can provide great relief from monotony with relatively minimal allocations. In our observations, considerable funds have been spent on landscape details that actually detracted from site aesthetics; by contrast, small budgets have been used to provide simple but extremely pleasing embellishments.

Green space. Large expanses of on-grade parking should be broken up with appropriate green space. Trees and shrubs do more to avoid impressions of an "asphalt sea" than does any other object.

Site lighting. Site lighting has assumed great importance in recent years for security reasons. No parking area should be left unlighted, and walkways and drives must be given special attention in this regard.

Water. If integrated into the landscape properly, in a manner creating a "clean" and "refreshing" effect, flowing water, fountains, and small lakes are useful as landscape details.

Avoiding stairs. Stairs, or steps, should be avoided in the "core" site area and, indeed, throughout the site if possible. The numbers of old, infirm, sick, and injured persons who may try to use them would seem to be precluding, despite the fact that appropriate access for the handicapped has been provided. Flights of steps from parking at the bottom of a hill to the hospital at the top of the hill can and should be avoided by proper building location and site grading, as well as the use of elevators under extreme site circumstances.

Design standards for the handicapped now largely preclude the long series of steps so commonly seen at entrances to older hospitals. However, on the site itself, codes are not so explicit, and the designer must realize that although steps often are a simple solution to grade problems, their use generally should be avoided on a hospital site.

Harmony. A variety of objects are used in detailing landscapes, such as sculptures, lighting standards, planters, seats, walls, fountains, trees, flowers, shrubs, and play objects for children. Among these, greatest success is usually achieved with the things of nature (water and vegetation), especially when budgets are limited.

In any event, the hospital structure itself usually sets the theme of the site, and incongruous landscape details, displeasing and distasteful to the eye, will be readily apparent. A harmonious relationship should be created among buildings and landscape objects.

Summary

Site planning represents one of the most important phases of hospital facility development, and if often receives less attention than merited by its importance, from both architects and hospital officials. It is in site planning that the future can be given appropriate account. Furthermore, a carefully developed master site plan will prevent the many problems confronting hundreds of existing hospitals for which poor site planning was accomplished.

It should be kept clearly in mind by hospital officials as the site plan is developed and reviewed that drawings merely represent lines on paper—all of which can be changed (except, of course, those depicting existing facilities and fixed site features). Many poor site plans have been allowed to be implemented, with built-in inconveniences for hosts of people over long periods of years, merely because of hesitancy to request design changes or because it was sincerely believed that a proposed location of one element shown on drawings precluded proper location of another when, in fact, both locations could have been changed. Deference to designers with regard to work volumes should not be a consideration in so important an aspect of design as the master site plan. Functional efficiency to serve the needs of people over long years, weighed against costs, should be the criterion by which judgments are made.

A master site plan should provide a long-term framework for facility development into which projects of individual phases can be logically fitted as they occur. Not to plan in this manner can only result in site problems that will cause serious inconveniences to the public and inefficiencies for staff members over the years. On the other hand, long-term site plans should not be regarded as a fixed guide for the future—they should be changed when necessary. Nevertheless, to opine that site planning is unimportant because "we don't know what is going to happen anyway" is to repudiate the importance of strategic plan forecasting.

Most medical center complexes and many large community hospitals are developed over long periods of time, in phases. Projected, sequenced phases, even if tentative, should be depicted in drawings; if multiple drawings are required to reflect the phases, an architect should prepare them, and additional fees should be allowed for this work as indicated. The cost of proper site planning for the long-range future is small compared with the long-term costs that will almost inevitably accrue when a formal plan is lacking.

Notes

1. James Lifton and Owen B. Hardy, *Site Selection for Health Care Facilities* (Chicago: American Hospital Association, 1982).
2. *Ibid.*, pp. 11–23.
3. *Ibid.*, pp. 33–35.
4. *Ibid.*, pp. 6–9.
5. *Guidelines for Construction and Equipment of Hospital and Medical Facilities.* Department of Health and Human Services Pub. No. (HRS-M-HF) 84-1A (Rockville, MD: DHHS Office of Health Facilities, 1984), p. 6.
6. *Energy Considerations for Hospital Construction and Equipment.* Department of Health and Human Services Pub. No. (HRS-M-HF) 84-1A (Rockville, MD: DHHS Office of Health Facilities, 1984), p. 15.

10

The Planning and Design Process

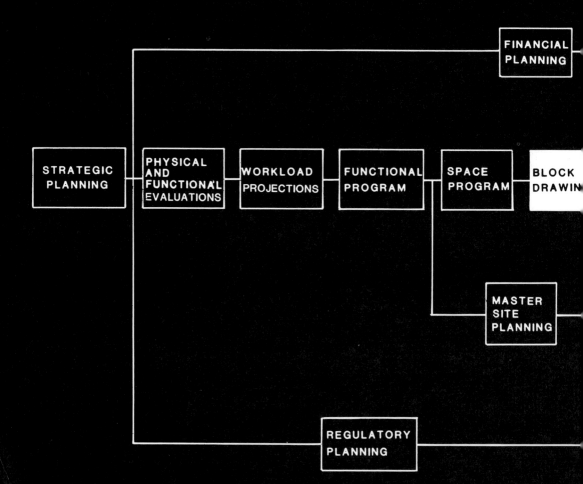

Preparation of block, schematic, and design development documents

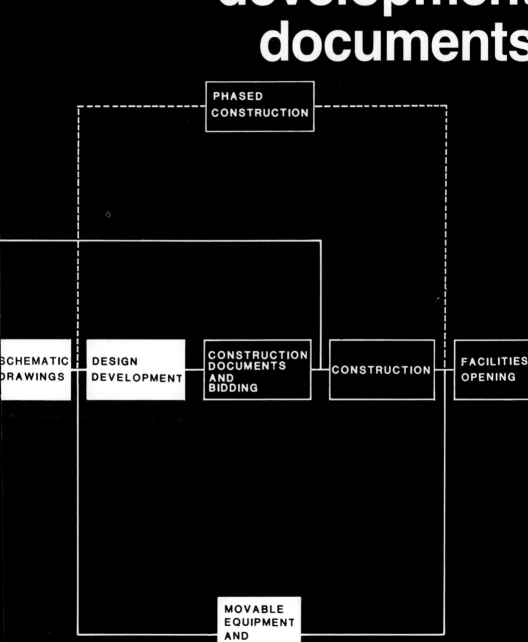

PHASED
CONSTRUCTION

SCHEMATIC
DRAWINGS

DESIGN
DEVELOPMENT

CONSTRUCTION
DOCUMENTS
AND
BIDDING

CONSTRUCTION

FACILITIES
OPENING

MOVABLE
EQUIPMENT
AND
INTERIORS
PLANNING

Prior to the development of definitive architectural drawings, the A&E firm should have available (1) a functional program of the type and character described in Chapter 7; (2) a space program at least of a quality comparable to that described in Chapter 8; (3) a closeness matrix similar to that displayed later in this chapter (Fig 10–3); (4) at least a topside construction and total project budget; and (5) a definitive site for placement of the proposed facilities, as well as appropriate data pertaining to the site. Not only should all these data be in possession of the A&E firm, but the designers who will be responsible for the development of drawings should be thoroughly conversant with all aspects of these documentations. If they are not, there is considerable likelihood that the design will not equate with functional planning standards, management control will be lost, and budget conformance will not be in evidence. As a result, considerable redesign effort may have to be expended.

It is a fact that designers, as do some writers and artists, take considerable pride in their accomplished work. When their drawings are subjected to considerable criticism, they may assume a defensive attitude, with the result that animosities are soon in evidence. Thus it is far better that design be developed from the start in an acceptable manner.

Before design begins, a design team, headed by the A&E firm's project manager, should be organized. In addition to the head as designated, the team should be composed of the following members: (1) the functional planner; (2) a representative of the owner, preferably the director of planning; (3) a construction-oriented cost estimator, representing the construction management firm; (4) engineers—civil, structural, electrical, and mechanical; and (5) the designers who will actually be performing the design work. After completion of the block and schematic design phases (before start of design development), both an equipment planner and an interior designer should be added to the team.

Not only should members of the A&E firm be thoroughly conversant with all documentations developed prior to this meeting, but all other named persons as well.

This team should first hold an organizational meeting, under auspices of the owners. The role each party is to play should be discussed and the responsibilities of each explained. A schedule of periodic meetings during the design process should be prepared and the location thereof fixed. Preferably, the location will be on the premises of the owner. How written communications are to be handled should be agreed upon, and it should be made clear that copies of all minutes, drawings, letters, and memoranda significant to the project, regardless of source, will be supplied to each independent party represented.

Following organization of the team, discussions related directly to the project and its scheduling should be held on a continuing basis (sometimes several days may be required) until all team members are satisfied that their respective concerns—both those expressed in immediate input and those relating to respective tasks as the design work proceeds— are understood by the others.

Especially, the designers should understand that design will be a team effort and that constraints as already documented and those discussed at predesign conferences must be observed. They must also understand that their drawings will be subject to critiques by the functional planning firm, which will provide the owner with a copy of its comments, and reviews by hospital users and officials. Cost estimating must be an ongoing process, and the cost estimator will render formal reports to the owner periodically, particularly at the conclusion of each design phase.

One of the prime purposes of predesign conferences is to provide the construction manager, or whoever is charged with project management planning in the absence of a bona fide construction manager, with information necessary to construct a project work schedule. As has been pointed out previously, such a schedule can be drawn up through the use of PERT, CPM, or a Gant chart, and in some simple constructions a mere listing of key task completion dates will suffice. It is quite probable that a knowledgeable construction manager will have already prepared a listing of most required tasks and will have anticipated reasonable completion dates for each. Even so, input from the remaining team members must be solicited and agreements reached by all that the plan is reasonable and satisfies individual constraints and limitations.

In the event that a decision has not already been reached among the owner, architect, and construction manager relative to a construction delivery approach, this determination should be made at the time of these predesign conferences. It is evident that a project schedule cannot be accurately prepared until this key decision is rendered. If phased construction is to be employed, the number and type of separate contracts will have to be identified and dates for the bidding of each established. If a traditional approach is undertaken, the schedule need only reflect a critical path for completion dates of block, schematic, design development, and construction drawings, as well as specifications. In each instance, reviews and authorizations by the owners and, as required, by outside agencies must be given appropriate account.

Block drawings

Block drawings are developed to reflect total building configuration and a design concept adapted to a particular site. Figures 10–1 and 10–2 show examples of preliminary and more detailed drawings, respectively.

Outside building entrances are shown and basic vehicular traffic patterns are established in a concurrent development of the total site plan. Gross departmental areas and gross areas of all functional entities are individually assigned to building levels and related one to the other within the context of demonstrated vertical and horizontal interdepartmental traffic patterns. Main intradepartmental corridors (e.g., within surgery and radiology) can be shown.

Designers base their drawings upon bay sizings, floor-to-floor measurements, and the selected construction materials as established at predesign conferences. All the operational systems that have been outlined in the functional program, given account in the space program, and approved by the governing board of the hospital must be reflected in the design, and the various known restrictions or constraints as they pertain to the site must be respected. The gross area of the design should not vary

**Preliminary block plan drawings
to establish
departmental relationships**

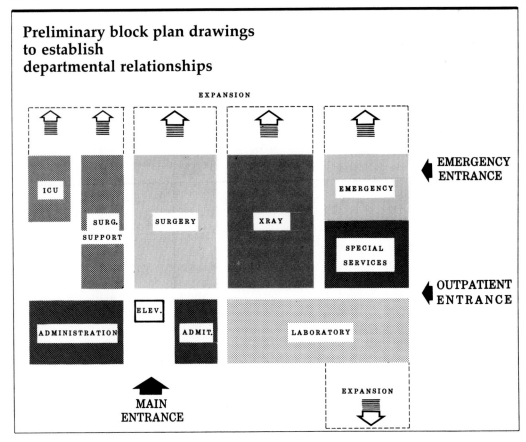

from the gross area of the approved space program by more than 5 percent. If it does, the designers should immediately return to the drawing board. The old cliché "we can correct that in schematics" ought not be allowed, because block drawings and the site plan should be approved by the governing board as finished, approved documentations to be used as the basis for further design work.

The concurrent development of a site plan and block drawings should be emphasized. Design as regards both site and structures at the time of block plan drawings is actually a single activity, although building design does involve many factors that are not site-related. Thus, most of the factors outlined in Chapter 9 with regard to master site planning have a direct bearing upon the development of block drawings.

Closeness matrix

The movement of people, supplies, and information throughout a hospital occasions a great deal of time and expense. Obviously the arrangement of departments or functional entities in such a manner as to shorten traffic distances and expedite traffic movements of all types will make for greater efficiencies. It follows, then, that a thorough, methodical analysis of the various types of traffic flows should be made prior to the start of block drawings.

Various functional planners have devoted a great deal of study to weighting traffic flows according to volume, importance, frequency, and criticality among departments or functional entities. The several quantifications as determined are then used to establish indexes of relative desirability for physical closeness between each two departments or functional entities. Expressed in terms of a simple priority ranking, the relative desirability for physical closeness between each two departments or functional entities can then be shown in a matrix form.

Two such matrixes are displayed in Figures 10–3 and 10–4. That in Figure 10–4 is, of course, a more highly quantified version of that in Figure 10–3.

Closeness matrixes prepared on interdepartmental bases are of great value to designers both as a guide and a control in block plan layout. After thorough study of the master program and with a good closeness matrix in hand, designers should encounter little difficulty in achieving appropriate relationships among departments or functional entities and in effecting optimal traffic flows.

Reviews

As the development of block drawings and site planning proceeds, plan reviews should be held with all members of the professional planning team and the director of planning (or other designated hospital representative) in attendance. The required number of reviews will vary depending upon the designers' ability to develop an acceptable plan. Critiques of block drawings should give careful account to total building expansibility, the proper separation of various categories of pedestrian traffic within the building, interdepartmental relationships, adequacy of vertical transportation, appropriateness of vehicular traffic flow to outside entrances, and conformance to the space program. Budget conformance should be a requisite during the entire process.

The director of planning may wish to carry forward alternative schemes for review by hospital committees and officials. In our judgment, more than one scheme is desirable, but more than three is undesirable. Thus, although multiple schemes can and, in most instances, should be developed and considered by the professional planning team, basic agreement should be reached on two or three schemes, which then are presented to hospital officials for review under a procedure established at the beginning of the entire planning and design process.

At formal reviews with hospital users and decision makers, the functional planner, construction manager, and architect should be present for answering pertinent questions.

At the conclusion of the hospital review process, the drawings and site plan should be returned to the architect with a statement of approval and binding signatures entered directly on the plans. With formal approval in hand, those involved in further planning and design work can proceed with confidence.

**Typical example
of
block plan
drawings**

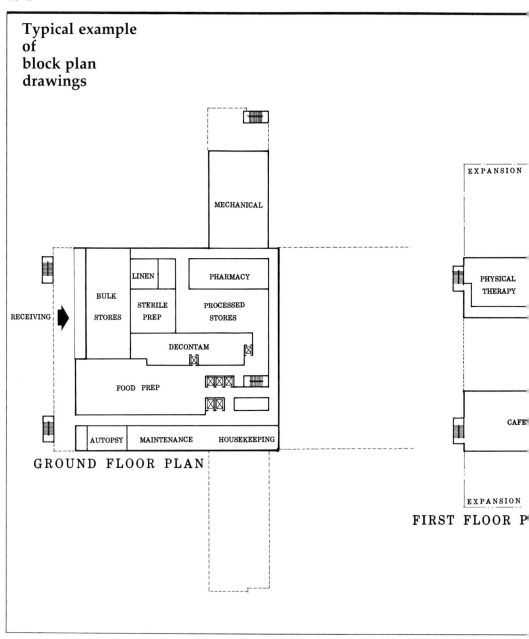

GROUND FLOOR PLAN

EXPANSION

EXPANSION

FIRST FLOOR P

Actually, drawings as originally submitted to the hospital are seldom approved without changes. Such is to be expected, but through a team approach to design as suggested hospital changes will usually be few. The fact of the matter is that in functional programming, space programming, and budget formulating, hospital officials have already determined the character and scope of the construction; in block drawings, the professional planning team is merely carrying out instructions previously set forth through approval of these documentations.

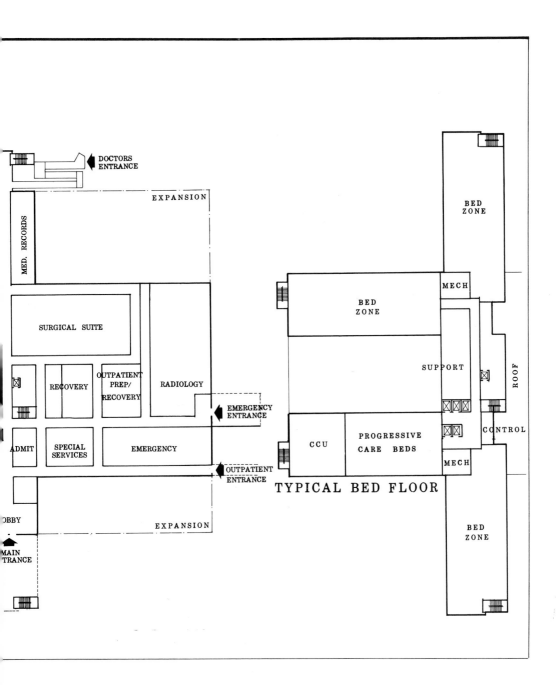

Models

In Chapter 9 mention was made of the use of models. These tools are useful in phased developments to show how a plan can evolve when additions and other changes are made. An example of a typical model showing such developmental phases is shown in Figure 10–5.

Certainly a model of any major construction program should be developed after approval of block drawings and a site plan, for a variety of reasons, not the least of which pertains to public relations. However,

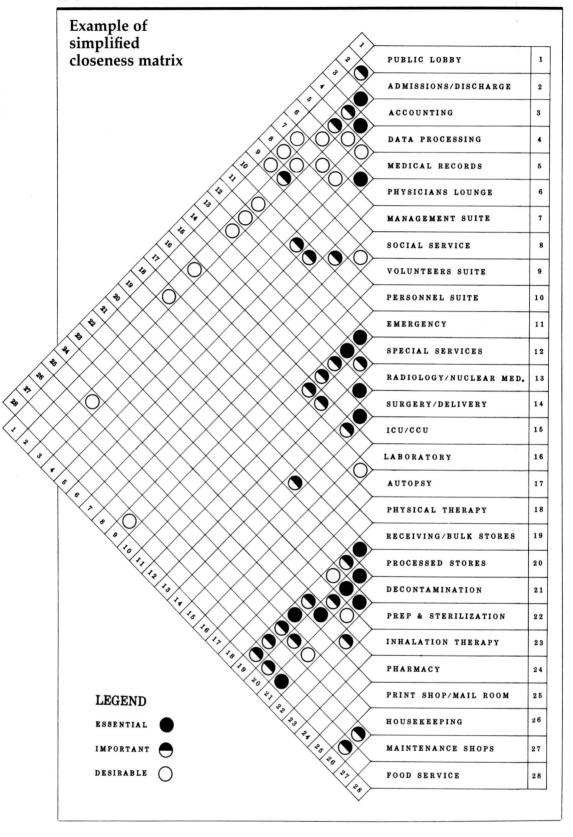

Example of simplified closeness matrix

LEGEND

ESSENTIAL	●
IMPORTANT	◐
DESIRABLE	○

PUBLIC LOBBY	1
ADMISSIONS/DISCHARGE	2
ACCOUNTING	3
DATA PROCESSING	4
MEDICAL RECORDS	5
PHYSICIANS LOUNGE	6
MANAGEMENT SUITE	7
SOCIAL SERVICE	8
VOLUNTEERS SUITE	9
PERSONNEL SUITE	10
EMERGENCY	11
SPECIAL SERVICES	12
RADIOLOGY/NUCLEAR MED.	13
SURGERY/DELIVERY	14
ICU/CCU	15
LABORATORY	16
AUTOPSY	17
PHYSICAL THERAPY	18
RECEIVING/BULK STORES	19
PROCESSED STORES	20
DECONTAMINATION	21
PREP & STERILIZATION	22
INHALATION THERAPY	23
PHARMACY	24
PRINT SHOP/MAIL ROOM	25
HOUSEKEEPING	26
MAINTENANCE SHOPS	27
FOOD SERVICE	28

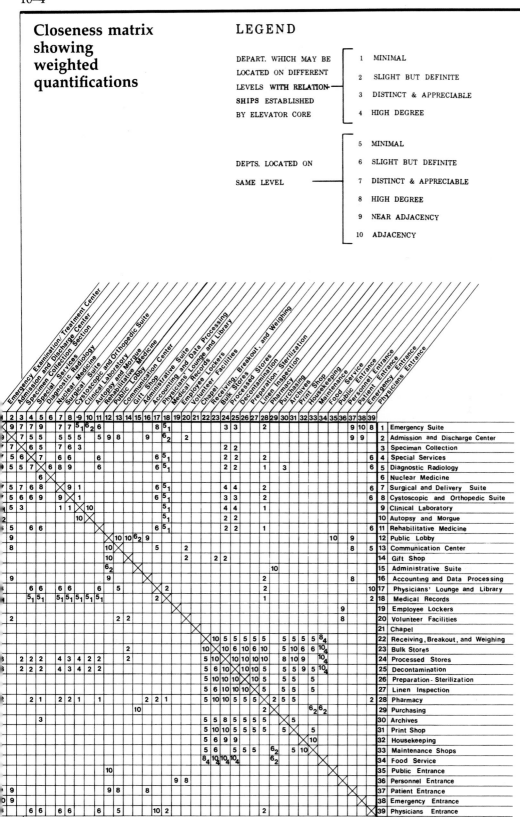

Photographs of a typical model

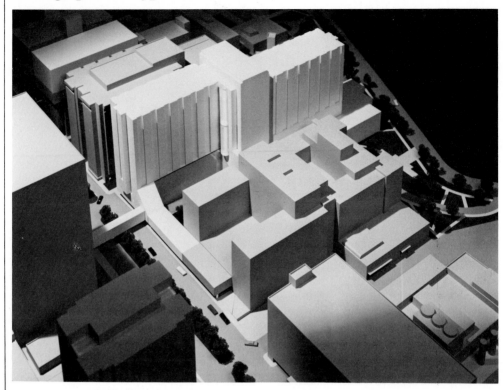

alternative models of block development can be made to assist in the hospital's decision-making process.

We have already mentioned the danger in modeling—that external aesthetics may become the dominant factor in decision making, especially if the board is composed of persons who do not understand the prime importance of many factors not readily apparent in models. Such factors include internal functionality, energy conservation, operating costs, and patient care and comfort.

Schematic drawings

The first definitive scheme of the project is reflected in single-line, level-by-level drawings known as *schematics*. These drawings represent a further development of block plan drawings and delineate every room in the net space program, as well as corridors, mechanical spaces, and all column locations. Beginning work is usually accomplished at ⅟₁₆-inch

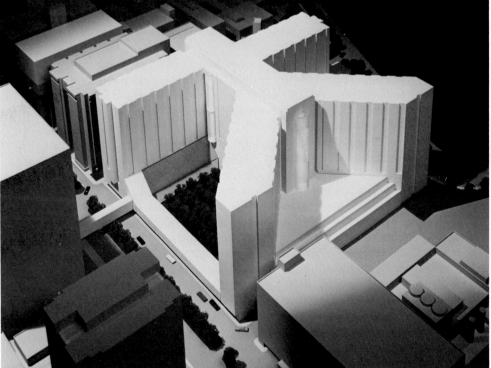

Source: Photographs of Methodist Hospital, Houston, Texas, courtesy of Morris Aubry Architects.

Closeness matrix detailing intradepartmental relationships

1	RECEIVING
2	BULK STORES
3	PROCESSED STORES
4	DECONTAMINATION
5	LINEN FINISHING
6	PACK & STERILIZATION
7	INHALATION THERAPY
8	PRINT SHOP
9	MAIL ROOM
10	PHARMACY

LEGEND

ESSENTIAL	◆
ESPECIALLY IMPORTANT	◇
IMPORTANT	◉
DESIRABLE	◈

scale (1 inch = 16 feet), with final versions being done at ⅛-inch scale (1 inch = 8 feet).

Some architects show door swings in schematic drawings, although this detail is usually left to the design development phase. It is common to show some fixed equipment, such as plumbing fixtures, but the definitive location of both fixed and movable equipment is also reserved for design development.

Schematic drawings provide a further delineation of interdepartmental traffic flows, in that respective entrances and control points to all departments and functional entities are shown. Intradepartmental room arrangements and corridor schemes are detailed.

Before designers begin this important design phase, the functional planner should provide them with intradepartmental closeness matrixes for respective major departments. Desirable room relationships within many functional entities, such as admitting, cashiering, and the main lobby complex, should be demonstrated with simple bubble diagrams. Examples of each of these two explanatory tools are shown in Figures 10–6 and 10–7, respectively.

Schematic drawings may provide some adjustments to the scope of the project as shown in block plan drawings, but upon completion of schematics both the scope and all relationships of project components (departments, functional entities, and rooms) should be fixed.

Schematic drawings display the ultimate character of the project, for it is not possible to complete them satisfactorily without first determining

**Bubble diagram
showing
intradepartmental
relationships**

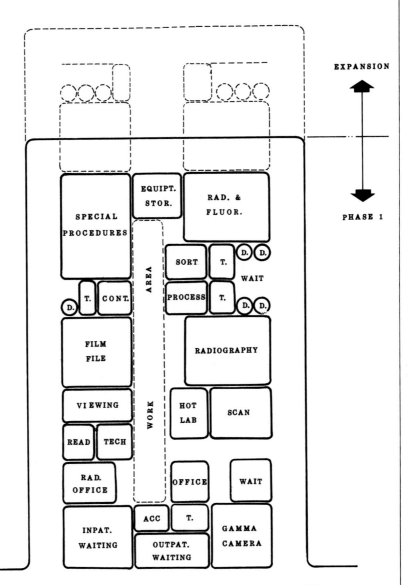

RADIOLOGY / NUCLEAR MEDICINE SUITE

Key: CONT = Controls
D   = Dressing
ACC = Administrative
          Control Center

Example of schematic design drawings

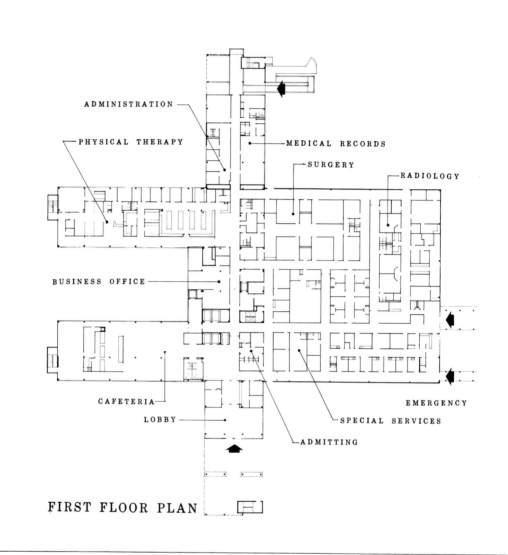

ADMINISTRATION

PHYSICAL THERAPY

MEDICAL RECORDS

SURGERY

RADIOLOGY

BUSINESS OFFICE

CAFETERIA

EMERGENCY

LOBBY

SPECIAL SERVICES

ADMITTING

FIRST FLOOR PLAN

all major operational concepts. Certainly, decisions should have been reached concerning operational concepts during functional programming, but approval of schematics ought to preclude any further changes in either systems or major features. Minor changes can be easily made even during design development, but major changes following formal approval of schematics should warrant a redesign fee for the A&E firm.

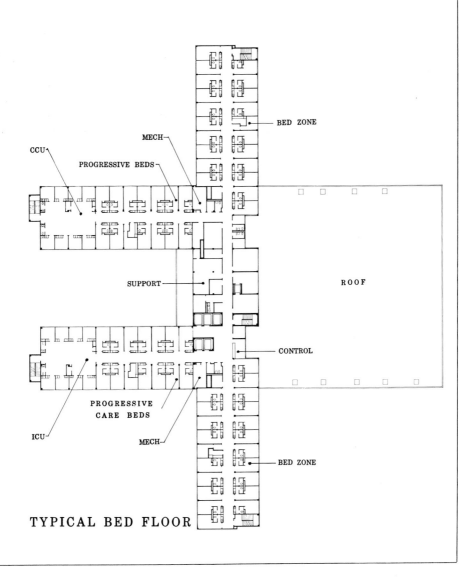

TYPICAL BED FLOOR

During the schematic design phase, the professional planning team must hold periodic meetings, preferably on a scheduled basis, and both the construction manager and the functional planner should be informally on call to the designers at all times. It is expected that electrical and mechanical engineers will be immediately available to render continuing input.

The functional planner should make a formal critique of drawings presented to each design conference and transmit same to owner, architect, and construction manager.

The construction manager should receive copies of the drawings presented at these sessions and update the first estimates of the costs of project components and possibly make reallocations among the budgets for each. Both cost estimates and changes in component budgets should be transmitted to the architect, owner, and functional planner.

Concurrent with estimating and budgeting, the construction manager can assist the architect in preparing outline specifications as schematic design proceeds, if phased construction is to be undertaken. When the drawings are finished, these summary specifications should be completed. If a traditional construction is undertaken, formal preparation of outline specifications will not be necessary at this time, although this is preferable inasmuch as the construction manager or other estimator must assume some selections of construction materials, fixed equipment, finishes, and so on for accurate cost estimating.

When the professional planning team reaches a consensus regarding the suitability of completed schematic drawings in terms of conformance to the functional program and space program and budget, the drawings (and outline specifications in the case of phased construction) should be presented to the hospital for review and approval. The director of planning, or other hospital representative who has the responsibility of liaison with the team, should take charge of the reviews and pursue the previously agreed-upon procedure to successful conclusion.

As in the case of block drawings, the hospital should enter a statement of approval on the finished documents, with appropriate signatures appended and updated. Upon their return to the A&E firm, work can begin on design development drawings, and in the case of a phased construction delivery approach, early bid packages can be immediately prepared.

Over the course of design conferences, if any impasse is reached among members of the planning team owing to differing professional opinions, the director of planning should resolve the matter. If it is of such weight that it does not fall within the scope of the director's delegated decision-making authority, this official should refer the matter to the proper point in the decision-making chain (with approval of the chief executive officer), as discussed in Chapter 2.

An example of schematic design drawings is shown in Figure 10–8.

Outline specifications

During the schematic design phase (sometimes in design development), either the architect or construction manager should prepare outline specifications for the proposed work, depending upon stipulations in individual contracts. Most often, the architect actually prepares the document, with advice from both the functional planner and the construction manager.

The purposes of outline specifications are usually (1) to describe to the owner a proposed quality of the construction and to secure his approval thereof, and (2) to provide more concrete bases for cost estimations. Outline specifications represent a decision point for the owner with regard to many building features. Once the decisions are made, further planning is based upon them. Outline specifications typically embrace the following summary descriptions:

1. project scope and description
2. pertinent points to be contained in the general conditions of the contract documents
3. site work
4. exterior foundations and walls
5. structural work
6. damp-proofing and vapor control
7. interior finishes
8. stairs
9. roof
10. flashing, sheet metal, and caulking
11. doors and frames
12. hardware
13. elevators
14. method of supply delivery
15. pneumatic tubes
16. casework systems
17. medical gases
18. dietary installation
19. cleaning and sterilizing equipment (fixed)
20. communications systems (including security)
21. linen system
22. trash disposal system
23. data processing system
24. plumbing work
25. heating, ventilating, and air-conditioning work
26. electrical work
27. energy management control system.

As in the case of the contract specifications, precise language should be used, and the outline specifications should be complete. For example, some systems are very costly, and their inadvertent omission can result in serious errors in cost estimating.

Design development

The *Standard Form of Agreement Between Owner and Architect*, published by the American Institute of Architects, contains the following provision relative to the design development phase:[1]

1.2 DESIGN DEVELOPMENT PHASE

1.2.1 Based on the approved Schematic Design Documents and any adjustments authorized by the Owner in the program or Project budget, the Architect shall prepare, for approval by the Owner, Design Development Documents consisting of drawings and other documents to fix and describe the size and character of the entire Project as to architectural, structural, mechanical and electrical systems, materials and such other elements as may be appropriate.

1.2.2 THE ARCHITECT SHALL SUBMIT TO THE OWNER A FURTHER STATEMENT OF PROBABLE CONSTRUCTIÓN COST.

With regard to paragraph 1.2.2, if the hospital has assembled a team whose membership includes an independent construction management (CM) firm, this provision would not, of course, apply. The separate construction manager would be charged with this responsibility. It would apply if the architect is to provide the cost estimating as a part of the A&E firm's design contract. In cases in which the architect provides CM services (usually through a subsidiary firm), cost estimating and formulation of the statement of probable construction cost, at least, would be accomplished under one aegis.

Prior to the start of design development drawings, the architect should devise a room-numbering system and apply it to the approved schematic drawings that will serve as a basis for design development. Environmental data sheets must then be prepared for each type of room in the project, with the sheets being keyed to the room numbers on the drawings.

These two points, room numbering and environmental data sheets, are extremely important. Room numbering allows ready identification of any specific room in the project throughout the course of the design work, and thus saves appreciable time and avoids mistakes. An environmental data sheet organizes pertinent information necessary to the design development of a specific room and provides a ready reference not only for the designers but for mechanical and electrical engineers as well. An example of a typical environmental data sheet appears in Exhibit 10–1.

Environmental data sheets may be prepared by either the architect or the functional planner. In either case, an experienced person should be assigned the responsibility. Typically, conferences should be held with department heads in preparation of sheets for each respective department room. The equipment planner, already selected, should also be in attendance at these conferences. The department head, of course, may bring to the conference various technical personnel as deemed advisable. Among the knowledge and experience of the architect or functional planner, and the equipment planner, plus that possessed by departmental personnel, state-of-the-art room attributes required for design development should be assured.

The preparer of the data sheets should consult frequently with the cost estimator, and prior to completion, the director of planning should indicate the owner's approval of the final products.

Exhibit 10–1

Example of environmental data sheet

HOSPITAL

DEPARTMENT: _____
ROOM NAME: _____

FUNCTION: _____ _____
ADJACENCY: _____ _____

ROOM NO.: _____
OCCUPANCY: _____
PAT./VISIT.: _____
STAFF: _____

FLOOR: _____
BASE: _____
WALLS: _____
CEILING: _____
CEILING HT.: _____

OPENINGS: _____
DOOR WIDTH: _____
MATERIAL: _____
HARDWARE: _____
HARDWARE: _____

REMARKS: _____

Architectural

DESCRIPTION	F/M	AMOUNT	FURN/INST.	SIZE	COMMENTS

Equipment

LIGHTING: ☐ FLUORESCENT ☐ INCANDESCENT ☐ TAMPERPROOF
RECEPTACLES: ☐ REGULAR ☐ TAMPERPROOF
SPECIALTIES: ☐ EMER. POWER ☐ CLOCK ☐ TV
COMMUNICATION: ☐ CCTV ☐ INTERCOM ☐ NURSECALL
☐ TELEPHONE ☐

REMARKS: _____

Electrical

WATER: ☐ WATER ☐ TEMP. CONTROL ☐
FIXTURES: ☐ FLOOR DRAIN ☐ HOSE BIB ☐ SHOWER
☐ TOILET ☐ TUB ☐ WATER COOLER
☐ SINK ☐ ☐

REMARKS: _____

Plumbing

MEDICAL GASES: ☐ GAS ☐ OXYGEN ☐ NITROUS OXIDE
☐ COMP. AIR ☐ NITROGEN ☐ VACUUM

REMARKS: _____

Gases

AIR CHANGES: ___ PER HOUR ☐ OUTSIDE ☐ RECIRCULATE
AIR PRESSURE: ☐ POSITIVE ☐ NEGATIVE ☐ EQUAL
CONTROLS: ☐ ROOM ☐ ZONE ☐

REMARKS: _____

HVAC

FIRE DETECT.: ☐ FIRE ALARM ☐ SMOKE DETECT. ☐ HEAT DETECT.
FIRE EXTING.: ☐ SPRINKLER ☐ FIRE HOSE ☐

REMARKS: _____

Fire

Lammers+Gershon   Environmental Data Sheet

A few functional planning firms and A&E firms have on file prepared environmental data sheets for all rooms in a typical complete hospital. A small portion of these firms have computerized the sheets for instantaneous recall. All such work is highly valuable, but it does possess one danger: "state of the art" may not be maintained owing to the time required for continuous updating. Thus, in our opinion, time should be taken as each project is accomplished to hold the departmental conferences as described here, with updatings of the base file as indicated.

As previously noted, environmental data sheets provide the hospital a means of providing input to the drawings in a form readily understood by all and allows the hospital excellent control over the development of each room in the structure. They also serve as a protection to the architect in that the hospital is committed to most vital features *before* design.

Essentially, design development documents are exactly what the name implies—they are a further development of the drawings and other documentations developed in the schematic design phase. Instead of single-line drawings, the exact dimensions and thickness of walls are shown, and drawings are usually done at ⅛-inch scale. Exact door sizes and swings are indicated. All electrical and mechanical spaces and structural elements are developed to precise dimensions. Floor-to-floor dimensions are precisely determined. Most of the features set forth in the environmental data sheets are included on the drawings. These drawings, then, provide the base for the finer details to be later shown in the construction drawings that will be used by all contractors and subcontractors in the actual construction of the building. Figure 10–9 depicts an example design development drawing.

The design development drawings should show most major movable equipment and all fixed equipment. Working directly with the functional planner and the equipment planner, the designers decide on the positioning of these items so as to reflect best functionality for the users. Intraroom design is determined *before* working drawings are executed, thus saving the architect valuable time later on, when design time may be extremely critical. This work in the design development phase also allows the owner an opportunity to view exactly the planned work flows in each individual work area.

During design development, the nature and scope of important systems are determined and reflected on the drawings or in other documents: medical gas systems; transportation systems (elevator and automatic or other supply delivery); sterilizer systems; housekeeping vacuum systems, if any; communication systems (nurse call, telephone, dictation, and intercom); lighting systems (in rooms and all examination-treatment areas); electrical service systems (including the voltages and outlets provided for each room); pneumatic tube systems; laundry equipment; plumbing fixtures; energy management control systems; and casework systems. In the review process, the owner has an opportunity for making known specific needs or wants; the functional planner can assist in these matters by bringing professional knowledge and expertise to bear in a positive manner.

In this phase, the architect further develops the structural and all features of the mechanical and electrical systems, thus providing the base for final working drawings and specifications in the construction document phase. The finishes throughout, the exterior "skin," and the quality

Example of design development drawing

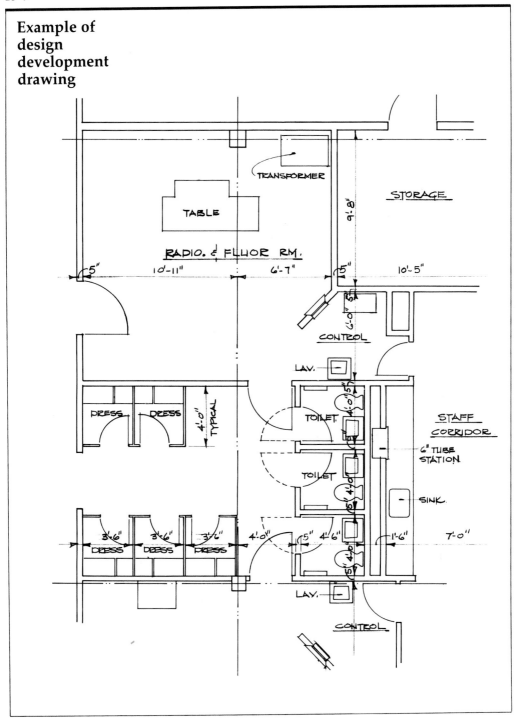

of all materials are determined and reflected in the several documents that are formulated. All these determinations are resolved in ongoing communications among the owner, functional planner, cost estimator, and the designers.

As the design development phase progresses, the construction manager advises on comparative costs of materials and items of fixed equipment and simultaneously refines the initial cost estimates. Tradeoffs among the several component budgets may be required as savings in one area are balanced against excesses in another. At the end of design development, a formal cost estimate should be prepared and submitted to the hospital along with the drawings and other documents prepared by the architect.

During the design development phase, several reviews will be made by departmental users, with the number depending upon the scope and complexity of the project, specific user demands, and the abilities of the professional planning team. The director of planning coordinates these reviews, with representatives from the A&E, the functional planning, and the CM firms in attendance.

When a basic consensus is reached among the members of the professional planning team and hospital users and officials regarding the acceptability of the design development documents as the basis for proceeding into the construction documents phase, the director of planning should initiate the procedure for securing hospital approval. When it is obtained, official signatures, dated and fixed directly on the documents, should so indicate. Instructions can then be given to start the construction documents phase.

In previous years, contracts between owner and architect often did not distinctly define a schematic design phase and a phase of design development. Instead, a "preliminary" design was specified during which drawings and other documents were to be developed sufficiently for proceeding into working drawings and specifications.

More recently, the American Institute of Architects has wisely spelled out a clear separation of schematic design and design development phases. Most intradepartmental and all intraroom functionality depends directly upon the work accomplished in the design development phase. If it is bypassed or given little attention, there will be great likelihood that all sorts of disutilities will be evidenced in the individual work areas throughout the completed construction.

Harold D. Hauf has clearly stated the case for a design development phase:[2]

> In general, recognition of both schematic and design development phases is greatly to the advantage of both owner and architect. This permits flexibility in studying solutions to the functional program in relation to alternative schemes for structural and mechanical systems without pursuing more detailed engineering design until a generally satisfactory overall scheme is approved. Then during [the] design development phase the principal quantitative engineering problems can be worked out and problems of coordination between functional requirements and engineering systems resolved. With this procedure the production of working drawings and specifications can proceed smoothly, since any changes required in the building program presumably will have been made before the owner's approval of the definitive design documents.

Phased construction

In the event that a decision was reached at the beginning of the entire design phase to pursue a phased construction approach, there can be a concurrent preparation of construction documents for each separate contract along with the design development work as described. Site work, foundations, and structural framing are typical work projects for which construction documents can be prepared and construction carried out without jeopardizing design development related to either functional or purely physical aspects of the structure. In fact, the construction documents phase can be carried forward related to all items listed in the first general contract, as set forth in Chapter 2 (Contract No. 2 for the Erie County Medical Center).

Working drawings can also be started on the several items under the second general contract (Contract No. 2 in Chapter 2), but the start of construction would not occur during the design development phase because of the time required for prior completion of site, foundation, structural, and other work noted under the first general contract.

Movable equipment planning

Most firms specializing in movable equipment planning desire to be contracted by the hospital or A&E firm at the start of schematic drawings. In fact, those firms that also specialize in fixed equipment planning may desire to be contracted even during space programming. Although we believe that such desires may result in worthwhile benefits on some projects, if the functional planner possesses a broad level of knowledge and experience (as should be the case), there is little reason to employ an equipment planner prior to the completion of schematic drawings. However, the dietary department is an exception, as are certain highly specialized equipment areas such as magnetic resonance imaging (MRI). Owing to the complexities involved in selecting and positioning kitchen and cafeteria equipment items, a dietary consultant, rather than a movable equipment planner, should be employed even before space programming is completed. Even in the case of specialized diagnostic equipment, however, the vendor of the equipment may provide planning services sufficient to allocate space, and the functional planner and the architect can certainly determine an optimal location. Thus, we see little reason to alter our long-held opinion that the start of design development is the logical time for a hospital to bring aboard the services of an equipment planning firm, unless the functional planner and the architect are deficient in knowledge that they, in reality, should possess.

At the start of design development, however, we believe that a reputable equipment planning firm should be employed. A professional fee basis is the only basis for such employment. Certainly a percentage of equipment purchased should never be the basis for compensation. Furthermore, the professional independence of the firm should be assured.

Design development demands resolution of movable equipment choices in many rooms owing to the fact that exact room dimensions, plumbing fixtures, and voltages of electrical outlets are determined directly by the selections made. As well, specialty features of some rooms are dictated by types of movable equipment, as in the case of thermography, MRI, electron microscopy, and so forth.

Some confusion exists as to the exact meaning of the term "movable equipment." Does it merely include all equipment items of a technical or scientific nature? Does it include those items as well as all items of furniture? Both connotations are used in the field today. As a result of this confusion, the hospital should be careful to define precisely all terms in any contracts signed with movable equipment planners or interior design firms.

In addition, the terms "Group I," "Group II," and "Group III," as referenced to hospital equipment, are still heard. These terms were originated by the U.S. Public Health Service a number of years ago. Group I equipment means all fixed equipment, excluding x-ray equipment; Group II means all movable equipment, including furniture, that would normally be included in depreciation schedules; and Group III equipment means all equipment that is not depreciated but regarded as being expendable, such as trash cans and pencil sharpeners.

The importance of a critical path schedule for movable equipment planning, geared to the total project schedule, must be stressed. This responsibility should be assigned to the equipment planner, who must work with the construction manager and director of planning in discharging it.

Although equipment planning firms vary widely in their capabilities and in their levels of sophistication regarding computerization, there seems to be a fairly standardized approach to the various tasks involved. This approach is described in the following list as a series of steps:

1. The equipment planner may be called upon to estimate movable equipment costs for the purpose of budgeting, as an initial task. This can be done from a study of completed schematic drawings and outline specifications. If such a budget or cost has already been set by the construction manager, as it may well have been, the equipment planner should affirm or modify these prior estimates.

2. The equipment planner should consult with the preparer of the environmental data sheets and the respective department heads during conferences about these sheets.

3. If there is an existing facility that is to be phased out, the movable equipment housed therein must be surveyed to determine those items suitable for transfer and use in the new construction. A categorized listing of all equipment to be transferred has to be made.

4. Using the room-numbering system as prepared by the architect at the beginning of design development (described previously), a composite room-by-room listing of all major movable equipment that will be required in the project is prepared, together with the quantity and estimated price, both unit and total. Items to be transferred from any existing facility are appropriately designated as to room and quantity.

5. Layouts of equipment must be made at ¼-inch scale for all rooms for which space requirements may be critical. We have encountered a number of instances in which this was not done: equipment was blindly ordered and delivered, and as might have been expected, some of it would not fit into the space for which it was planned. The result was not only embarrassment for all concerned but time and money lost in the ensuing corrective transactions. It is safe to say that no person is capable of "eyeballing" specific spaces on ⅛-inch scale drawings and fitting equipment and furniture thereto without appreciable chance of serious error.

6. The equipment planner must work closely with users, through the director of planning, to prepare the room equipment listing. Review time is necessary. Color schemes must be coordinated with those planned by the person charged with the responsibility for interior design.

7. Precise specifications for all equipment items must be prepared and categorized, and consolidated listings must be made. This means that from the individual room listings, all like items must be accumulated and total quantities determined. Appropriate supplier catalog numbers and specifications then have to be compiled or verified.

8. For competitive bidding, items of the same general nature are grouped in the same listing. For example, all office equipment is usually grouped to afford office suppliers the opportunity of bidding. It is obvious, for example, that an office supplier could not bid on a listing that contained a variety of medical and surgical items. Laboratory items, x-ray items, bedroom furniture, waiting rooms, and lobby furniture are typical examples of groupings often made. It should be pointed out, however, there are now a number of general supply houses that will bid on any item, regardless of its nature, normally purchased by a hospital. In these instances, of course, careful judgments have to be made relating to both groupings and the list of suppliers who will be asked to bid.

9. Separate cards or other documentations should be prepared describing like items, respective quantities, and the room in which each individual item will be placed. This list will facilitate placement upon delivery and help the hospital in formulating depreciation schedules.

10. Ongoing cost estimates have to be prepared. These are given to the construction manager or other person charged with total project budgeting and estimating. This work is of considerable importance owing to the fact that movable equipment costs have advanced over the past two decades (including x-ray equipment) from approximately 20 percent of construction costs to a level now in excess of 30 percent.

11. Bid packages must be prepared and sent to selected suppliers. The forms used in this regard have become rather standardized, but clauses containing specific instructions to the bidders must be set

forth along with the general conditions of the contract including such items as materials and labor, permits and regulations, indemnification, necessary insurances, modifications, guaranties, deliveries, storage, installations, transmittal of invoices, and so on.

12. Bids are received and judgments made as to successful bidders.

13. Purchase orders are prepared and sent to the successful bidders, specifying dates and methods of delivery, as well as all other general and specific terms of the purchase. This work must respect procurement priorities and required lead times.

14. The equipment must be received, uncrated, inspected, and placed. The equipment planner should monitor installation and prepare lists of exceptions to specifications. In many instances, temporary storage space must be procured by the hospital pending completion of the construction project; this possibility should be anticipated and a plan formulated either on a definite or contingency basis.

15. The equipment planner should assume responsibility for assuring that all equipment and equipment layouts and placements will be in compliance with current Occupational Safety and Health Act (OSHA), National Fire Protection Association (NFPA), and local code standards.

16. Regarding placement of equipment in rooms, much confusion and misplacement sometimes occurs, with the result that some items are actually "lost" from the outset. A simple technique employed by one of the investor-owned systems[3] involves placing in each room, prior to the receipt of equipment, a listing of every item that is to be placed or installed in that room. Then, as each item is put into the room, the person placing it there initials the item on the list. The chances of placing "wrong" items in a room are then greatly reduced.

Interior design services

Providers

Interior design services are provided by either the hospital-appointed architect or a separate contractor. In recent years, provision by separate contractors specializing in these services has become prevalent, especially in the case of larger projects.

Certainly, there is no reason that competent architects cannot perform quality interior design services, and the American Institute of Architects publishes a suggested model contract for this service.[4] However, few individuals are highly competent in greatly diversified activities, and many otherwise competent architects do not have the training or experience that may characterize individuals in specialized interior design firms. Some of the large A&E firms have organized distinct interior design departments and, of course, can compete directly with the separate specialty firm.

It is well to note here also that some movable equipment planners and interior designers have now merged their services into one firm. Such a merger would seem to be advantageous, provided competent personnel are in evidence.

Services

The services for which a hospital can contract under the general heading of interior design services can vary quite widely in scope and nature. However, the great thrust should be toward interior aesthetics. Simply put, even a highly functional hospital can be extremely displeasing from the standpoint of interior aesthetics.

Usually, the interior design firm (if a contractor other than the architect is used) coordinates its services with the architect in design development. Coordination must also be effected with the movable equipment planner.

A basic interior design plan typically specifies the following:

1. space planning—that is, planning as to how a given room will be arranged, divided, and furnished in order to achieve both aesthetic appeal and functionality

2. color coordination of furnishings, floors, and walls, as well as medical equipment, and other design features, including fabrics, draperies, woods, vinyls, and carpets

3. graphic design, usually including both a signage program and wall graphics.

This information provided by the interior design service is usually presented to hospital officials in the form of mock-up presentation renderings and boards.

In addition to the basic services outlined here, most interior design firms provide a purchasing service for many of the decorating materials, as well as an installation service.

Results

Any hospital should strive to avoid a stereotypical institutional appearance. Over the course of the past decade, interior designers have made great strides in assisting hospitals to provide a warm-appearing, attractive environment for their users. Certainly the therapeutic process would seem to be accelerated if patients are brought into a pleasant atmosphere in which surroundings make a positive contribution, as contrasted with an austere world of institutional life, drab color, and ill-arranged furnishings.

Summary

Design should be the responsibility of a team, headed by the A&E firm's project manager. The team should be composed of the functional planner; an owner's representative (usually the director of planning); an independent cost estimator (probably representing the CM firm); engineers—civil, structural, electrical, and mechanical; and the design architect actually responsible for accomplishing the drawings.

Supplementing the various documents already produced by the functional planner for design guidance, predesign conferences should be held to determine organization, to outline the role to be fulfilled by each team member, to decide or affirm the type of construction delivery approach to be used, and to prepare a detailed design schedule.

Block drawings, definitively related to a master site plan, must be prepared initially and approved by the owner following appropriate reviews. Models of at least two design alternatives should be prepared during the final stages of block drawings to assist the owner in designating an approved design.

After blocks are officially approved, schematic drawings, based directly upon the functional and space programs, can be undertaken. Schematic design can be greatly facilitated through the use of matrixes and bubble diagrams, prepared by the functional planner, depicting intradepartmental room relationships.

A set of outline specifications should be prepared by either the architect or the construction manager and approved by the design team and the owner. These specifications, together with the finished schematic drawings, can be used by the cost estimator to supply an accurate estimate of construction costs at this time.

After approval of schematic design, the design development phase is started. This phase is guided by environmental data sheets prepared by either the architect or the functional planner, working with the owner, department heads, the director of planning, and the equipment planner. The environmental data sheets provide the owner with an opportunity to control the design development phase and to be assured that "state of the art" is maintained in the project.

Movable equipment planning starts at the beginning of the design development phase, and the person designated as the movable equipment planner should be added to the design team. The person responsible for interior design services should also join the team when design development starts.

Over the course of design development, several reviews will be made of the drawings by departmental users, including medical staff representatives. The director of planning coordinates these reviews. Following the several department approvals and a consensus among the members of the design firm that the drawings are acceptable and complete, official hospital approval can be obtained.

The work accomplished in preparing block, schematic, and design development documents sets the stage for construction documents. Major owner input is required to supplement that supplied by all other named members of the design team. If the process outlined is diligently followed, a "state-of-the-art" project, delivered on schedule and within budget, will be assured as long as the construction documents phase is accomplished efficiently.

Notes

1. *Standard Form of Agreement Between Owner and Architect*, AIA Document B141, 1977 ed. (Washington, DC: American Institute of Architects, 1977), p. 3.
2. Harold D. Hauf, *Building Contracts for Design and Construction* (New York: John Wiley & Sons, 1968), p. 23.
3. Hospital Corporation of America employs this technique.
4. *Standard Form of Agreement for Interior Design Services*, AIA Document B171, 1977 ed. (Washington, DC: American Institute of Architects, 1977).

11

The Planning and Design Process

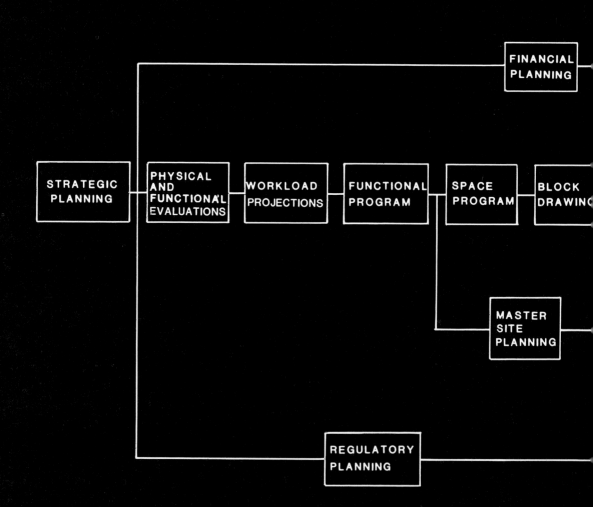

Construction documents and bidding phases

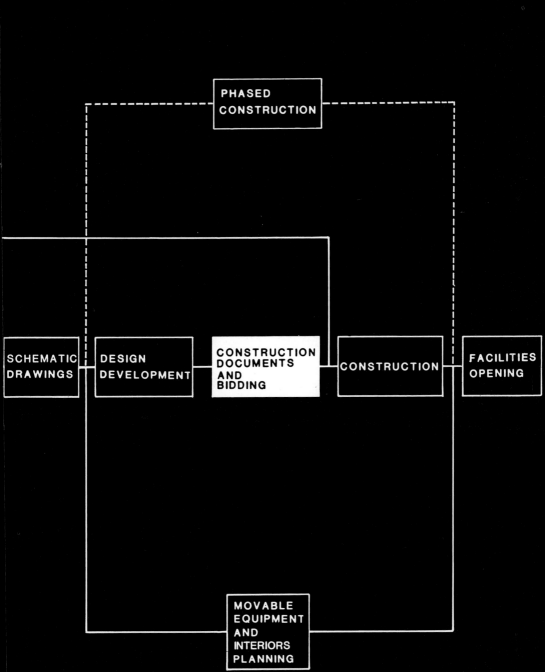

PHASED CONSTRUCTION

SCHEMATIC DRAWINGS

DESIGN DEVELOPMENT

CONSTRUCTION DOCUMENTS AND BIDDING

CONSTRUCTION

FACILITIES OPENING

MOVABLE EQUIPMENT AND INTERIORS PLANNING

Construction documents represent the culmination of all efforts of the planning team. If they do not faithfully represent commitments made in the block plan and schematic and design development phases, the character and quality of the completed facilities will not be as expected by the client. The onus rests squarely upon the A&E firm to prepare drawings and specifications that clearly represent the previous decisions of hospital officials.

Bidding requirements and the form of agreement are not a part of the construction documents, but both are prepared in the construction documents phase and are given brief comment in this chapter. The form of agreement is the uniting mechanism for all parts of the contract and is a part of the contract documents.

Construction documents phase

Construction documents consist of three basic parts, all of which are incorporated into the contract between the owner and builder: (1) specifications, (2) drawings, and (3) conditions of the contract. Each is discussed in this section.

For a contract of any type to be binding upon the parties involved, the contract documents must indicate unequivocally the responsibilities of each. The working drawings and specifications represent contract provisions, and without complete clarity, intents will be clouded, thus opening the way for disputes, interminable explanations by the architect, further negotiations, and added costs to the owner.

George T. Heery has rightly stated that the major aspects of clarity are the completeness, accuracy, and form of the contract drawings and specifications.[1] It is, then, the achievement of "clarity" that Heery suggests should constitute a major objective in the preparation of construction documents.

Some of the major advantages in achieving "clarity" in drawings and specifications are as follows:

1. accuracy in cost estimating prior to bidding

2. assurance of precise, competitive bidding

3. facilitation of decision making by the architect relative to the contract work

4. simplification of supervision of the work by the contractor and monitoring by the architect or construction manager

5. avoidance of time-consuming misunderstandings and disputes, some of which may terminate in costly legal contests

6. assurance of work performance as intended

7. elimination of corrective change orders.

Certainly, the best interests of all parties directly involved with the contract—the owner, the contractor, and the architect—will be served by documentations possessing "clarity." Moreover, the work of all those who must interpret them from time to time will be greatly simplified.

The *Standard Form of Agreement between Owner and Architect* (AIA Document B141, 1977 edition) states the following relative to the construction documents phase:

1.3   CONSTRUCTION DOCUMENTS PHASE

1.3.1   Based on the approved Design Development Documents and any further adjustments in the scope or quality of the Project or in the Project budget authorized by the Owner, the Architect shall prepare, for approval by the Owner, Construction Documents consisting of Drawings and Specifications setting forth in detail the requirements for the construction of the Project.

1.3.2   The Architect shall assist the Owner in the preparation of the necessary bidding information, bidding forms, the Conditions of the Contract, and the form of Agreement between the Owner and the Contractor.

1.3.3   The Architect shall advise the Owner of any adjustments to previous Statements of Probable Construction Cost indicated by changes in requirements or general market conditions.

1.3.4   The Architect shall assist the Owner in connection with the Owner's responsibility for filing documents required for the approval of governmental authorities having jurisdiction over the Project.[2]

Thus it is evident that the A&E firm is charged with actual preparation of (1) drawings and (2) specifications, to include necessary bidding information for the project, and with *assisting* in the preparation of instruments incident to bidding and the award of a contract. This consultant shall also keep project cost information up to date (if the A&E firm retains that responsibility) and shall *assist* in filing whatever documents are required for obtaining approval from appropriate governmental agencies.

Because the greatest time involvement by the architect pertains to the preparation of drawings and specifications, our comments deal primarily with this portion of the contract documents.

Richard H. Clough, noted authority on construction contracting, has stated, "Drawings, or plans, . . . portray the physical aspects of the structure, showing the arrangement, dimensions, construction details, materials, and other information necessary for estimating and building the project. . . . specifications describe how the project is to be constructed and what results are to be achieved."[3]

Harold J. Rosen, an expert in the field of specifications writing, has noted the basic content of contract drawings and specifications:[4]

Drawings should generally show the following information:

1. Extent, size, shape, and location of component parts.

2. Location of materials, equipment and fixtures.

3. Detail and overall dimensions.

4. Interrelation of materials, equipment and space.

5. Schedules of finishes, windows and doors.

6. Sizes of equipment.

7. Identification of class of material at its location.

8. Alternates.

Specifications should generally describe the following items:

1. Type and quality of materials, equipment and fixtures.

2. Quality of workmanship.

3. Methods of fabrication, installation and erection.

4. Test and code requirements.

5. Gauges of manufacturers' equipment.

6. Allowances and unit prices.

7. Alternates and options.

Rosen has explicitly pointed out the undesirability of overlap between specifications and drawings: "Specifications should not overlap or duplicate information contained in the drawings. Duplication, unless repeated exactly, word for word, is harmful because it can lead to contradiction, confusion, misunderstanding and difference of opinion. Duplication, word for word, is redundant."[5] He also has described a significant difference between contract drawings and specifications:[6]

Also, the drawings, except for structural, mechanical and electrical drawings, make no attempt at segregating the work of the various trades, and all of the architectural work is shown on them as an integrated whole. The specifications, on the other hand, segregate the information depicted on the drawings into the various specification sections so that a contractor can generally let his subcontracts on the basis of the specification breakdown of sections.

Specifications

In the event that any discrepancies exist in the contract documents among drawings and specifications, the specifications take precedence. Language is the *sine qua non* of any contract, and written and printed words (in that order) stand as preferred evidence before the courts. It is for this reason that we have elected to discuss specifications prior to drawings.

Types of specifications

Generally, there are two types of specifications: (1) descriptive (method-oriented) and (2) performance (results-oriented). In each instance, the "reference specification" is used and is one that "refers to a standard established for either a material, a test method, or an installation procedure."[7] The term "proprietary specification" is also common in the field and can be defined as "one in which the specifier states outright the actual make, model, catalogue number, and so on, of a product or the installation instructions of a manufacturer."[8]

Descriptive specifications have been and are used predominantly for the great majority of constructions on this continent, including hospitals, and we predict this situation will continue to apply. The ambiguities inherent in results-oriented specifications will prevent their widespread application. However, with "the advent of systems building using major assemblies and sub-assemblies, there [has] developed a need for more sophisticated procedures to specify end results."[9] Thus, it is quite likely that some parts of specifications for many hospitals will continue to be of the performance types.

Achieving "clarity"

There are two types of ambiguities that often appear in contract specifications, both of which should be avoided:

1. *patent ambiguities*, which occur where words are omitted or are, on their face, contradictory

2. *latent ambiguities*, which are not ascertained until performance is undertaken.

Ambiguities in specifications can be avoided by (1) the employment of precise terms, and avoidance of generalizations; (2) designating completely, as opposed to partially; (3) utilization of a format that avoids repetitive designations expressed dissimilarly; and (4) specifying so clearly, completely, and definitively that interpreters must understand the intent whether or not it is to their advantage to do so.

Because specifications constitute possibly the most important part of the contract between the hospital and the construction contractor, the need for clarity and completeness stands unquestioned. Despite all attempts to achieve both, however, interpretation is sometimes required. This situation pertains not only in cases wherein motives are not altogether honest, but in cases in which both architect and contractor are sincerely striving to resolve objectively held viewpoints.

Thus, it seems that any writer of specifications should know and understand pertinent statutes and decisions regarding the rules of interpretation for contracts. This knowledge and understanding will assist in the selection of words and phrases and the complete construction of sentences, paragraphs, and sections in such a way as to avoid the ultimate need for legal interpretation. If that need arises, however, the writer, by knowing the applicable rules of interpretation, will be more likely to have written in a manner that results in an outcome favorable to the owner without unfair penalty to the contractor.

Since most state statutes derive from the English common law, they are similar in many respects, and this is true in the case of contract law. Certainly an examination here of individual state statutes is not feasible, but a brief discussion of the rules of interpretation, as they generally apply, would seem to be helpful. The reader is urged to consult statutes for individual states in which project contract interests may lie.

The following has been extracted from the Code of Georgia:[10]

1. Parol [oral] evidence is inadmissible to add to, take from, or vary a written contract. All the attendant and surrounding circumstances may be proved, and if there is an ambiguity, latent or patent, it may be explained; so if a part of a contract only is reduced to writing . . . , and it is manifest that the writing was not intended to speak the whole contract, then parol evidence is admissible.

2. Words generally bear their usual and common significance; but technical words, or words of art, or [words] used in a particular trade or business, will be construed, generally, to be used in reference to this peculiar meaning. The local usage or understanding of a word may be proved in order to arrive at the meaning intended by the parties.

3. The custom of any business or trade shall be binding only when it is of such universal practice as to justify the conclusion that it became, by implication, a part of the contract.

4. The construction which will uphold a contract in whole and in every part is to be preferred, and the whole contract should be looked to in arriving at the construction of any part.

5. If the construction is doubtful, that which goes most strongly against the party executing the instrument, or undertaking the obligation, is generally to be preferred.

6. The rules of grammatical construction usually govern, but to effectuate the intention they may be disregarded; sentences and words may be transposed, and conjunctions substituted for each other. In extreme cases of ambiguity, where the instrument as it stands is without meaning, words may be supplied.

7. When a contract is partly printed and partly written, the latter part is entitled to most consideration.

Written language can be made very precise; in specification writing, it must be precise, and the writer should be a person whose knowledge of true word meanings has been clearly proved. Words that are intrinsically ambiguous should be avoided.

The following words and phrases are often found in specifications:[11]

"as required," "when required," "if required," "as needed," "as necessary," "such as," "similar," "equal to and similar," "as needed," "usual," "customary," "suitable for the intended service," "large areas," "for purpose of early removal," "in accordance with the best practice," "correct dimensions," "properly located to insure proper operation," "correct fit," "where possible," "for the best appearance," "suitable allowance," "sufficient strength to support safely," "in such manner as to insure safety," "adequate for the total load," "finished in such a manner as to produce an attractive texture," "reasonably air tight," "snug," "thoroughly compacted," "when required," "as directed," "braced where necessary," "with minimum rubbing," "in general," "a little fancy brick work here and there," "a safe and secure installation," "adequately braced," "which positively prevent dust," "change in temperature and changes in humidity cannot be tolerated in the existing building," and "contractor shall take precautions to maintain integrity of the existing building . . . ," "adequate," "sufficient," "in compliance with the underwriter's criteria," "with least inconvenience to occupants," "in a manner satisfactory to the architect," "all applicable codes," "shall be installed strictly in accordance with the manufacturer's recommendations," "without setting forth the 'date of the doctrine,' . . . that is, the exact title, number or edition, date and page number of the bulletin, circular or catalog in which the manufacturer's printed recommendations appear."

On their face, they are generalities and subject to various interpretations. Needless to say, their use in specifications is not desirable.

On the other hand, the following designations are quite precise:[12]

Color	Graduation	Height
Extent	Thickness	Length
Pitch	Equivalence	Breadth
Proportion	Substance	Compass
Rate	Measure	Number
Amplitude	Percent	Evenness
Quantity	Dimension	Range
Balance	Degree	Degree of tolerance
Scale	Regularity	Size
Amount	Scope	Weight
Gauge	Standard	Caliber
Pounds	Distance	Direction

Temperature	Time	Inches
Date	Humidity	Days
Location	Amount of advance notice in calendar days	Duration in hours, days, etc.
Volume	Depth	Strength
Limitation as to date	Chart	Date of published recommendations of manufacturer
Maximum	Minimum	Level
Ounces	Test, specified	Commercial
Space	Ratio	Standard Number
ASTM designation	Federal specification number	Catalog number

These designations should be used where appropriate. It is obvious that "any member of the class shall serve as its own yardstick in that it is a specification with such marks as are peculiar to a member and thus distinguish it from any other individual in the class."[13]

Certainly, the architect's use of words of specificity and definitive criteria will eliminate the need for questions and oftentimes time-consuming explanations as well. In cases in which the architect must render a decision, this task is made infinitely more simple. Although all descriptions cannot be reduced to precisely quantified criteria, a specification writer should be skilled "in the use of terms which denote, differentiate, and come to the point as distinguished from terms which suggest, connote, and imply."[14]

In addition to precise language, the writer is obligated to set forth complete descriptions. Designations and descriptions that are set forth should be sufficiently detailed that no doubt is left in a reasonable mind as to the methods and materials intended.

With regard to building, electrical, and mechanical codes, the general conditions of the contract documents should state that the work shall be done in accordance with applicable codes, and that both architects and engineers shall certify that their drawings and specifications comply. The mere designation of a code, however, is a generality that ethically should not be relied upon as an all-inclusive demand on the contractor. Specifications and drawings should be so executed that the documentations themselves definitively designate the work, qualitatively as well as quantitatively.

Because the writing of specifications has grown to be a science unto itself, with entire volumes having been published with regard thereto, our comments here are limited. Without going into lengthy discussion, the following additional points are noted with regard to the achievement of "clarity":

1. Materials, products, equipment, and articles should not be designated merely by trade name; instead, where possible, a number, a commercial standard, federal specification, or other recognized designation should be used. If this is not possible, the item should be designated

by manufacturer's name, catalog number, model number, or serial number.

2. The format and content sequence of the specification should be uniform from one building trade section to another.

3. Specifications should designate "what," rather than "who." The writer should leave the responsibility for performance to the contractor.

4. Provisions that are not expected to be enforced should not be put in the specifications.

5. Specifications should not designate what is *not* required. Their "clarity" should be such that no doubt remains as to what *is* required.

Form

The Construction Specification Institute (CSI) has devised a systematic format for organizing specifications. The most recent update is the CSI *Masterformat*,[15] presented here as Exhibit 11–1. The American Institute of Architects (AIA) has now organized its own specification work sheets and filing system according to the *Masterformat* system. In this system, the technical sections are prepared as they were previously, except that these sections are then placed under a fixed division, and each is assigned a five-digit section number (see Exhibit 11–1). Some specifications writers use an alphanumeric section number (e.g., 2A and 2B, or 5A and 5B) in lieu of the fixed five-digit number. If local trade practices or conditions of the specific project so dictate, the specifications writer has the prerogative to alter the location of the information and the section.[16]

The obvious advantages of this system of organizing the specifications have been stated by Rosen:[17]

> In preparing his specification section, the specifier no longer needs to be concerned with whether the architect or the engineer adds or deletes certain materials or trades as he develops his drawings. Previously, this change in design meant the deletion of a specification section, or the inclusion at the last moment of a specification section, placed entirely out of sequence. Under the *Masterformat* such revisions do not impose hardships since a section can be added to or deleted from a specific division without radically upsetting the sequence and numbering system. The specifier can write or prepare sections long before the drawings are completed and assign numbers to them immediately. In addition, the specification writer can now file material, shop drawings, correspondence, technical data, literature, samples, estimates, and a host of office memoranda under a similar numbering system. The contractor, manufacturer, estimator, and inspector can more readily find those items in the specifications with which he or she is concerned.

Use of this standardized format is advantageous not only for the specifier but also for the estimators during bidding. Order is brought to

Exhibit 11–1

CSI format: *Masterformat*

Division 0—Bidding Requirements, Contract Forms, and Conditions of the Contract

00010 Pre-Bid Information
00100 Instructions to Bidders
00200 Information Available to Bidders
00300 Bid Forms
00400 Supplements to Bid Forms
00500 Agreement Forms
00600 Bonds and Certificates
00700 General Conditions
00800 Supplementary Conditions
00850 Drawings and Schedules
00900 Addenda and Modifications

Division 1—General Requirements

01010 Summary of Work
01020 Allowances
01025 Measurement and Payment
01030 Alternates/Alternatives
01040 Coordination
01050 Field Engineering
01060 Regulatory Requirements
01070 Abbreviations and Symbols
01080 Identification System
01100 Special Project Procedures
01200 Project Meetings
01300 Submittals
01400 Quality Control
01500 Construction Facilities and Temporary Controls
01600 Materials and Equipment
01650 Starting of Systems/Commissioning
01700 Contract Closeout
01800 Maintenance

Division 2—Sitework

02010 Subsurface Investigation
02050 Demolition
02100 Site Preparation
02140 Dewatering
02150 Shoring and Underpinning
02160 Excavation Support Systems
02170 Cofferdams
02200 Earthwork
02300 Tunnelling
02350 Piles, Caissons
02450 Railroad Work
02480 Marine Work
02500 Paving and Surfacing
02590 Ponds and Reservoirs
02600 Piped Utility Materials
02660 Water Distribution
02680 Fuel Distribution
02700 Sewage and Drainage
02760 Restoration of Underground Pipelines
02770 Ponds and Reservoirs

02780 Power and Communications
02800 Site Improvements
02900 Landscaping

Division 3—Concrete

03100 Concrete Formwork
03200 Concrete Reinforcement
03250 Concrete Accessories
03300 Cast-in-Place Concrete
03370 Concrete Curing
03400 Precast Concrete
03500 Cementitious Decks
03600 Grout
03700 Concrete Restoration and Cleaning
03800 Mass Concrete

Division 4—Masonry

04100 Mortar
04150 Masonry Accessories
04200 Unit Masonry
04400 Stone
04500 Masonry Restoration and Cleaning
04550 Refractories
04600 Corrosion-Resistant Masonry

Division 5—Metals

05010 Metal Materials
05030 Metal Finishes
05050 Metal Fastening
05100 Structural Metal Framing
05200 Metal Joists
05300 Metal Decking
05400 Cold-Formed Metal Framing
05500 Metal Fabrications
05580 Sheet Metal Fabrications
05700 Ornamental Metal
05800 Expansion Control
05900 Hydraulic Structures

Division 6—Wood and Plastics

06050 Fasteners and Adhesives
06100 Rough Carpentry
06130 Heavy Timber Construction
06150 Wood-Metal Systems
06170 Prefabricated Structural Wood
06200 Finish Carpentry
06300 Wood Treatment
06400 Architectural Woodwork
06500 Prefabricated Structural Plastics
06600 Plastic Fabrications

Divison 7—Thermal and Moisture Protection

07100 Waterproofing
07150 Damp-proofing
07200 Insulation
07250 Fireproofing

Exhibit 11–1 continued

07300 Shingles and Roofing Tiles
07400 Preformed Roofing and Cladding/
      Sliding
07500 Membrane Roofing
07570 Traffic Topping
07600 Flashing and Sheet Metal
07700 Roof Specialties and Accessories
07800 Skylights
07900 Joint Sealants

Division 8—Doors and Windows

08100 Metal Doors and Frames
08200 Wood and Plastic Doors
08250 Door Opening Assemblies
08300 Special Doors
08400 Entrances and Storefronts
08500 Metal Windows
08600 Wood and Plastic Windows
08650 Special Windows
08700 Hardware
08800 Glazing
08900 Glazed Curtain Walls

Division 9—Finishes

09100 Metal Support Systems
09200 Lath and Plaster
09230 Aggregate Coatings
09250 Gypsum Wallboard
09300 Tile
09400 Terrazzo
09500 Acoustical Treatment
09540 Special Surfaces
09550 Wood Flooring
09600 Stone Flooring
09630 Unit Masonry Flooring
09650 Resilient Flooring
09680 Carpet
09700 Special Flooring
09760 Floor Treatment
09800 Special Coatings
09900 Painting
09950 Wall Covering

Division 10—Specialties

10100 Chalkboards and Tackboards
10150 Compartments and Cubicles
10200 Louvers and Vents
10240 Grilles and Screens
10250 Service Wall Systems
10260 Wall and Corner Guards
10270 Access Flooring
10280 Specialty Modules
10290 Pest Control
10300 Fireplaces and Stoves
10340 Prefabricated Exterior Specialties
10350 Flagpoles
10400 Identifying Devices
10450 Pedestrian Control Devices
10500 Lockers

10520 Fire Protection Specialties
10530 Protective Covers
10550 Postal Specialties
10600 Partitions
10650 Operable Partitions
10670 Storage Shelving
10700 Exterior Sun Control Devices
10750 Telephone Specialties
10800 Toilet and Bath Accessories
10880 Scales
10900 Wardrobe Specialties

Division 11—Equipment

11010 Maintenance Equipment
11020 Security and Vault Equipment
11030 Teller and Service Equipment
11040 Ecclesiastical Equipment
11050 Library Equipment
11060 Theater and Stage Equipment
11070 Instrumental Equipment
11080 Registration Equipment
11090 Checkroom Equipment
11100 Mercantile Equipment
11110 Commercial Laundry and Dry Cleaning
      Equipment
11120 Vending Equipment
11130 Audio-Visual Equipment
11140 Service Station Equipment
11150 Parking Equipment
11170 Solid Waste Handling Equipment
11190 Detention Equipment
11200 Water Supply and Treatment
      Equipment
11280 Hydraulic Gates and Valves
11300 Fluid Waste Treatment and Disposal
      Equipment
11400 Food Service Equipment
11450 Residential Equipment
11460 Unit Kitchens
11470 Darkroom Equipment
11480 Athletic, Recreational, and Therapeutic
      Equipment
11500 Industrial and Process Equipment
11600 Laboratory Equipment
11650 Planetarium Equipment
11660 Observatory Equipment
11700 Medical Equipment
11780 Mortuary Equipment
11850 Navigation Equipment

Division 12—Furnishings

12050 Fabrics
12100 Artwork
12300 Manufactured Casework
12500 Window Treatment
12600 Furniture and Accessories
12670 Rugs and Mats
12700 Multiple Seating
12800 Interior Plants and Plantings

Exhibit 11–1 continued

Division 13—Special Construction

13010 Air-Supported Structures
13020 Integrated Assemblies
13030 Special Purpose Room
13080 Sound, Vibration, and Seismic Control
13090 Radiation Protection
13100 Nuclear Reactors
13110 Observatories
13120 Pre-engineered Structures
13150 Pools
13160 Ice Rinks
13170 Kennels and Animal Shelters
13180 Site Constructed Incinerators
13200 Liquid and Gas Storage Tanks
13220 Filter Underdrains and Media
13230 Digestion Tank Covers and
       Appurtenances
13240 Oxygenation Systems
13260 Sludge Conditioning Room
13300 Utility Control Systems
13400 Industrial and Process Control Systems
13500 Recording Instrumentation
13550 Transportation Control Instrumentation
13600 Solar Energy Systems
13700 Wind Energy Systems
13800 Building Automation Systems
13900 Fire Supervisory Systems

Division 14—Conveying Systems

14100 Dumbwaiters
14200 Elevators
14300 Moving Stairs and Walks
14400 Lifts

14500 Material Handling Systems
14600 Hoists and Cranes
14700 Turntables
14800 Scaffolding
14900 Transportation Systems

Division 15—Mechanical

15050 Basic Materials and Method
15250 Mechanical Insulation
15400 Plumbing
15500 Heating, Ventilating, and Air
       Conditioning
15550 Heat Generation
15650 Refrigeration
15750 Heat Transfer
15880 Air Distribution
15950 Controls
15990 Testing, Adjusting, and Balancing

Division 16—Electrical

16050 Basic Electrical Materials and Methods
16200 Power Generation
16300 High Voltage Distribution (Above 600
       Volt)
16400 Service and Distribution (600 Volt and
       Below)
16500 Lighting
16600 Special Systems
16700 Communications
16850 Electric Resistance Heating
16900 Controls
16950 Testing

Source: Reproduced by permission of The Construction Specification Institute, Inc., Alexandria, Va., 22314.

---

the bidding process, and chances for duplications and overlaps are almost eliminated.

Design/build methodology
In recent years, the design/build (D/B) method of implementing hospital construction has been employed to some extent. Under this approach, discussed more fully in Chapter 2, it has been common to see highly abbreviated specifications, since the designers also usually undertake construction, and there may be no competitive bidding other than that advantageous to the D/B firm for specific subcontractor work. Although the general quality of specifications may be improving on most D/B projects, owing to owner demands and the entry of ethical professionals into the field, any hospital considering D/B should assure itself that the work is specified with clarity and in detail. (Owners should also place controls on the extent and nature of bidding and on job-site supervision.) If the work is not precisely specified, the chances of receiving a quality

product may be greatly reduced since the finished structure will depend almost directly on whims of the D/B firm and the profit it can or desires to make at a given point in time.

Working drawings

Current status

To the average layperson, and even to the typical hospital administrator, other hospital executives, and governing board members, working drawings represent a maze of largely unintelligible lines and symbols. Some directors of planning, by either experience or training, may be able to make a worthwhile interpretation, but as a rule, few hospital staff or governing board members can be expected to read working drawings intelligently or to adjudge their "clarity." In view of the importance of achieving "clarity," it seems that there should be some easy means of assuring it.

However, architecture and engineering are inherently specialized and complicated disciplines. This fact, together with the basic complexity of a hospital structure and the lack of language in the owner-architect contract defining and specifying work quality, means that the greatest assurance of "clarity" lies in initially contracting with the best A&E firm possible through an appropriate selection process.

The functional planner and construction manager can counsel architects and engineers in preparing these drawings, but it is uncommon that such persons are more technically qualified in this area than staff members of an A&E firm. Some functional planning firms now have experienced architects and engineers on staff who can exercise a degree of control for the owner and can lend valuable advice to A&E firms that are relatively inexperienced in hospital design. Some construction managers can assist in like manner. However, in the preparation of working drawings, architects and engineers are truly practicing the disciplines for which they have been highly trained; thus, from all aspects, best assurance for "clarity" seems to lie, as stated, in commissioning a reputable, experienced firm.

Working drawings (see Figure 11–1) should legibly show all construction, fixed equipment, and mechanical and electrical systems as-built or as-installed. They present, through fully and precisely dimensioned orthographical drawings (Figure 11–2) and elevations (Figure 11–3), the scope of the work and the details of what is to be done. Graphical symbols and characteristic lines are used to designate details and location. Written or printed schedules are used to present types and characteristics of finishes, windows, doors, and items of equipment.

As we have previously pointed out, the purposes of drawings and specifications are different, and they should not contain duplicate information. Information that is best conveyed graphically should be presented in the drawings; information that can be most lucidly conveyed by language should go in the specifications. Time has confirmed this approach, and it has been said that drawings "portray the physical aspects of the structure, showing the arrangement dimensions, construction details, materials and other information necessary for bidding and building the project."[18]

Example of working drawings

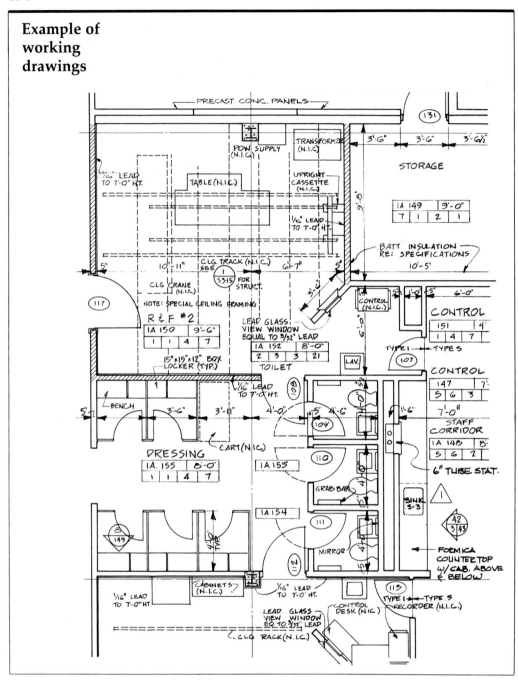

With regard to rules of interpretation as they relate specifically to the drawings, written dimensions are preferred to scaled dimensions; large-scale drawings are preferable to small-scale drawings; and writing has preference over typing. Generally, if there is conflict between drawings and specifications, the specifications will hold, as previously noted.

Various scales are used in the execution of working drawings, but, generally, site plans are designated by 1 inch = 20 feet or larger scale.

Example of detailed room plan

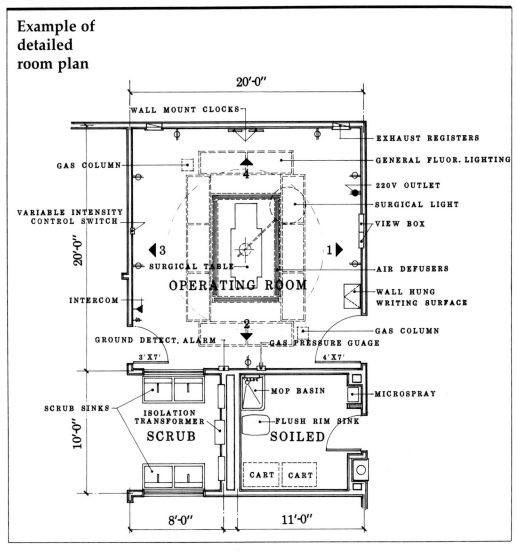

Depending upon requirements for "clarity" in presenting overall building configurations and close detail, scales from ⅟₁₆ inch = 1 foot to ½ inch = 1 foot are not uncommon; ⅛ inch = 1 foot is usually used for electrical and mechanical drawings. It is not unusual to see five or six different scales used on the same sheet, especially among the architectural drawings, depending upon the optimal presentation for a particular section or other detail.

In Canada, conversion has recently been made to metric scales, and in Europe metric scales are used exclusively. Little or no advances have been made in this nation toward the use of metric scales. The U.S. Department of Defense, with its overseas interests, has made some preparations in this regard, but we predict that the current use of inches and feet will continue in the United States for the foreseeable future.

As an example of the volume of work required on a project of rather limited scope, the following table lists numbers and types of drawings

Examples of wall elevations

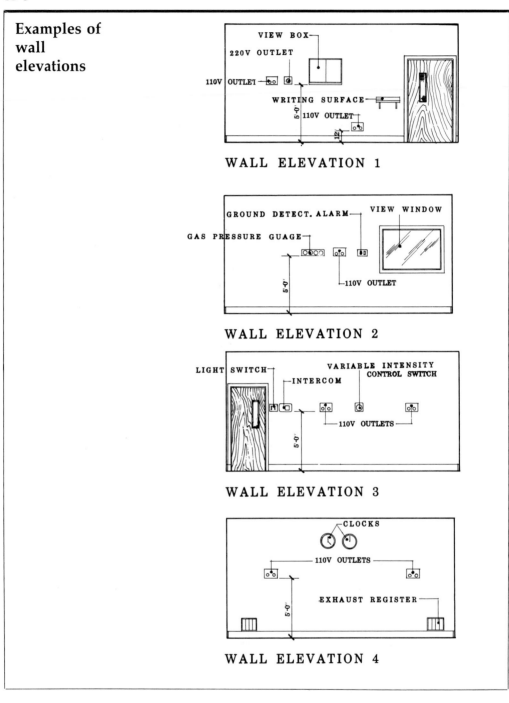

WALL ELEVATION 1

WALL ELEVATION 2

WALL ELEVATION 3

WALL ELEVATION 4

required for a single contract for additions and alterations to an existing hospital:

Drawings	Sheets
Site plan	2
Architectural	42

Structural	14
Utilities site plan	2
Mechanical plan	2
Plumbing	24
Mechanical	30
Electrical	25
Total	141

The construction cost of this project, for which the contract was let in 1983, was $15 million.

It is our experience that American architects (including those in Canada) execute the finest-quality drawings in the world; we attribute this primarily to their independent, professional status.

The Occupational Safety and Health Act (OSHA) has further complicated the formulation of working drawings. This is an area in which both hospital executives and architects must be knowledgeable. The subject is too complex for discussion here, and the reader is merely referred to *Designer's Guide to OSHA*, by Peter S. Hopt.[19]

Change orders

One of the purposes of making construction documents clear and complete is the avoidance of change orders. The quality of drawings and specifications is subject to gross measurement, ex post facto, by the number of change orders among projects of similar scope.

Owners cannot expect that there will be no change orders, however, for architects and engineers, like other human beings, are not perfect. The myriad of complex details that must make up drawings for modern hospitals virtually assures that no project of more than a million or so dollars in cost will be constructed without several change orders.

Actually, the greatest source of change orders is unrelated to clarity of the construction documents. This source is additional owner decisions reached after construction is started.

For a project with a capable A&E firm and construction manager, the magnitude of change order–related costs that can be presumed reasonable is about 5 percent of all construction costs. For all reasons, this was the approximate percentage recently reported by the Associated General Contractors of America on five highly prestigious projects with total construction costs of some $116 million.[20]

Role of the functional planner

The role of the functional planner is reduced considerably in the construction documents phase. However, this consultant remains on call to the architect and, as specified in the contract with the client, usually supplies formal critiques of the drawings at the 50, 75, 90, and 100 percent stages of completion. Review of the specifications by the functional planner is desirable as well. These reviews should be performed promptly so as not to delay the work progress of the architect.

As has been pointed out, the contract documents phase is largely an A&E activity, and it is an activity reflecting, primarily, decisions made in previous phases. The functional planner can advise as to proposed changes and, if the A&E firm contracted for the project is inexperienced in hospital design, can also lend invaluable assistance by furnishing example documentations (such examples can be acquired, with permission, from past projects).

Role of the construction manager

The construction manager assumes responsibility for managing the project during construction in much the same way as the general contractor traditionally has done. The Associated General Contractors of America has published CM guidelines and states the following regarding the functions of the construction manager during the construction phase:[21]

> a. He will maintain competent supervisory staff to coordinate and provide general direction of the work and progress of the contractors on the Project.
> b. He will observe the work as it is being performed, until final completion and acceptance by the Owner, to assure that the Materials furnished and work performed are in accordance with working drawings and specifications.
> c. He will establish an organization and lines of authority in order to carry out the overall plans of the Construction Team.
> d. He will establish procedures for coordination among the Owner, Architect-Engineer, contractors and Construction Manager with respect to all aspects of the Project and implement such procedures. He will maintain job site records and make appropriate progress reports.
> e. In cooperation with the Architect-Engineer, he will establish and implement procedures to be followed for expediting and processing all shop drawings, samples, catalogs, and other Project documents.
> f. He will implement an effective labor policy in conformance with local, state, and national labor laws. He will review the safety and EEO programs of each contractor and make appropriate recommendations.
> g. He will review and process all applications for payment by involved contractors and material suppliers in accordance with the terms of the contract.
> h. He will make recommendations for and process requests for changes in the work and maintain records of change orders.
> i. He will furnish either with his own forces or others all General Conditions items as required.
> j. He will perform portions of the work with his own forces if requested by the Owner to do so.
> k. He will schedule and conduct job meetings to ensure the orderly progress of the work.
> l. When the Project is of sufficient size and complexity, the Construction Manager will provide data processing services as may be appropriate.
> m. He will refer all questions relative to interpretation of design intent to the Architect-Engineer.
> n. He will continue the close monitoring of the Project progress schedule, coordinating and expediting the work of all of the

contractors and his own forces and provide periodic status reports to the Team.

o. He will establish and maintain an effective cost control system, monitoring all Project costs. He will schedule and conduct appropriate meetings to review costs and be responsible for providing periodic reports to the Team on cost status.

If phased construction is undertaken, it becomes obligatory upon the construction manager to provide estimates on every contract at the time of bidding each individual one. In this manner, accuracy can be maintained and possibly increased because the reestimates are made ever closer to the time of bidding.

Some years ago, we were associated with one rather large "fast-track" project in which estimates were made of all separate contracts only at the time of bidding the first. A year and a half later, budgets were greatly exceeded by one award after another. Had contract estimating been accomplished, the owner at least would have had no surprises and, more important, could have taken measures of economy judiciously in several bid packages *before* they were advertised to contractors.

Hospital actions

When the working drawings and specifications are complete and when the construction manager has made a last estimate and the functional planner a final critique, the architect should request review and approval by the hospital. The director of planning or other designated person should take charge and make whatever presentation is requested by the governing board. Usually, if the planning and design process has been organized and conducted properly, board approval will be a perfunctory matter, in the case of either a single general contract or one of several separate contracts in phased construction.

Conditions of the contract

The AIA publishes a sample document specifying general conditions of the contract, which are nearly universally used for construction contracts in this nation. This document, entitled *General Conditions of the Contract for Construction* (AIA Document A201), has stood the test of time, and any architect or owner is well advised to use the latest version of it, with amendments being made as necessary in individual situations.

Richard Clough has described the purposes of this portion of the contract:[22]

The general conditions . . . set forth the manner and procedures whereby the provisions of the contract are to be implemented according to accepted practices in the construction industry. These conditions are intended to govern and regulate the obligations of the formal contract. . . . They are not intended to regulate the internal workings of either party to the agreement, except insofar as the activities of one may affect the contractual right of the other party or the proper execution of the work.

General conditions
Essentially, the "general conditions" of the contract represent the bases of the contract between an owner and a construction contractor. However, this portion of the contract also outlines the role of the architect who, while being an agent of the owner, is supposed to administer the contract in an impartial manner. The fact that contractors have acceded to these conditions for decades attests both to the efficiency of the arrangement and to the professional integrity of architects.

The article headings from the "Table of Articles" in the AIA's *General Conditions of the Contract for Construction*, together with brief statements regarding the most pertinent points cited under each, are set forth in the following listing:[23]

1. "Contract Documents." The initial article defines the contract documents, the contract, the work, and the project, together with the method of execution, correlation among the several documents, the intention of the documents, and the method of interpretation. A statement that all drawings, specifications, and copies thereof remain the property of the architect, with restrictions on their use, has also been included.

2. "Architect." A definition of the term "architect" and a description of this consultant's role, authority, and responsibilities are set forth.

3. "Owner." The term "owner" is defined, and owner's rights and responsibilities are identified.

4. "Contractor." The term "contractor" is defined, and contractor's rights and responsibilities are spelled out with regard to most aspects of the work.

5. "Subcontractors." A definition of subcontractors is given; how awards for subcontract and changes in subcontractors will be made is spelled out, and the relationship that must exist between the contractor and subcontractor is explained.

6. "Work by Owner or by Separate Contractors." The owner's right to perform work and to award separate contracts is established; the mutual responsibility of contractors in coordinating work is specified; and the owner's right to perform clean-up work is explained.

7. "Miscellaneous Provisions." This article outlines provisions related to governing laws, successors and assigns, written notices, claims for damages, performance bond and labor and material payment bond, rights and remedies, royalties and patents, tests, interest on monies due and not paid, and arbitration.

8. "Time." Definitions of "contract time," "date of commencement," and "date of substantial completion of the work" are set forth. A statement specifies that time limits stated in the contract documents are of the essence of the contract. How delays and extensions of time will be handled is explained.

9. "Payments and Completion." This article defines contract sums and sets forth requirements of a submittal by the contractor to the architect of a "Schedule of Values," based on the relative worth of the various portions of the contract work, for use in making payments to the contractor. It also outlines how progress payments will be made, how the architect will issue certificates of payment to the owner, the bases on which payments to the contractor may be withheld and the methodology for doing so. The actions the contractor may take in the event of unjustified nonpayment of the "Application for Payment" are explained. The method by which substantial completion of the work or portions thereof will be established is outlined, and actions pertaining to the architect's inspections and final approval are detailed, including the method for securing final payment for the contractor. Verification and other actions the contractor may consummate in obtaining final payment and other details incidental to completing the work and settling the contract are described. Final explanations clarify the bases for waiving of claims, both by the contractor and owner (with exceptions).

10. "Protection of Persons and Property." Explanations here relate to the contractor's responsibilities regarding safety precautions; the prevention of damages, injury, or losses; the contractor's compliance with applicable laws and regulations; and the contractor's necessary actions regarding safeguards and protection from a variety of standpoints. What the contractor should do in the event of dangerous emergencies is specified. Other descriptions outline remedies to be effected by the contractor for damages and losses by reason of the contractor's liability.

11. "Insurance." This article describes types and requirements of insurance policies that the contractor and the owner must maintain. Manner of proof of insurance coverage, how losses are handled, and how monies received from insured losses will be handled are also covered here.

12. "Changes in the Work." Descriptions here outline the methodology regarding the handling of owner-initiated change orders and the manner in which costs will be adjusted by reason thereof. Other language details the way the contractor shall make claim for increases in the contract sum; how the architect shall order minor changes in the work; and the architect's actions in preparation and issuance of field orders.

13. "Uncovering and Correction of Work." This article describes circumstances related to uncovering work for inspection by the architect; the contractor's responsibilities and actions in correcting defective work and the time frame relating thereto; the possible consequences attaching to the contractor's failures in correcting defective work; and the owner's right to accept defective work under a change order procedure.

14. "Termination of the Contract." The final article outlines circumstances under which either the contractor or the owner may terminate the contract, together with the rights of each regarding monies involved.

Supplementary conditions

Because the general conditions, as cited, cannot be applied in toto to a specific project, "supplementary conditions" have to be formulated. Generally, these supplementary conditions effect conformance to specific situations not covered under the general conditions and provide a way to modify the general conditions. Heery has cited a number of examples of supplements to general conditions related to such items as time extension, substantial completion and beneficial occupancy, requirements of the contractor job superintendent, extension of time in change orders, and other matters.[24]

Liquidated damages

A decade or so ago many architects believed that contractual clauses related to liquidated damages were better omitted, for various reasons. The inclusion of such clauses was said to result in elevated bids. The difficulty in enforcement also was cited, and some expressed doubt as to the legality of these provisions. Another line of reasoning assumed, falsely, that the contractor is always just as anxious as the owner to finish the project. However, after a number of undesirable outcomes received wide publicity, interest in liquidated damages again heightened.

One approach to the problem of liquidated damages is to allow a perfectly reasonable time for finishing the work. Then for each day beyond scheduled completion, allowing for extensions properly calculated, the contractor would be required to pay the hospital's daily losses due to incompletion. Daily losses, however, should be expressed contractually as a certain sum, so that there can be no arguments related to calculations. Also, the sum should be large enough to provide a stimulus for expediting the work and finishing the project.

Bidding phase

The construction work for most hospital projects is awarded through a competitive bid process, and despite the inroads made by D/B firms, it is safe to say that the competitive process will continue to predominate. Competition has been the heart of this nation's capitalistic form of economy, and there is no reason to predict its demise.

The appropriate management of the bid process is critical. Hira N. Ahuja has stated, "If care is not exercised in obtaining the lowest cost in awarding contracts, economy achieved in design can be destroyed. In inviting bids, it is vitally important to obtain a bid from the hungry contractor."[25] Our experience directly corroborates this statement.

Two aspects of bidding phase activities are discussed here: (1) bidding requirements and (2) managing the process.

Bidding requirements

Rosen has succinctly described those documentations required in bidding:[26]

> Bidding requirements consist of documents that are used in the solicitation of bids by an owner or an agency. The documents are directed to bidders who might be interested in submitting bids for a project. These documents consist of three essential forms dealing with advertising, or notifying interested bidders of the existence of a proposed project; instructions pertaining to the submission of a proposal or bid; and the sample form on which the bid is to be executed by a bidder.

Invitation to bid

Documents notifying potential bidders about a proposed construction have taken a number of forms, but all must contain the same pertinent information. Generally, the following must be included in an "invitation to bid":

1. the fact that sealed bids are invited

2. the name of the project and its location by site, city, and state

3. the name and address of the owner and the name and address of the architectural firm preparing the construction documents

4. the exact time and location of prebid conferences, if any

5. the exact time deadline for receipt of bids and the exact time and place of opening, as well as the place where bids will be delivered and opened

6. the several places where bid documents may be examined and the hours of the day during which they may be examined

7. the conditions under which bid documents may be obtained, including costs and the methodology for securing refunds

8. the nature of the contract—that is, whether or not a part of phased construction or a single contract on a lump sum basis

9. the length of time during which the proposal must stand as submitted

10. the type and amount of bid bond or guarantee

11. the owner's reservations as to the conditions under which bids may be rejected, the waiving of formalities in bidding, and reservations regarding contract awards, if any.

A sample of a typical invitation to bid is set forth in Exhibit 11–2.

Exhibit 11–2

A typical invitation to bid

INVITATION TO BID

All prequalified bidders are invited to submit sealed bids for the construction of the New Medical Center Hospital to be located on the northwest corner of Main Street and Center Avenue in the Town of Reston, Virginia.

The owner of the project is the Medical Center Hospital, Inc., 475 Center Avenue, Reston, Virginia 22090. The architectural firm preparing the construction documents is LGA Architects, 11333 Sunset Hills Road, Reston, Virginia 22090.

A pre-bid conference is scheduled for 1:30 PM E.S.T., October 22, 1986 at the office of the architect.

Bids will be received at Suite 311, Medical Center Hospital, Inc., 475 Center Avenue, Reston, Virginia 22090 until 2:00 PM E.S.T. on the third day of November, 1986, where all bids will be opened and read aloud. No bids will be accepted after this time.

Plans and specifications may be examined at the architect's office or copies may be obtained from the architect upon deposit of $300.00 per set. Deposits will be refunded upon return of same in good condition and within (20) days after date of opening of bids.

The awarding of the contract shall be on a lump-sum basis and may not be withdrawn for a period of (30) days after the opening date of the bids. A bid bond in the amount of 5% of the base bid is required.

The owner reserves the right to reject any and all bids.

Instruction to bidders
"Instructions to bidders" are exactly what the name implies. They usually consist of the following:

1. the terms of eligibility of bidders

2. the form of bid submitted, the number of copies to be submitted, and the manner in which they will be executed, including the information to be contained on the outside of the enclosing sealed bid cover

3. references to the information contained in the invitation to bid; special conditions (e.g., completion dates, liquidated damage); and general and supplementary conditions

4. how and to whom prospective bidders will make inquiries and the manner in which responses will be made

5. method for resolving contradictions or omissions in the documents, together with the issuance of addenda and later incorporation of same

6. a directive specifying the necessity to achieve familiarization with all conditions affecting the work regarding both documents and site, together with a recitation of the most important conditions

7. how oral, telephonic, and telegraphic proposals or modifications will be handled; how bids can be withdrawn

8. the requirements related to bid bonds, and time and method of return of same to bidders not successful

9. A description of the manner in which acceptance or rejection of bids will be made

10. the requirements for bidding qualifications and the method of proving same

11. a statement as to ownership of documents, the cost of single and additional sets, and methods of refund upon return.

Although there are other forms widely used, the AIA has issued sample *Instructions to Bidders* (AIA Document A701, 1978), which is set forth here as Exhibit 11–3.

Bid form
Many architects use the designation "form of proposal" rather than "bid form." The purpose of the form, of course, is to ensure similarity in submittals and resultant ease in interpretation. Essentially, the bid form, when it is executed by a bidder, represents a response to the invitation to bid, in conformance with the instructions to bidders, which the bidder has previously received and acknowledged. The executed copy is, then, the bid itself.

The primary aspects of a bid form include the following:

1. the name and address of the owner to whom the executed bid will be addressed

2. blanks for name and address of the bidder from whom the bid is being delivered

3. a description of the construction for which the bid is being submitted by title of the contract document

4. blanks for the time and date of mailing of the bid, preferably by registered mail

Exhibit 11–3

Instructions to Bidders: AIA Document A701, 1978

THE AMERICAN INSTITUTE OF ARCHITECTS

AIA Document A701

Instructions to Bidders

1978 EDITION

Use only with the 1976 Edition of AIA Document A201, General Conditions of the Contract for Construction

TABLE OF ARTICLES

1. DEFINITIONS

2. BIDDER'S REPRESENTATIONS

3. BIDDING DOCUMENTS

4. BIDDING PROCEDURES

5. CONSIDERATION OF BIDS

6. POST-BID INFORMATION

7. PERFORMANCE BOND AND LABOR AND MATERIAL PAYMENT BOND

8. FORM OF AGREEMENT BETWEEN OWNER AND CONTRACTOR

9. SUPPLEMENTARY INSTRUCTIONS

Exhibit 11–3 continued

INSTRUCTIONS TO BIDDERS

ARTICLE 1
DEFINITIONS

1.1 Bidding Documents include the Advertisement or Invitation to Bid, Instructions to Bidders, the bid form, other sample bidding and contract forms and the proposed Contract Documents including any Addenda issued prior to receipt of bids. The Contract Documents proposed for the Work consist of the Owner-Contractor Agreement, the Conditions of the Contract (General, Supplementary and other Conditions), the Drawings, the Specifications and all Addenda issued prior to and all Modifications issued after execution of the Contract.

1.2 All definitions set forth in the General Conditions of the Contract for Construction, AIA Document A201, or in other Contract Documents are applicable to the Bidding Documents.

1.3 Addenda are written or graphic instruments issued by the Architect prior to the execution of the Contract which modify or interpret the Bidding Documents by additions, deletions, clarifications or corrections.

1.4 A Bid is a complete and properly signed proposal to do the Work or designated portion thereof for the sums stipulated therein, submitted in accordance with the Bidding Documents.

1.5 The Base Bid is the sum stated in the Bid for which the Bidder offers to perform the Work described in the Bidding Documents as the base, to which work may be added or from which work may be deleted for sums stated in Alternate Bids.

1.6 An Alternate Bid (or Alternate) is an amount stated in the Bid to be added to or deducted from the amount of the Base Bid if the corresponding change in the Work, as described in the Bidding Documents, is accepted.

1.7 A Unit Price is an amount stated in the Bid as a price per unit of measurement for materials or services as described in the Bidding Documents or in the proposed Contract Documents.

1.8 A Bidder is a person or entity who submits a Bid.

1.9 A Sub-bidder is a person or entity who submits a bid to a Bidder for materials or labor for a portion of the Work.

ARTICLE 2
BIDDER'S REPRESENTATIONS

2.1 Each Bidder by making his Bid represents that:

2.1.1 He has read and understands the Bidding Documents and his Bid is made in accordance therewith.

2.1.2 He has visited the site, has familiarized himself with the local conditions under which the Work is to be performed and has correlated his observations with the requirements of the proposed Contract Documents.

2.1.3 His Bid is based upon the materials, systems and equipment required by the Bidding Documents without exception.

ARTICLE 3
BIDDING DOCUMENTS

3.1 COPIES

3.1.1 Bidders may obtain complete sets of the Bidding Documents from the issuing office designated in the Advertisement or Invitation to Bid in the number and for the deposit sum, if any, stated therein. The deposit will be refunded to Bidders who submit a bona fide Bid and return the Bidding Documents in good condition within ten days after receipt of Bids. The cost of replacement of any missing or damaged documents will be deducted from the deposit. A Bidder receiving a Contract award may retain the Bidding Documents and his deposit will be refunded.

3.1.2 Bidding Documents will not be issued directly to Sub-bidders or others unless specifically offered in the Advertisement or Invitation to Bid.

3.1.3 Bidders shall use complete sets of Bidding Documents in preparing Bids; neither the Owner nor the Architect assume any responsibility for errors or misinterpretations resulting from the use of incomplete sets of Bidding Documents.

3.1.4 The Owner or the Architect in making copies of the Bidding Documents available on the above terms do so only for the purpose of obtaining Bids on the Work and do not confer a license or grant for any other use.

3.2 INTERPRETATION OR CORRECTION OF BIDDING DOCUMENTS

3.2.1 Bidders and Sub-bidders shall promptly notify the Architect of any ambiguity, inconsistency or error which they may discover upon examination of the Bidding Documents or of the site and local conditions.

3.2.2 Bidders and Sub-bidders requiring clarification or interpretation of the Bidding Documents shall make a written request which shall reach the Architect at least seven days prior to the date for receipt of Bids.

3.2.3 Any interpretation, correction or change of the Bidding Documents will be made by Addendum. Interpretations, corrections or changes of the Bidding Documents made in any other manner will not be binding, and Bidders shall not rely upon such interpretations, corrections and changes.

3.3 SUBSTITUTIONS

3.3.1 The materials, products and equipment described in the Bidding Documents establish a standard of required function, dimension, appearance and quality to be met by any proposed substitution.

3.3.2 No substitution will be considered prior to receipt of Bids unless written request for approval has been re-

---

Exhibit 11–3 continued

ceived by the Architect at least ten days prior to the date for receipt of Bids. Each such request shall include the name of the material or equipment for which it is to be substituted and a complete description of the proposed substitute including drawings, cuts, performance and test data and any other information necessary for an evaluation. A statement setting forth any changes in other materials, equipment or other Work that incorporation of the substitute would require shall be included. The burden of proof of the merit of the proposed substitute is upon the proposer. The Architect's decision of approval or disapproval of a proposed substitution shall be final.

3.3.3 If the Architect approves any proposed substitution prior to receipt of Bids, such approval will be set forth in an Addendum. Bidders shall not rely upon approvals made in any other manner.

3.3.4 No substitutions will be considered after the Contract award unless specifically provided in the Contract Documents.

3.4 **ADDENDA**

3.4.1 Addenda will be mailed or delivered to all who are known by the Architect to have received a complete set of Bidding Documents.

3.4.2 Copies of Addenda will be made available for inspection wherever Bidding Documents are on file for that purpose.

3.4.3 No Addenda will be issued later than four days prior to the date for receipt of Bids except an Addendum withdrawing the request for Bids or one which includes postponement of the date for receipt of Bids.

3.4.4 Each Bidder shall ascertain prior to submitting his bid that he has received all Addenda issued, and he shall acknowledge their receipt in his Bid.

ARTICLE 4
BIDDING PROCEDURE

4.1 **FORM AND STYLE OF BIDS**

4.1.1 Bids shall be submitted on forms identical to the form included with the Bidding Documents, in the quantity required by Article 9.

4.1.2 All blanks on the bid form shall be filled in by typewriter or manually in ink.

4.1.3 Where so indicated by the makeup of the bid form, sums shall be expressed in both words and figures, and in case of discrepancy between the two, the amount written in words shall govern.

4.1.4 Any interlineation, alteration or erasure must be initialed by the signer of the Bid.

4.1.5 All requested Alternates shall be bid. If no change in the Base Bid is required, enter "No Change."

4.1.6 Where two or more Bids for designated portions of the Work have been requested, the Bidder may, without forfeiture of his bid security, state his refusal to accept award of less than the combination of Bids he so stipulates. The Bidder shall make no additional stipulations on the bid form nor qualify his Bid in any other manner.

4.1.7 Each copy of the Bid shall include the legal name of the Bidder and a statement that the Bidder is a sole proprietor, a partnership, a corporation, or some other legal entity. Each copy shall be signed by the person or persons legally authorized to bind the Bidder to a contract. A Bid by a corporation shall further give the state of incorporation and have the corporate seal affixed. A Bid submitted by an agent shall have a current power of attorney attached certifying the agent's authority to bind the Bidder.

4.2 **BID SECURITY**

4.2.1 If so stipulated in the Advertisement or Invitation to Bid, each Bid shall be accompanied by a bid security in the form and amount required by Article 9 pledging that the Bidder will enter into a contract with the Owner on the terms stated in his Bid and will, if required, furnish bonds as described hereunder in Article 7 covering the faithful performance of the Contract and the payment of all obligations arising thereunder. Should the Bidder refuse to enter into such Contract or fail to furnish such bonds if required, the amount of the bid security shall be forfeited to the Owner as liquidated damages, not as a penalty. The amount of the bid security shall not be forfeited to the Owner in the event the Owner fails to comply with subparagraph 6.2.1.

4.2.2 If a surety bond is required it shall be written on AIA Document A310, Bid Bond, and the attorney-in-fact who executes the bond on behalf of the surety shall affix to the bond a certified and current copy of his power of attorney.

4.2.3 The Owner will have the right to retain the bid security of Bidders to whom an award is being considered until either (a) the Contract has been executed and bonds, if required, have been furnished, or (b) the specified time has elapsed so that Bids may be withdrawn, or (c) all Bids have been rejected.

4.3 **SUBMISSION OF BIDS**

4.3.1 All copies of the Bid, the bid security, if any, and any other documents required to be submitted with the Bid shall be enclosed in a sealed opaque envelope. The envelope shall be addressed to the party receiving the Bids and shall be identified with the Project name, the Bidder's name and address and, if applicable, the designated portion of the Work for which the Bid is submitted. If the Bid is sent by mail the sealed envelope shall be enclosed in a separate mailing envelope with the notation "SEALED BID ENCLOSED" on the face thereof.

4.3.2 Bids shall be deposited at the designated location prior to the time and date for receipt of Bids indicated in the Advertisement or Invitation to Bid, or any extension thereof made by Addendum. Bids received after the time and date for receipt of Bids will be returned unopened.

4.3.3 The Bidder shall assume full responsibility for timely delivery at the location designated for receipt of Bids.

4.3.4 Oral, telephonic or telegraphic Bids are invalid and will not receive consideration.

4.4 **MODIFICATION OR WITHDRAWAL OF BID**

4.4.1 A Bid may not be modified, withdrawn or canceled by the Bidder during the stipulated time period following the time and date designated for the receipt of Bids, and each Bidder so agrees in submitting his Bid.

AIA DOCUMENT A701 • INSTRUCTIONS TO BIDDERS • THIRD EDITION • MAY 1978 • AIA® • ©1978
THE AMERICAN INSTITUTE OF ARCHITECTS, 1735 NEW YORK AVE., N.W., WASHINGTON, D. C. 20006

Exhibit 11–3 continued

4.4.2 Prior to the time and date designated for receipt of Bids, any Bid submitted may be modified or withdrawn by notice to the party receiving Bids at the place designated for receipt of Bids. Such notice shall be in writing over the signature of the Bidder or by telegram; if by telegram, written confirmation over the signature of the Bidder shall be mailed and postmarked on or before the date and time set for receipt of Bids, and it shall be so worded as not to reveal the amount of the original Bid.

4.4.3 Withdrawn Bids may be resubmitted up to the time designated for the receipt of Bids provided that they are then fully in conformance with these Instructions to Bidders.

4.4.4 Bid security, if any is required, shall be in an amount sufficient for the Bid as modified or resubmitted.

ARTICLE 5

CONSIDERATION OF BIDS

5.1 OPENING OF BIDS

5.1.1 Unless stated otherwise in the Advertisement or Invitation to Bid, the properly identified Bids received on time will be opened publicly and will be read aloud. An abstract of the Base Bids and Alternate Bids, if any, will be made available to Bidders. When it has been stated that Bids will be opened privately, an abstract of the same information may, at the discretion of the Owner, be made available to the Bidders within a reasonable time.

5.2 REJECTION OF BIDS

5.2.1 The Owner shall have the right to reject any or all Bids and to reject a Bid not accompanied by any required bid security or by other data required by the Bidding Documents, or to reject a Bid which is in any way incomplete or irregular.

5.3 ACCEPTANCE OF BID (AWARD)

5.3.1 It is the intent of the Owner to award a Contract to the lowest responsible Bidder provided the Bid has been submitted in accordance with the requirements of the Bidding Documents and does not exceed the funds available. The Owner shall have the right to waive any informality or irregularity in any Bid or Bids received and to accept the Bid or Bids which, in his judgment, is in his own best interests.

5.3.2 The Owner shall have the right to accept Alternates in any order or combination, unless otherwise specifically provided in Article 9, and to determine the low Bidder on the basis of the sum of the Base Bid and the Alternates accepted.

ARTICLE 6

POST BID INFORMATION

6.1 CONTRACTOR'S QUALIFICATION STATEMENT

6.1.1 Bidders to whom award of a Contract is under consideration shall submit to the Architect, upon request, a properly executed AIA Document A305, Contractor's Qualification Statement, unless such a Statement has been previously required and submitted as a prerequisite to the issuance of Bidding Documents.

6.2 OWNER'S FINANCIAL CAPABILITY

6.2.1 The Owner shall, at the request of the Bidder to whom award of a Contract is under consideration and no later than seven days prior to the expiration of the time for withdrawal of Bids, furnish to the Bidder reasonable evidence that the Owner has made financial arrangements to fulfill the Contract obligations. Unless such reasonable evidence is furnished, the Bidder will not be required to execute the Owner-Contractor Agreement.

6.3 SUBMITTALS

6.3.1 The Bidder shall, within seven days of notification of selection for the award of a Contract for the Work, submit the following information to the Architect:

.1 a designation of the Work to be performed by the Bidder with his own forces;

.2 the proprietary names and the suppliers of principal items or systems of materials and equipment proposed for the Work;

.3 a list of names of the Subcontractors or other persons or entities (including those who are to furnish materials or equipment fabricated to a special design) proposed for the principal portions of the Work.

6.3.2 The Bidder will be required to establish to the satisfaction of the Architect and the Owner the reliability and responsibility of the persons or entities proposed to furnish and perform the Work described in the Bidding Documents.

6.3.3 Prior to the award of the Contract, the Architect will notify the Bidder in writing if either the Owner or the Architect, after due investigation, has reasonable objection to any such proposed person or entity. If the Owner or Architect has reasonable objection to any such proposed person or entity, the Bidder may, at his option, (1) withdraw his Bid, or (2) submit an acceptable substitute person or entity with an adjustment in his bid price to cover the difference in cost occasioned by such substitution. The Owner may, at his discretion, accept the adjusted bid price or he may disqualify the Bidder. In the event of either withdrawal or disqualification under this Subparagraph, bid security will not be forfeited, notwithstanding the provisions of Paragraph 4.4.1.

6.3.4 Persons and entities proposed by the Bidder and to whom the Owner and the Architect have made no reasonable objection under the provisions of Subparagraph 6.3.3 must be used on the Work for which they were proposed and shall not be changed except with the written consent of the Owner and the Architect.

ARTICLE 7

PERFORMANCE BOND AND LABOR AND MATERIAL PAYMENT BOND

7.1 BOND REQUIREMENTS

7.1.1 Prior to execution of the Contract, if required in Article 9 hereinafter, the Bidder shall furnish bonds covering the faithful performance of the Contract and the payment of all obligations arising thereunder in such form and amount as the Owner may prescribe. Bonds may be secured through the Bidder's usual sources. If the furnish-

Exhibit 11–3 continued

ing of such bonds is stipulated hereinafter in Article 9, the cost shall be included in the Bid.

7.1.2 If the Owner has reserved the right to require that bonds be furnished subsequent to the execution of the Contract, the cost shall be adjusted as provided in the Contract Documents.

7.1.3 If the Owner requires that bonds be obtained from other than the Bidder's usual source, any change in cost will be adjusted as provided in the Contract Documents.

7.2   TIME OF DELIVERY AND FORM OF BONDS

7.2.1 The Bidder shall deliver the required bonds to the Owner not later than the date of execution of the Contract, or if the Work is to be commenced prior thereto in response to a letter of intent, the Bidder shall, prior to commencement of the Work, submit evidence satisfactory to the Owner that such bonds will be furnished.

7.2.2 Unless otherwise required in Article 9, the bonds

shall be written on AIA Document A311, Performance Bond and Labor and Material Payment Bond.

7.2.3 The Bidder shall require the attorney-in-fact who executes the required bonds on behalf of the surety to affix thereto a certified and current copy of his power of attorney.

ARTICLE 8

FORM OF AGREEMENT BETWEEN OWNER AND CONTRACTOR

8.1   FORM TO BE USED

8.1.1 Unless otherwise required in the Bidding Documents, the Agreement for the Work will be written on AIA Document A101, Standard Form of Agreement Between Owner and Contractor, where the basis of payment is a Stipulated Sum.

ARTICLE 9
SUPPLEMENTARY INSTRUCTIONS

5   A701-1978   AIA DOCUMENT A701 • INSTRUCTIONS TO BIDDERS • THIRD EDITION • MAY 1978 • AIA® • ©1978
THE AMERICAN INSTITUTE OF ARCHITECTS, 1735 NEW YORK AVE., N.W., WASHINGTON, D. C. 20006

5. a form for recitation of the "bid schedule," including the following:

- all alternates by number, with blanks for pricing of each

- a statement regarding areas of work (if any) where unit pricing is requested, together with blanks for the actual pricing

- a statement of acknowledgement of addenda, by number and date, with blanks for the listing of addenda received

- a statement regarding agreement to finish the work within the time schedule (if any) set forth in the "Special Conditions" of the specifications, with blanks for the dates of completion to be filled in by the bidder

- a statement of acknowledgement by the bidder of stipulations regarding changes in the work as may have been promulgated in the general or supplementary conditions

- statements regarding bid securities to be attached, with blanks for the bidder to fill in the amount

- statements regarding the terms of acceptance by the owner and the actions the bidder, if successful, must take in executing a contract

- statements regarding the furnishing of performance and payment bonds and disposition of the bid bond

- blanks for the bidder to execute stating where a notice of acceptance can be delivered, usually by one of several designated means

- the names of subbidders, together with the classification of respective areas of work and the license numbers of respective principals

- blanks for the signature of an authorized principal or other agent of the bidder

- blanks for listing any attachments (e.g., bid bonds)

- blanks for describing the nature of the bidder's firm (e.g., partnership, corporation) together with other desired information referenced to financial or other qualifications.

An example copy of a bid form for a small project is set forth in Exhibit 11–4.

Managing the process

The primary objective of the bidding process is to obtain a bid from a contractor who is professionally and financially competent to perform the work specified, at a price within the hospital's budget. A secondary objective is to establish a climate of professional rapport among the architect, the construction manager, and all the firms bidding on the

Exhibit 11–4

Typical bid form

(SAMPLE PROPOSAL FORM FOR A SMALL PROJECT)

Section Number_____   Section Title_____

(Name and Address of Owner)

Gentlemen:

We, the undersigned bidder, having familiarized ourselves with the site, local conditions affecting the cost of the Project and with the Contract Documents including Addendum Nos. _____ where applicable in a section of work, for the construction of _____ prepared by Henkel, Hovel and Schaefer, Architects and Engineers, do hereby propose to provide and furnish all labor, materials, necessary tools, expendible equipment, and all utility and transportation services required by said contract documents for Section No. _____ Section Title _____ to complete such items of work as are hereinafter designated, for the sum of money enumerated for said items, the said amount constituting the total bid for this Section of Work.

Include within total bid all Allowances, where applicable in a Section of Work, etc., as specified in "SPECIAL CONDITIONS."

We (the Contractor) will purchase, maintain and file with the Owner prior to commencement of the work, Certificates of Insurance, as specified in the "SUPPLEMENTARY GENERAL CONDITIONS," acceptable to the Owner.

Total Bid for Section No. _____ $ _____
_____ Dollars
Add or Deduct Alternate Bid Item:
(Where applicable in a section of work)
List Description for Alternate Work.   Item No. 1 — $ _____
_____   _____ Dollars
                                        Item No. 2 — $ _____
_____   _____ Dollars
                                        Item No. 3 — $ _____
_____   _____ Dollars

These sums shall include the cost of all State and/or Local Sales and/or Use Taxes, all Federal Taxes and *all* charges or duties of any nature applicable to the Project (other than special assessments as noted in the SUPPLEMENTARY GENERAL CONDITIONS—Page   ).

73-9 (Job Number)   TTH/ks
                                                   Proposal Form — 1

Completion Time

The Work to be performed under this Section of the Work will be commenced after the Contract is signed. After the Contract is signed, the Work to be completed under this Section of the Contract will be commenced upon notification to proceed from the Construction Manager on _____ (date) which is shown in the Critical Path Schedule. The Critical Path Schedule as herein noted and as contained in these Specifications is to be used by each Contractor as a guide in establishing the date of commencement and time needed to complete his work. At the pre-award Conference, the Construction Manager and the successful bidders shall amend the Critical Path as required to schedule the work of the separate Contractors to meet the completion date of the Project. Any variations proposed, from the C.P.S. of the date to proceed or the time to complete shall be noted on the appropriate spaces to be filled in on the proposal form. The work shall be completed to its entirety within _____ calendar days unless delayed by general strikes, act of God, or national emergency.

Exhibit 11–4 continued

Unit Prices — (These unit prices, where applicable in a Section of Work, to include all labor, materials, equipment, tools and installation, and apply for such more or less Work that may be required.)

Section I

1. Hand excavation. $ _____/cu. yd.

2. Mechanical excavation (earth). $ _____/cu. yd.

3. Selected Earth Backfill (from site) compacted in place. $ _____/cu. yd.

4. Granular backfill compacted in place. $ _____/cu. yd.

5. Trucked removal of excess soil from site. $ _____/cu. yd.

6. Load, distribution and spreading of on site top-soil on site as directed by C.M. $ _____/cu. yd.

7. Compacted aggregate base. $ _____/cu. yd.

73-9 (Job Number)   TTH/ks
                              Proposal Form — 2

Section II

1. 3000# concrete $ _____/cu. yd.

2. Reinforcing steel. $ _____/lb.

3. Welded wire mesh. $ _____/sq. ft.

4. Concrete finishing — wood float. $ _____/sq. ft.

5. Concrete finishing — steel trowel. $ _____/sq. ft.

It is agreed that this proposal shall be irrevocable for a period of thirty (30) days after the specified date for receiving bids.

Official Address   Firm Name _____

_____ By _____

_____ Title _____

_____ Date _____

Also include the names of any subcontractors doing work for you under this section of **the work,** if such work done is by workmen not in your direct employment.

Subcontractors

_____

_____

_____

73-9 (Job Number)   TTH/ks
                              Proposal Form — 3

This document has been reproduced with the permission of Henkel, Hovel and Schaefer, Architects and Engineers.

project, of whom one will be successful; in this instance, professional rapport is construed to include the give-and-take in seeking and gaining understanding of all construction documents and the satisfactory resolution of diverse viewpoints.

The best and most serious bidding by contracting firms depends on a host of factors peculiar to individual situations related to place, time, and project size, as well as on the efforts of whoever is charged with the management of the bidding process (architect or construction manager). We merely describe here a typical management process in which achievement of an optimal result is assumed to be obtainable.

Bidder psychology

Psychology often plays a large part in creating a competitive bidding climate. The following are common observations related to this matter:

1. Too few bidders will reduce the probability of highly competitive bidding and raise the probability of harmful collusion among bidders. "Too few" can usually be construed to mean on the order of two to four.

2. Too many bidders will reduce the probability of sharp bidding. Each firm involved in the bidding may assume that its chances for success are lessened by the large number of bidders and, therefore, will not commit sufficient estimating time to assure its best bid. "Too many" can usually be construed to mean more than eight firms that are competent to perform the work.

3. Most contractors in a local area will know the workload, capabilities, and resources of their competitors. Competitive bidding will be encouraged by a set of bidders who all genuinely want the work and who are competent to perform it from all aspects.

4. A completely professional handling of the bidding process, in which there is no indication that those managing the process "favor" or "like" one bidder better than another, will encourage competitive bidding. We were involved in one project in which the architect was suspected of having informed only one bidder that many additive change orders would be forthcoming on the project. Of course, the low bidder proved to be the architect's personal friend. The profitable change orders did develop. The unsuccessful bidders were observant of the whole situation. To make the point, a "buddy-buddy" relationship between the manager of the bidding process and any of the bidders will discourage a competitive atmosphere.

5. The bidding period is a critical time and must be sufficiently long, in view of the scope and complexity of the construction, to allow a competent, capable bidder to obtain prices from vendors and subcontractors, properly estimate costs, and prepare a bid. If pressed with an unreasonable deadline, the bidder will pad the bid to ensure protection from the "unknowns" that there was insufficient time to investigate. Conversely, too long a bidding period, besides delaying the work itself, will cause some bidders to assume a lackadaisical

attitude and implement a long, uncoordinated estimation process that results in inaccurate bidding.

Management of the bidding process should create a psychological climate among prospective bidders that is most conducive to competitive bidding. The architect or construction manager should strive toward that end, while considering the points just laid out, and should use best judgment in individual situations.

Prebid activities

Prospective bidders should be studied, evaluated, and identified well before the construction documents are finished, and upon their completion, the invitation to bid should be mailed to those so identified. If the hospital is a governmental or quasi-governmental institution, the bidding must be advertised. The proposed construction documents must be delivered to those who request to bid, under the process outlined for the invitation to bid.

The prebid conference has grown popular in recent years and is frequently stipulated in the invitation to bid. The time of this conference should be set so as to give bidders ample opportunity to have studied the documents after receiving them and to have formulated any questions pertinent thereto. Likewise, there should remain time before bid openings for the architect to issue necessary addenda and to elicit interest on the part of additional firms, in the event that the prebid conference reveals that a desirable number of serious, qualified bidders is not in evidence.

During the bid preparation period, the architect should maintain contact with each bidder, typically at weekly intervals. The dialogue should be carried forward on a professional basis, and it should yield indications as to the seriousness of bidders and their requirements for information.

Most large projects should be designed to accept both deductive and additive alternatives so as to provide better assurance of equating the contract price and budget. Late in the prebid period, the professional planning team and hospital executives should hold a "what if" meeting to ascertain actions based on possible bid ranges. During this meeting, there should be some indication as to the bidding range, and quite realistic discussions are possible.

Bid receipt and opening

Bidders should always gain evidence of the deliverance of their bids and the time thereof to the person designated to receive same. The person charged with receipt of bids should carefully protect them, sealed, until the designated time of opening.

Both the AIA and the Association of General Contractors of America recommend that the "afternoon of a Tuesday, Wednesday, Thursday, or Friday, but not on a legal holiday or the day following"[27] be set for bid opening. "It is also desirable that there be cooperation among A&E offices to avoid, insofar as practical, conflict of bid opening duties for important projects in the area."[28]

Date setting for bid opening, of course, will have been determined early and set forth in the invitation to bid.

All competitive bids should be opened publicly. If they are not, collusion may be charged whether or not it did, in fact, exist. There is no excuse for the private opening of bids on a hospital project.

The bid opening should be conducted according to a formal sequence well established in the building industry. Each bid is opened, the bidder's name called, the bidder's acknowledgement of having received published addenda stated, identification of the bid bond read, and the amount of the bid on every bid item called.

Pricing on all bid items is recorded on bid tabulation forms distributed to all present. At the conclusion of the opening and tabulations, the person conducting the opening adjourns the meeting without any disclosure of the identity of the low bidder, although this fact is usually apparent. However, we have attended several openings at which the apparent low bidder proved not to be so upon subsequent closer examination of prices on alternatives and the manner in which the hospital chose to accept them.

Contract award

After the architect or the construction manager has studied the bids carefully for possible mistakes or irregularities, a conference should be held among authorized hospital representatives and all members of the professional planning team. If there are mistakes and irregularities to be resolved, the process for resolving them should be determined. If there are none, a decision to award the contract can be made, and the successful bidder is sent an official notice of award. In contract law, this notice constitutes "acceptance" and sets the stage for official signing of the contract. The date of the contract signing and the beginning of construction are the same, unless otherwise stated in the contract.

The hospital can set the time of signing of the contract for any time during the period designated for all bids to remain as open offers. The date of actual signing may depend upon a number of factors, including the hospital's receipt of monies from the sale of bonds.

Form of agreement

The AIA publishes several examples of a *Standard Form of Agreement Between Owner and Contractor*, each of which is adapted for different situations. All these examples contain an article in which every element of the contract document is specifically named. For the *Standard Form of Agreement Between Owner and Contractor* AIA Document A101, 1977 edition, this article reads as follows:

> The Contract Documents consist of this Agreement, the Conditions of the Contract (General, Supplementary and other Conditions), the Drawings, the Specifications, all Addenda issued prior to and all Modifications issued after execution of this Agreement. These form the Contract, and all are as fully a part of the Contract as if attached to this Agreement or repeated herein. An enumeration of the Contract Documents appears in Article 7.[29]

Thus, one of the prime purposes of the "form of agreement" is to incorporate all the construction documents into the contract as integral elements thereof.

The form of agreement serves to set forth the formalities inherent to a formal contract, names the contract price, states the contract time, sets forth the method of payment, and provides appropriate spaces for owner and contractor signatures to be affixed and sealed.

The various articles of the form of agreement are largely self-explanatory, so rather than engage in lengthy discussion of them, we have elected to reproduce here, as Exhibit 11–5, the previously noted AIA Document A101.

Summary

Construction documents consist of specifications, drawings, and conditions of the contract. Each should represent the best clarity that drawings and language can express in order to provide for precise bidding and, after contract award, to avoid friction and provide for the owner's complete protection.

Construction drawings portray the completed building, and specifications describe construction materials and how the project is to be constructed. Because language is the basis for all contracts, specifications take precedence over drawings in case of conflict between the two.

Descriptive specifications serve to express directions relating to materials to be used and how the structure is to be built better than any other type. However, performance specifications (merely describing results to be achieved) are now being used to some extent. It is unlikely that description specifications will be replaced by those of the performance type.

Ambiguities should be avoided in specification writing, and descriptions should be precise and complete. Only persons with proven language capabilities should engage in specification writing.

The Construction Specification Institute (CSI) publishes a format for the organization of specifications that is now almost exclusively used throughout this nation. This standardized format has greatly facilitated the process of bidding and the construction process itself.

Construction drawings, also called working drawings, precisely depict all aspects of the building. They serve to portray the finished product, and they should be complete. Because of their complexity, the best protection available to an owner for assuring a quality product is a thorough architect selection process at the outset.

Some change orders are to be expected in the process of construction, but they can be held to a minimum by clarity in drawings and specifications and by reducing "mind-changing" on the part of the owners to a minimum.

The functional planner has a minor role during preparation of construction documents, but this consultant should remain on call to both owner and architect.

Exhibit 11–5

Standard Form of Agreement Between Owner and Contractor, AIA Document A101

THE AMERICAN INSTITUTE OF ARCHITECTS

AIA Document A101

Standard Form of Agreement Between Owner and Contractor

where the basis of payment is a

STIPULATED SUM

1977 EDITION

THIS DOCUMENT HAS IMPORTANT LEGAL CONSEQUENCES; CONSULTATION WITH AN ATTORNEY IS ENCOURAGED WITH RESPECT TO ITS COMPLETION OR MODIFICATION

Use only with the 1976 Edition of AIA Document A201, General Conditions of the Contract for Construction.

This document has been approved and endorsed by The Associated General Contractors of America.

AGREEMENT

made as of the   day of   in the year of Nineteen
Hundred and

BETWEEN the Owner:

and the Contractor:

The Project:

The Architect:

The Owner and the Contractor agree as set forth below.

AIA DOCUMENT A101 • OWNER-CONTRACTOR AGREEMENT • ELEVENTH EDITION • JUNE 1977 • AIA®
©1977 • THE AMERICAN INSTITUTE OF ARCHITECTS, 1735 NEW YORK AVE., N.W., WASHINGTON, D. C. 20006   **A101-1977   1**

Exhibit 11–5 continued

ARTICLE 1

THE CONTRACT DOCUMENTS

The Contract Documents consist of this Agreement, the Conditions of the Contract (General, Supplementary and other Conditions), the Drawings, the Specifications, all Addenda issued prior to and all Modifications issued after execution of this Agreement. These form the Contract, and all are as fully a part of the Contract as if attached to this Agreement or repeated herein. An enumeration of the Contract Documents appears in Article 7.

ARTICLE 2

THE WORK

The Contractor shall perform all the Work required by the Contract Documents for
(Here insert the caption descriptive of the Work as used on other Contract Documents.)

ARTICLE 3

TIME OF COMMENCEMENT AND SUBSTANTIAL COMPLETION

The Work to be performed under this Contract shall be commenced

and, subject to authorized adjustments, Substantial Completion shall be achieved not later than

(Here insert any special provisions for liquidated damages relating to failure to complete on time.)

Exhibit 11–5 continued

ARTICLE 4

CONTRACT SUM

The Owner shall pay the Contractor in current funds for the performance of the Work, subject to additions and deductions by Change Order as provided in the Contract Documents, the Contract Sum of

The Contract Sum is determined as follows:
(State here the base bid or other lump sum amount, accepted alternates, and unit prices, as applicable.)

ARTICLE 5

PROGRESS PAYMENTS

Based upon Applications for Payment submitted to the Architect by the Contractor and Certificates for Payment issued by the Architect, the Owner shall make progress payments on account of the Contract Sum to the Contractor as provided in the Contract Documents for the period ending the   day of the month as follows:

Not later than   days following the end of the period covered by the Application for Payment   percent (%) of the portion of the Contract Sum properly allocable to labor, materials and equipment incorporated in the Work and   percent (%) of the portion of the Contract Sum properly allocable to materials and equipment suitably stored at the site or at some other location agreed upon in writing, for the period covered by the Application for Payment, less the aggregate of previous payments made by the Owner; and upon Substantial Completion of the entire Work, a sum sufficient to increase the total payments to   percent (%) of the Contract Sum, less such amounts as the Architect shall determine for all incomplete Work and unsettled claims as provided in the Contract Documents.

(If not covered elsewhere in the Contract Documents, here insert any provision for limiting or reducing the amount retained after the Work reaches a certain stage of completion.)

Payments due and unpaid under the Contract Documents shall bear interest from the date payment is due at the rate entered below, or in the absence thereof, at the legal rate prevailing at the place of the Project.
(Here insert any rate of interest agreed upon.)

(Usury laws and requirements under the Federal Truth in Lending Act, similar state and local consumer credit laws and other regulations at the Owner's and Contractor's principal places of business, the location of the Project and elsewhere may affect the validity of this provision. Specific legal advice should be obtained with respect to deletion, modification, or other requirements such as written disclosures or waivers.)

AIA DOCUMENT A101 • OWNER-CONTRACTOR AGREEMENT • ELEVENTH EDITION • JUNE 1977 • AIA®
©1977 • THE AMERICAN INSTITUTE OF ARCHITECTS, 1735 NEW YORK AVE., N.W., WASHINGTON, D. C. 20006   **A101-1977 3**

Exhibit 11–5 continued

ARTICLE 6

FINAL PAYMENT

Final payment, constituting the entire unpaid balance of the Contract Sum, shall be paid by the Owner to the Contractor when the Work has been completed, the Contract fully performed, and a final Certificate for Payment has been issued by the Architect.

ARTICLE 7

MISCELLANEOUS PROVISIONS

7.1 Terms used in this Agreement which are defined in the Conditions of the Contract shall have the meanings designated in those Conditions.

7.2 The Contract Documents, which constitute the entire agreement between the Owner and the Contractor, are listed in Article 1 and, except for Modifications issued after execution of this Agreement, are enumerated as follows:

(List below the Agreement, the Conditions of the Contract (General, Supplementary, and other Conditions), the Drawings, the Specifications, and any Addenda and accepted alternates, showing page or sheet numbers in all cases and dates where applicable.)

SAMPLE

This Agreement entered into as of the day and year first written above.

OWNER   CONTRACTOR

_____   _____

_____   _____

_____   _____

AIA DOCUMENT A101 • OWNER-CONTRACTOR AGREEMENT • ELEVENTH EDITION • JUNE 1977 • AIA®
©1977 • THE AMERICAN INSTITUTE OF ARCHITECTS, 1735 NEW YORK AVE., N.W., WASHINGTON, D. C. 20006   **A101-1977 4**

The construction manager has a major role during the construction document phase, including preparing cost estimates, giving advice in materials selection, and doing value engineering work.

The owner must give final approval to the construction documents and should be advised by the construction manager in doing so after appropriate explanations by the A&E firm.

Conditions of the contract specify the relationship among the parties involved and their rights and responsibilities. They are the stipulations that actually form the contract and make the drawings and specifications an integral part of it. General conditions are published by the AIA and are widely used in contracts. Supplementary conditions are those that relate to unique features of each project.

The bidding phase should be guided by the A&E firm, and full explanations should be provided to all bidders either in written bidding instructions or in scheduled conferences with bidders.

When bids are taken, every effort should be made to avoid the appearance of improprieties, and each bidder should receive fair treatment. After thorough examination of each bid the most desirable one should be selected and an award made.

Notes

1. George T. Heery, *Time, Cost and Architecture* (New York: McGraw-Hill, 1975), p. 175.
2. *Standard Form of Agreement Between Owner and Architect*, AIA Document B141, 1977 ed. (Washington, DC: American Institute of Architects, 1977), p. 3.
3. Richard H. Clough, *Construction Contracting* (New York: John Wiley & Sons, 1981), pp. 58, 59.
4. Harold J. Rosen, *Construction Specifications Writing* (New York: John Wiley & Sons, 1981), pp. 9, 10.
5. *Ibid.*, p. 10.
6. *Ibid.*, p. 1.
7. *Ibid.*, p. 27.
8. *Ibid.*, p. 28.
9. *Ibid.*, p. 27.
10. The Code of Georgia of 1933, Section 20-704.
11. *The Rainbow Memorandum of Policy*, Georgia Building Authority Form No. BGA-5 (m-GBA), Section 26, Schedule 1.
12. *Ibid.*, Schedule 4.
13. *Ibid.*
14. *Ibid.*
15. CSI *Masterformat* (Alexandria, VA: The Construction Specification Institute, 1981).
16. Rosen, *Construction Specifications Writing*, p. 17.
17. *Ibid.*
18. Clough, *Construction Contracting*, p. 58.
19. Peter S. Hopt, *Designer's Guide to OSHA* (New York: McGraw-Hill, 1975), p. 289.
20. *Construction Management (CM) Delivery Systems for Hospital Facilities—Five Case Studies*, report of a joint AGC–Purdue University Symposium in Construction Management, Indianapolis, May 18–20, 1983 (Washington, DC: Associated General Contractors of America, 1983), p. 176.
21. *Ibid.*, p. 174.
22. Clough, *Construction Contracting*, pp. 60–61.

23. *General Conditions of the Contract for Construction*, AIA Document A201, 1976 ed. (Washington, DC: American Institute of Architects, 1976), pp. 5–19.

24. Heery, *Time, Cost and Architecture*, pp. 129–139.

25. Hira N. Ahuja, *Successful Construction Cost Control* (New York: John Wiley & Sons, 1980), p. 172.

26. Rosen, *Construction Specifications Writing*, p. 41.

27. Harold Hauf, *Building Contracts for Design and Construction* (New York: John Wiley & Sons, 1978), p. 231.

28. *Ibid.*, p. 169.

29. *Standard Form of Agreement Between Owner and Contractor*, AIA Document A101, 1977 ed. (Washington, DC: American Institute of Architects, 1977), p. 2.

12

The Planning and Design Process

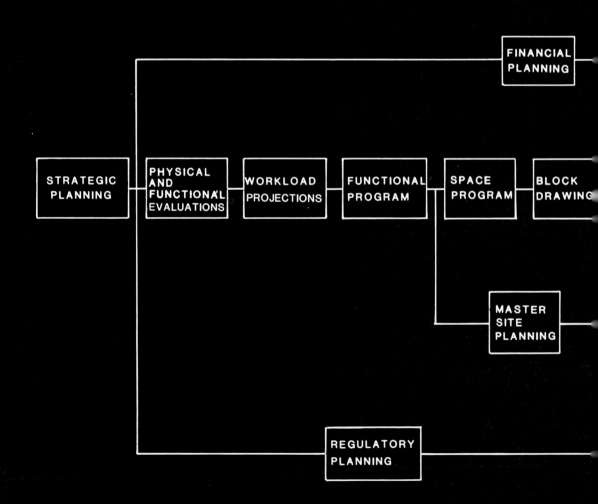

Construction phase and facilities opening

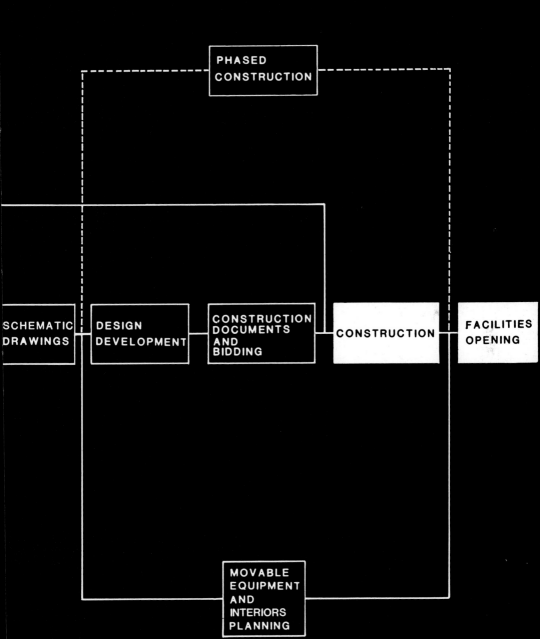

Traditionally, the construction phase has been carried forward under a contract between an owner and a general contractor, with an A&E firm serving as the agent of the owner while assuming the major professional role of decision maker relative to ensuring adherence to contract provisions by both parties. This approach to construction continues as a viable option, but the use of construction managers to serve in one of several roles is now evidenced in a majority of major hospital constructions.

Construction manager roles

Typically, during construction, the prime role of a construction manager is in coordination of the different contractors involved on the project; this role is performed by a general contractor on projects for which the traditional lump-sum approach is used. The construction manager generally oversees competitive bidding on the individual trade contracts and handles the scheduling of a phased construction approach. In addition "the construction manager can provide on-site quality control, cost control through regular budget status updates and approval of contractor payments, administration of the 'general conditions,' and various post-construction services, such as systems testing and warranty follow-up."[1]

The American Institute of Architects has published example terms and conditions in a *Standard Form of Agreement Between Owner and Construction Manager* (AIA Document B801). This document outlines basic services of a construction manager during the construction phase, as follows:

1.2 CONSTRUCTION PHASE
The Construction Phase will commence with the award of the initial Construction Contract or purchase order and, together with the Construction Manager's obligation to provide Basic Services under this Agreement, will end 30 days after final payment to all Contractors is due.
1.2.1
Unless otherwise provided in this Agreement and incorporated in the Contract Documents, the Construction Manager, in cooperation with the Architect, shall provide administration of the Contracts for Construction as set forth below and in the 1980 Edition of AIA Document A201/CM, General Conditions of the Contract for Construction, Construction Management Edition.
1.2.2
Provide administrative, management and related services as required to coordinate Work of the Contractors with each other and with the activities and responsibilities of the Construction Manager, the Owner and the Architect to complete the Project in accordance with the Owner's objectives for cost, time and quality. Provide sufficient organization, personnel and management to carry out the requirements of this Agreement.
1.2.2.1
Schedule and conduct pre-construction, construction and progress meetings to discuss such matters as procedures, progress,

problems and scheduling. Prepare and promptly distribute minutes.

1.2.2.2

Consistent with the Project Construction Schedule issued with the Bidding Documents, and utilizing the Contractors' Construction Schedules provided by the separate contractors, update the Project Construction Schedule incorporating the activities of Contractors on the Project, including activity sequences and durations, allocation of labor and materials, processing of Shop Drawings, Product Data and Samples, and delivery of products requiring long lead time procurement. Include the Owner's occupancy requirements showing portions of the Project having occupancy priority. Update and reissue the Project Construction Schedule as required to show current conditions and revisions required by actual experience.

1.2.2.3

Endeavor to achieve satisfactory performance from each of the Contractors. Recommend courses of action to the Owner when requirements of a Contract are not being fulfilled, and the non-performing party will not take satisfactory corrective action.

1.2.3

Revise and refine the approved estimate of Construction Cost, incorporate approved changes as they occur, and develop cash flow reports and forecasts as needed.

1.2.3.1

Provide regular monitoring of the approved estimate of Construction Cost, showing actual costs for activities in progress and estimates for uncompleted tasks. Identify variances between actual and budgeted or estimated costs, and advise the Owner and the Architect whenever projected costs exceed budgets or estimates.

1.2.3.2

Maintain cost accounting records on authorized work performed under unit costs, additional Work performed on the basis of actual costs of labor and materials, or other Work requiring accounting records.

1.2.3.3

Recommend necessary or desirable changes to the Architect and the Owner, review requests for changes, assist in negotiating Contractors' proposals, submit recommendations to the Architect and the Owner, and if they are accepted, prepare and sign Change Orders for the Architect's signature and the Owner's authorization.

1.2.3.4

Develop and implement procedures for the review and processing of Applications by Contractors for progress and final payments. Make recommendations to the Architect for certification to the Owner for payment.

1.2.4

Review the safety programs developed by each of the Contractors as required by their Contract Documents and coordinate the safety programs for the Project.

1.2.5

Assist in obtaining building permits and special permits for permanent improvements, excluding permits required to be obtained directly by the various Contractors. Verify that the Owner has paid applicable fees and assessments. Assist in obtaining approvals from authorities having jurisdiction over the Project.

1.2.6

If required, assist the Owner in selecting and retaining the professional services of surveyors, special consultants and testing laboratories. Coordinate their services.

1.2.7

Determine in general that the Work of each Contractor is being performed in accordance with the requirements of the Contract Documents. Endeavor to guard the Owner against defects and deficiencies in the Work. As appropriate, require special inspection or testing, or make recommendations to the architect regarding special inspection or testing, of Work not in accordance with the provisions of the Contract Documents whether or not such Work be then fabricated, installed or completed. Subject to review by the Architect, reject Work which does not conform to the requirements of the Contract Documents.

1.2.7.1

The Construction Manager shall not be responsible for construction means, methods, techniques, sequences and procedures employed by Contractors in the performance of their Contracts, and shall not be responsible for the failure of any Contractor to carry out Work in accordance with the Contract Documents.

1.2.8

Consult with the Architect and the Owner if any Contractor requests interpretations of the meaning and intent of the Drawings and Specifications, and assist in the resolution of questions which may arise.

1.2.9

Receive Certificates of Insurance from the Contractors, and forward them to the Owner with a copy to the Architect.

1.2.10

Receive from the Contractors and review all Shop Drawings, Product Data, Samples and other submittals. Coordinate them with information contained in related documents and transmit to the Architect those recommended for approval. In collaboration with the Architect, establish and implement procedures for expediting the processing and approval of Shop Drawings, Product Data, Samples and other submittals.

1.2.11

Record the progress of the Project. Submit written progress reports to the Owner and the Architect including information on each Contractor and each Contractor's Work, as well as the entire Project, showing percentages of completion and the number and amounts of Change Orders. Keep a daily log containing a record of weather, Contractors' Work on the site, number of workers, Work accomplished, problems encountered, and other similar relevant data as the Owner may require. Make the log available to the Owner and the Architect.

1.2.11.1

Maintain at the Project site, on a current basis: a record copy of all Contracts, Drawings, Specifications, Addenda, Change Orders and other Modifications in good order and marked to record all changes made during construction; Shop Drawings; Product Data; Samples; submittals; purchases; materials; equipment; applicable handbooks; maintenance and operating manuals and instructions; other related documents and revisions which arise out of the Contracts or Work. Maintain records, in duplicate, of principal building layout lines, elevations of the bottom of footings, floor levels and key site elevations certified by a qualified surveyor or professional engineer. Make all records available to the Owner and the Architect. At the completion of the Project, deliver all such records to the Architect for the Owner.

1.2.12

Arrange for delivery and storage, protection and security for Owner-purchased materials, systems and equipment which are a part of the Project, until such items are incorporated into the Project.

1.2.13

With the Architect and the Owner's maintenance personnel, observe the Contractors' checkout of utilities, operational systems and equipment for readiness and assist in their initial start-up and testing.

1.2.14

When the Construction Manager considers each Contractor's Work or a designated portion thereof substantially complete, the Construction Manager shall prepare for the Architect a list of incomplete or unsatisfactory items and a schedule for their completion. The Construction Manager shall assist the Architect in conducting inspections. After the Architect certifies the Date of Substantial Completion of the Work, the Construction Manager shall coordinate the correction and completion of the Work.

1.2.15

Assist the Architect in determining when the Project or a designated portion thereof is substantially complete. Prepare for the Architect a summary of the status of the Work of each Contractor, listing changes in the previously issued Certificates of Substantial Completion of the Work and recommending the times within which Contractors shall complete uncompleted items on their Certificate of Substantial Completion of the Work.

1.2.16

Following the Architect's issuance of a Certificate of Substantial Completion of the Project or designated portion thereof, evaluate the completion of the Work of the Contractors and make recommendations to the Architect when Work is ready for final inspection. Assist the Architect in conducting final inspections. Secure and transmit to the Owner required guarantees, affida-

vits, releases, bonds and waivers. Deliver all keys, manuals, record drawings and maintenance stocks to the Owner.
1.2.17
The extent of the duties, responsibilities and limitations of authority of the Construction Manager as a representative of the Owner during construction shall not be modified or extended without the written consent of the Owner, the Contractors, the Architect and the Construction Manager, which consent shall not be unreasonably withheld.

Following the construction phase and extending into the facilities opening phase, the construction manager may perform additional services, some of which relate directly to opening. These are as follows:[3]

1. prepare as-built drawings (showing the inclusion of all changes made during the course of construction)

2. oversee equipment and systems testing and start-up and recommend maintenance schedules

3. submit operations manuals and warranties

4. perform warranty follow-up if required

5. provide continuing consultation to the hospital, especially regarding contractor claims and disputes.

Each of these activities is highly important as we stress later in the chapter, and hospital officials will do well to contract for most of them at the outset, when bargaining capabilities related to fees may be better.

All the provisions as outlined previously were devised for situations in which the services of a general contractor are not contemplated—either projects involving multiple prime contracts, awarded on a phased or simultaneous basis, or those in which the construction manager assumes the role of the general contractor on a single-contract basis.

In projects for which a general contractor is engaged, a construction manager can still be employed to assume some of the tasks previously accomplished by the architect, as outlined in AIA Document B141 under Construction Phase—Administration of the Construction Contract.

Construction phase

Preconstruction conference

Any major construction contract should begin with a preconstruction conference of general nature as has been outlined by George T. Heery in *Time, Cost and Architecture*. Attended by representatives of the owner, the architect, the construction manager, the contractor's job-site superintendent and project manager, and other contractor representatives, this conference has as its prime purpose "to re-confirm the proper channels of communication and assist the contractor in understanding various methods and procedures that will help him in expediting drawings, requests for payments, and other paper work."[4] In addition to pointing out the need for owner representation at the job site, Heery also specifies the responsibility of the construction manager at this point:[5]

> . . . [drawing] the attention of the contractor to the various time-control contract provisions, such as payment scheduling, liquidated damage provisions, superintendent requirements, contract time-extension rulings, etc., that are contained in the general and special conditions of the contract.
>
> It will be crucial, at this meeting, for the construction manager . . . not only to point out these provisions but to be convincing to the contractor that he will fully administer the contract fairly and completely and that he will keep a complete record of the job to allow him to do so in a proper manner. This kind of clear understanding at the outset can save the contractor, as well as the owner, a great deal of trouble later on. . . .

All of Heery's remarks are corroborated by conclusions drawn from the findings of eight recent case studies reported by the Institute for Health Planning in Madison, Wisconsin. One of these conclusions states, "Thus, to measure the effectiveness of the delivery of a complex structure like a hospital, one must look to the effectiveness of the team involved. The key characteristics of an effective hospital project team (architect, engineers, construction manager, contractors, and owner) are its expertise, its commitment, and its level of communications."[6] Certainly, the preconstruction conference is the first step in achieving coordination and close communication among the key team members throughout the project.

Facilitating construction

Assuming that hospital officials have done their job well in assembling a quality planning and design team, which is extended through construction, and that a competent construction manager has been made a part of the team at the appropriate design phase, the following question can be logically asked: "What are the factors that have greatest effect upon facilitating the construction phase?" This question assumes exercise of optimal cost and quality control.

Although many personal opinions, from consultants, construction managers and architects (including ourselves), have been offered in this regard, the conclusions drawn by the Institute for Health Planning in a recent study of a number of projects may be more valid, since they are drawn from supposedly unbiased observations. We list here the factors observed by the Institute's study team and also briefly summarize the comments made in the discussion of each factor:[7]

1. team commitment. The commitment of the hospital itself to the project is emphasized through the assignment of a full-time representative to the construction project (e.g., the planning director, if qualified, or a specially appointed expeditor who has both hospital experience and a construction background). The commitment of other team members was also accentuated by on-site personnel. Paren-

thetically, one of the most successful jobs with which we have recently been associated, had full-time on-site representatives of each team member, including the hospital.

2. team communication.   Frequency was listed as an important measure of communication, but quality of communication and its documentation were noted as being even more important attributes. Participation in weekly meetings was cited as the best vehicle for solving and avoiding construction problems.

3. cooperation, competition, and coexistence.   As summarized by the Institute, " . . . those methods that worked established a system of checks and balances between the interests of owner, designer, and builder. . . . [The] competition of professional ideas and the competition among prices (bidders) were important means of protecting the hospital's interests in what was essentially a cooperative enterprise."[8]

Those who actually perform the work on a project, regardless of the important contributions of each member of the construction team, are the trade contractors. In the case of either a single general contractor or an individual trade contractor, the most important person placed on site by any contractor is the job superintendent. If any key contractor places a superintendent on the job who obviously is incompetent, or who does not diligently attend to required tasks, there should be some means of effecting the removal of that person. Procedures can be piled upon procedures, but if a superintendent is not capable of exercising constant leadership and control at the job site, the activities involved will suffer either quantitatively or qualitatively, and probably both.

The owner also has one prime responsibility that, if failed, can have serious repercussions on work efforts: the prompt payment of sums due contractors after proper approval has been effected. Procedures relative to payments should be clearly spelled out in the contract documents, and the owner, like the other parties involved, should adhere strictly to specified policy. If the proper procedures are not followed, the architect or construction manager should immediately "go to bat" for the contractor.

The importance of appropriate scheduling in the construction manager's coordination of the various contractors involved on a project cannot be overemphasized. Although phased construction certainly has a number of benefits for the owner, if the work is not scheduled in a timely manner, quality of construction can suffer, costs can increase, and project delivery dates will be missed. Most construction managers have grown very sophisticated in the use of scheduling techniques, and for hospital officials, at least, a more simple form of schedule summary may be desirable. This point was stressed in the cited recent study by the Institute for Health Planning.[9] In any event, the quality of scheduling has a profound effect in facilitating the construction of any major project.

Completing construction

Over the course of a hospital construction project, which can range from one year in the case of minor projects to more than five years for some of the largest, a tremendous amount of data relating to the various systems and equipment installed in the completed structure will be accumulated. Most of these data are not well-organized and therefore are not readily usable by those who will occupy and operate the building. The various communications of the functional planner regarding the myriad details of operational concepts may also remain unorganized. In some instances, officials of the hospital may have changed so that those who helped plan the building are no longer around when it is opened. For all of these reasons, there should be a concerted effort, commissioned and paid for by the hospital, to effect an organization of technical data pertaining to the completed facility, beginning as early as 18 months before opening. These data should be assembled into two basic groups of information: (1) information about the building as a physical system, especially with regard to any fixed or movable subsystem requiring power or maintenance, and (2) information about the functional use of the building and each of the operational concepts around which it was designed. All this information should be in the hands of appropriate hospital officials several months before occupancy.

With regard to the first group of data, the construction manager can be commissioned to perform the necessary modifications. With regard to the second group, the functional planning firm should be charged in its original contract with implementing employee orientation programs during the final months of the construction phase. This assignment of responsibility to the party most familiar with the intended operation of the facilities should result in an easy opening and occupancy. Without appropriate orientation, new faces at the hospital, in ignorance of functions which should now follow form, may attempt to force a *modus operandi* into facilities that were designed to accommodate totally different procedures.

Harold Hauf provides an excellent description of the wind-up of a project:[10]

> The process leading to final completion and final payment begins when the contractor requests the architect-engineer to issue a certificate of substantial completion. At this time, a "punch list" of items yet to be completed or corrected is prepared and an inspection made. This leads to the issuing of the certificate of substantial completion . . . . It should be stated specifically that failure to include any items on this list does not relieve the contractor of responsibility for completing all work in accordance with the contract documents. When the items on the list have been accomplished, the contractor requests final inspection and presents his final application for payment. If the work is found acceptable and complete, the architect issues the final certificate for payment which includes release of the retainage. Actual payment under the final certificate, however, is made contingent upon the furnishing of additional documents by the contractor as follows.
>
> At time of final payment, the contractor must submit releases or waivers of liens from all subcontractors, material vendors, and other parties to the construction; an affidavit that the releases and waivers furnished include all labor, materials and equipment for which a lien could be filed, a consent to final

payment by the surety underwriting the performance and payment bonds; and any other data substantiating payment of obligations that the owner may require. Items in this last category should be named in the Supplementary Conditions or in the General Requirements division of the specifications. Provision is normally included in the General Conditions to cover cases where final completion of the work is materially delayed through no fault of the contractor. This permits payment to be made for that portion of the work that is completed and accepted but does not terminate the contract.

The making of final payment by the owner constitutes a waiver of all claims by him except those arising from unsettled liens, terms of special guarantees and warranties required by the contract, and latent defects attributable directly to the contractor's failure to follow plans and specifications. Acceptance of final payment by the contractor constitutes a waiver of all claims by him except those previously presented but still unresolved.

Facilities opening

Each facilities opening is unique, but most can be categorized under one of the following basic situations:

1. a new hospital built where none previously existed

2. a new hospital that replaces an existing facility in its entirety, usually because of complete obsolescence of an existing plant or a decision to relocate

3. major additions and alterations in which the new addition will serve as the nucleus of a new plant, with old facilities being phased from use over a period of time

4. major additions and alterations that merely represent an expansion of an existing plant

5. minor additions or alterations.

The last two situations will present problems relative to opening, but certainly they will not be of the magnitude usually encountered with the first three. For that reason, the discussions here apply primarily to the first three situations.

Assuring a successful opening
In any major facility opening, the following points are worthy of consideration.

Scheduling
A definitive schedule for all activities related to opening should be prepared well in advance of opening. In view of the many activities and the

complexity of some of them, a proven scheduling technique—either the PERT or the CPM—should be used. This schedule should be kept updated constantly and should extend over two or three months after opening to provide a planned approach to handling the unforeseen problems that usually arise.

Early hiring and ongoing review
Key personnel should be employed full-time well in advance of opening, and there should be weekly meetings to review the schedule and to keep abreast of progress and problems.

In the case of a new hospital built where none existed before, a chief executive officer should be employed and the nucleus of a medical staff formed at the same time that a professional planning team is assembled. In many instances the hiring of an assistant to the chief executive, who may serve as the director of planning, can be justified.

Many years ago, Malcolm T. MacEachern, in writing about the opening of a new hospital, stated, "Usually he [the administrator] will not be engaged until plans are fairly well commenced, but certainly he should be placed in charge before working drawings are completed so that, as a representative of the hospital organization, he may be familiar with the details of planning and construction."[11] This advice may have been valid when it was written, but it could not be more erroneous at present, in view of the complexity that typifies today's physical facilities and operations. Moreover, failure to have an executive on board from the beginning may result in situations apparent in many older hospitals throughout the nation—illogical arrangements, inadequate space, poor sites, and spartan amenities of all types.

We will not attempt to outline the time sequence for hiring other key persons since much has been written on this subject. However, as a whole, the literature seems more concerned with saving dollars *prior* to opening, rather than after, through smooth, economical work processes.

Staff orientation
There should be a definitive program of staff orientation concerning the conceptual nature of the new facilities, referenced directly to procedures that the facility was designed to support. No more chaotic opening and shakedown of a new building can be anticipated than when the personnel do not understand the concepts of operation designed into the structure.

With regard to the physical systems of the building, key members of the engineering and maintenance staff should have participated in the testing and shakedown of all physical systems prior to opening. Over the whole course of construction, the chief engineer should make at least two or three visits to the site weekly in order to gain intimate knowledge about the individual systems and their integral parts.

At the present time, the Veterans Administration (VA)—still the owner of the largest system of hospitals in the nation—is concerned with the quality of its facilities openings and is trying to avoid the problems referred to in this book. Accordingly, the VA has funded a state-of-the-art study to be performed by the National Institute of Building Sciences (NIBS) in the interest of assessing the need to provide better guidance to design professionals, hospital administrators, and particularly operations and maintenance personnel regarding intended operations of a new facility.[12] As a result of this funding, NIBS, with the assistance of prestigious members of its volunteer facility start-up project committee, is currently in the process of preparing a series of model manuals to guide successful openings of new facilities; four volumes are planned, to cover the following topics:[13]

- building description and system design intent

- start-up

- operations

- maintenance.

This series of model manuals will soon be available to the public and may well be worth procuring by all those currently engaged in a major design and construction project to guide their own efforts in preparing for a smooth building opening.

With regard to operational concepts and the numerous procedures required to support them throughout the new facility, staff orientation should begin nine months to a year prior to opening. Every department should be engaged in the preparation of procedures manuals; furthermore, each department head should have a copy of the functional program that guided the design of the entire hospital, as well as a copy of the several architectural drawings relevant to the department and the building level on which it is located.

Delegation of responsibility to department heads
The responsibility for opening each department and effecting efficient operation in the new facility should be placed squarely upon each department head. Although many tasks can be delegated to persons to perform on a hospital-wide basis, such as moving in and placing equipment, this should never relieve the department head from seeing that everything in that department is ready to operate and does operate.

Operational shakedown
Portions of the building, especially those possessing complex equipment systems, should undergo an operational shakedown before they are occupied. In the interest of patient care and in anticipation of possible malpractice suits, it is necessary to achieve certainty that everything is in working order before patients are moved in.

On-site representation of the planning, design, and construction team
For several days prior to opening, on opening day, and for several days thereafter, every planning, design, and construction team member should have a competent representative on site.

Review of supplies and equipment operability

On-site repair representatives: Suppliers of complex equipment, upon which the basic operation of the hospital may depend, should be required to have competent repair representatives on site at opening and for several days thereafter. Equipment such as supply monorails, electronic robots, pneumatic tubes, complex washer-sterilizers, laundry equipment, communications equipment, and the like have a way of becoming inoperable just at opening. Their failure may cause great impatience and result in completely unjustified criticism of a highly cost-effective total operation.

Spare parts inventory: Well before opening, optimal levels of spare parts should be determined for all equipment, and they should be stored in the maintenance and engineering department in such a manner as to assure both protection and ready accessibility. Manufacturers can give appropriate advice in this regard but in some instances may not do so for a number of ulterior motives related to sales or service, or both. It is up to the chief engineer to use proper judgment in this matter.

Procedures manuals

By the time of opening, detailed procedures manuals for every department in the hospital should have been prepared to delineate the functions for which the building has been planned. Employees should have been well indoctrinated in the content and should have access to those appropriate to the nature of assigned work.

It is a fact that some hospitals in this nation are, in reality, "running themselves." Each department may operate primarily according to the personality, knowledge, and frame of reference of its head, with nothing in writing specifying how work is to be done. For example, we are well acquainted with a university teaching hospital in which each nursing floor operates as an entity unto itself, entirely upon the basis of its head nurse's decisions. (It is interesting to note that this hospital currently is seeking buyers among the investor-owned systems.) This state of affairs is deplorable even for a hospital whose operations were perhaps not specified but merely more or less evolved (as many have), but when a new, advanced facility is opened and personnel move in with no specification of procedures in writing, only bedlam and chaos can be expected.

Operations manuals

Although all manufacturers may promise to have operations manuals for their equipment in the hands of the hospital's maintenance and engineering department at opening, this frequently is not the case, even though contract specifications may have been clear on this point. The schedule of activities as outlined under Scheduling should allow for the obtaining of such manuals well before opening, and they should be placed in a protected, orderly file. In addition, maintenance personnel should have had proper orientation to these manuals by the manufacturer's representative and actual exposure to the equipment prior to opening.

Maintenance and engineering program

Qualified chief engineer and maintenance staff: The chief engineer and the maintenance staff are key figures to any opening. The first and most important criterion in selecting a chief engineer is proven executive ability; the second criterion, technical competence and experience; and the third, diligence and willingness to work. Under the chief engineer's supervision must be an appropriately sized staff with high educational and skill levels.

The complexity of systems now installed in new hospitals has spelled the end of blue-denimed, grease-stained "engineers" of yesteryear and requires a new breed of highly educated, specialized mechanics who perform much of the work as a team.

Preventive maintenance: A program of preventive maintenance should be established before the opening occurs and should be continued from the first day.

Maintenance and repair request forms: There should be a formal system for making written requests for repair work so that requests can be "logged in," categorized, and assigned appropriate priority. If work requests are received via telephone by whoever happens to answer the telephone in the "shop," with no formal log being maintained, confusion will assuredly reign.

Continued monitoring by the functional planner: administrative checklists

The functional planner's responsibility should extend throughout the opening period according to terms of the initial contract with that firm. A knowledgeable representative of the firm should meet with appropriate hospital staff members many times during the years prior to opening. This representative can point out problems experienced in other openings, arrange trips to hospitals of similar conceptual nature, and give good general advice about scheduling.

Additionally, the functional planner will probably have developed checklists of key activities that must be performed by each department before and during the opening process. Such checklists are essential to the smooth opening of each department. A sample page from a checklist developed by one functional planning firm and used successfully for several years is displayed in Exhibit 12–1.

An administrative checklist also assures that items pertaining to the entire hospital will not be overlooked. One of the largest of the investor-owned systems employs an extremely simple checklist that has been used in scores of new plant openings. This list merely specifies all the items that must be accomplished by top management on a week-by-week basis, for each week prior to opening, beginning six months in advance. The total list is updated weekly, with items that were not accomplished on schedule being carried forward as required and with new items being added as ascertained. Every new hospital, of course, has the list from previous openings available, and there is small chance of anything important being overlooked.

The primary role of the functional planner is to provide advice when needed and to monitor the hospital's activities to assure that important aspects of planning for opening are not omitted.

Case studies

Between the years 1970 and 1985, we have had occasion to observe a great number of hospital openings. Five are reported here, with two representing what might be regarded as unsuccessful openings and three representing what would be regarded as successful openings.

Exhibit 12–1

Sample checklist used in hospital opening

Department	Item	Participants	Date required	Date completed and approved
Maintenance and Engineering	Preventive maintenance program to include 24-hour coverage with men properly trained in the maintenance of the supply systems. Scheduled inspection of the following: sterilizers, stills, ultrasonic cleaners, washers, ironers, and other equipment not covered by a service contract, to become a chapter of the Engineering Manual.	Chief Engineer		
	Maintenance Request Form to include date, time, location, trouble and space for priority to be given by Engineering Department.	Chief Engineer Nursing Service		
	Safety Inspection Schedule to include: cleaning agents piped gases sterilizers hot plates and gas burners trash and laundry chutes general environment automatic supply cartlifts supply carts waste treatment system conveyors cart washer automatic doors	Chief Engineer		

Source: This document has been adapted with the permission of Friesen International, Inc., Washington, D.C.

Four of the hospitals were existing and were moved from obsolete facilities to completely new plants. For the fifth hospital, the nucleus of a new plant was added, with the old facilities being renovated and adapted thereto.

All five hospitals embody highly advanced operational concepts, and each is extensively automated. All possess the capability of being very cost-effective, and in truth, all are now operating as exemplary models in the areas where they are located.

Unsuccessful openings
Hospital A (208 beds) and hospital B (369 beds)—the two regarded as having unsuccessful openings—were not operating smoothly after even a full year of operation. Each had been relieved of two administrators during this period, and many key department heads had resigned or been fired. Census had been restricted, and both had lost sizable sums of money. Each hospital, however, was finally fortunate enough to employ an administrator who "got tough" with equipment suppliers who had not performed their responsibility in making equipment satisfactorily operational, instituted procedures compatible with the concepts around which the building had been designed, undertook appropriate staff orientation (a year late, of course), and brought back for consultation the functional planner whom the original administrator had elected not to use for opening advice.

As noted, these two hospitals are now models of success, but many troublesome months were spent in reaching this point.

Successful openings
Hospitals C (245 beds), D (545 beds), and E (309 beds) were highly successful from the start. In each of these instances, the hospital administrator was dedicated to appropriate staff education and orientation and took pains to ensure that written procedures, tailored to the concepts of operation around which the buildings were designed, were completed by opening date. Each administrator was insistent that equipment manufacturers fulfill their obligations in following up their installations with operational instructions, and all sought advice from the functional planner who started the projects. In each instance, opening activities were formally scheduled well in advance of facilities completion. Owing to the success of these hospitals in opening, their procedures are now used as models for openings in other hospitals.

Implications
The lesson is that executive officers cannot close their eyes to the fact that facilities opening can be a highly complicated event that, without proper planning and control, may result in complete confusion, monetary loss, and embarrassment. On the other hand, with proper planning, it can be accomplished smoothly and elicit the admiration of all concerned.

Summary

Construction in which construction management is employed in one way or another now dominates in the hospital field. This is due to the complexity of hospital construction and the usual necessity to divide the total effort into coordinated phases. The tasks of the construction manager usually involve the coordination of the various trades on the job, as well as a number of other activities formerly performed by either the A&E firm or the general contractor.

Recent research has proved the value of frank and frequent communications among project team members assembled for planning, design, and construction. Full-time job site representatives have been found to be invaluable in facilitating construction with regard to time, cost, and quality. Especially important is the presence on the site of a full-time hospital representative.

During the final year of construction, data should be organized that will assure a successful opening of the facility and subsequent successful operations. Two prime areas are involved: (1) the physical plant and the various physical systems and (2) the functional concepts around which the facility was designed and was intended to operate.

The many detailed activities necessary to a successful opening must be carefully coordinated, requiring frequent communication among top management officials and department heads. In a major facility opening, most of these activities are related to the following:

- appropriate and timely scheduling

- sufficient orientation of personnel

- the fixing of responsibilities as appropriate, not the least of which is to require department heads to accept the responsibility for successfully opening their respective departments

- advance "shakedown" of all major equipment

- the advance preparation of all procedures manuals, operations manuals, safety checklists, and checklists of necessary specific actions.

Experience has shown that opening new, major constructions must be accorded sufficient time, money, and personnel to avoid a host of pitfalls, some of which, such as malpractice suits, can be extremely harmful to the institution.

Notes

1. Institute for Health Planning, *Administrators' Guide to Hospital Construction Delivery Approaches*, prepared under HRSA contract (Madison, WI: 1984), p. ix.
2. *Standard Form of Agreement Between Owner and Construction Manager*, AIA Document B801, 1980 ed. (Washington, DC: American Institute of Architects, June 1980), pp. 2–4.
3. Institute for Health Planning, *Administrators' Guide*, p. 22.
4. George T. Heery, *Time, Cost and Architecture* (New York: McGraw-Hill, 1975), p. 198.
5. *Ibid.*, p. 199.
6. Institute for Health Planning, *Administrators' Guide*, p. XIII.
7. *Ibid.*, pp. XIV–XVI.
8. *Ibid.*, p. XV.
9. *Ibid.*
10. Harold Hauf, *Building Contracts for Design and Construction* (New York: John Wiley & Sons, 1978), p. 121.
11. Malcolm T. MacEachern, *Hospital Organization and Management* (Berwyn, IL: Physicians Record Co., 1962), p. 50.
12. Cited by Ted Mariani to members of its Facility Start-Up Project Committee in a memorandum from the National Institute of Building Sciences, June 25, 1984.
13. Cited in correspondence from the National Institute of Building Sciences to members of its Facility Start-Up Project Committee, November 16, 1984.

13

The Planning and Design Process

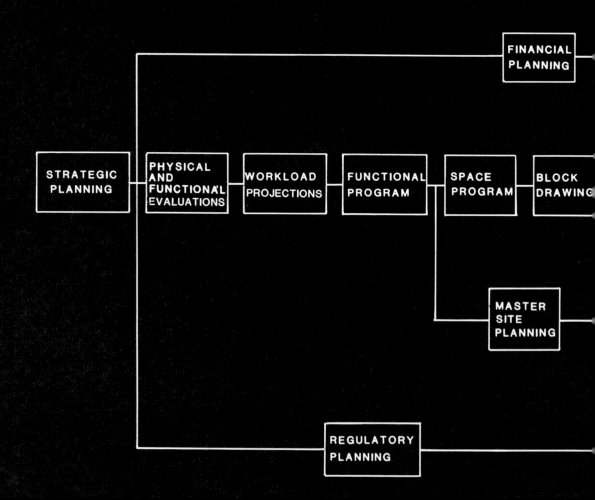

FINANCIAL
PLANNING

STRATEGIC
PLANNING

PHYSICAL
AND
FUNCTIONAL
EVALUATIONS

WORKLOAD
PROJECTIONS

FUNCTIONAL
PROGRAM

SPACE
PROGRAM

BLOCK
DRAWING

MASTER
SITE
PLANNING

REGULATORY
PLANNING

Modernization and expansion

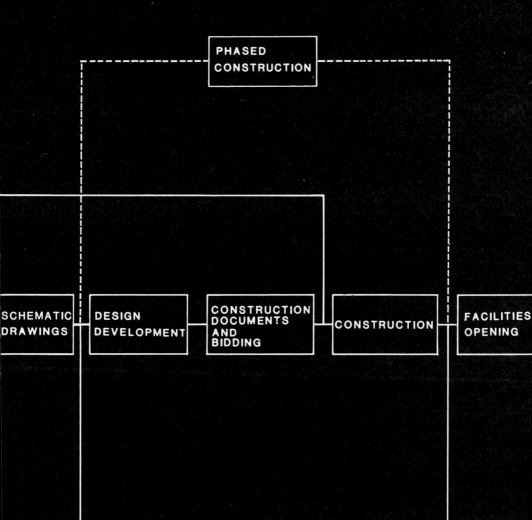

PHASED
CONSTRUCTION

SCHEMATIC
DRAWINGS

DESIGN
DEVELOPMENT

CONSTRUCTION
DOCUMENTS
AND
BIDDING

CONSTRUCTION

FACILITIES
OPENING

MOVABLE
EQUIPMENT
AND
INTERIORS
PLANNING

Our purpose in this chapter is to provide some insight for management personnel of hospitals regarding programs of modernization and expansion, from the standpoint of both future needs and immediate necessity. Concern for future needs should be a consideration in planning for any new or replacement hospital and should continue throughout the life of the structure. When service needs suggest that a specific program of modernization or expansion should be implemented, real-world circumstances will require further evaluation in terms of both immediate and future facility needs.

Before we address these specific concerns, we examine future construction trends as they relate to facilities upgrading and also present some important definitions.

Upgrading facilities: future trends

The prospective pricing of services based on DRGs and the trend toward greater reliance on ambulatory care will probably slow the rate of expansion of hospital beds across the nation. In fast-growing urban areas and in states for which rapid growth has been projected, hospitals will continue to expand their inpatient facilities, because population growth more than accounts for the decline in patient days per 1000 population. Even here, however, owing to the need to use facilities as intensively as possible, the rate of bed expansion will probably slow for an undetermined period.

At the same time, hospitals are engaged in intense competition, and facilities and their quality are very definite factors in attracting the practice of admitting physicians. Thus, it would seem that programs of alterations and modernization will be considered by a substantial percentage of existing hospitals in the immediate years ahead. As these programs are undertaken, bed numbers may be adjusted either upward or downward, according to foreseen need, but we believe that the prime impetus for change will be to provide for patient comfort and convenience and to maintain state-of-the-art physical plant technology and medical equipment, both fixed and movable.

The need for vertical integration of other services with acute hospital care will also cause changes in physical facilities.

We believe that the majority of new hospitals (those built where none previously existed) will be constructed by the investor-owned systems. These systems have the decision-making ability to initiate such programs, as well as readily available capital finances. However, compared with previous decades, the coming decade will see proportionately fewer new hospitals, owing to the fact that the nation is already fairly well supplied with hospitals insofar as location is concerned.

Replacement hospitals promise to be a substantial part of total hospital construction. The often prohibitive cost of modernizing older facilities, particularly in the Northeastern and Midwestern states, will cause many hospitals to consider seriously a program of replacement when the need to modernize becomes acute.

Note: Portions of this chapter were originally authored by Owen B. Hardy, James Phalen, and Lawrence P. Lammers, "Modernization and Expansion: A Concern for the Decade Ahead." Some sections appeared untitled in *Modern Health Care,* March 1975.

During the period 1977–1984, the regulatory agencies were at the height of their power, and most of them firmly held the objective of slowing hospital expansion. That they were successful to some extent is evidenced by the fact that in this same period about 48 percent of short-term acute care hospitals listed by the American Hospital Association for both 1977 and 1984 showed no appreciable changes in bed capacities; moreover, 15 percent showed an actual reduction in beds. Thirty-seven percent, however, showed increases of sufficient scope that one could conclude that an expansion program probably had been completed.[1]

Of the 63 percent that showed either a reduction in beds or no appreciable change, we cannot say how many initiated programs of modernization, alterations, or expansion that did not entail bed expansions. Undoubtedly, some did, so that it might be surmised that at least 50 percent of all existing hospitals undertook and completed a construction program over the seven-year period. Even so, this percentage is considerably reduced from earlier periods.[2]

The possibility exists that there is a considerable "pent-up" need to upgrade existing facilities throughout the nation. If this is, indeed, a fact, we believe that despite several clearly contravening factors, a majority of such hospitals will seek solutions to their problems in the immediate future.

Certainly, there are clear indications that, compared with the figures cited for 1977–1984, the number of existing hospitals that will undertake changes of one type or another in the immediate future will increase rather than decrease. Some programs will be small and will be carried out by in-house staff; others will entail large expenditures and will involve levels of complexity exceeding even those of new plant construction. In either case, considerable planning talent will be required in order to assure optimal life cycle building costs and effective implementation of service programs.

Definitions

Although the word expansion is seldom ambiguously interpreted, modernization has been defined variously. In the context of this narrative, a *modernization* means any program whereby extensive alterations or renovations, or both, in an existing plant are undertaken. Such alterations and renovations may occur for a number of reasons, including those related to changes resulting from additions, program changes, functional obsolescence, and physical obsolescence. "Retrofitting" for energy conservation will certainly be a major feature of many modernizations.

We have already pointed out that there are two basic types of additions (expansions): *minor* and *major*. The distinction between the two is usually based on the relationship between the scope of the proposed addition and that of existing facilities. Scope can be interpreted in terms of either costs of construction or size, or both.

The character of many major additions should be carefully projected on the basis of the need to start the nucleus of a new plant (the first step in regeneration) or merely to perpetuate and expand the character of existing facilities. In planning most major additions, alternative solutions should be composed. An orderly methodology for comparing such alternatives, regardless of whether or not plant regeneration will be considered, should be employed. An approach that we have frequently used and consider appropriate is called a *cost-benefit analysis*, which involves both life cycle costing and factor analyses.

Life cycle costing reduces all the costs associated with specific alternatives that are being considered for construction and operation over a distinct time period, or indefinitely, to a common denominator called *present worth*, or *present value dollars*. Its purpose is to allow cost comparisons on an exactly common basis. "Dissimilar projects fulfilling a similar functional requirement can be compared directly despite any dissimilarities in their materials, methods, and cash flow."[3]

Factor analysis involves the assignment of value weights to specific noncost benefits desired to be realized with each program alternative. Each alternative is subjectively "scored" in terms of its expected ability to deliver the weighted benefit. The point scorings for each benefit are added to determine a total point score for that alternative. The total scores for each alternative can then be directly compared.

With both costs and noncost benefits quantified in terms of similar factors, valid comparisons are possible, and the likelihood of making a better decision is substantially increased. Both of these aspects of the evaluation are discussed in greater detail later in this chapter.

Prospective concerns

The original physical facilities of a hospital, as constructed, should represent the first phase of a response to programs of service projected for an approximate 15- to 20-year period. Long-range strategic planning should be continually updated thereafter so that modernization or expansion, as required, can also be made in consideration of long-term program needs. Thus it is reasonable to assume that if constructions are always undertaken on the basis of not only immediate but also future needs, life cycle costs of a building will be decreased, for two reasons: (1) changes will probably be required less frequently, and (2) when they *are* required, the cost will probably be relatively smaller.

Despite proper strategic program planning and optimal interpretation of projected service needs in physical facilities, the need for unanticipated building changes can be expected. Additionally, the life of a building can be conservatively estimated at 40 years, and good long-range programming rarely extends beyond 20 years. Thus, design should feature flexibility and easy expansibility, in addition to good accommodation of foreseeable programs of service.

Site selection and master site planning

Planning for optimal flexibility and expansibility, in the face of unknowns and unknowables regarding building utilizations, starts with original site selection and master site planning.

Factors related to site selection that affect optimal facility planning and use over the years include site access points, zoning ordinances, site restrictions, site size, site configuration, and easements. Although each of these can affect flexibility and expansibility, *site size* has stood as the foremost restraint over the years. Errors of the past loom large and speak a distinct lesson for planners in this regard.

Master site planning, accomplished by a professional planning team (including a functional planner, architect, and mechanical, civil, and electrical engineers), is the approach by which building expansibility can be assured and objectionable aspects of "boxing-in" avoided. A clear site is the obvious ingredient of both expansion and long-term plant regeneration, but it is surprising that there exists today a large number of hospitals that cannot be expanded owing to this lack. In most instances, an appropriate site selection methodology and master site planning would have precluded the predicament.

Flexibility

As a matter of prospective concern, flexibility can be achieved in some of the following ways:

1. A standard planning module, as conceptualized in Figure 13–1, should be utilized in design where possible. In recent years such modules have been used, especially in outpatient areas and laboratories, to good advantage. Clearly, it is not possible to employ a universal module, but a few types can serve the needs of most departments.

2. Design should locate the fixed elements of a building (such as stairways, elevator shafts, and mechanical elements) so as to allow free space of a size and shape that will accommodate a variety of hospital functions.

3. Good utility service accessibility should be provided to appropriately sized functional spaces. Interstitial spaces should be considered as an alternative in particular instances.

4. Demountable metal partitioning systems, office landscaping components, and operable area dividers should be evaluated.

5. Fixed casework should be kept to a minimum, and movable casework and "shelves-on-wheels" employed where feasible.

6. Varying degrees of flexibility are achievable through design of mechanical, electrical, and structural systems. Inasmuch as innovations are constant in each of these areas, suffice it to say that respective disciplines should be consulted regarding the future flexibility of all proposed systems in each construction program.

Expansibility

Expansibility, prospectively regarded, may be enhanced by consideration of the following:

1. An assessment should be made of the various rates and frequencies of expansion of all departments. Those shown to have a high probability of expansion should always adjoin an outside wall.

Conceptual
use of
modular spaces

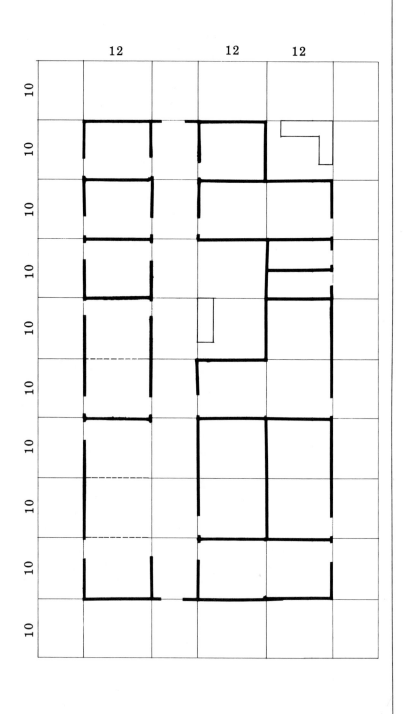

2. Where a multilevel structure is involved, services identified as most likely to expand that are located on different levels should be placed one above the other.[4]

3. Owing to the usual need to change existing areas when expansion occurs, it can be concluded that good flexibility, previously discussed, promotes good expansibility.

4. The original design should incorporate an interdepartmental corridor scheme, which in later years can simply be extended as required, with intradepartmental branches being added as indicated. Additional vertical circulation cores should be included in the initial master plan. The basic idea to be reflected in design is to allow growth through minimum disruption of ongoing activities and to provide for the independent growth of a single department.

5. The power plant should be located in a separate expansible building that does not block the expansion of other site structures.

6. Although it can usually be shown that oversizing utilities to any great extent is not feasible, especially with regard to standby units, consideration should be given to plans for expansion of all such services in construction programs. If the design evolved precludes future expansion, it should certainly be peremptorily discarded.

Choosing an appropriate program

Although past planning teams may have done their jobs in the best manner possible, and although existing facilities may exhibit the best features of such efforts, each modernization and expansion program is almost always unique. However, the decisions involved in various aspects of evaluation (as required) and in basic planning can be facilitated through the use of largely common methodologies.

Preparation of a functional program and an architectural space program as a distinct part of a long-range program plan is the first undertaking when any program of modernization and expansion is to be considered, except in rare instances of modernization where the single objective is to correct specific aspects of physical obsolescence.

In many instances, functional programming and space programming will be followed by schematic design or other simple drawings, with construction then carried out by in-house staff. In others, schematic design will be followed by preparation of construction documents so that bids can be received from outsiders who will effect the construction desired. Such straightforward programs, requiring minimal consideration of alternatives, probably constitute the majority of constructions completed each year. That serious planning and design errors have been made in these programs, however, is apparent, as revealed in numerous plant evaluations we have conducted.

As noted, many modernization and expansion projects are relatively simple. In certain situations, however, intensive evaluations and complex modeling of alternatives are required:

- when the program, for whatever reason, is so extensive that relocating the hospital to a new plant must be considered

- when a replacement facility has already been ruled out, but several alternatives for a major program of modernization (possibly to include alterations, additions, and renovations) exist

- when a program for alleviating widespread obsolescence is needed.

Considerations involved in evaluating each of these situations are presented in the following discussion.

Replacement versus modernization or expansion

Consideration of any extensive program of modernization must be initiated by physical and functional evaluations. These studies compare features of the existing building and its systems to recognized governmental standards that are currently being applied to new construction, and deficiencies are tabulated to allow accurate cost estimation of corrective measures later in the evaluation process. In addition, inconveniences and discomforts that may exist for building inhabitants, as well as deterrents to meeting objectives of patient care programs, should be accurately described so that later cost-benefit judgments can be made to determine feasible improvements for inclusion in the modernization program.

After the information inherent to the cited evaluations is obtained, the basic problem of deciding whether to modernize or expand, as indicated, or to relocate to a new facility can be attacked. A cost-benefit study, previously defined, must be performed.

In order to quantify the costs of the two alternatives, accurate descriptions of the work required under each must be formulated. Typically, a gross space program for a new facility should be prepared along with abbreviated outline specifications. The work decided upon in terms of modernization can be derived from the physical and functional evaluations, and if expansions are involved, required gross space must be calculated and outline specifications prepared.

Several decision models have been evolved for comparing these alternatives. One example is shown as Figure 13–2.

Recall that a cost-benefit analysis entails life cycle costing and factor analysis. Six factors are involved in life cycle costing:

1. initial construction costs, which alone may indicate an obvious decision in view of limited funding capabilities

2. lost revenues, a common problem in programs of modernization or expansion, when services may have to be temporarily reduced, or in relocation from an old to a new structure

Decision model for considering modernization and expansion projects

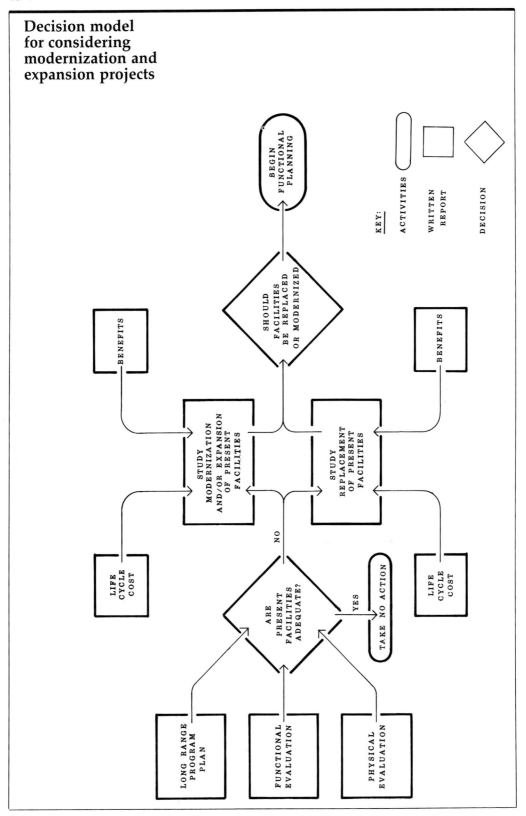

3. costs of relocation, related to the actual move of personnel, patients, and equipment to new facilities or from one area in an existing plant to another

4. costs of each alternative program relating to operation, maintenance, and repair over a projected life cycle

5. salvage or resale value of the existing facility, which in some instances may be a negative value owing to demolition expense

6. salvage value at the end of the projected life cycle of the new facilities identified under each alternative.

In order to provide a common basis for comparing net life cycle costs, and because costs are usually incurred at different times under each alternative, future costs are discounted to present value in calculations using a present-worth discount factor. The statistical formulations to accomplish such conversions to comparable net cost are quite complicated, but they have been computerized, thus allowing rapid calculations to be accomplished.[5]

For a detailed explanation of a typical model, the reader is referred to a recognized landmark research study by Battelle Memorial Institute, which focused on whether an existing naval facility should be replaced or continued in use by modernization.[6]

If possible, noncost benefits (if they are not considered equal) should also be quantitatively compared. A factor analysis should be accomplished so that decision makers can agree upon various weights assigned to listed benefits.

With both costs and benefits quantified, rationality can be brought to the process, and the probability of making the best decision will be considerably enhanced.

Alternative programs of modernization or expansion

Preliminary evaluation of a program of modernization or expansion often requires consideration of alternative courses of action, owing to several factors:

1. problems related to funding

2. the numerous facets of obsolescence as exhibited in most older buildings

3. the wide differences in costs as related to benefits in alleviating obsolescence to varying degrees

4. the several options usually extant in considering the long-term future of an institution.

In order to formulate alternative courses of action, the strategic future of the institution must be considered, and each formulation should allow pursuance of established program goals.

Each alternative should be identified in terms of room and space programs; formal block drawings (if required); and, at a minimum, outline specifications. The findings of functional and physical evaluations, previously accomplished, prove invaluable when definitive identifications of appropriate alternatives are being prepared.

Again, life cycle cost analyses must be performed on each alternative to compare the economies of each. Usually, factor analyses should also be performed. Methodologies now being utilized are closely similar to those described under the previous heading.

Although life cycle cost analyses almost invariably reveal the alternative that makes best economic sense, on some occasions the best alternative may never even be introduced for consideration. For example, additions sufficient in extent to be organized as the nucleus of a new plant (regeneration) may not be so organized but instead may be tacked on an existing plant in a seemingly "best" way. The problem with this approach, as contrasted with the regeneration approach, is that the life of any construction tied intimately into an existing plant is immediately compromised by the span of life remaining in the existing. For example, suppose that a 30-year-old patient pavilion is expanded directly by approximately 50 percent through new construction. The life of the new construction, in most instances, will be shortened by 30 years owing to the fact that it cannot be used in the absence of the old and, therefore, will be razed at the same time. In contrast, if the new bed construction had been integrated into the nucleus of a regenerated plant, its full life potential could have been realized.

Certainly, the possibilities for plant regeneration should never be overlooked when major additions and alterations are being considered.

Outside professional assistance is usually required in large programs of modernization. Although expenditures for such expertise may seem high, they are usually justified in view of the long-term institutional role and the significant variation in life cycle costs for different alternatives. Certainly, personnel who are busily engaged in day-to-day hospital management and who are inexperienced in the ramifications of facility planning cannot be expected to bring to these complicated tasks either the level of competency or the time commitments that are required.

Correcting widespread obsolescence

Many hospitals do not need to expand and need relatively few major alterations. These hospitals may simply need to update their various operational systems and to correct physical obsolescence, such as features relating to energy conservation, HVAC systems, transportation systems, and so on.

A typical approach in correcting a broad number of obsolete features is first to establish an upper-limit budget. Each discrete obsolete feature should be listed and a cost for correction fairly accurately estimated. Hospital officials can then arrange the various items and their costs in a priority ranking based on factor analyses. If the total cost overruns the budget, those items for which correction is least desirable can be eliminated.

Life cycle costing can be employed to compare alternative methods of correcting some of the items on the list. Historically, however, programs of this nature have not seen widespread use of life cycle costing, owing to time involved and the fact that there may not be wide cost differentials among alternative approaches.

Summary

Modernizations and expansions promise to compose a majority of hospital constructions in the decade ahead. Accordingly, hospital officials should make sure that the professional planning team assembled possesses the skills required to implement such programs efficiently. Nearly every program of modernization or expansion is unique, and a number of alternative solutions can be considered. In many instances, cost-benefit analyses, featuring life cycle costing and factor analysis, should be undertaken to assure that the most feasible selection is made.

There are three primary situations that may require intensive evaluation with complex modeling of alternatives: (1) situations in which the condition of the physical plant in relation to program requirements is so deficient that plant replacement must be considered; (2) those in which there are two or more approaches to accomplishing a major program of modernization and additions; and (3) those in which there is widespread obsolescence, with a broad number of items requiring upgrading, but no expansion is required. The necessary evaluation should be based on appropriate modeling and employment of life cycle costing and factor analysis.

Notes

1. Study by O.B. Hardy based on a 25 percent sampling of acute care hospitals listed in both the 1977 and 1984 editions of the *American Hospital Association Guide to the Health Care Field* (Chicago, IL: American Hospital Association).
2. For the eight-year period, 1965 to 1973, about 85 percent of hospitals apparently made facility changes; this figure is based on a 15 percent sampling of acute care hospitals listed in both the 1965 and 1973 editions of the *American Hospital Association Guide to the Health Care Field*.
3. Hira N. Ahuja, *Successful Construction Cost Control* (New York: John Wiley & Sons, 1980), p. 172.
4. Herbert McLaughlin et al., "Remodeling and Expansion: Study Tells Which Areas Change Most Often and Why," *Modern Healthcare*, March 1973, p. 100.
5. Comptroller General of the United States, *Study of Health Facilities Construction Costs* (Washington, DC: U.S. Government Printing Office, 1972), p. 2.
6. Battelle Memorial Institute, *The Development of an Economic Method to Determine Whether an Existing Naval Facility Should Be Replaced or Continued in Use by Modernization* (September 1966; Distributed by National Technical Information Service, U.S. Department of Commerce).

14

The Planning and Design Process

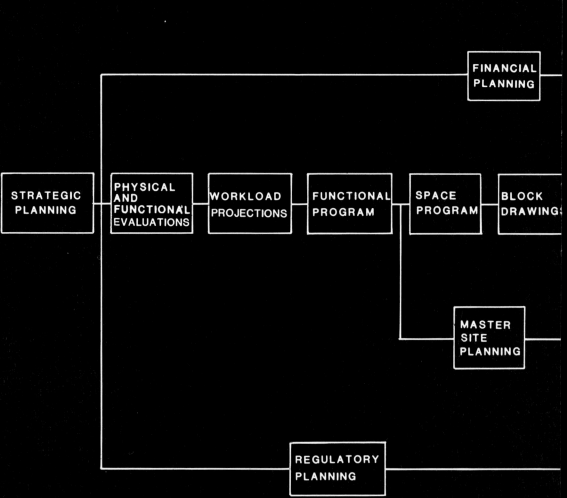

| STRATEGIC PLANNING | PHYSICAL AND FUNCTIONAL EVALUATIONS | WORKLOAD PROJECTIONS | FUNCTIONAL PROGRAM | SPACE PROGRAM | BLOCK DRAWING |

FINANCIAL PLANNING

MASTER SITE PLANNING

REGULATORY PLANNING

Design efficiency: key to construction cost savings

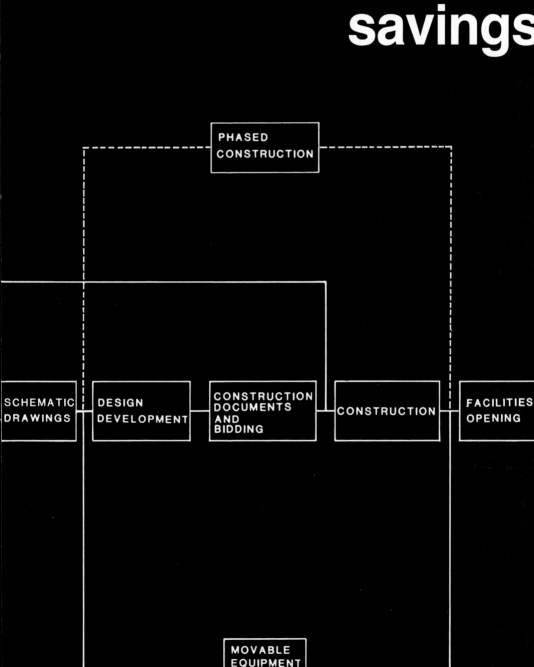

PHASED CONSTRUCTION

SCHEMATIC DRAWINGS

DESIGN DEVELOPMENT

CONSTRUCTION DOCUMENTS AND BIDDING

CONSTRUCTION

FACILITIES OPENING

MOVABLE EQUIPMENT AND INTERIORS PLANNING

Design efficiency, defined as achieving a high ratio of net usable space to total gross building space, has the potential of reducing hospital construction costs in many cases by 10 percent or more. Thus, for a typical 200-bed hospital, with 900 gross square feet per bed, savings can approximate well over $1 million through attention to simple and basic, but often overlooked, design characteristics. This savings can be additional to those obtained through more frequently used cost containment methodologies.

Although the rise in per-unit construction costs has moderated in the preceding few years, certainly these costs are extremely high and will tax the budgets of most hospitals undertaking major projects. Every feasible means of reducing these costs should be investigated, and we believe that the thesis here pursued is worthy of serious consideration by architects, hospital executives, consultants, and all other members of planning and design teams.

A number of significant studies have been accomplished to consider means of reducing the cost of constructing health care facilities. Notable among these is the *Study of Health Facilities Construction Costs*,[1] completed in 1972 by the General Accounting Office of the United States government. This study focused primarily on hospitals and, most properly, considered not only initial construction costs but operating costs as a function of design and construction materials used.

The Veterans Administration (VA) has consistently investigated the possibilities for reducing construction costs. In 1968, the Research Staff of the VA Office of Construction located in Washington, D.C., performed an in-depth analysis of construction costs in a research study report entitled *Integration of Mechanical, Electrical, Structural and Architectural Systems in VA Hospital Facilities*.[2] Since 1980, the VA has sponsored studies related to streamlining the design and construction process and to standards that will meet codes but not exceed them to degrees of unreasonable excess. The studies related to standards have pertained to fire and safety and to the basic quality of buildings and equipment.

Also, the VA is presently investigating the use of prototype buildings with maximum use of computer-aided design (CAD) systems. This approach has obvious implications, for the VA is the nation's largest owner of health facilities, with reference to not only CAD but also many other factors pertaining to mass purchase of component building elements and their assembly.

Results of all these studies are available, or will be shortly, and are not reviewed here. Undoubtedly the recommendations flowing from such studies will assist health care institutions in receiving more cost-effective structures for today's dollar. As experience is accumulated in testing the various techniques and methodologies of planning, design, and construction that have been suggested, it is reasonable to expect that added efficiency in achieving economically built facilities of required quality and functionality will be evidenced.

Note: Major portions of this chapter were originally written by Owen B. Hardy, Lawrence P. Lammers, and Chester Minkalis. An edited version appeared in *Hospitals, JAHA,* March 16, 1976, as the article "Build Less Total Space but More Usable Space."

The net-to-gross area ratio

Potential cost savings

Among the studies we reviewed, however, design achievement of a high ratio of net usable space to gross space has not been given the attention it deserves in relationship to obvious potential savings. As stated previously, through *efficiency in design alone*, we believe the possibility exists, for hospitals of various size ranges, to achieve increased net usable space—of 10 percent or more beyond the currently accepted amount—in the same area of gross space. Conversely, the implication is apparent that gross space can be reduced significantly yet still provide the necessary net area detailed by the hospital's functional and space programs.

Finished building construction costs are typically compared in a unit cost format (e.g., $100 per gross square foot). The same unit is usually used in comparing costs of similar buildings. However, when such comparisons are made among hospitals of a given bed range, insufficient consideration is given to the net-to-gross ratio, and quantified data relating to the exact effect, if any, exerted by this parameter are largely lacking. However, in considering various cost factors involved in the provision of net space as contrasted with those items that make up gross area, we can conclude only that little difference would exist between the unit cost of a building with a net-to-gross ratio, for example, of 62 percent and the unit cost of another with a 52 percent ratio. Even if there were a cost differential of any significance, it would not approach the proportion of 62 to 52. We are of the opinion that, under similar conditions of construction, so long as two hospitals in a certain bed range have the same gross square footage, their respective costs will be very similar. The building with the higher net-to-gross ratio, of course, will provide greater amounts of usable area at little or no increase in cost.

Current interest

In recent years we have noticed a distinct upsurge of interest in the net-to-gross ratio, and architects are, in fact, coming to recognize the importance of the matter. Hospital officials must also become more aware of the significant savings possible. We cannot estimate the effects of our research and findings (although reports of our work have been widely published). We have noted with satisfaction the progress being made; nevertheless, increased efforts should be exerted in every construction project to achieve an optimal ratio, with little or no sacrifice of functionality or aesthetics.

Research

We emphasize that our research into this matter has not been accomplished to the necessary extent, in view of the cost savings possibilities. However, the significance of our analysis and findings should point the way for further study by both ourselves and others.

Our research effort was prompted during the course of a facilities evaluation of a large teaching hospital. This institution, evolving over more than a 50-year period and possessing some 18 separate buildings, exhibited among its various structures designs that achieved a net assignable area of only 46 percent of gross space, on the low end of the range,

**Example of design
with low
net-to-gross ratio**

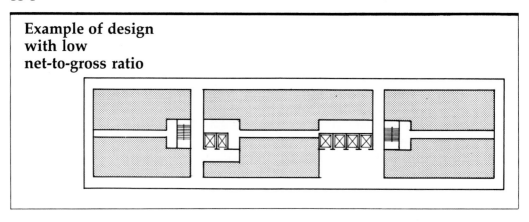

and a high of 76 percent. The wide variations observed, as well as their obvious causes, elicited our interest in seeking a population of hospitals that had been analyzed properly with regard to ratios of net to gross and that was large enough to formulate valid conclusions.

Graphic portrayals of the designs that yielded the low and high ratios are set forth here as Figures 14–1 and 14–2, respectively. The design in Figure 14–1 shows a "racetrack" corridor scheme in a long and narrow configuration subdivided into small room areas. Thus there are high ratios of perimeter wall to floor area, of corridor space to net usable area, and of space occupied by partitions to usable areas. Figure 14–2 shows a building shaped as a square, with a low ratio of perimeter wall to floor area; waiting spaces for departmental and other functional areas are located directly off an elevator core lobby. Thus, in the latter design, corridor space is nearly nonexistent, and interior wall space and other areas composing gross space have been reduced to a minimum. It was our recognition of this apparently advantageous design feature that inspired us to pursue further analysis.

**Example of design
with high
net-to-gross ratio**

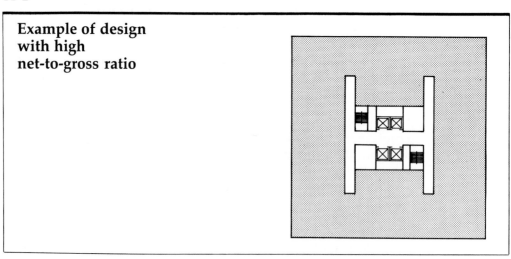

From the Office of Architecture and Engineering of the Department of Health, Education and Welfare (DHHS) in Washington, D.C., we obtained appropriate data on a sample of 85 new hospitals constructed between 1960 and 1967. Although it can be stated that these data are not as current as would be desirable, reflective thought reveals that the *cause* of the variations in net-to-gross ratios remains the same today, and, in fact, will always be the same owing to certain geometric considerations. Additional data, pertaining to certain departmental areas and referenced to 43 of the 85 HEW hospitals, were obtained from the Center for Environmental Research in Boston.

Analyses of data received from the HEW Office of Architecture and Engineering were directed toward the hospitals as whole entities, and data from the Center for Environmental Research were studied from the standpoint of individual departments. All these data are especially significant since space measurements ("takeoffs") from finished drawings were accomplished by the same team using similar methodologies. Previously published data regarding ratios of net-to-gross areas have been regarded as possibly invalid and unreliable, owing to the fact that space measurements were done by different individuals employing dissimilar methodologies and interpretations.

Following are definitions of the terms used in analyses of the data studied:[3]

- *gross area*—total building gross area measured from exterior faces of exterior walls; as related to departments, the gross area forming the department

- *net area*—the area of rooms or spaces as measured from inside wall to inside wall and assigned to functional use by occupants in accomplishment of work related to patient care, research, education or other institutional objectives

  total net area—the sum of all net areas in the hospital

  departmental net area—the sum of net spaces in a department

- *mechanical area*—main boiler room and other mechanical and electrical areas; included in gross areas and excluded in net areas

- *circulation area*—entrances, vestibules, corridors, passages, elevators, escalators, stairs, and so on; included in gross areas and excluded in net areas

- *construction area*—areas taken up by interior and exterior walls, columns, thresholds, doorways, openings in walls, and all plumbing and mechanical chases of which the inside clear area is less than 10 square feet; included in gross areas, excluded in net areas

- *percentage of net to gross*—net/gross × 100.

Groupings by number of beds were constructed among the 85 HEW study hospitals as follows: 75–150; 151–250; 251–350; and 351–550.

Table 14–1

Comparison of total net-to-gross ratios

Bed size grouping	No. of hospitals in grouping	% of Net Space		
		Range	Mean	Median
75–150	45	50.8–65.0	58.9	59.3
151–250	23	46.5–61.6	56.2	55.7
251–350	12	52.2–63.2	58.5	57.0
351–550	5	52.7–61.2	57.2	57.8

We first examined the total net-to-gross ratios among the hospitals in these bed groupings. These findings are shown in Table 14–1, and regardless of relevant factors that could have produced the variances between high and low percentages, it is clear that the wide ranges possess significance.

In the 75–150 bed grouping, for example, the hospital at the top of the range shows 22 percent more net space than does the lowest. In the 151–250 bed grouping, the high figure represents a 25 percent advantage in net space achieved. In the 251–350 bed grouping, a difference of 18 percent between the high and low is shown. As might be expected, a somewhat more narrow range is exhibited among the five hospitals in the 351–550 bed grouping, but even here an 11 percent greater amount of net space in the hospital at the top of the range represents a significant advantage.

In searching for reasons for exhibited variations in achieved net areas, as cited, we examined two major segments of gross space: circulation area and construction area. We noted that circulation areas ranged from a low of 17.56 percent total gross area to a high of 26.67 percent among the 45 units in the 75–150 bed group. Construction areas ranged from a low of 6.84 percent to a high of 16.53 percent for the same grouping.

Although parameters for circulation and construction areas were significant when considered separately, they proved even more significant when the data were combined, owing to the fact that these areas constitute such a large part of the total. Combining the percentages of the total gross area cited for the 75–150 bed group, for example, yields a range of 26.60 to 39.93 percent, with both the mean and the median equaling approximately one third of the entire gross area.

In Table 14–2 we have shown parameters for circulation and construction areas, separately and combined.

We divided arrayed data on percentages of net assignable area for the 45 hospitals in the 75–150 bed group into quartiles and then selected the median figures in the lowest and highest quartiles for comparison. The median for the lowest quartile was 54.90 percent, and that for the highest was 62.84 percent. Assuming two 115-bed hospitals, each with 850 gross square feet per bed, and an equal cost of $100 per square foot, we calculated a total project cost for each of $9,775,000. However, the hospital with a net assignable area of 54.90 percent could theoretically have been reduced in size by 12.6 percent, by using the more efficient design,

Table 14–2

Circulation and construction areas as percentages of gross areas

Area	75–150 Beds (45 hospitals)	151–250 Beds (23 hospitals)	251–350 Beds (12 hospitals)	351–550 Beds (5 hospitals)
Circulation				
Range	17.6–26.7	19.0–25.2	20.7–25.3	21.3–28.3
Mean	21.5	22.0	22.8	23.9
Median	21.2	22.0	23.0	23.1
Construction				
Range	6.8–16.5	5.8–15.8	4.0–15.4	5.2–12.7
Mean	11.6	11.7	10.9	9.0
Median	11.5	11.6	10.9	8.7
Combined Circulation and Construction				
Range	26.6–39.9	28.3–38.5	27.0–39.4	28.2–36.9
Mean	33.0	33.7	33.6	33.0
Median	32.4	33.3	33.8	34.0

and still have retained the same amount of net assignable area. A 12.6 percent reduction in the total area would amount to a savings of $1,231,700.

We performed similar statistical procedures and calculations for the 23 hospitals in the 151–250 bed group. Assuming a 200-bed hospital at 900 gross square feet per bed with a construction cost of $100 per square foot, we determined that the median hospital in the lower quartile could have been reduced in size by 23,220 square feet for a savings of $2,322,000, with use of a design as efficient as that for the median institution in the upper quartile.

We do not cite similar calculations for the other two groupings owing to small sample sizes. Suffice it to say that results were closely similar but could be invalid.

Although arguments can be developed to question the simplistic specificity of these calculations, the conclusion *is* warranted that efficiency in design with regard to attainment of net usable area can result in appreciable total savings in costs over those for an inefficient design. Conversely, inattention to this factor can result in an inefficient design and a high premium for net usable space.

It will be noted that we have not accomplished an analysis of mechanical areas. Even though areas so assigned influenced the net assignable areas to some extent, our review of raw data led to the belief that direct comparisons among the hospitals in this regard would not be valid. Owing to climate differences in the several sections of the nation, requirements for heating and cooling equipment vary, and space provisions logically correlate with the type of these installed equipment elements. Furthermore, we suspected that some hospitals, even in the same climate areas, were air-conditioned to a greater degree than others. We *can* specifically say, however, that no inverse correlation between net assignable areas and areas assigned to mechanical spaces could be ascertained.

It is clear that, to some extent, a hospital as a whole must be a summation of its individual departments. The information obtained from the Center on Environmental Research on the net area of each of seven major hospital departments as a percentage of gross has been assembled and is shown in Table 14–3. For the sake of brevity, only the parameters for large space consumers have been reported, but we can state that other functional areas were similarly composed.

A cursory review of means and medians reveals that they are much higher throughout than those for total net assignable areas reported for the larger 85-hospital sample from DHHS' Office of Architecture and Engineering. We can conclude only that combined *interdepartmental* circulation areas, construction areas, and mechanical areas play a great role in reducing total net assignable area, with nonassignable *intradepartmental* areas being another major contributor. Thus, the inference is clear that the scheme by which the total hospital is configured, as well as the design for each individual department, has a definite effect upon the total percentage of net assignable area achieved.

Other pertaining factors

The question of whether a low ratio of net area to gross provides any increase in functionality, cost effectiveness, or other specific benefit, for either the short- or long-term future, needs to be addressed. Although there are some departmental areas, such as nursing levels, the emergency suite, and surgery, where particular corridor schemes designed either to reduce walking distances or to separate categories of traffic may be productive of somewhat reduced net areas as compared with others, we believe that, on balance, a design that effects a high net area ratio will be more functional and cost effective than one that is productive of a low ratio.

Many nonassignable gross areas, for example, must be heated, air-conditioned, and cleaned. Moreover, the increased size of a building with a low ratio of net to gross will usually be productive of greater walking distances among the net areas. These factors all tend to produce higher operational costs per unit of service and lowered cost effectiveness.

It is doubtful that any major claims for increased expansibility or flexibility could be substantiated for structures with low percentages of net area. In the case of mechanical areas, where the amount of space provided depends in great part upon design, we certainly believe that ample space must be provided, regardless of its effect on the net-to-gross ratio. The provision of space defined as "ample," however, needs to be controlled quantitatively, on the basis of the equipment installed. In the case of nursing areas, all single bedrooms have an adverse effect upon the net-to-gross ratio (occasioned by greater circulation and construction areas), and this effect must be weighed against the many advantages of building all single rooms, one of which is achieving a higher occupancy rate among the same number of beds, thus theoretically reducing bed needs.

Table 14–3

Net-to-gross percentages for seven major hospital services

Service	75–124 Beds (10 hospitals)	125–174 Beds (16 hospitals)	175–224 Beds (10 hospitals)	225–274 Beds (7 hospitals)
Administration				
Range	69.66–98.89	61.47–94.77	79.89–96.66	76.42–98.93
Mean	78.66	82.14	88.24	86.84
Median	79.98	77.61	90.35	86.73
Pathology				
Range	79.81–100	74.20–100	79.39–98.43	78.02–100
Mean	86.75	88.83	87.58	84.07
Median	90.98	89.93	89.69	97.23
Radiology				
Range	70.22–100	66.21–100	66.25–83.33	77.27–87.42
Mean	80.11	84.35	73.93	81.46
Median	80.20	86.22	70.49	87.42
Surgery				
Range	67.47–81.89	67.45–95.56	67.61–83.02	64.14–87.55
Mean	76.09	80.43	75.10	78.05
Median	75.47	84.03	72.68	72.65
Obstetrics				
Range	61.96–86.38*	63.77–95.18†	59.34–83.33	61.03–96.60
Mean	74.96	75.66	72.96	72.17
Median	75.39	78.79	69.62	66.62
Dietary				
Range	79.39–100	82.39–100	91.68–100	92.31–100
Mean	92.77	96.56	98.06	96.00
Median	96.79	91.12	95.57	92.31
Nursing (Inpatient Bed Units)				
Range	66.13–77.53	65.54–82.97	64.54–77.58	70.19–75.24
Mean	71.70	73.54	72.40	72.90
Median	71.31	73.07	73.57	70.19

* 7 hospitals only.
† 15 hospitals only.

Design considerations

If a high ratio of net area to gross is indeed desirable, the designer should consider how to attain it and, as well, how to avoid the pitfalls productive of a low ratio. Further research toward these ends needs to be performed, but the following basic observations are pertinent:

1. Other than that attainable with a circle (and configurations closely akin to a circle), the square is productive of the least amount of wall space per square foot of floor space. Although possibilities for utilization of square configurations in hospital design seldom occur, owing to many constraints, this simple geometric fact should preclude the use of long narrow rectangles, both internally and overall, in most designs. See Figure 14–3 for a comparison of specific configurations in this regard.

2. The ratio of linear feet of wall space to floor areas increases as floor area decreases. For example, a $300' \times 300'$ configuration contains 75 square feet per linear foot of exterior wall—that is, a 75:1 ratio; a $100' \times 100'$ space has a ratio of only 25:1; and a $10' \times 10'$ space further reduces this ratio to 2.5:1. Thus, it is well to consider the adverse implications of small separate structures and small, inflexible internal spaces.

3. Single-loaded corridors (those with net assignable areas aligned only on one side) produce exactly twice the ratio of corridor space to net area as that for double-loaded corridors, all conditions being equal. It follows that single-loaded corridor situations should be closely scrutinized and avoided in most instances.

14–3

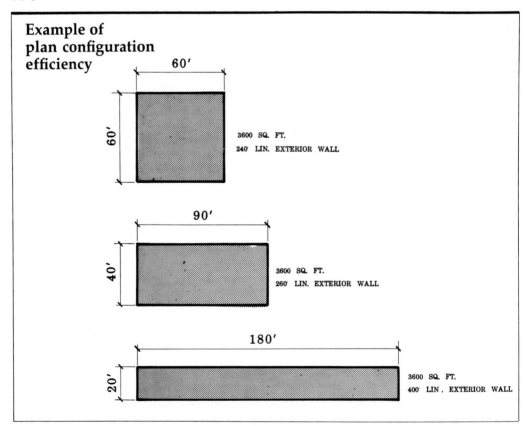

Example of plan configuration efficiency

60'
60'
3600 SQ. FT.
240' LIN. EXTERIOR WALL

90'
40'
3600 SQ. FT.
260' LIN. EXTERIOR WALL

180'
20'
3600 SQ. FT.
400' LIN. EXTERIOR WALL

4. The ratio of net area to the corridor space it borders varies directly with the depth of the net space. Thus, an 8-foot-deep net space bordering an 8-ft corridor has a 1:1 ratio; a 16-ft-deep net space increases this ratio to 2:1, and a 32-ft-deep net space, to 4:1. The implication is that corridors—normally, double-loaded—should service the deepest net space on each side that is functionally feasible. Invariably, schematic plans showing a maze of corridors with shallow bordering usable area will exhibit a low net-to-gross ratio. This type of poor design will also usually be lacking in functionality and flexibility.

5. Although many constraining factors are involved in selecting span and bay requirements, construction areas (as well as internal inflexibility) are increased by use of short spans and small bays. In addition, mechanical space is increased by small span and bay sizes, owing to requirements for a greater number of vertical chases; thus, net assignable area is proportionately reduced.

6. Approximately a third of the gross area in a hospital today is provided for bed areas. When bed levels are stacked one above the other in a tower, the ratio of net assignable area to gross is almost always greater with larger bed numbers per level. For example, in a 240-bed hospital, the provision of 40 beds per level will require six levels. Eighty beds per level will require three levels. In the 40-bed configuration, the amount of exterior wall space per unit of floor space is greater; the space required for exit stairs also is greater (under most designs); and the amount of mechanical areas is usually increased.

   About two thirds of total hospital gross area is provided for support, administration, and diagnostic and treatment services. Design geometrics previously explained apply here also. The trend has been to locate these services in a broad one- to three-level chassis, but in some hospitals, particularly those located in dense urban areas, the "straight-up" configuration is still seen. In these instances, a considerable premium is being paid relative to the net-to-gross ratio. In the chassis design, many factors are involved, too numerous to discuss here, but achievement of a high net-to-gross ratio is one that is of considerable importance and often ignored.

7. Design flexibility is invariably compromised by constricted sites; and accordingly, a high ratio of net area to gross becomes more difficult to achieve. Small, oddly configured sites force the design of small, often oddly shaped or "straight-up" buildings, which usually possess a low net-to-gross ratio and reduced functionality as well. Thus, site selection to provide enough building space so that design flexibility will be allowed is greatly desirable.

8. Although a good case can be made for a multiple-building complex at large medical centers, the separate-building concept nearly always reduces the net-to-gross ratio owing to the need for "connectors" of one type or another and to the increased amount of outside perimeter walls. Decisions regarding separate buildings should take into

account design concepts that are productive of high ratios of net to gross in the case of each building considered. Usually, the total number of buildings in such instances can be held to a minimum with no loss of original objectives.

9. Hospital designs that are effected from the vantage point of a grand concept (based on size) to obtain operational objectives, as contrasted with ones that are evolved as a series of departments fitted together in the most advantageous manner, will usually result in an overall configuration that is productive of a high net-to-gross ratio. This is not to say that a particular plant form should be selected and functions forced into it; it is to say that planners should have in mind a total skeletal scheme that can be fitted to a given site (one that affords design freedom, desirably) and will allow a coordinated operating whole with multiple options in departmental design.

10. Construction area is invariably increased by provision of many small, and usually inflexibly used, spaces. The 10' × 12' module is, in our opinion, the smallest modular net space that should be provided in a hospital structure (excepting toilets, janitors' closets, and baths), and these should be used as sparingly as is functionally feasible.

    Many hospitals, for example, are provided with separate areas on nursing levels for clean linen storage, supplies, and equipment. One large space, rather than three small ones, will require considerably less wall area and possibly less circulation space, as well as other savings. Functionality will, in fact, also be increased.

11. We have worked with several architects who wished to "design on the 45°." We have also observed several hospitals actually built under this design, in which interdepartmental corridors run at a 45° angle to outside walls (usually in a rectangular chassis), with intradepartmental corridors then angled at 90° to the interdepartmental corridors. This type of design usually results in a low net-to-gross ratio, especially where nursing units are designed at the grade level. Of course, these must be designed with interdepartmental corridors running parallel to outside walls so that each patient room can have windows and be accessed by an internal corridor.

    Not only does this design reduce the net-to-gross ratio, but some amounts of net space are always unusable owing to the fact that some triangular areas usually result. Since triangular furniture and equipment are not made, this net space is wasted (but paid for by the hospital).

    An added disadvantage to "designing on the 45°" is that the resulting building is always confusing to users, especially visitors when they attempt to ascertain directions to points of internal destination.

12. Office landscaping, with liberal use of prefabricated work carrels installed in large, open rectangular areas, not only assists in achieving a high net-to-gross ratio but also yields flexibility and more productive use of space.

Summary

There are many ways to reduce unit costs of a hospital structure and maximize cost effectiveness. Achievement of a high ratio of net area to gross is one of them, and a highly important one. Too little attention is being paid to this ratio from outset of planning to design concept and throughout actual designs.

We emphasize that design should be evaluated in the schematic drawing stage. It is relatively simple to revise drawings at this point, whereas in later stages great difficulties will be experienced on the part of all concerned.

Architects, particularly, should be prompted to evaluate design approaches and to seek more efficient solutions with regard to overall building configurations and departmental layouts. Hospital management should assume the posture of evaluating schematic designs in terms of their relationships of total net usable areas to gross areas; inefficient percentages of net areas should be rejected, and insistence upon achieving efficient percentages should be positive.

Notes

1. *Study of Health Facilities Construction Costs.* 1972. (Washington, DC: General Accounting Office).
2. *Integration of Mechanical, Electrical, Structural and Architectural Systems in VA Hospital Facilities.* 1968. (Washington, DC: Veterans Administration, Office of Construction).
3. Derived from definitions published by the Center for Environmental Research, Boston, MA.

15

The Planning and Design Process

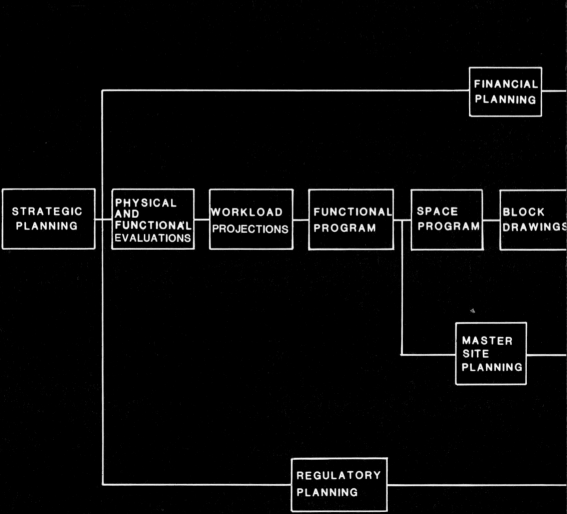

| | STRATEGIC PLANNING | PHYSICAL AND FUNCTIONAL EVALUATIONS | WORKLOAD PROJECTIONS | FUNCTIONAL PROGRAM | SPACE PROGRAM | BLOCK DRAWINGS |

FINANCIAL PLANNING

MASTER SITE PLANNING

REGULATORY PLANNING

Establishing management control over the process

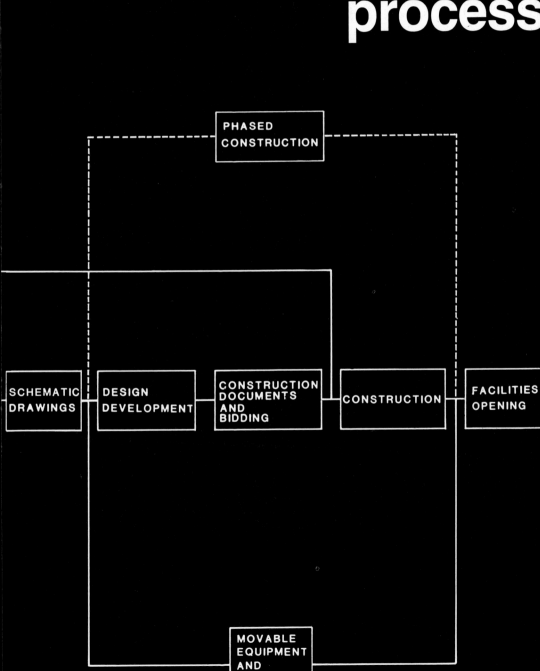

Typically, hospital executive officers and governing board members are not skilled in tasks of facility planning, and only occasionally do such individuals possess the competence required for an appropriate evaluation of architectural and engineering documentations. However, our experience indicates that in many cases, hospital officials are not cognizant of their deficiencies in these regards and, accordingly, fail to implement appropriate management control measures over the facility planning and design process.

The need for control

Without management control measures over the process, quality of planning and design oftentimes falls far below that which might reasonably be expected. Not infrequently, schedules fail to be met, costs far exceed estimates, and confusion compounds confusion.

One of the precise reasons why the design/build (D/B) approach has gained credence in the hospital field is that some hospital officials hope to reduce their control responsibilities during construction projects. In fact, many D/B projects are undertaken as a "crash" solution when disastrous results are being realized during the course of planning and design under other approaches. However, even with the D/B construction approach, control measures should never be relaxed and, in our opinion, should be even more vigorously applied in such cases to assure both quality and the basic nature of the initially promised product.

The Institute for Health Planning recently made these observations about its study of two successful D/B projects:[1]

> However, each hospital took care to build checks and balances [control measures] into its process in order to off-set any potential disadvantages of the design/build approach. These actions of the hospitals included hiring a consultant architect, careful competitive selection of the design/build firm, separate contracts for the design and construction phases so that construction services could be competitively bid, and strong participation of hospital management throughout the design and construction process. This participation is particularly critical to note since some hospitals may consider design/build because they seek to reduce hospital management responsibilities during their construction projects. However, all methods fare best when the hospital is fully involved.

Our own association with horror experiences has been drastically reduced over the years since publication of the first edition of this book. The reason has been that, whether it was our responsibility or not, we have informed our clients of the many pitfalls associated with insufficient control measures, and they have heeded our warnings. However, reports of projects in deep trouble owing to management's failure to implement proper control measures still come to our attention.

Three case studies of constructions during the early and mid 1970s are reported here as examples of highly undesirable situations:

Case A: Project had to be reduced by 30 percent (a reduction of approximately $10 million) upon conclusion of schematic design, with a 1-year delay occurring in project delivery. Causes related to lack of control over space programming, absence of a fixed upper-limit budget, inadequate project scheduling, and failure to control planning and design time.

Case B: Project exceeded original budget in excess of $30 million, and planning, design, and construction time consumed more than 10 years. Causes stemmed from failure to schedule time properly, inaccurate cost estimating, absence of adequate cost controls, and failure to coordinate properly the activities of planning team members.

Case C: In excess of $1.5 million was expended on planning and architectural design, and the project was finally abandoned owing to excessive costs. Causes related to lack of a fixed upper-limit budget, absence of adequate cost controls, failure to control planning and design time, and inaccurate cost estimating.

Even though best judgments have been exercised in selecting every member of the planning team, management control should not be abrogated. That this has been done to a considerable extent in the past, however, is verified by the mute testimony of hundreds of illogically arranged hospital structures, found throughout the North American continent, that cannot support efficient operations (see Figure 15–1 for an extreme example). The toll exacted in increased costs has never been determined, but it is bound to be considerable. These hospitals, of course, do not speak well for their professional planning teams, but, in the final analysis, responsibility for planning and design rests with hospital management. As is the case with responsibility for quality of patient care, it cannot be delegated.

Establishing control

How can management establish a satisfactory degree of control over the planning and design process? There are a number of answers, and in this section we suggest some of them. Our discussion here is based upon a classic interpretation of management control as a three-step process:

1. establishing standards for measuring results (within the context of quality, cost, or time)

2. comparing or measuring results against the standards

3. taking corrective actions to bring deviations in line with the plans or standards as established.

This process is reflected in each of the following suggested control measures.

Control 1: organizing for planning

Conscious efforts on the part of top-level management must be made in order to accommodate properly planning for a major building program.

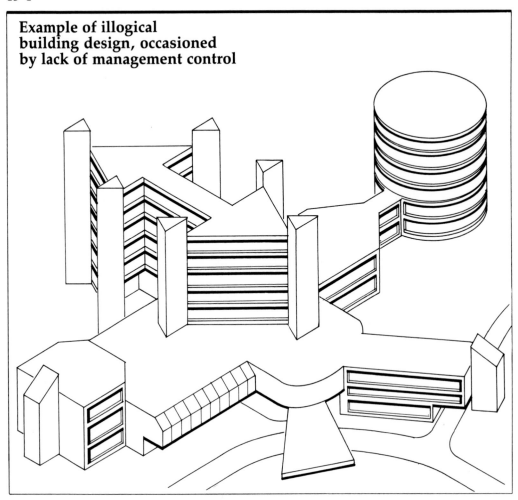

**Example of illogical
building design, occasioned
by lack of management control**

As we have pointed out in previous pages, officials often believe that existing organizational structures can respond to the exigencies of construction planning, design, and implementation—but this is seldom so.

Several actions must be accomplished in this step. While we have noted these in more detail in Chapter 2, we believe that they are important enough to repeat.

- Appointment of a planning director or person who devotes the major portion of his or her time to managing the process. The management of a major building program now demands an exclusive allocation of executive time which cannot be met through the reactions of an existing organizational management structure geared merely to operating the hospital.

- Development of a definitive decision-making process. Types of decisions which must be made during the course of a project should be identified and the authority for making them should be fixed at the outset.

- Organizing for internal review of planning documentations. This structure nearly always includes persons separate and apart from the process of definitive decision making.

- Selection of the professional planning team. A typical planning team for a large project now includes a hospital consultant (with functional planning capabilities), a financial feasibility consultant, an architect/ engineer, and an experienced person or firm with construction management capabilities.

- Organizing the planning team and formulating operating procedures. The relationships among the members of the team must be clearly established from the start, or else animosities may develop and time will be lost.

Control 2: establishing a project schedule

As discussed previously, a project schedule should be prepared in early planning stages, approved by the hospital, and published for all planning participants. This schedule should set forth a timetable, specify tasks, and assign individual responsibilities. Constant updating will be required as circumstances change, and the schedule should be reviewed on a continuing basis to see that work as assigned is being accomplished on time. If it is not, corrective actions should be taken.

PERT and CPM are the most effective scheduling techniques, but in the absence of capabilities to prepare such documentations, a Gant chart or a mere chronological listing of tasks can be effective.

Appropriate scheduling and adherence to schedules on the part of all concerned, including the hospital, means *dollars saved*. The control of time stands as one of the basic aspects of cost control.

Control 3: budgeting and establishing financial feasibility

Perhaps cost control is more efficiently applied than any other control in the facility planning and design process. Even here, however, management has failed in many instances. Certainly it is not uncommon to learn of projects being "overbudget," and entire building programs have been shelved indefinitely for this reason. Usually, thousands of dollars for planning and design have been wasted; such waste could have been avoided through application of appropriate control measures.

For a relatively minor facility construction program that will pose no financial strain, it is an easy matter to prepare a project budget; to establish checkpoints for cost estimating by a reliable estimator throughout the planning, design, and construction period; and to proceed to project completion. If the budget is exceeded, the hospital has the choice of reducing the scope of the project or increasing the budget; the latter choice is most commonly selected. However, in the case of a project for which costs may exceed the limit of the hospital's borrowing capacity and for which there is no source of additional funds, the matter of control becomes critical.

Strategic plans sometimes indicate programs that, when translated into physical facilities, far exceed capital funding capabilities. In such instances, it appears unwise to engage in active facility planning and design. Thus, priorities should be established among programs indicated in the strategic plan, and only facilities that can be designed within attainable capital funds should be considered for construction.

We have been associated with projects for which, despite advice to the contrary, the client carried forward extensive planning and design activities without considering budget limitations. Finally, when funding capabilities were tested, facility reductions by as much as 40 percent were required. Besides loss of time, inflation had taken its toll, and a redesign fee had to be paid. Planning team members, understandably, were psychologically enervated, and work on the second time around was not of the highest quality. Invariably, the conclusion on the part of all concerned was that a realistic budget should have been established at the beginning.

It is assumed that the upper limit of a budget has been established at the time of functional programming, and the functional planner should make recommendations in consideration thereof. When the construction manager or other estimator presents a cost estimate upon completion of a space program and outline specifications, if the project is not within budget, the program should be reduced or additional funds allocated. Certainly, it is inadvisable to enter into design phases with a program that cannot be funded.

The financial feasibility consultant, through a detailed study of anticipated income and expense during space programming and early design, provides the "fine tuning" of budgeting. This consultant's work defines net revenue available to satisfy requirements of debt retirement, and thus provides the basis for accurately budgeting total project costs and the elements thereof. Ongoing comparisons between budget figures and estimated project costs (based on plans and drawings), both of which are being refined as the project progresses, are allowed.

In summary, at several points during project activities, it is particularly important to set or to refine project budgets:

1. on completion of the strategic plan when only the general parameters of the project are known but when budget limits have been set, usually according to a debt capacity analysis

2. on completion of a functional program and space program

3. on completion of schematic drawings and outline specifications

4. on completion of design development

5. at periodic intervals during the construction documents phase.

Certainly, every facility planning and design activity should always be accomplished within the context of a feasible budget at any given point in time.

Control 4: cost control measures

A "percentage of construction" fee, still charged by many A&E firms, is not conducive to serious and determined design cost control. This fact, as well as other considerations, has spawned several other methods of establishing design fees and has assisted in bringing a new discipline to the forefront in modern-day construction—construction management (CM).

A&E firms that possess the capabilities have organized CM firms, and many general contractors either have turned entirely to CM or provide the service. These firms, involved from early planning and design phases to project completion, establish cost controls through continual cost estimating, value engineering, and refined scheduling.

Brady and coauthors in *CM for the General Contractor*, published by the Associated General Contractors of America, Inc., state: "Cost estimating is performed throughout the entire duration of the project, and actually becomes a very important part of the design process. Cost estimates are prepared in increasing detail as more specific information concerning the project becomes available, and each estimate becomes a control budget for the next state of project development."[2] Clearly, and as corroborated by our experience, when design changes that put the project over budget are made, other changes must be made to keep the project within budget.

Value engineering, performed by either the A&E firm or the CM firm, or both, is one of the techniques employed to control costs. A noted practicing construction engineer has defined value engineering as follows: "Value engineering is the review of plans and specifications with the goal of making cost cutting substitutions."[3] A professor of engineering and applied sciences has stated, "Value engineering is a system of obtaining optimum value for every dollar spent. It is concerned with the elimination or modification of anything that adds to the cost of a system without adding to its function."[4]

Perhaps the definition espoused by the Associated General Contractors of America, Inc., remains the most meaningful: "Value engineering is a systematic effort directed at analyzing the functional requirements of systems, facilities, procedures, and supplies for the purpose of achieving the essential functions at lowest total cost, consistent with needed performance, reliability, quality, maintainability, aesthetics, safety, and fire protection."[5]

Our experience indicates that the failures of cost controls have occurred most frequently in the early stages of the project. CM has the potential for preventing such failures, and in this regard, Brady and coauthors state:[6]

> The cost estimates which are prepared during the preconstruction stages provide reliable forecasts of the cost of each significant part of the project, as well as of the project in its entirety. Cost reduction studies and value engineering tradeoffs can be made at a very early stage, well before significant monetary commitments have been made by the owner.

Many owners play a somewhat passive role in the preparation of contracts with members of their professional planning team. This represents a poor approach. Hospital officials should make positive stipulations about the responsibilities of each such team member and have them clearly spelled out in a definitive manner. The requirements that both the A&E firm and the construction manager should employ ongoing value engineering based on recognized engineering methodologies should be such a stipulation.

Control 5: the functional program

Broadly, it can be said that management can effect control by requiring certain documentations, in a form understandable by both officers and users, before definitive architectural design begins. The functional program is such a documentation and can be prepared by a qualified functional planner with assistance of hospital staff. As described in Chapter 7, the functional program should explain how intended construction will operate; set forth the desirability for physical closeness among departments and functional entities based on functional relations; and discuss the rationale for other design parameters and constraints, particularly traffic flows. As each departmental area is discussed and operational processes are explained, options for achieving physical closeness among departments, as well as other design alternatives, should be outlined. After study and approval of this documentation, management should then deliver it to the architect for guidance in design.

As drawings are produced, they should either conform to the intentions of management or present a clearly superior solution. If they do neither, corrective actions can be taken.

Control 6: space programs

Net and gross space programs give management needed control in two basic ways, the first being related to cost (as discussed in Chapter 14). Although construction costs can vary quite widely among projects with identical space provisions owing to a host of factors, the construction manager or other estimator, by assuming materials of reasonable quality throughout and employing competent component estimating, can predict construction costs from a space program with a high degree of accuracy. At the least, there will be small risk of inability to bring the project into budget conformance during design stages if estimates at this point indicate that the space program is compatible with current budget figures. On the other hand, if compatibility does not exist, it is unwise to proceed further without reductions.

It should be clearly remembered that it is usually less complicated to add space to a project than to reduce space, especially after design starts. As well, it certainly will be less embarrassing to all concerned.

Net space programs allow management control over the make-up of the project as a whole and with regard to every department or functional entity. The architectural designer has the responsibility to see that all rooms included in the space program are shown in drawings and that each is given a size closely approximating that assigned in the space program. If the designer fails to do so, management can immediately use the space program as a control device.

Control 7: closeness matrixes

Another tool for giving design a positive direction is a closeness matrix, usually prepared just prior to definitive design work. (Examples of such matrixes are set forth in Chapter 10.) This documentation gives a weighted priority for physical closeness among all departments and independent functional entities, as well as programmed entrances and staff and public elevators. Weightings can be formulated by statistical calculations, but more often, senior consultants who possess a broad background of hospital operational experience prepare them.

The finalized matrix should, of course, be approved after full study and consideration by management and then delivered to the architect for guidance. Although design determinants include other factors, some as demanding as requirements for physical closeness, use of the matrix as a guide in design increases the probability that functionality will be attained, thus providing a positive control.

Control 8: tracing traffic flows

Although the functional program narrative and closeness matrix give management a hand in guiding design and establishing a degree of control, they do not eliminate actual need to evaluate schematic designs in terms of relationships achieved among departments and functional entities. With the limited knowledge usually possessed by management in this area, how can effective interpretations be accomplished? The answer lies in a methodical tracing, during the schematic design phase, of the most important flows of patients, staff, visitors, and supplies that will occur within the structure. Figure 15–2 shows one example of this technique.

Interdepartmental traffic flow patterns that should be traced and given definitive account range in number from about 35 in a community-type hospital to 50 in a university teaching hospital, for all categories. *Intra-departmental* flow patterns must also be considered for the same categories and range in number from one or two for some small departments or functional entities to over a dozen for some of the large departments, such as radiology and surgery. All types of *vehicular* traffic flows to and from the site should also be traced.

In sessions with the architect and consultants, management can have each flow traced on the drawings presented, and it can indeed be surprising how often illogical flow patterns will surface in a design effected by the most skilled planning team. In such demonstrations, even the most unaccustomed eye can detect improper departmental relationships, unnecessarily long pedestrian treks, and failures to separate incompatible flows—none of which should be tolerated. It is true that the perfect functional design is difficult to achieve, but close scrutiny of these flows will allow management a control that cannot be denied and that will disallow establishment of grossly inefficient relationships.

Control 9: determination of net-to-gross ratio

We pointed out in Chapter 14 the considerable importance of achieving a high ratio of net usable area to total gross area.

Upon conclusion of schematic design, the architect and construction manager should be requested to submit calculations of ratios of net usable area to total gross area for each departmental area and for the building as a whole. If the design proves to be unacceptably inefficient, the fact should be forthrightly stated, and a redesign at no cost to the hospital should be requested.

If designers are apprised that their responsibility includes achievement of an efficient ratio before design begins, they will accept this requirement as professionals should, and there will be little likelihood that an inefficient ratio will result.

Plotting internal traffic patterns: a technique of management control over design

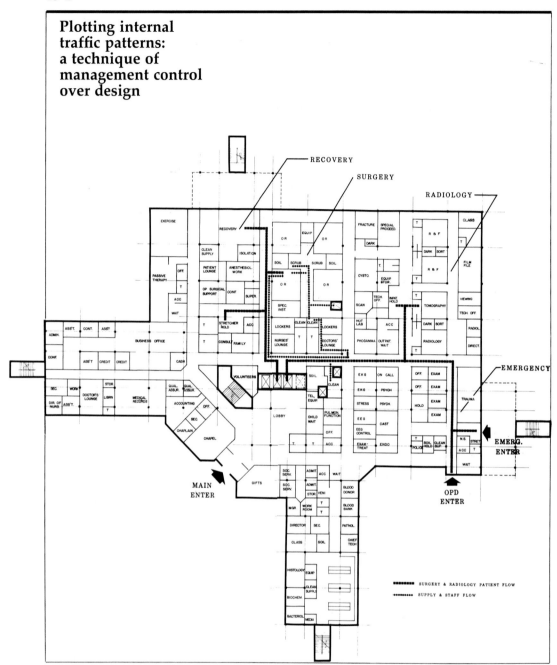

Control 10: environmental data sheets

Managers who have opened a new hospital construction may be familiar with instances in which the finished product failed to possess many features that were thought to have been included in plans. For example, the lack of needed electrical outlets, the omission of plumbing fixtures or installation of an unanticipated type, the use of finishes not expected, and the installation of undesirable lighting fixtures occur with a considerable degree of regularity. Such situations may result when the architect is not sufficiently experienced, or when guidance for design or specification of these features is largely verbal or given on a hit-or-miss basis. To minimize the occurrence of such eventualities, management can require preparation of environmental data sheets to guide design development drawings and working drawings. This documentation can be accomplished by interaction among hospital personnel, the architect, and the functional planner, as explained in Chapter 10. (Exhibit 10–1 displays one format of an environmental data sheet.)

Environmental data sheets present information regarding detailed features of every different type of room in the hospital, in a form that hospital officials can readily understand. These data sheets specify pertinent architectural characteristics, types of fixed and movable equipment (including casework), and the key features of plumbing, electrical, medical gas, HVAC, and fire protection systems that should appear in respective rooms. When completed and properly approved by hospital officials, data sheets constitute a formal directive to the architect.

Environmental data sheets not only provide a guide to design but also allow a control when specifications and working drawings are submitted. Management, with documentation in hand rather than memories of discussions, can quiz the design team with regard to key points set forth on the data sheets, on a room-by-room basis. Only a few such control discussions are required, and serious embarrassments can be avoided on completion of construction.

Control 11: written approvals

Reporting is a central element in any management control process, and the larger and more impersonal an organization becomes, the more importance this element assumes. In large, complicated projects the policy of reporting in writing becomes critical. To avoid repetitive work on the part of planning team members and to allow them to proceed with a high degree of assurance of the acceptability of their work, the results of all reviews should be reduced to writing. Free discussions among planning team members and the various hospital groups can and should occur, but when the discussions are terminated, the hospital should reduce opinions, recommendations, and decisions to writing. If this is not done, the chances are considerably enhanced that misunderstandings will occur.

For example, all user groups who review the functional program should formulate their comments in writing. They may then call upon the functional planner to give verbal explanations, and lengthy discussions sometimes ensue. Regardless of the outcome, when the discussions are finished, the report of the group should be formally recorded in writing. The planning director then assembles all comments and recommendations and is charged with making reconciliations as appropriate. Finally, board-approved decisions that will be incorporated into the final program are delivered to the functional planner.

Over the course of a large project there will be perhaps ten formal reviews of various planning team documentations, depending upon the number of repeat reviews required after incorporation of changes. In every instance, review proceedings, formal acceptance, and authority to proceed further should be made a part of a written reporting system.

Summary

In numerous instances, it can be stated that hospital management, in the absence of adequate technical knowledge of functional and architectural planning, has abdicated a rightful and proper control of the facility planning and design processes. The tools do exist, however, to establish appropriate control measures, and the discussions here point the way to some of them. Reasonable capital costs, operational efficiency, and functionality are characteristics that any public, utilitarian structure should possess, especially hospitals, and they are characteristics that management can assure by exercise of one vital management process over another—control over planning.

Notes

1. Institute for Health Planning, *Administrators' Guide to Hospital Construction Approaches*, prepared under HRSA Contract (Madison, WI: 1984), p. XXVI.
2. Thomas Brady et al., *CM for the General Contractor* (Washington, DC: Associated General Contractors of America, Inc., 1974), p. 41.
3. King Royer, *The Construction Manager in the 80's* (Englewood Cliffs, NJ: Prentice-Hall, 1981), p. 117.
4. Hira H. Ahuja, *Successful Construction Cost Control* (New York: John Wiley and Sons, 1980), p. 172.
5. Brady et al., *CM for the General Contractor*, p. 48.
6. *Ibid.*, p. 42.

Index

Entries in *italics* donote figures; entries followed by "t" denote tables.

About the authors

Owen B. Hardy, FACHE, FAAHC, has provided consulting services to some of the world's most prestigious medical centers, including Rush-Presbyterian-St. Luke's Medical Center in Chicago, Illinois; Tulane University Medical Center and Ochsner Foundation Hospital, both in New Orleans, Louisiana; Erie County Medical Center in Buffalo, New York; University of Cologne Hospital in Cologne, West Germany; Ottawa General Hospital in Ottawa, Ontario; and The Washington Hospital Center in Washington, D.C.

Over a 20-year span of consulting, Mr. Hardy has supervised the preparation of hundreds of reports in every aspect of hospital planning. The value of hospital construction for which he has provided planning services runs into billions of dollars.

For eight years Mr. Hardy has held the position of National Health Care Planning Advisor with the firm of Ernst & Whinney, Chicago, Illinois. He formerly was president of Medicus Planning, Inc., and vice president of Friesen International, Inc. He stands eminently qualified to coauthor a resource volume on planning such as this text. Mr. Hardy is a frequent contributor to the nation's top hospital professional publications and is widely known throughout the United States and abroad.

Lawrence P. Lammers, AIA, FAAHC, is the president of Lammers + Gershon Associates, Inc., a hospital planning and consulting firm in Reston, Virginia. Mr. Lammers has been involved in hospital planning and design for more than 20 years. He has directed some of the most dynamic and complex hospital projects in the world and has planned and consulted on over 150 hospital projects (both new and expanded), including medical schools, clinics, ambulatory care centers, and psychiatric facilities. Mr. Lammers is also involved in materials handling systems development; in this area he has developed programs for many hospitals and many products manufactured specifically for the health care field.

Mr. Lammers holds a National Council of Architectural Registration Boards certificate. He is a guest lecturer, specializing in hospital planning, at many architectural schools and graduate programs.